DICTIONARY OF
ENVIRONMENT
& ECOLOGY

FIFTH EDITION

Also published by Bloomsbury Reference:

Visit our website for full details of all our books
www.bloomsbury.com/reference

DICTIONARY OF
ENVIRONMENT & ECOLOGY

FIFTH EDITION

P.H. Collin

BLOOMSBURY

A BLOOMSBURY REFERENCE BOOK

www.bloomsbury.com/reference

Originally published by Peter Collin Publishing

First published 1985
Second edition published 1992
Third edition published 1995
Fourth edition published 2001
Fifth edition published 2004

Bloomsbury Publishing Plc
38 Soho Square, London W1D 3HB

British Library Cataloguing-in-Publication Data
A catalogue record for this book is available from the British Library

ISBN 0 7475 7201 1

Text production and proofreading
Katy McAdam, Joel Adams, Charlotte Regan,
Sarah Lusznat, Heather Bateman, Emma Harris

All papers used by Bloomsbury Publishing are natural, recyclable
products made from wood grown in well-managed forests. The paper used
in this book is 100% recycled and contains 20 - 25% post-consumer waste
material which was de-inked using chlorine free methods. The
manufacturing processes conform to the environmental regulations of the
country of origin.

Text processing and computer typesetting by Bloomsbury
Printed and bound in Italy by Legoprint

Contents

Introduction

Few things in the universe are constant over thousands or millions of years, not the orbit of the Earth around the sun, the height of eroding mountains, the distribution of boreal forests, or the abundance of a particular species. As we shift our attention from the stellar and global to the regional and local, then the more likely it is that we will encounter things that change over even short spans of time.

Dictionaries contribute to communication by providing definitions which deliver consistency of meaning. But consistency is not the same as constancy. With the passage of time, new dictionaries, or new editions of old ones, are necessary, because new subject areas develop, new terms are introduced or the meanings of words change. Examples of all of these developments are to be found in the following pages, as is to be expected in such dynamic fields of study as environment and ecology. In documenting change, dictionaries not only record developments in language and human endeavour, but also reflect the reality of the natural world.

As this dictionary goes to press it is perhaps global climatic change and the high rate of extinction of species which are the best exemplars of this. Change can be a challenge to those with an interest in ecology or the environment, as that interest rightly engenders a commitment to seek to conserve what we know and value. It can also create tensions between competing interests within the same field, as conflict between the protection of bird life and the perceived need for offshore wind farms has illustrated. But the entities we are aware of are more than features in their own right, they are also the products of fundamental processes which seem remarkably constant over time. These processes, such as glaciation, erosion, mutation, evolution, competition and decay have created the landscapes, communities, plants and animals we observe and study. As ecologists and environmentalists it is primarily these processes which we study, and it is perhaps these which we should value and conserve as much as their temporary products. This shift in emphasis may be one of the future developments in thinking in ecology and environment and a change to be recorded in later editions of this dictionary.

Dr John Harvey
Secretary, Eurosite

Preface

This dictionary provides the user with a wide range of vocabulary from across the fields of environment and ecology, and also includes general terms frequently used in scientific documents and reports, as well as some more informal terms seen in the media. Words and phrases cover many aspects from contaminated land and landfill sites to climate change and biofuels.

The dictionary is designed for anyone who needs to check the meaning of an environmental or ecological term, but especially for those for whom English is an additional language. Each entry is explained in clear straightforward English and examples are given to show how the words are used in normal contexts. Quotations from reports and publications give recent uses of some words. In some cases, additonal information about a word is added in a Note, or a wider context is offered in a Comment. Irregular plurals and verb forms, and other helpful usage points are included.

Thanks are due to Dr John Harvey, Professor Graham Jellis, Judith Cheney, Steven Griffiths and Susan Jellis for valuable comments and advice on the text for this fifth edition.

A

abate *verb* to become less strong or intense ○ *The wind has abated.*

abatement *noun* a reduction in strength or intensity ○ *water pollution abatement*

abiotic *adjective* not relating to a living organism

abiotic factor *noun* something which influences the environment but which is not produced by living organisms, e.g. wind, temperature or rainfall. Compare **biotic factor**

abiotic stress *noun* stress caused by the physical and chemical aspects of an organism's environment

abiotic stress resistance *noun* resistance in organisms to stress arising from non-biological causes such as drought or salinity

ablation *noun* **1.** the removal of the top layer of something **2.** the removal of snow or ice from the surface of a glacier by melting or by the action of the wind

abort *verb* **1.** to stop a process or the development of something before it is finished, or to stop developing ○ *The flowers abort and drop off in hot, dry conditions, with no fruit developing.* **2.** to give birth before the usual end of a pregnancy (*technical*) Also called **miscarry**

abrasion *noun* the wearing away by friction of a material, especially the erosion of rock by the action of particles suspended in water, ice or wind

abscission *noun* the shedding of a leaf or fruit due to the formation of a layer of cells between the leaf or fruit and the rest of the plant (NOTE: It occurs naturally in autumn, e.g. leaf fall, or at any time of the year in response to stress.)

absolute *adjective* **1.** very great ○ *absolute confidence in the results* **2.** complete or total ○ *No absolute correlation with climate change has yet been established.* **3.** measured relative to a standard ■ *noun* an unchanging principle

absorb *verb* to take something in ○ *Warm air absorbs moisture more easily than cold air.* ○ *Salt absorbs moisture from the air.*

absorbent *adjective* able to absorb

absorption *noun* the process of taking in water, dissolved minerals and other nutrients across cell membranes

absorptive capacity *noun* the ability of a substance or part of an organism to take up something such as moisture or nutrients

abstract *noun* a short summary of a document ○ *It's quicker to search through the abstracts than the full text.* ■ *verb* **1.** to remove water from a river or other source for industrial, horticultural or agricultural use **2.** to take something such as gas, oil, mineral resources or gravel from the ground

abstraction *noun* **1.** the removal of water from a river or other source for industrial, horticultural or agricultural use **2.** the removal of something such as gas, oil, mineral resources or gravel from the ground

abstraction licence *noun* a licence issued by a regulatory body to allow abstraction, e.g. of water from a river, lake or aquifer for domestic or commercial use such as irrigation

abundance *noun* **1.** a large amount or number of something ○ *The area supports an abundance of wildlife.* **2.** a measure of quantity applied to plants or animals, often based on density or frequency

abundant *adjective* occurring or available in large quantities ○ *a region of abundant rainfall* ○ *The ocean has an abundant supply of krill.*

abyss *noun* a very deep part of the sea

abyssal *adjective* referring to the deepest part of the sea

abyssobenthic *adjective* referring to an organism living on the floor of the deepest part of a sea or lake

abyssopelagic *adjective* referring to an organism living in the deepest part of a sea or lake, at depths greater than 3000m

acaricide *noun* a substance used to kill mites and ticks. Also called **acaridicide**

acarid *noun* a small animal which feeds on plants or other animals by piercing the outer skin and sucking juices, e.g. a mite or tick

Acarida *noun* the order of animals including mites and ticks. Also called **Acarina**

acaridicide *noun* same as **acaricide**

Acarina *noun* same as **Acarida**

acceptable daily intake *noun* the quantity of a substance such as a nutrient, vitamin, additive or pollutant which a person or animal can safely consume daily over their lifetime. Abbr **ADI**

acceptable limits *plural noun* the upper and lower limits within which something is generally regarded as suitable by a large number of people or by legislation ○ *The noise from the road falls within acceptable limits.* ○ *The acceptable limits for such chemicals in food and animal feed are strictly regulated.*

access *noun* **1.** a place of entry, or the right of entry, to somewhere **2.** the right of the public to go onto uncultivated private land for recreation. ◊ **Countryside and Rights of Way Act**

access order *noun* a court order which gives the public the right to go on private land

access road *noun* a road that allows only the properties on it to be reached and is not for general traffic

acclimatisation, acclimatization, acclimation *noun* the process of adapting to a different environment (NOTE: This process is known as **acclimatisation** if the changes occur naturally and **acclimation** if they are produced in laboratory conditions.)

acclimatise, acclimatize *verb* **1.** to make an organism become used to a different environment, usually a change in climate **2.** to become used to a different sort of environment

accretion *noun* **1.** the growth of inorganic objects by the attachment of material to their surface **2.** the growth of a substance around an object ○ *an accretion of calcium round the joint* **3.** an accumulation of sediments

accumulate *verb* **1.** to collect and increase ○ *Cold air flows downwards and accumulates over low ground.* ○ *Sediment and debris accumulate at the bottom of a lake.* **2.** to gather several things together over a period of time ○ *We have gradually accumulated a large collection of plant specimens.*

accumulation *noun* **1.** the process of becoming greater in size or quantity over a period of time ○ *the risk of accumulation of toxins in the food chain* **2.** something that has accumulated

acer *noun* a maple or sycamore tree. Genus: *Acer*.

achene *noun* a dry single-seeded fruit that does not split open (NOTE: Achenes are produced by plants such as dandelions and sunflowers.)

acid *noun* a chemical compound containing hydrogen which dissolves in water and forms hydrogen ions, or reacts with an alkali to form a salt and water, and turns litmus paper red

acid aerosol *noun* an acidic liquid or solid particles that are small enough to be propelled through the air

acid deposition *noun* ◊ **acid rain**

acid fallout *noun* an acid which forms in the atmosphere and falls as particles, without any water

acid grassland *noun* a type of vegetation that is typical especially on soils that drain freely and are low in mineral nutrients, and may also occur on post-industrial sites. The range of plant species found is small. ◊ **calcareous grassland**

acidic *adjective* referring to acids ○ *has acidic properties*

acidic rock *noun* a rock which contains a high percentage of silica

acidification *noun* the process of becoming acid or of making a substance more acid ○ *Acidification of the soil leads to the destruction of some living organisms.*

acidify *verb* to make a substance more acid, or to become more acid ○ *Acid rain acidifies the soils and waters where it falls.* ○ *The sulfur released from wetlands as sulfate causes lakes to acidify.*

acidifying compound *noun* a compound that contributes to acidification, e.g. sulfur oxides, sulfates, nitrogen oxides, nitrates and ammonium compounds

acidity *noun* the proportion of acid in a substance ○ *The alkaline solution may help to reduce acidity.*

acid mine drainage *noun* water containing acids, which drains from mine workings or from heaps of mine refuse and enters water courses

acid mine water *noun* water in mine workings which contains acid from rocks

acid-neutralising capacity *noun* the ability of water to neutralise acids, measured by the amount of bicarbonate it contains. Abbr **ANC**

acid precipitation *noun* same as **acid rain**

acid-proof *adjective* able to resist the harmful effects of an acid

acid pulse *noun* a sudden increase in acidity in rainwater or river water

acid rain *noun* precipitation such as rain or snow which contains a higher level of acid than normal. Also called **acid deposition**, **acid precipitation**

COMMENT: Acid rain is mainly caused by sulfur dioxide, nitrogen oxide and other pollutants being released into the atmosphere when fossil fuels such as oil or coal containing sulfur are burnt. Carbon combines with sulfur trioxide from sulfur-rich fuel to form particles of an acid substance. The effects of acid rain are primarily felt by wildlife. The water in lakes becomes very clear as fish and microscopic animal life are killed. It is believed that it is acid rain that kills trees, especially conifers, making them gradually lose their leaves and die. Acid rain can damage surfaces such as stone buildings when it falls on them.

acid soot *noun* acid carbon particles which fall from smoke from chimneys

acorn *noun* the fruit of an oak tree

acoustician *noun* a person who specialises in the study of sound

acoustics *noun* the study of sound, especially noise levels in buildings

ACP *abbr* Advisory Committee on Pesticides

acquired character *noun* a characteristic that develops in response to the environment

acquis *noun* in the European Union, a set of laws that potential member states have to adopt ○ *an environmental acquis*

acre *noun* a unit of measurement of land area, equal to 4840 square yards or 0.4047 hectares

ACRE *abbr* Advisory Committee on Releases to the Environment

acreage *noun* the area of a piece of land measured in acres

acrid *adjective* having a strong bitter smell or taste ○ *acrid fumes*

actinide *noun* one of the radioactive elements which are in the same category as uranium in the periodic table and have atomic numbers from 89 to 104

actinium *noun* a natural radioactive element, produced by the decay of uranium-235 (NOTE: The chemical symbol is **Ac**; the atomic number is **89** and the atomic weight is **226**.)

actinomycete *noun* a bacterium shaped like a rod or filament. Order: Actinomycetales. (NOTE: Some actinomycetes cause diseases while others are sources of antibiotics.)

action *noun* **1.** something done or to be done ○ *Appropriate action should be taken to avoid contamination.* **2.** the effect that something has ○ *worn away by the action of rain* ○ *the action of the drug on the nervous system* □ **to take action against something or to stop something** to work to prevent something happening ○ *The government is taking action to stop the spread of pollution.*

action plan *noun* a detailed statement of how something that needs to be done will be carried out ○ *an action plan for conserving species*

activate *verb* to start a process or to make something start working

activated sludge *noun* solid sewage containing active microorganisms and air, mixed with untreated sewage to speed up the purification process

activation *noun* the act of making something start to work

activator *noun* a substance which activates a process ○ *a compost activator*

active *adjective* **1.** doing something, usually energetically, or being alert ○ *Kiwis are only active after dark.* **2.** in action or in use **3.** (*of a volcano*) likely to erupt from time to time

active ingredient *noun* the main effective ingredient of something such as an agrochemical, as opposed to the base substance. Abbr **AI**

active organic matter *noun* organic matter in the process of being broken down by bacteria. Abbr **AOM**

active packaging *noun* food packaging that interacts chemically or biologically with its contents so that shelf-life is longer or the product is modified during storage

activity *noun* **1.** the actions that humans and other living things undertake ○ *research activities* ○ *The hillside showed signs of human activity.* ○ *We saw no activity around the nest in several hours.* **2.** the effect that something has ○ *Biopesticides are being evaluated for their biological activity in a range of environments.* **3.** an action or movement ○ *volcanic activity*

act on, act upon *verb* (*of force*) to produce an effect on something

acute exposure *noun* exposure to a pollutant or radioactive substance for a short period

acute health effect *noun* a health problem which lasts a short time, following exposure to a pollutant or radioactive substance

acute toxicity *noun* the concentration of a toxic substance which is high enough to make people seriously ill or can cause death

adapt *verb* **1.** to change to suit new conditions ○ *People adapt to the reduced amounts of oxygen available at high altitudes.* **2.** to change or modify something for special use ○ *The engine has been adapted to use the new fuel.* **3.** to experience a heritable change in structure or function that makes an organism better able to survive and reproduce, as part of the process of evolution

adaptation, adaption *noun* **1.** the act of changing, or of modifying something for special use **2.** a heritable change in an organism so that it is better able to survive and reproduce in an environment, as part of the process of evolution

adaptive radiation *noun* the development of different species from a single ancestor in such a way that the different forms have adapted to suit different environmental conditions

ADAS *noun* a commercial research-based organisation that offers technical advice on agricultural, food and environmental matters to rural industries. Former name **Agricultural Development and Advisory Service**

additive *noun* **1.** a chemical which is added to food to improve its appearance or to keep it fresh ○ *The tin of beans contains a number of additives.* ○ *These animal foodstuffs are free from all additives.* **2.** a chemical which is added to something to improve it ○ *A new fuel additive made from plants could help reduce energy costs.*

COMMENT: Colour additives are added to food to improve its appearance. Some are natural organic substances like saffron, carrot juice or caramel, but others are synthetic. Other substances added to food to prevent decay or to keep the food in the right form are emulsifiers, which bind different foods together as mixtures, and stabilisers, which can keep a sauce semi-liquid and prevent it from separating into solids and liquids. The European Union allows some additives to be added to food and these are given E numbers.

ADI *abbr* acceptable daily intake

adiabatic *adjective* referring to a change in temperature in a mass of air as a result of compression or expansion caused by an increase or decrease in atmospheric pressure without loss or gain of heat to or from its surroundings

adjust *verb* to change something to be more suitable or so that it works better ○ *We will have to adjust the next trial to take account of recent results.*

adjustment *noun* **1.** a change to improve the setting or position of something ○ *The brightness needs adjustment.* **2.** a process of physical change in response to external environmental changes

adjuvant *noun* something added to improve the effectiveness of something else, e.g. a substance added to a pesticide to make it stick to waxy leaves

adsorb *verb* (*of a solid*) to bond with a gas or vapour which touches its surface

adsorbent *adjective* capable of adsorption

adsorber *noun* a device which removes volatile organic compounds from gas by adsorbing them to a carbon filter

adsorption *noun* the bonding of a solid with a gas or vapour which touches its surface

adult *adjective* having reached maturity ○ *takes two years to reach the adult stage* ■ *noun* an organism that has reached maturity

advanced gas-cooled reactor *noun* a type of nuclear reactor, in which carbon dioxide is used as the coolant and is passed into water tanks to create the steam which will drive the turbines. Abbr **AGR**

advection *noun* a movement of air in a horizontal direction □ **advection fog** fog which forms when warmer moist air moves over a colder surface (land or sea) ▶ compare **convection**

adventitious *adjective* **1.** on the outside or in an unusual place **2.** referring to a root which develops from a node on a plant stem and not from another root

adverse *adjective* **1.** bad or poor ○ *Adverse weather conditions delayed planting.* **2.** harmful or unfavourable ○ *adverse effects* **3.** moving in the opposite direction ○ *adverse winds*

adverse health effect *noun* a harmful effect on a person's health as a result of coming into contact with pollutants or allergens

advisory *adjective* giving advice and information

advisory board, advisory committee *noun* a group of specialists who can give advice

Advisory Committee on Pesticides *noun* a statutory body set up under the UK Food and Environment Protection Act 1985 to advise on all matters relating to the control of pesticides. Abbr **ACP**

Advisory Committee on Releases to the Environment *noun* an independent advisory committee giving statutory advice to UK Government Ministers on the risks to human health and the environment from the release and marketing of genetically modified organisms (GMOs). It also advises on the release of some non-GM species of plants and animals that are not native to Great Britain. Abbr **ACRE**

AE *abbr* assimilation efficiency

AEA *noun* ♦ **UKAEA**

AEBC *abbr* Agriculture, Environment and Biotechnology Commission

AEC *abbr* Atomic Energy Commission

aeon *noun* ♦ **geological aeon**

AEPS *abbr* Arctic Environmental Protection Strategy

aerate *verb* to allow air to enter a substance, especially soil or water ○ *Worms play a useful role in aerating the soil.*

aeration *noun* the process of putting air into a substance ○ *aeration of the soil*

COMMENT: The process of aeration of soil is mainly brought about by the movement of water into and out of the soil. Rainwater drives out the air and then, as the water drains away or is used by plants, fresh air is drawn into the soil to fill the spaces. The aeration process is also assisted by changes in temperature, good drainage, cultivation and open soil structure. Sandy soils are usually well aerated; clay soils are poorly aerated.

aerator *noun* a device to put a gas, especially carbon dioxide or air, into a liquid. ◊ **de-aerator**

aerial *adjective* referring to the air ○ *Some orchids have aerial roots.*

aerobe *noun* a living thing, particularly a microorganism, that needs oxygen for metabolism. Compare **anaerobe**

aerobic *adjective* needing oxygen for its existence or for a biochemical reaction to occur. Compare **anaerobic**

aerobic digester *noun* a digester which operates in the presence of oxygen

aerobic digestion *noun* the processing of waste, especially organic waste such as manure, in the presence of oxygen

aerobiosis *noun* a biological activity which occurs in the presence of oxygen

aerogenerator *noun* a windmill with fast-moving sails used to generate mechanical power or electricity

aerolisation, aerolization *noun* the transmission of a substance in the form of a vapour or fine particles in the air

aerosol *noun* **1.** a quantity of tiny particles of liquid suspended in a gas under pressure, sprayed from a container **2.** a can of liquid with a propellant gas under pressure, which is used to spray the liquid in the form of tiny drops **3.** a quantity of tiny particles of liquid or powder which stay suspended in the atmosphere

aesthetic argument *noun* reasoning for conservation based on the view that the beauty of scenery or nature should be preserved

aesthetic injury level *noun* the level at which the amenity benefits of pest control become acceptable. Abbr **AIL**

aestivation *noun* **1.** dormancy in some animals such as lungfish during the summer or periods of drought. Compare **hibernation 2.** the arrangement of sepals and petals in a flower bud

aetiological agent *noun* an agent which causes a disease

aetiology *noun* the causes of a disease, or the study of those causes

affect *verb* to have an influence on or to change something. Compare **effect**

affluent *adjective* referring to water which is flowing freely ■ *noun* a stream which flows into a river

afforest *verb* to plant an area with trees

afforestation *noun* **1.** the growing of trees as a crop ○ *There is likely to be an increase in afforestation of upland areas if the scheme is introduced.* **2.** the planting of trees on land previously used for other purposes

aflatoxin *noun* a toxin produced by species of the fungus *Aspergillus*, especially *Aspergillus flavus*, which grows on seeds and nuts and affects stored grain

afrormosia *noun* a hardwood tree from West Africa, now becoming scarce. Latin name: *Pericopisis elata*.

afterburner *noun* a device which reduces pollution by burning out organic gases

aftercare *noun* **1.** arrangements for preventing future pollution from an environmentally sensitive activity that has ceased **2.** the continuing management of the soil or vegetation of an area that has been restored or replanted ○ *vegetation management practices during aftercare* ○ *an aftercare agreement to restore a disturbed site*

aftershock *noun* a weaker shock which follows the main shock of an earthquake. Compare **foreshock**

agency *noun* **1.** an organisation or company that acts as a representative for a person or business **2.** a government organisation with a specific role **3.** the act of causing something to happen ○ *The disease devel-*

ops through the agency of bacteria present in the bloodstream.

Agenda 21 *noun* a global environmental programme and statement of principles concerning sustainable development for the 21st century, agreed in 1992 at the Earth Summit in Rio de Janeiro, Brazil

agent *noun* **1.** a chemical substance which causes a change ○ *an anti-icing agent* **2.** a substance or organism which causes a disease or condition ○ *They identified the disease agent.*

agglomerate *noun* a rock made up of fragments of lava fused together by heat

aggravate *verb* to make something worse ○ *The effects of acid rain on the soil have been aggravated by chemical runoff.*

aggregate *noun* **1.** crushed stones used to make concrete or road surfaces **2.** a mass of soil and rock particles stuck together ■ *verb* to make up a whole or total ○ *Ice crystals aggregate to form snowflakes.*

aggregation *noun* a dispersal pattern of plants or animals, where the individuals remain quite close together

AGR *abbr* advanced gas-cooled reactor

Agreement on the conservation of small cetaceans of the Baltic and North Seas *noun* an agreement made between European countries in 1991. Abbr **ASCOBANS**

agri- *prefix* referring to agriculture or to the cultivation or management of land. ◊ **agro-**

agribusiness *noun* a large-scale farming business run along the lines of a conventional company, often involving the processing, packaging and sale of farm products

agricultural *adjective* referring to farming

agricultural burning *noun* the burning of agricultural waste as part of farming practice, e.g. stubble burning

agriculturalist *noun* a person trained in applying the principles of science to farming

agricultural waste *noun* waste matter produced on a farm, e.g. plastic containers for pesticides

Agricultural Waste Stakeholders' Forum *noun* a group that includes representatives of government, farming organisations, waste companies and farm suppliers with the aim of identifying and dealing with issues of waste management in agriculture

agriculture *noun* the cultivation of land, including horticulture, fruit growing, crop and seed growing, dairy farming and livestock breeding

Agriculture, Environment and Biotechnology Commission *noun* the UK Government advisory body on biotechnology issues affecting agriculture and the environment

agri-environmental indicator *noun* an indicator designed to provide information on the complex interactions between agriculture and environment

agri-environment scheme *noun* a financial incentive given to farmers to adopt environmentally beneficial land management practices, e.g. the Countryside Stewardship Scheme

agro- *prefix* referring to agriculture or to the cultivation or management of land. ◊ **agri-**

agrobiodiversity *noun* the aspects of biodiversity that affect agriculture and food production, including within-species, species and ecosystem diversity

agrochemical industry *noun* the branch of industry which produces pesticides and fertilisers used on farms

agrochemicals *plural noun* pesticides and fertilisers developed for agricultural use

agroclimatology *noun* the study of climate and its effect on agriculture

agroecology *noun* the ecology of a crop-producing area

agroecosystem *noun* a community of organisms in a crop-producing area

agroforestry *noun* the growing of farm crops and trees together as a farming unit

agroindustry *noun* an industry dealing with the supply, processing and distribution of farm products

AI *abbr* **1.** active ingredient **2.** artificial insemination

aid *noun* **1.** something which helps someone do something ○ *The computer is a great aid to rapid processing of large amounts of information.* ○ *Crop sprayers are useful aids in combating insect-borne disease.* **2.** help such as food, medicines, equipment or people offered to somewhere that has experienced difficult conditions or a disaster ○ *sent food aid to the famine zone* ■ *verb* to help or give support to someone or something ○ *They were aided in their research by the detailed records kept by observers.* ○ *Changing to lead-free petrol has aided the fight against air pollution.*

AIL *abbr* aesthetic injury level

aim *noun* a goal or objective ■ *verb* to intend or to try to do something

air *noun* a mixture of gases forming the Earth's atmosphere, which cannot be seen

air basin *noun* an area of land which has uniform climate and geographical features

air bladder *noun* an air-filled sac that helps the fronds of a seaweed to float in the water

airborne *adjective* carried in the air ○ *airborne particles* ○ *airborne spores*

airborne lead *noun* particles of lead carried in the air, causing pollution

air gas *noun* a mixture of carbon monoxide and nitrogen made by passing air over hot coke or the like and used as a fuel. Also called **producer gas**

air monitoring *noun* the taking of regular samples of air to check pollution levels

air pollutant *noun* a substance such as gas or smoke that contaminates the air in a specific place or the Earth's atmosphere. Also called **atmospheric pollutant**

air pollution *noun* the contamination of the air by substances such as gas or smoke. Also called **atmospheric pollution**

air quality *noun* the state of the air in a specific place in terms of the degree of pollution measured

Air Quality Framework Directive *noun* a European Commission directive that provides a framework for setting limits for a range of pollutants, for assessing their concentrations and for managing air quality so that it remains within the set limits

air quality index *noun* a numerical scale that indicates how polluted the air is in a specific place

air quality monitoring station *noun* a facility that measures the concentration of pollutants in the air of a specific place

air quality standards *plural noun* legal limits on specific pollutants in the air

air stripping *noun* a technique for removing pollutants from water in which water is split into minute particles

Al *symbol* aluminium

albedo *noun* a measurement of the ability of a surface to reflect light, shown as the proportion of solar energy which strikes the Earth and is reflected back by a particular surface

alder *noun* a hardwood tree in the birch family. Genus: *Alnus*. (NOTE: The wood is resistant to decay in wet conditions.)

aldrin *noun* an organochlorine insecticide that is banned in the European Union

alga *noun* a tiny single-celled or multicellular organism living in water or in moist conditions, which contains chlorophyll but has no stems, roots or leaves (NOTE: The plural is **algae**.)

COMMENT: Algae were formerly regarded as plants because they contain chlorophyll, but are now classified separately. Seaweeds are forms of algae. Algae grow rapidly in water which is rich in phosphates and/or nitrates. When these levels increases, for example when fertiliser runoff enters the water, the algae multiply to form huge floating mats called blooms, blocking out the light and inhibiting the growth of other organisms. When the algae die, they combine with all the oxygen in the water so that other organisms suffocate.

algaecide *noun* same as **algicide**

algal *adjective* referring to algae ○ *Algal populations increase rapidly when phosphates are present.*

algal bloom *noun* a mass of algae which develops rapidly in a lake as a result of eutrophication

algal control *noun* the prevention of the growth of algae

algicide *noun* a substance used to kill algae

algoculture *noun* the growing of algae commercially or for scientific purposes

alien *adjective* same as **exotic** ○ *A fifth of the area of the national park is under alien conifers.* ○ *Alien species, introduced by settlers as domestic animals, have brought about the extinction of some endemic species.* ■ *noun* same as **exotic**

alkali *noun* a substance which reacts with an acid to form a salt and water. It may be either a soluble base or a solution of a base that has a pH value of more than 7. (NOTE: The plural is **alkalis**; an alternative US plural is **alkalies**.)

alkaline *adjective* containing more alkali than acid and having a pH value of more than 7

alkalinity *noun* the amount of alkali in something such as soil, water or a body ○ *The alkalinity of the soil makes it unsuitable for growing rhododendrons*

alkaloid *adjective* similar to an alkali ■ *noun* one of many poisonous substances found in plants which use them as a defence against herbivores (NOTE: Many alkaloids such as atropine, morphine or quinine are also useful as medicines.)

alkyl benzenesulfonate, alkyl benzenesulphonate *noun* a surface-acting agent used in detergents, which is not biodegradable and creates large amounts of foam in sewers and rivers

Allee effect *noun* an effect of population density on population growth, by which there is a fall in reproductive rate at very low population densities and a positive relationship between population density and the reproduction and survival of individuals

allele *noun* one of two or more alternative forms of a gene, situated in the same area (**locus**) on paired chromosomes and controlling the inheritance of the same characteristic

allelopathy *noun* the release by one plant of a chemical substance that restricts the germination or growth of another plant

Allen's rule *noun* a rule that shows that warm-blooded animals from cold regions have smaller ears and legs than animals from warmer regions, reducing the ratio of body volume to body surface

allergen *noun* a substance which produces a hypersensitive reaction in someone. Allergens are usually proteins, and include foods, the hair of animals and pollen from flowers, as well as dust.

allergenic *adjective* producing an allergy ○ *the allergenic properties of fungal spores*

allergic *adjective* affected by an allergy ○ *allergic to penicillin*

allergy *noun* a sensitivity to substances such as pollen or dust, which cause a physical reaction ○ *She has an allergy to household dust.* ○ *He has a penicillin allergy.*

alleviate *verb* to reduce or lessen the harmful effect of something

alleviation *noun* a reduction or lessening of the harmful effect of something

alley cropping *noun* the planting of crops such as maize or sorghum between trees (NOTE: The trees help to prevent soil erosion, especially on slopes, and may benefit soil fertility if the leaves are used as mulch or they are legumes.)

Alliance of Small Island States *noun* a group of states made up of islands or low-lying areas in the Pacific, Caribbean and Indian Oceans that negotiate within the United Nations to show how vulnerable they are to climate change. Abbr **AOSIS**

allo- *prefix* different

allochthonous *adjective* relating to flora, fauna, material or inhabitants that have moved from elsewhere to the region in which they are found. Compare **autochthonous**

allogenic succession *noun* the establishment of different communities in a particular area as a result of external environmental factors such as climatic change

allopatric *adjective* referring to plants of the same species which grow in different parts of the world and so do not cross-breed

allopatric speciation *noun* the development of new species which are geographically isolated from each other

alluvial *adjective* referring to alluvium

alluvial deposit *noun* a deposit of silt formed on the bed of a river or lake and carried and laid down elsewhere, often on flood plains. Also called **alluvial soil**

alluvial fan *noun* a fan-shaped deposit of sediment built up by a river where the slope of the bed becomes less steep

alluvial flat *noun* a flat area along a river where silt is deposited when the river floods. Also called **alluvial plain**

alluvial mining *noun* the extraction of minerals from alluvial deposits, e.g. panning for gold

alluvial plain *noun* same as **alluvial flat**

alluvial soil *noun* same as **alluvial deposit**

alluvial terrace *noun* a flat plain left when a river cuts deeply into the bottom of a valley. Also called **river terrace**

alluvium *noun* the silt deposited by a river or a lake

alpha diversity *noun* the number of species occurring in a small area

alpine *adjective* referring to the European mountains known as the Alps, or to other high mountains ■ *noun* a plant that grows on mountains between the tree line and the snow line

alternate *adjective* referring to flowers, buds, or leaves that are arranged singly at different heights on either side of a stem, rather than being in pairs or groups

alternative *adjective* **1.** different ○ *an alternative means of achieving the same result* **2.** not traditional or conventional ○ *searching for alternative sources of energy*

alternative energy *noun* the energy produced by tidal, wind, or solar power, or by burning biomass rather than by fossil fuels or nuclear power

alternative fuel *noun* a fuel which is promoted as a cleaner alternative to petrol, e.g. methanol

alternative technology *noun* the use of traditional techniques and equipment and materials that are available locally for agriculture, manufacturing and other processes

alternator *noun* a device for producing alternating current electricity that can be driven by a motor, or by water or wind power

altimeter *noun* a pressure or radio instrument for measuring vertical distance or altitude

altitude *noun* the height of an object above sea-level

altitudinal zonation *noun* changes in the structure of plant or animal communities in zones according to altitude

altocumulus *noun* a layer of small white cumulus clouds at moderate altitude above 3000m, usually resulting in fair weather. Compare **stratocumulus**

altostratus *noun* a high thin uniform cloud above 3000m, usually seen as a front is approaching

altruism *noun* the behaviour of an animal that reduces its chances of survival or of producing offspring, but increases those chances for another closely related individual of the same species

aluminium *noun* a metallic element extracted from the ore bauxite (NOTE: The chemical symbol is **Al**; the atomic number is **13** and the atomic weight is **26.98**.)

Am *symbol* americium

AMAP *abbr* Arctic Monitoring and Assessment Programme

amber *noun* a yellow translucent substance that is the fossilised resin of conifers. It sometimes contains fossilised insects.

ambient *adjective* referring to background conditions

ambient air *noun* the air around a building or other point

ambient climate *noun* the atmospheric conditions surrounding a specific geographical point

ambient conditions *plural noun* the atmospheric conditions such as humidity, temperature or air pressure in which something exists ○ *The ambient conditions are ideal for the development of fungi.*

ambient environment *noun* the environment which surrounds an ecosystem

ambient quality standards *plural noun* the levels of acceptable clean air which a regulatory body tries to enforce

ambient temperature *noun* the temperature of the air surrounding something

amelioration *noun* an improvement or the process of improving something ○

There has been some amelioration in pollution levels.

amenity *noun* something which makes surroundings more pleasant, e.g. a park, swimming pool or sports centre

amenity society *noun* a group of people who are concerned about the protection and improvement of their local surroundings

amenity value *noun* the degree to which something makes its surroundings more pleasant ○ *A particular hedgerow has historic, archaeological, wildlife, landscape or amenity value.*

amensalism *noun* symbiosis between two different species that is harmful to one but not the other

amensualism *noun* a situation where a species is adversely affected by another

americium *noun* an artificial radioactive element (NOTE: The chemical symbol is **Am**; the atomic number is **95** and the atomic weight is **243**.)

amino acid *noun* a chemical compound which is a component of proteins

ammonia *noun* a gas with an unpleasant smell that is easily soluble in water. Formula: NH_3.

ammonification *noun* the treatment or soaking of something with ammonia

ammonium *noun* an ion formed from ammonia

amorphous *adjective* with no regular shape

amount *noun* a quantity of something ○ *Global warming and climate change caused by increasing amounts of greenhouse gases will have wide-ranging consequences.*

Amphibia *plural noun* a class of egg-laying animals which live partly in water and partly on land and whose larvae live in water (NOTE: Amphibia include frogs, toads and newts.)

amphibian *noun* **1.** an animal which lives both in water and on land, e.g. a frog, toad or newt **2.** a vehicle which can travel both on water and on land ■ *adjective* referring to an organism which lives both in water and on land

amphibious *adjective* **1.** referring to an animal which lives both in water and on land **2.** referring to a vehicle which can travel both on water and on land

anabatic wind *noun* a stream of wind currents which are caused by solar heating of the land and rise up south-facing mountainsides. Compare **katabatic wind**

anabolism *noun* the process of building up complex chemical substances on the basis of simpler ones

anadromous *adjective* referring to a species of fish such as salmon which hatches in fresh water and becomes adult in salt water. Compare **catadromous**

anadromy *noun* a form of migration of fish such as salmon which hatch in fresh water, migrate to the sea and then return to fresh water to spawn. Compare **catadromy**

anaerobe *noun* a microorganism which lives without oxygen, e.g. the tetanus bacillus or blue-green algae. Compare **aerobe**

anaerobic *adjective* not needing oxygen for existence. Compare **aerobic**

anaerobic decomposition *noun* the breakdown of organic material by microorganisms without the presence of oxygen

anaerobic digester *noun* a digester which operates without oxygen ○ *Anaerobic digesters can be used to convert cattle manure into gas.*

COMMENT: Anaerobic digesters for pig, cattle and poultry waste feed the waste into a tank where it breaks down biologically without the presence of oxygen to give off large amounts of methane. This gas is then used to generate electricity. The remaining slurry can be applied directly to the land.

anaerobiosis *noun* a biological activity which occurs without the presence of oxygen

analyse *verb* **1.** to examine something in detail ○ *We'll need to analyse the effect of the new reporting procedures.* **2.** to separate a substance into its parts ○ *The laboratory is analysing the soil samples.* ○ *When the water sample was analysed it was found to contain traces of bacteria.*

analysis *noun* **1.** the process of examining something in detail **2.** the process of breaking down a substance into its parts in order to study them closely ○ *Samples of material were removed for analysis.* ◊ **data analysis**

analyst *noun* **1.** a person who examines samples of substances to find out what they are made of **2.** a person who carries out a study of a problem ○ *a health and safety analyst*

analyte *noun* the chemical for which tests are made on a sample

ANC *abbr* acid-neutralising capacity

ancient forest *noun* a forest which has existed for many years, containing very old trees and of great biological interest

ancient tree *noun* a tree, generally in a place where it is not surrounded by other trees, that is of great age and biological interest

ancient woodland *noun* a wooded area which has been covered with trees for many hundreds of years

anemograph *noun* an instrument which maintains a continuous recording of wind direction and speed on a graph

anemometer *noun* an instrument, usually attached to a building, which provides wind-speed information

aneroid barometer *noun* a device that shows the changes in atmospheric pressure

angiosperm *noun* a plant in which the sex organs are carried within flowers and seeds are enclosed in a fruit. Compare **gymnosperm**

animal *noun* an organism which can feel sensations and move voluntarily ■ *adjective* referring to organisms which can feel sensations and move voluntarily

animal ecology *noun* the study of the relationship between animals and their environment

animal inspector *noun* an official whose job is to inspect animals to see if they have notifiable diseases and are being kept in acceptable conditions

animal kingdom *noun* the category of all organisms classed as animals

anion *noun* an ion with a negative electric charge

Annex I parties *plural noun* industrialised countries which, as parties to the Framework Convention on Climate Change, agreed to reduce their greenhouse-gas emissions to 1990 levels by the year 2000

annoyance scale *noun* a system of classifying the amount of nuisance, harm or offence caused by something

annoyance sound level *noun* the point at which a noise begins to cause a nuisance or become offensive

annual *adjective* happening or done once a year ■ *noun* a plant whose life cycle of germination, flowering and fruiting takes place within the period of a year. ◊ **biennial, perennial**

annual ring *noun* a ring of new wood formed each year in the trunk of a tree which can easily be seen when the tree is cut down. ◊ **dendrochronology**. Also called **growth ring, tree ring** (NOTE: As a tree grows, the wood formed in the spring has more open cells than that formed in later summer. The difference in texture forms the visible rings. In tropical countries, trees grow all the year round and so do not form rings.)

COMMENT: As a tree grows, the wood formed in the spring has more open cells than that formed in later summer. The difference in texture forms the visible rings. In tropical countries, trees grow all the year round and so do not form rings.

anomaly *noun* something which differs from the expected order or range ○ *Any anomalies in the results will be detected during checking.*

anoxia *noun* a complete lack of oxygen ○ *The investigation established that the cause of death was anoxia.*

anoxic *adjective* referring to water which lacks oxygen

anoxybiosis *noun* a biological activity occurring where there is a lack of oxygen

Antarctic *noun* the area of land around the South Pole, largely covered with snow and ice ■ *adjective* referring to the Antarctic

Antarctica *noun* the continent at the South Pole

'About 90 per cent of the world's fresh water is held in Antarctica and, if it all melted, sea levels could rise as much as 60 metres' [*Times*]

Antarctic Circle *noun* the parallel running round the Earth at latitude 66°32'S, to the south of which lies the Antarctic region

Antarctic Treaty *noun* a treaty signed by all countries with territorial claims to the Antarctic continent, by which military use of the continent and dumping of nuclear waste are prohibited

anther *noun* the part of the stamen of a flower that produces pollen

anthocyanin *noun* a water-soluble plant pigment responsible for blue, violet and red colours

anthracite *noun* a type of shiny hard black coal which burns well and does not produce much smoke

anthropogenic *adjective* caused by or resulting from human activities

anti- *prefix* against or opposing

antibacterial *adjective* preventing or reducing the growth of bacteria

anticline *noun* (*in rock formations*) a fold where the newest layers of rock are on the surface. Compare **syncline**

anticondensation paint *noun* a paint which prevents the formation of condensation

anticyclone *noun* an area of high atmospheric pressure, usually associated with fine dry weather in summer and fog in winter (NOTE: Winds circulate round an anticyclone clockwise in the northern hemisphere and anticlockwise in the southern hemisphere.)

anticyclonic *adjective* **1.** referring to anticyclones **2.** referring to the opposite direction to the rotation of the Earth

anticyclonically *adverb* in the opposite direction to the rotation of the Earth

antidote *noun* a substance which controls the effects of a poison ○ *There is no satisfactory antidote to cyanide.*

antifoam, anti-foaming agent *noun* a chemical substance added to a detergent or to sewage to prevent foam from forming

antifouling paint *noun* a pesticide painted onto the bottom of a ship to prevent organisms growing on the hull. ◊ **TBT** (NOTE: It may be toxic enough to pollute sea water.)

antifungal *adjective* referring to a substance which kills or controls fungi

antigen *noun* a substance in the body which makes the body produce antibodies to attack it, e.g. a virus or germ

antigenic *adjective* referring to antigens

antigenic stability *noun* the condition of an individual who has been infected by a disease, and then remains immune to further infection in later life. This is the case in most childhood diseases.

antiknock additive *noun* a substance which is added to petrol to improve engine performance, e.g. tetraethyl lead

antioxidant *noun* a substance which prevents oxidation, used to prevent materials such as rubber from deteriorating and added to processed food to prevent oil going bad (NOTE: In the EU, antioxidant food additives have numbers E300–321.)

antipodes *plural noun* two points on opposite sides of the Earth

anti-pollution *adjective* intended to reduce or stop environmental pollution

anti-pollution legislation *noun* a set of laws designed to control pollution

anti-predator net *noun* a net designed to prevent predators from entering an area

AOM *abbr* active organic matter

AONB *abbr* Area of Outstanding Natural Beauty

AOSIS *abbr* Alliance of Small Island States

aphicide *noun* a pesticide designed to kill aphids on plants

aphid *noun* an insect that sucks sap from plants and can multiply very rapidly, e.g. a greenfly (NOTE: Aphids are pests of some garden plants such as roses and may transmit virus diseases in crops such as potatoes and sugarbeet.)

Aphis *noun* the genus of insects which comprises aphids

aphotic zone *noun* a region in a sea or lake below about 1500m, so deep that sunlight cannot penetrate it. Compare **euphotic zone**

apical meristem *noun* the actively dividing tissue at the tip of a shoot or root that produces the new tissue for growth

apomict *noun* an organism that reproduces asexually

apomictic *adjective* reproducing asexually

apomixis *noun* a form of asexual reproduction in which embryos are formed from unfertilised ova

aposematic *adjective* referring to markings on an animal which are very conspicuous and serve to discourage potential predators

apparatus *noun* equipment used in a laboratory or elsewhere for experiments or scientific study ○ *a self-contained apparatus which provides a efficient and convenient method for conducting safety tests* (NOTE: no plural: *a piece of apparatus*; *some new apparatus*)

application *noun* **1.** a formal request ○ *an application for research funds* **2.** the act of putting a substance on a surface ○ *The crop received two applications of fungicide.* **3.** the act or instance of using an existing ability ○ *the application of knowledge and skills* **4.** a particular use ○ *This new technology has many applications.* **5.** a piece of computer software that fulfils a particular job

apply *verb* **1.** to make a formal request for something ○ *You can apply for a research grant.* **2.** to put something on a surface **3.** to use existing knowledge or skills ○ *Apply the same method as in the example.* **4.** (of rules, regulations, orders, instructions, etc.) to be relevant ○ *The rules which apply to the measurement of wind velocities on isobaric charts apply equally to contour charts.* (NOTE: **applying – applies – applied**)

approach *noun* a path towards something ○ *The approach to the site was blocked by an overturned lorry.*

appropriate assessment *noun* a step in the decision-making process which must be undertaken for plans or projects which would be likely to have a significant effect on a site of conservation importance, so that any unfavourable impact can be avoided

appropriate dose *noun* the amount of a substance required to be effective, e.g. the amount of a fungicide required to control a disease

appropriate technology *noun* a technology that is suited to the local environment, usually involving skills or materials that are available locally ○ *Biomethanation is an appropriate technology for use in rural areas.*

aqua- *prefix* water. ◊ **aqui-**

aquaculture, aquafarming *noun* same as **fish farming**

aquarium *noun* a container with water and a display of fish and other animals or plants that live in water

aquatic *adjective* referring to water

aquatic animal *noun* an animal that lives in water

aquatic ecosystem *noun* an ecosystem that is based on water, e.g. a river, pond, lake or ocean

aquatic plant *noun* a plant that grows in water

aqui- *prefix* water. ◊ **aqua-**

aquiclude *noun* a body of rock or soil such as clay through which water passes very slowly

aquiculture *noun* same as **fish farming**

aquifer *noun* a body of porous rock or soil through which water passes and in which water gathers

Ar *symbol* argon

arable *adjective* referring to land on which crops are grown

arable weed *noun* a weed that grows on or near land that has been cultivated for crops, e.g. poppy

arachnid *noun* an animal with four pairs of legs and a body with two segments. Class: Arachnida. (NOTE: Spiders, scorpions and mites are arachnids.)

Arachnida *noun* a class of animals that have eight legs, e.g. spiders and mites

arbor- *prefix* tree

arboreal *adjective* referring to trees

arboreal animal *noun* an animal which lives in trees

arboretum *noun* a collection of trees from different parts of the world, grown for scientific study (NOTE: The plural is **arboreta**.)

arboricide *noun* a chemical substance which kills trees

arboriculture *noun* the study of the cultivation of trees

arborist *noun* a person who studies the cultivation of trees

archipelago *noun* a group of islands

Arctic *adjective* referring to the area around the North Pole ■ *noun* the area of the Earth's surface around the North Pole, north of the Arctic Circle

arctic air *noun* a mass of cold air which forms over the Arctic region and then moves south

Arctic Circle *noun* a parallel running round the Earth at latitude 66°32N to the north of which lies the Arctic region

Arctic Council *noun* the eight Arctic countries (Canada, Finland, Denmark, Iceland, Norway, Sweden, Russia and the United States) which follow the Arctic Environmental Protection Strategy

Arctic Environmental Protection Strategy *noun* a plan followed by the Arctic Council to monitor and protect the Arctic environment. Abbr **AEPS**

Arctic Monitoring and Assessment Programme *noun* a programme that provides information on the status of, and threats to, the Arctic environment as well as scientific advice on action to be taken to prevent or recover from contaminants. Abbr **AMAP**

Arctogea *noun* one of the main biogeographical regions of the Earth, comprising the Palaearctic, Nearctic, Oriental and Ethiopian regions. ◊ **Neogea, Notogea**

area *noun* **1.** the measurement of the space taken up by something, calculated by multiplying the length by the width ○ *The area of this office is 3400 square feet.* ○ *We are looking for an area of about 100 square metres.* **2.** a region of land ○ *The whole area has been contaminated by waste from the power station.*

area of low pressure *noun* an area in which the atmospheric pressure is low and around which the air turns in the same direction as the Earth

Area of Outstanding Natural Beauty *noun* in England and Wales, a region which is not a National Park but which is considered sufficiently attractive to be preserved from unsympathetic development. Abbr **AONB**

Area of Special Scientific Interest *noun* in Northern Ireland, an area of land which is officially protected to maintain its fauna, flora or geology. Abbr **ASSI**

arête *noun* a sharp ridge between two valleys

argon *noun* an inert gas, which occurs in air and of which isotopes form in the cooling systems of reactors. It is used in electric light bulbs. (NOTE: The chemical symbol is **Ar**; the atomic number is **18** and the atomic weight is **39.95**.)

arid *adjective* referring to soil which is very dry, or an area of land which has very little rain

aridity *noun* the state of being extremely dry

arithmetic mean *noun* a number calculated by adding together several figures and dividing by the number of figures added. Also called **average**

aromatic *adjective* having a pleasant smell

aromatic compound, aromatic hydrocarbon *noun* a compound such as benzene, with a ring of carbon atoms held by single and double bonds

arrest *noun* a sudden stoppage

arrester *noun* a device or substance which prevents or stops something from happening

arroyo *noun* a gully with a stream at the bottom, found in desert regions of the US. Compare **wadi**

arsenic *noun* a grey semimetallic chemical element that forms poisonous compounds such as arsenic trioxide, which was formerly used in some medicines (NOTE: The chemical symbol is **As**; the atomic number is **33** and the atomic weight is **74.92**.)

arsenide *noun* a compound of arsenic and a metallic element

artefact, artifact *noun* a human-made object

artesian well *noun* a well which has been bored into a confined aquifer, the hydrostatic pressure usually being strong enough to force the water to the surface

artifact *noun* another spelling of **artefact**

artificial *adjective* made by humans and not existing naturally

artificial community *noun* a plant community kept by people, as in a garden

artificial fertiliser *noun* a fertiliser manufactured from chemicals. Also called **chemical fertiliser**

artificial insemination *noun* a method of breeding livestock by injecting sperm from specially selected males into a female. Abbr **AI**

artificial recharge *noun* the introduction of surface water into an underground aquifer through a recharge well

As *symbol* arsenic

asbestos *noun* a fibrous mineral substance that causes lung disease if inhaled. It was formerly used as a shield against fire and as an insulating material in many industrial and construction processes.

asbestosis *noun* a disease of the lungs caused by inhaling asbestos dust

ASCOBANS *noun* an agreement made between European countries in 1991. Full form **Agreement on the conservation of small cetaceans of the Baltic and North Seas**

asexual *adjective* not involving sexual reproduction

ash *noun* **1.** a hardwood tree. Genus: *Fraxinus*. **2.** a grey or black powder formed of minerals left after an organic substance has been burnt

aspect *noun* a direction in which something faces ○ *a site with a northern aspect*

aspen *noun* a hardwood tree with leaves that tremble in the wind. Genus: *Populus*.

asphalt *noun* a black substance formed from bitumen

assessment *noun* **1.** careful consideration of something to make a judgment about it **2.** a judgment based on evidence

ASSI *abbr* Area of Special Scientific Interest

assimilate *verb* to take into the body's tissues substances which have been absorbed into the blood from digested food

assimilation *noun* the action of assimilating food substances

assimilation efficiency *noun* the percentage of food energy which is taken into the gut of a consumer and assimilated through the wall of the gut. Abbr **AE**

associate *verb* to be linked to or accompanied by something ○ *Turbulence is often associated with strong winds.*

association *noun* **1.** a group of people with similar interests **2.** a link between two things ○ *They were looking for an association between specific chemicals and the disease.* **3.** same as **biological association**

astatine *noun* a natural radioactive element (NOTE: The chemical symbol is **At**; the atomic number is **85** and the atomic weight is **210**.)

Asteraceae *plural noun* a common and very large family of plants with flat flowers that consist of many florets arranged around a central structure. Former name **Compositae**

asulam *noun* a herbicide used around trees and fruit bushes

At *symbol* astatine

Atlantic Conveyor Belt *noun* same as **North Atlantic Conveyor**

Atlantic Ocean *noun* the ocean to the north of the Antarctic, south of the Arctic, west of Europe and Africa and east of North and South America

atmosphere *noun* **1.** a mass of gases surrounding the Earth or any astronomical object such as a planet or star **2.** a unit of measurement of pressure, equal to 101325 pascals or equal to a height of 760 mm of mercury

atmospheric *adjective* referring to the atmosphere

atmospheric contamination *noun* pollution of the air with harmful substances

atmospheric lifetime *noun* same as **lifetime**

atmospheric pollutant *noun* same as **air pollutant**

atmospheric pollution *noun* same as **air pollution**

atoll *noun* an island in warm seas, made of coral and shaped like a ring

atom *noun* a fundamental unit of a chemical element and the smallest part of an element that can exist independently

Atomic Energy Authority *noun* ▶ United Kingdom Atomic Energy Authority, International Atomic Energy Agency

Atomic Energy Commission *noun* US an agency responsible for nuclear energy in the US. Abbr **AEC**

atomic fission *noun* the splitting of the nucleus of an atom such as uranium-235 into several small nuclei which then release energy and neutrons. Also called **nuclear fission**

atomic power station *noun* a power station in which nuclear reactions are used to provide energy to run turbines that generate electricity

atomic waste *noun* radioactive waste from a nuclear reactor, including spent fuel rods and coolant

atomise, atomize *verb* to reduce liquids to a fine spray

atrazine *noun* a herbicide used especially on maize crops that kills germinating seedlings. It is a contaminant of ground water and is banned in the European Union, but still allowed for essential use in the UK.

atropine *noun* a poisonous plant compound (**alkaloid**), found in *Atropa belladonna*, that affects heart rate and is used medically to relax muscles

attend *verb* to exist or happen in connection with something else (*formal*) ○ *Serious consequences may attend this decision.*

attend to *verb* **1.** to deal with something or someone ○ *We need to attend to the feedback first of all.* **2.** to pay attention to something (*formal*) ○ *Please attend to this safety advice immediately.*

attract *verb* to cause something to draw near ○ *If two magnets, with unlike poles are brought together, they will attract each other.* ○ *An animal may attract a mate with a courtship display.*

attractant *noun* a chemical that attracts an organism. ◊ **pheromone**

attraction *noun* the act or an instance of being drawn near to someone or something ○ *The strength of the magnetic force will depend, amongst other things, on the magnitude of attraction at the magnetic source.*

attribute *noun* a characteristic or quality

Au *symbol* gold

audio-, audi- *prefix* hearing or sound

audit *noun* a check on figures, scientific data or procedures

Aurora Australis *noun* same as **Southern Lights**

Aurora Borealis *noun* same as **Northern Lights**

autecology *noun* the study of an individual species in its environment. Compare **synecology**

authority *noun* **1.** the power to act □ **to abuse your authority** to use powers in an illegal or harmful way **2.** an official body that controls an area or a specific activity ○ *You will have to apply to the local planning authority.* **3.** a person or body with specialised knowledge of a subject

auto- *prefix* automatic or automated

autochthonous *adjective* referring to flora, fauna or other matter which is produced by the community in which it is found. Compare **allochthonous**

autocidal control *noun* a form of pest control, especially of insects, by which sterile males are introduced in order to stop the population breeding

autoecology *noun* same as **autecology**

autogenic succession *noun* **1.** succession that follows biological processes, and can include colonisation and changes to the environment **2.** the establishment of different communities in a particular area as a result of biological changes, including colonisation and changes to the environment

'In the absence of natural ecological processes of grazing, fire and water-level fluctuations, autogenic succession tends to build dense stands of emergent hydrophytes in many wetlands' [*Northern Prairies Wildlife Research Center*]

autolysis *noun* the action of cells destroying themselves with their own enzymes

autotroph, autotrophic organism *noun* an organism which manufactures its own organic constituents from inorganic materials, e.g. a bacterium or green plant. Compare **chemotroph, heterotroph**

autumn *noun* the season of the year, following summer and before winter, when days become shorter and the weather progressively colder (NOTE: The US term is **fall**.)

autumnal *adjective* referring to the autumn

autumn colour *noun* the bright red and yellow colours produced in the leaves of some plants by chemical changes as the days shorten and become colder

avalanche *noun* a large mass of snow that becomes detached and falls down the side of a mountain

average *adjective* **1.** typical or usual ○ *of average ability* ○ *below average performance* **2.** referring to the arithmetic mean ○ *average cost per unit* ○ *average price* ○ *average sales per representative* ■ *noun* same as **arithmetic mean** ○ *the average for the last three months* ○ *sales average* ■ *verb* to produce as an average figure

Aves *noun* the class that comprises birds

avian *adjective* relating to birds

aviary *noun* a cage or large enclosure for birds

avicide *noun* a substance that kills birds

avifauna *noun* all the birds that live naturally in a specific area (NOTE: The plural is **avifauna** or **avifaunas**.)

azobacter *noun* a nitrogen-fixing bacterium belonging to a group found in soil

B

B *symbol* boron

Ba *symbol* barium

bacillary *adjective* referring to a bacillus

bacillus *noun* a bacterium shaped like a rod (NOTE: The plural is **bacilli**.)

back *verb* (*of wind*) to change direction, anticlockwise in the northern hemisphere and clockwise in the southern hemisphere. Opposite **veer**

backbone *noun* in vertebrate animals, a series of bones (**vertebrae**) linked together to form a flexible column running from the pelvis to the skull

background *noun* a set of conditions which are always present in the environment, but are less obvious or less important than others

background concentration *noun* same as **background pollution**

background extinction rate *noun* the usual rate at which some species become extinct as other species develop, not caused by the actions of human beings

background noise *noun* **1.** a general level of noise which is always there in the environment ○ *The other machines around this device will produce a lot of background noise.* **2.** (*in an electronic instrument*) noise which is present along with the required signal ○ *The modem is sensitive to background noise.*

background pollution *noun* the general level of air pollution in an area, disregarding any specifically local factors, e.g. the presence of a coal-fired power station

backscatter *noun* the sending back of radiation ○ *Backscatter contributes to an increase in albedo.* ■ *verb* to send back radiation ○ *A proportion of incoming solar radiation is backscattered by air in the atmosphere.*

backshore *noun* the part of a beach between the foreshore and where permanent vegetation grows

backswamp *noun* a marshy area in a flood plain

back-to-nature *adjective* relating to a simple self-sufficient way of life with very little use of modern technology. ◊ **nature**

backwash *noun* the flow of seawater down a beach. Compare **swash**

backwater *noun* **1.** stagnant water connected to a river or stream **2.** the water held behind a dam, or kept back by a current

bacteria *plural noun* submicroscopic organisms, belonging to a large group, some of which help in the decomposition of organic matter, some of which are permanently in the intestines of animals and can break down food tissue and some of which cause disease (NOTE: The singular is **bacterium**.)

bacterial *adjective* referring to or caused by bacteria ○ *a bacterial disease*

bactericidal *adjective* destroying bacteria

bactericide *noun* a substance that destroys bacteria

bacteriology *noun* the scientific study of bacteria

bacteriophage *noun* a virus that affects bacteria

bacterium *noun* ♦ **bacteria**

badlands *plural noun* areas of land which are or have become unsuitable for agriculture

bag *noun* a filter made of cloth or artificial fibre, used to remove particles of matter from waste gas from industrial processes

bagged waste *noun* mixed waste which has been collected from households and other sources

baghouse *noun* a device for cleaning gas by forcing it through large bags which trap particulates

balance *noun* **1.** a state in which weights or forces are evenly distributed **2.** a state in which proportions of substances are correct ○ *to maintain a healthy balance of vitamins in the diet*

balanced diet *noun* a diet which provides all the nutrients needed in the correct proportions

balance of nature *noun* a popular concept that relative numbers of different organisms living in the same ecosystem may remain more or less constant without human interference □ **to disturb the balance of nature** to make a change to the environment which has the effect of putting some organisms at a disadvantage compared with others

baleen *noun* a series of plates like a comb, which hang down from the upper jaw of some whales and act like a sieve

baleen whale *noun* a whale that has two breathing holes and feeds by sucking in water and then forcing it out with the tongue through the baleen, which traps plankton. Suborder: Mysticeti. (NOTE: Baleen whales are the larger of the two groups of whales; the others are the toothed whales or Odontoceti.)

balsa wood *noun* a very soft tropical wood, used for making lightweight models. Latin name: *Ochroma pyramidalis*.

ban *noun* an official statement forbidding something, or saying that something should not be done ■ *verb* to say that something should not be done ○ *The use of CFCs in aerosols is banned.* ○ *Importing some plants is banned under CITES regulations.*

band *noun* **1.** a strip or loop of fabric, metal or plastic ○ *A jet stream is a narrow band of high-altitude strong winds.* **2.** a narrow area that is different in colour from other areas **3.** a layer of rock

banded *adjective* **1.** referring to rock arranged in layers **2.** showing bands of colour

bank *noun* **1.** a piece of land at the edge of water such as a river or lake **2.** a long heap of sand or snow, e.g. a sandbank in shallow water or a snowbank along the side of a road **3.** a place where something is collected for a particular use, e.g. a seed bank or a bottle bank. ◊ **bottle bank, can bank**

BAP *abbr* Biodiversity Action Plan

bar *noun* **1.** a unit of atmospheric pressure, equal to 1000 millibars or $10^{5\,Pa.}$ ◊ **millibar** **2.** a long bank of sand submerged at high tide at the entrance to a harbour, river or bay

barium *noun* a chemical element that forms poisonous compounds (NOTE: The chemical symbol is **Ba**; the atomic number is **56** and the atomic weight is **137.34**.)

bark *noun* **1.** the outer layer of a tree trunk or branch **2.** the cry of an animal of the dog family, e.g. a wolf or fox

barley *noun* a cereal crop used as animal feed and for making malt for beer or whisky. Latin name: *Hordeum sativum*.

baro- *prefix* referring to weight or pressure

barograph *noun* an instrument that records changes in atmospheric pressure by a pen attached to a barometer which records fluctuations in pressure on a roll of paper

barometer *noun* an instrument which measures changes in atmospheric pressure and is used to forecast changes in the weather

barometric *adjective* referring to a barometer

barometrically *adverb* by use of a barometer

barrage *noun* a construction to prevent or regulate the flow of tides, used either to prevent flooding or to harness tidal power

barrel *noun* **1.** a large cylindrical container for liquids such as beer, wine and oil **2.** the amount of a liquid contained in a standard barrel of 42 US gallons, used as a measure of the quantity of crude oil produced and equal to 159 litres or 35 imperial gallons

barren *adjective* unable to support plant or animal life ○ *a sparse and barren landscape at high altitude*

barrier *noun* a structure that prevents something going from one place to another. ◊ **geographical barrier, species barrier**

basal *adjective* **1.** being the base or bottom of something **2.** forming the basis of something

basalt *noun* a hard black volcanic rock

basaltic *adjective* referring to or containing basalt (NOTE: Most volcanic lava is basaltic.)

base *noun* **1.** the original, lowest or first position **2.** the main ingredient of something such as a paint or an ointment **3.** a substance that reacts with an acid to form a salt ■ *verb* **1.** to start to calculate from a position ○ *We based our calculations on the rate of change we observed.* **2.** to develop something from something else ○ *Field identification of plants is based on morphological characters.*

base level *noun* **1.** the lowest level of something, from which other levels are calculated **2.** the depth below which erosion would be unable to occur

baseline *noun* the point from which change can be measured

baseline conditions *plural noun* (*in economic analyses*) the health, environmental, economic or other conditions that exist before any accidental or deliberate changes occur ○ *return the damaged land to baseline conditions*

baseline emission *noun* the level of emission of a gas such as a greenhouse gas that would occur without a change in policy

basement *noun* the lowest level of rock, which has been covered by sediment

base metal *noun* a common metal, e.g. copper, lead or tin. Compare **noble metal**

basic *adjective* **1.** from which everything else comes ○ *This chapter provides a basic understanding from which the study of meteorology can develop.* ○ *The basic structure is the same for all models in this range.* **2.** relating to a chemical which reacts with an acid to form a salt

basic reproductive rate *noun* the number of eggs produced per individual over the period of a cycle, calculated by dividing the total number of eggs produced by the number of individuals at the beginning of the cycle

basin *noun* a large low-lying area of land, drained by a large river system or surrounding an ocean ○ *Thousands of tributaries drain into the Amazon basin.* ○ *A ring of volcanoes lies around the edge of the Pacific basin.*

Batesian mimicry *noun* a form of mimicry where one species mimics another which is poisonous, so as to avoid being eaten

bathing water *noun* a seawater or freshwater area used for swimming in for which specific water quality standards exist under EU law

bathy- *prefix* referring to the part of the seabed between 200 and 2000 m deep

bathyal *adjective* referring to the deep part of the sea

bathylimnetic *adjective* referring to the deepest part of a lake

BATNEEC *noun* a principle applied to the control of emissions into the air, land and water from polluting processes, in order to minimise pollution without the use of advanced technology or expensive methods. Full form **best available technology not entailing excessive cost**

battery *noun* a chemical device which produces electrical current

battery farming *noun* a system of keeping thousands of chickens in a series of small cages

battery hen *noun* a chicken which spends its life confined in a small cage

bauxite *noun* a mineral that contains aluminium ore

bay *noun* a wide curved coastline, partly enclosing an area of sea

Be *symbol* beryllium

beach *noun* an area of sand or small stones at the edge of the sea, a lake or a river ■ *verb* to come or bring out of the sea or a lake onto a beach ○ *Many whales die after beaching themselves on coasts.*

Beaufort scale *noun* a scale rising from 0 to 12, used to refer to the strength of wind ○ *The meteorological office has issued a warning of force 12 winds.*

beck *noun* a mountain stream

becquerel *noun* the SI unit of measurement of radiation, 1 becquerel being the amount of radioactivity in a substance where one nucleus decays per second. Symbol **Bq**. ◊ **rad** (NOTE: now used in place of the **curie**)

bed *noun* **1.** the bottom of a river, lake or the sea **2.** a layer of sediment in rock ○ *The cliffs show clearly several beds of sandstone.* ■ ♦ **filter bed**

bedding *noun* sediment in different layers

bedrock *noun* the rock which is found under a layer of ore or coal

bee *noun* a flying insect with a hairy body (NOTE: Bees pollinate some types of plant.)

beech *noun* a common temperate hardwood tree. Genus: *Fagus*.

beetle *noun* an insect with hard covers on its wings. Order: Coleoptera.

beetle bank *noun* an uncultivated ridge left in the middle of large fields for insects and spiders which survive there during winter and then spread rapidly into the crop in the following spring to eat pests such as aphids

behaviour *noun* the way in which a living organism responds to a stimulus

behavioural *adjective* referring to behaviour

behavioural ecology *noun* the study of patterns of behaviour in animals

behavioural strategy *noun* a strategy adopted by an animal as a response to a predator, e.g. attack, escape or hiding

belt *noun* a long, narrow area ○ *a belt of trees* ◊ **Green Belt**

benchmark *noun* a level or standard against which increases or decreases can be measured ■ *verb* to establish a level or standard against which increases or decreases can be measured

benthic *adjective* on or living on the bottom of the sea or of a lake

benthic fauna *plural noun* animals living on the bottom of the sea or a lake

benthic organism *noun* an organism living on the bottom of the sea or of a lake

benthos *noun* a collection of organisms living on the bottom of the sea or a lake

benzene *noun* a simple aromatic hydrocarbon produced from coal tar that is very carcinogenic. Formula: C_6H_6.

benzene hexachloride *noun* the active ingredient of the pesticide lindane

benzpyrene *noun* an inflammable substance found in coal tar, produced in exhaust fumes from petrol engines and coal- and oil-burning appliances, and from smoking tobacco. It is carcinogenic.

Bergmann's rule *noun* the principle that warmblooded animals from cold regions have larger bodies than animals of the same species from warmer regions, thus reducing the ratio of their body volume to body surface

Bern Convention, Berne Convention *noun* ◆ Convention on the Conservation of European Wildlife and Natural Habitats

berry *noun* a small fleshy indehiscent fruit with several seeds, e.g. a tomato or a grape

berylliosis *noun* poisoning caused by breathing in dust or fumes containing particles of beryllium or beryllium compounds

beryllium *noun* a metallic element. It is used in making various alloys. (NOTE: The chemical symbol is **Be**; the atomic number is **4** and the atomic weight is **9.01**.)

best-before date *noun* a date stamped on foodstuffs sold in supermarkets, which is the last date when the food is guaranteed to be in good condition. Compare **sell-by date**

beta diversity *noun* the number of species in a wide region

Betz limit *noun* the maximum power that can be produced by a wind turbine

Bhopal *noun* a town in India that was the scene of an accident in 1984, when methyl isocyanate gas escaped from a chemical plant and caused many deaths

BHT *abbr* butylated hydroxytoluene

bicarbonate *noun* same as **hydrogen carbonate**

biennial *adjective* happening every two years ■ *noun* a plant that completes its life cycle over a period of two years. ◊ **annual, perennial**

bight *noun* a wide curve in a shoreline

bilharzia *noun* **1.** a flatworm which enters the bloodstream from infected water and causes schistosomiasis. Genus: *Schistosoma*. **2.** same as **schistosomiasis**

bilharziasis *noun* same as **schistosomiasis**

billion *noun* a number equal to one thousand million (NOTE: In the US it has always meant one thousand million, but in the UK it formerly meant one million million, and it is still sometimes used with this meaning. With figures it is usually written **bn**: *5 bn*.)

bind *verb* to form a chemical bond

binding agent *noun* a substance that causes two or more other substances to stick together or combine

binding target *noun* an environmental standard that must be met in the future

binomial classification *noun* the scientific system of naming organisms devised by the Swedish scientist Carolus Linnaeus (1707–78)

COMMENT: The Linnaean system of binomial classification gives each organism a name made up of two Latin words. The first is a generic name referring to the genus to which the organism belongs, and the second is a specific name referring to the particular species. Organisms are usually identified by using both their generic and specific names, e.g. *Homo sapiens* (human), *Felis catus* (domestic cat) and *Sequoia sempervirens* (redwood). A third name can be added to give a subspecies. The generic name is written or printed with a capital letter and the specific name with a lowercase letter. Both names are usually given in italics or are underlined if written or typed.

bio- *prefix* referring to living organisms

bioaccessible *adjective* able to be taken up by any organism

bioaccumulate *verb* (of toxic substances) to accumulate in increasing amounts up the food chain

bioaccumulation *noun* the accumulation of substances such as toxic chemicals in increasing amounts up the food chain

bioaeration *noun* the treatment of sewage by pumping activated sludge into it

bioassay *noun* a test of a substance by examining the effect it has on living organisms

bioaugmentation *noun* the addition of microorganisms to human or industrial waste to reinforce natural biological processes

bioavailability *noun* the degree to which a nutrient or other chemical can be metabolised by an organism

biocatalysis *noun* the process of a chemical reaction being aided by a biochemical agent such as an enzyme

biocatalyst *noun* a biological agent such as an enzyme that aids a chemical reaction

biocatalytic *adjective* referring to biocatalysis

biochemical *adjective* referring to bio-chemistry

biochemical oxygen demand *noun* same as **biological oxygen demand**

biochemist *noun* a scientist who special-ises in biochemistry

biochemistry *noun* the chemistry of liv-ing tissues

biocide *noun* a substance that kills living organisms ○ *Biocides used in agriculture run off into lakes and rivers.*

biocide pollution *noun* pollution of lakes and rivers caused by the runoff from fields of herbicides and other biocides used in agriculture

bioclimatic *adjective* referring to the re-lationship between climate and living or-ganisms, or to the study of bioclimatology

bioclimatology *noun* the study of the ef-fect of climate on living organisms

biocoenosis *noun* **1.** a varied communi-ty of organisms living in the same small area such as the bark of a tree **2.** the rela-tionship between the organisms in such a community (NOTE: [all senses] The US spelling is **biocenosis**.)

biocomposite *noun* a material that is made from a plant fibre such as hemp fixed within a resin made from a fossil fuel. ◊ **ecocomposite**

biocontrol *noun* same as **biological con-trol**

bioconversion *noun* the changing of or-ganic waste into a source of energy, e.g. the production of methane gas from the decom-position of organic matter

biodegradability *noun* the degree to which material such as packaging can be decomposed by natural processes

biodegradable *adjective* easily decom-posed by organisms such as bacteria or by natural processes such as the effect of sun-light or the sea ○ *biodegradable household waste such as potato peelings* ○ *Biode-gradable cartons can be made from potato starch.* ○ *Organochlorines are not biode-gradable and enter the food chain easily.*

biodegradable packaging *noun* ma-terial such as boxes, cartons or bottles that can be decomposed by organisms such as bacteria or by natural processes such as the effect of sunlight or the sea

biodegradation *noun* the breaking down of a substance by natural processes, e.g. the breakdown of activated sludge by bacteria

biodegrade *verb* to decay as the result of natural processes

biodiesel *noun* a substitute for diesel fuel made wholly or partly from organic prod-ucts, especially oils extracted from plants such as oilseed rape

biodigestion *noun* the use of microor-ganisms to break down food and organic waste

biodiverse *adjective* containing a large number of species ○ *a biodiverse area of rainforest*

biodiversity *noun* the range of species, subspecies or communities in a specific habitat such as a rainforest or a meadow. Also called **biological diversity**

'Modern intensive farming is probably the main cause of declining biodiversity in the country-side. (Delivering the evidence. Defra's Science and Innovation Strategy 2003–06)'

Biodiversity Action Plan *noun* a de-tailed scheme to maintain the biological di-versity of a specific area. Abbr **BAP**

biodiversity hotspot *noun* a threat-ened region with a large range of endemic plant species (at least 1500) but where more than 70% of the original habitat has been lost because of human activities. Typ-ically, the diversity of endemic vertebrates is also high.

biodiversity indicator *noun* a factor that allows change in the environment over time to be assessed. Also called **bioindica-tor**

biodiversity prospecting *noun* the process of searching among wild organ-isms for new species or genetic characteris-tics that may have potential commercial value

biodome *noun* a very large greenhouse or similar structure with a controlled internal environment in which plants and animals from much warmer or colder regions are kept in conditions similar to nature

biodynamic agriculture *noun* a view of agriculture based on a holistic and spirit-ual understanding of nature and humans' role in it, which considers a farm as a self-contained evolving organism, relying on home-produced feeds and manures with external inputs kept to a minimum

biodynamics *noun* the study of living organisms and the production of energy

bioecology *noun* the study of the rela-tionships among organisms and between them and their physical environment, with particular emphasis on the effect of humans on the environment

bioenergetics *noun* same as **biodynam-ics**

bioenergy *noun* energy produced from biomass

bioengineering *noun* the use of biochemical processes on an industrial scale to produce drugs and foodstuffs or to recycle waste

bioerosion *noun* erosion or decay due to the action of living organisms

bioethanol *noun* a fuel for internal-combustion engines that is made by fermenting biological material to produce alcohol (NOTE: Typically 5–10% bioethanol is added to petrol.)

biofilter *noun* a filter system that uses microorganisms to convert the organic compounds of a pollutant to carbon dioxide, water and salts

biofuel *noun* a fuel produced from organic domestic waste or other sources such as plants (NOTE: Coppiced willow is sometimes grown for biofuel.)

biogas *noun* a mixture of methane and carbon dioxide produced from fermenting waste such as animal dung ○ *Farm biogas systems may be uneconomic unless there is a constant demand for heat.* ○ *The use of biogas systems in rural areas of developing countries is increasing.*

biogenic *adjective* relating to plants and animals

biogenic source *noun* a plant or animal which emits air pollutants

biogeochemical *adjective* relating to biogeochemistry

biogeochemical cycle *noun* a process in which nutrients from living organisms are transferred into the physical environment and back to the organisms (NOTE: This process is essential for organic life to continue.)

biogeochemistry *noun* the study of living organisms and their relationship to the chemical components of the Earth such as its soil, rocks and minerals

biogeographer *noun* a scientist who studies regions that have their own fauna and flora

biogeographical region, biogeographical zone *noun* a region of the Earth that has its own special fauna and flora, separated from other regions by a natural barrier or change in environmental conditions

biogeography *noun* the study of the relationship between organisms and the geography of the region where they occur, including how they originally came to that region

biogeosphere *noun* the top layer of the Earth's crust, which contains living organisms

biohazard *noun* a risk to human beings or their environment presented by something that is toxic or infectious

biohydrology *noun* the study of the interactions between the water cycle and plants and animals

bioindicator *noun* same as **biodiversity indicator**

bioinformatics *noun* the use of computers to extract and analyse biological data

bioinsecticide *noun* an insecticide developed from natural plant toxins, e.g. pyrethrum. ◊ **microbial insecticide**

biological *adjective* referring to biology

biological association *noun* a group of organisms living together in a large area, forming a stable community

biological control *noun* the control of pests by using predators and natural processes to remove them. Also called **biocontrol**

biological desert *noun* an area where there is no life (NOTE: Heavy pollution can turn the bottom of a lake into a biological desert.)

biological diversity *noun* same as **biodiversity**

Biological Diversity Convention *noun* one of two binding treaties agreed at the Earth Summit, in Rio de Janeiro in June 1992, requiring states to take steps to preserve ecologically valuable areas and species

biological efficiency *noun* the ratio of the productivity of an organism or community of organisms to that of its supply of energy

biological half-life *noun* the time taken for half of an amount of radioactive material to be eliminated naturally from a living organism

biological indicator *noun* an organism that is known to respond to specific changes in the environment

biologically decomposable *adjective* same as **biodegradable**

biological magnification *noun* same as **bioaccumulation**

biological mass *noun* same as **biomass**

biological monitoring *noun* the process of checking the changes that take place in a habitat over time

biological oxygen demand *noun* the amount of pollution in water, shown as the amount of oxygen needed to oxidise the polluting substances. Abbr **BOD**

   COMMENT: Diluted sewage passed into rivers contains dissolved oxygen, which is utilised by bacteria as they oxidise the pollutants in the sewage. The oxygen is replaced by oxygen from the air. Diluted sewage should not absorb more than 20 ppm of dissolved oxygen.

biological pesticide *noun* same as **biopesticide**

biological pump *noun* the process by which carbon sinks from the surface to the depths of the oceans, so reducing the levels of carbon dioxide in the atmosphere

biological wastewater treatment *noun* the use of aerobic or anaerobic microorganisms to produce effluents and separated sludge containing microbial mass together with pollutants, often as well as using mechanical processes

biologist *noun* a scientist who specialises in biology

biology *noun* the study of living organisms

bioluminescence *noun* the production of light by organisms such as fireflies or sea animals, as a result of an enzymic reaction (NOTE: Bioluminescence is found in many deep-sea animals, fireflies and some bacteria and fungi.)

biomagnification *noun* same as **bioaccumulation**

biomanipulation *noun* the action or process of changing the environment to improve the survival of wildlife

biomarker *noun* a distinctive indicator of a biological or biochemical process, e.g. a chemical whose occurrence shows the presence of a disease

biomass *noun* **1.** the sum of all living organisms in a given area or at a given trophic level, usually expressed in terms of living or dry mass **2.** organic matter used to produce energy (NOTE: Willow and miscanthus are grown as biomass for fuel.)

biomass boiler *noun* a device that burns biomass as a fuel to heat water

biomass energy *noun* the energy produced by burning renewable materials such as wood or waste

biomaterial *noun* a biodegradable material of plant origin

biome *noun* a large ecological region characterised by its vegetation and climate and the organisms adapted to live in it

   COMMENT: The ten principal biomes are: mountains, polar regions, tropical rainforest, grasslands, deserts, temperate forests, monsoon forests, deciduous forests, coniferous forests and evergreen shrub forests.

biometeorology *noun* the scientific study of the weather and its effect on organisms

biomethanation *noun* a system of producing biogas for use as fuel

   'Biomethanation is attractive for use in rural areas for several reasons: it is an anaerobic digestion process, which is the simplest, safest way that has been found for treating human excreta and animal manure.' [*Appropriate Technology*]

biometrical *adjective* referring to biometrics

biometrics *noun* the use of statistical techniques on biological data (NOTE: takes a singular verb)

biomonitoring *noun* the measurement and tracking of a chemical substance in an organism or in biological material such as blood or urine, in order to monitor exposure to pollution, chemicals or other hazards

bion *noun* a single living organism in an ecosystem

biopesticide *noun* a pesticide produced from biological sources such as plant toxins that occur naturally. ◊ **microbial insecticide**

biophyte *noun* a plant that obtains nutrients from the decomposing bodies of insects which it traps and kills, e.g. a sundew

biopiracy *noun* the commercial development of genetic resources such as plants with medicinal properties or genes for resistance to disease without allowing the people or government of the area where they were originally discovered to share in financial benefits

bioprospecting *noun* the process of looking for plants that contain potentially useful pharmaceutical compounds

bioregion *noun* an area defined in environmental terms rather than by geopolitics

bioremediation *noun* the use of organisms such as bacteria to remove environmental pollutants from soil, water or gases (NOTE: Bioremediation is used to clean up contaminated land and oil spills.)

biosecurity *noun* the management of the risks to animal, plant and human health posed by pests and diseases

bioseparation *noun* the use of biological agents such as plants, enzymes, or biological membranes in separating the different components of something, e.g. in the purification of proteins or water, or in making food and pharmaceutical products

biosolids *plural noun* a nutrient-rich organic material, solid or semi-solid before processing, that is derived from sewage as a product of wastewater treatment and used as a fertilizer

biosphere *noun* same as **ecosphere**

biosphere reserve *noun* an environmentally sensitive area with protected status managed primarily to preserve natural ecological conditions (NOTE: Biosphere reserves may be open to tourists.)

biospheric cycle *noun* a natural cyclical process that supports life on Earth, e.g. the oxygen cycle, carbon cycle, nitrogen cycle or water cycle

biostimulation *noun* the addition of nutrients to polluted waste or ground in order to enhance the remedial activity of microorganisms

biosynthesis *noun* the production of chemical compounds by a living organism

biota *noun* the flora and fauna of a region

biotechnology *noun* the use of biological processes in industrial production, e.g. the use of yeasts in making beer, bread or yoghurt. ◊ **genetic modification**

biotic *adjective* referring to the living constituents of an environment. Compare **abiotic**

biotic barrier *noun* a set of conditions which prevent members of a species moving to other regions

biotic carrier potential *noun* an assessment of the maximum increase in the number of individuals in a species, not considering the effects of competition and natural selection

biotic climax *noun* a plant community produced by a permanent influence or combination of influences of organisms, including people, e.g. woodland

biotic community *noun* a community of organisms in a specific area

biotic factor *noun* an organism that has an effect on a specific environment. Compare **abiotic factor**

biotic index *noun* a scale for showing the quality of an environment by indicating the types of organisms present in it

biotic potential *noun* same as **biotic carrier potential**

biotic pyramid *noun* a graphical representation of the structure of an ecosystem in terms of which organism eats which. Also called **ecological pyramid** (NOTE: The base is composed of producer organ-

isms, usually plants, then herbivores, then carnivores. It may be measured in terms of number, biomass or energy.)

biotic succession *noun* the sequence of changes that takes place in the composition of a group of organisms under the influence of their changing environment

biotope *noun* a small area with uniform biological conditions such as climate, soil or altitude

biotroph *noun* a parasite which only feeds on living organisms. Compare **necrotroph**

biotype *noun* a group of similar individuals within a species

biphenyl *noun* a white or colourless crystalline substance, used as a fungicide, in the production of dyes and as a preservative applied to the skins of citrus fruit. Formula: $C_6H_5C_6H[[SUB]]5$. (NOTE: The preservative has E number E230.)

birch *noun* a common hardwood tree found in northern temperate zones. Genus: *Betula.*

bird *noun* a warm-blooded animal that has wings, feathers and a beak and lays eggs
 'Birds are sensitive to even small climate changes. For instance the North Atlantic Oscillation – the Atlantic's version of El Niño – has subtle effects on weather. These go unnoticed by most humans, but research shows that as the oscillation waxes and wanes, populations of larks and sandpipers rise and fall. (Climate Change, UK farmland birds and the global greenhouse. RSPB 2001)'

birder *noun* same as **birdwatcher**

bird haven *noun* same as **bird sanctuary**

bird of prey *noun* a bird that kills and eats other birds or small animals

bird reserve *noun* same as **bird sanctuary**

bird sanctuary *noun* a place where birds can breed and live in a protected environment

Birds directive *noun* a European Union directive relating to the conservation of all species of naturally occurring wild birds

birdsong *noun* singing calls made by birds to communicate with each other

birdwatcher *noun* a person who observes and studies birds as a leisure activity. Also called **birder**

birdwatching *noun* observing and studying birds as a leisure activity

birth *noun* the event of being born

birthrate *noun* the number of births per year, shown per thousand of the population ○ *a birthrate of 15 per thousand* ○ *There has been a severe decline in the birthrate.*

bison *noun US* a type of large cattle found in North America, now largely restricted to protected areas because of hunting. Also called **buffalo**

bitumen *noun* a solid hydrocarbon contained in coal. Also called **tar**

bituminous coal *noun* coal containing a high percentage of tar

bituminous sand, bituminous shale *noun* same as **oil sand**

bivalve *noun* an invertebrate animal with a shell composed of two halves joined at one place. Bivalves such as oysters or mussels may live in fresh or salt water.

black carbon *noun* carbon in the form of fine particles which rise in the smoke produced by the burning of fossil fuels such as coal, wood or oil

black earth *noun* same as **chernozem**

bladder *noun* **1.** an inflated modified leaf of a plant that traps insects, e.g. bladderwort, or an inflated fruit, e.g. senna pod **2.** same as **air bladder**

blade *noun* **1.** a flattened part of a propeller, rotor or wind turbine **2.** a thin flat leaf, e.g. a leaf of a grass, iris or daffodil

blanket bog *noun* a wide area of marshy ground that may occur in lowland or upland areas (NOTE: In the UK, they occur mainly at high altitude in the north and west.)

blast *noun* the impact from an explosion ○ *Thousands of people would be killed by the blast.*

blast effect *noun* a result of the impact from an explosion, e.g. damage caused

blaze *noun* a mark put on a tree to show that it needs to be felled or to indicate a path through a forest

bleaching *noun* **1.** the removal of colour by the action of a chemical or sunlight **2.** a process in which coral loses its colour or loses its symbiotic algae ○ *There have been several incidents of coral bleaching on reefs around Easter Island and northeastern Australia.*

bleed *verb* **1.** to exude blood or sap from a wound **2.** to remove liquid or gas from a system

blight *noun* **1.** a disease caused by different fungi, that rapidly destroys a plant or plant part **2.** □ **(urban) blight** excessive building development, or the occurrence of dilapidated and unattractive areas in a city or town ■ *verb* to ruin or spoil the environment ○ *The landscape was blighted by open-cast mining.*

blizzard *noun* a heavy snowstorm with wind, or lying snow which is blown by strong wind ○ *There were blizzards in the highlands during the weekend.*

bloom *noun* a flower ○ *The blooms on the orchids have been ruined by frost.* ■ *verb* to flower ○ *The plant blooms at night.* ○ *Some cacti only bloom once every seven years.*

blow *verb* (*of air or wind*) to move ○ *The sea breeze may blow almost parallel to the coast.*

blow-by *noun* unburnt fuel mixed with air and other gases that escapes past the piston rings in an internal combustion engine

blowhole *noun* **1.** a hole in the roof of a cave by the sea, leading to the surface of the cliff above, through which air and water are sent out by the pressure of the waves breaking beneath **2.** the nostril of a cetacean such as a whale, situated towards the back of the skull, through which the whale releases air and water

blowout *noun* a sudden rush of oil or gas from an oil well

blubber *noun* fat lying in a thick layer under the skin of marine animals such as whales

blue flag beach *noun* a beach with sea water that meets the cleanliness requirements of the European Commission and has been awarded the symbol of a blue flag

blue-green alga *noun* ♦ **cyanobacterium**

blue whale *noun* a large whale with no teeth, which feeds by straining large amounts of water through its baleen and so retaining plankton and other food

board of inquiry *noun* a group of people who carry out a formal investigation when there has been an accident, or something has gone wrong

BOAT *abbr* byway open to all traffic

BOD *abbr* **1.** biochemical oxygen demand **2.** biological oxygen demand ○ *The main aim of sewage treatment is to reduce the BOD of the liquid.*

body burden *noun* the amount of a chemical contained in a human or animal body

bog *noun* soft wet land, usually with moss growing on it, which does not decompose, but forms a thick layer of acid peat (NOTE: The mosses that grow on bogs live on the nutrients that fall in rain.)

boggy *adjective* soft and wet like a bog

bogland *noun* an area of bog

boil *verb* to heat a liquid until it reaches a temperature at which it changes into gas

bole *noun* the wide base of a tree trunk

bond *noun* same as **chemical bond** ■ *verb* **1.** (*of two substances*) to link together ○ *Adsorption is the bonding of a gas to a solid surface.* **2.** (*of atoms*) to form a chemical bond

bone *noun* **1.** one of the calcified pieces of connective tissue which make up the skeleton, e.g. a leg bone **2.** a hard substance of which the parts of the skeleton are formed

bonemeal *noun* a fertiliser made of ground bones or horns, reduced to a fine powder

boom *noun* a sudden loud noise, especially one caused by an aircraft travelling at speeds greater than the speed of sound

boom town *noun* a town where the population and number of buildings is increasing very quickly, or a town where business is thriving ○ *The oil industry has turned this once sleepy port into a boom town.*

booster *noun* a device which increases the force or amount of something

Bordeaux mixture *noun* a mixture of copper sulfate, lime and water, used to spray on plants to prevent infection by fungi

bore *noun* **1.** a measurement across the inside of a pipe or hole ○ *The central heating uses small-bore copper piping.* ○ *The well has a 2-metre bore.* **2.** a tidal wave which rushes up the estuary of a river at high tide ■ *verb* to make a round hole in the ground ○ *They have bored six test holes to try to find water.*

boreal *adjective* referring to the climate in the northern hemisphere between 60° and 40° N with short hot summers and longer cold winters

boreal forest *noun* a forest in the tundra areas around the North Pole, consisting primarily of black spruce and white spruce trees with balsam fir, birch and aspen

boreal region *noun* one of the biogeographical regions of Europe, in the north east between the Arctic and the continental region

borehole *noun* **1.** a hole bored deep into the ground to survey for the presence of oil, gas or water, or to establish the nature of ground structure ○ *The borehole is intended to test the geology of the site to see what sort of foundation the building will need.* **2.** a hole bored into the water table for the extraction of water ○ *Boreholes supply water of excellent quality.*

-borne *suffix* carried by ○ *wind-borne pollen of grasses*

boron *noun* a chemical element. It is essential as a trace element for healthy plant growth. (NOTE: The chemical symbol is **B**; the atomic number is **5** and the atomic weight is **10.81**.)

botanic, botanical *adjective* referring to botany

botanical garden, botanic garden *noun* a place where plants are grown for showing to the public and for scientific study

botanical horticulture *noun* the activity of growing different species of plants to study and maintain them

botanical insecticide *noun* an insecticide made from a substance extracted from plants, e.g. pyrethrum, derived from chrysanthemums, or nicotine, derived from tobacco plants

botanical specimen *noun* a plant collected for study

botanist *noun* someone who studies plants as a scientific or leisure activity

botany *noun* the study of plants as a scientific or leisure activity

bottle bank *noun* a large container into which people put empty glass bottles and jars which can then be recycled into new glass

bottled gas *noun* a gas produced from refining crude oil and sold in pressurised metal containers for use in domestic cooking or heating, or as vehicle fuel

bottom *noun* **1.** the floor of a sea, lake or river **2.** a flat area along a river where silt is deposited when the river floods

bottom feeder *noun* an organism such as a fish which collects food on the bottom or in the deepest water of the sea, a lake or river

bottom-up control *noun* the system of regulation of trophic levels by which the abundance of individuals in the higher trophic levels is determined by factors in the lower levels. Compare **top-down control**

boulder *noun* a large rounded piece of rock

Bovidae *plural noun* the largest class of even-toed ungulates, including cattle, antelopes, gazelles, sheep and goats

bovine *adjective* referring to cattle

bovine spongiform encephalopathy *noun* full form of **BSE**

Bq *symbol* becquerel

Br *symbol* bromine

bracken *noun* a tall fern with large triangular fronds that grows on hillsides and in woodland. Latin name: *Pteridium aquilinum*. (NOTE: no plural)

brackish *adjective* referring to water which contains some salt, though less than seawater, and is not good to drink

bract *noun* a small green leaf at the base of a flower or flowering stem

braided river *noun* a river that is divided into a pattern of many channels with small areas of dry land between them

braiding *noun* the process of a river becoming divided into many channels with small areas of dry land between them

bran *noun* the outside covering of a cereal grain (NOTE: It is removed from wheat in making white flour, but is an important source of roughage in the human diet and is used in muesli and other breakfast cereals.)

branch *noun* **1.** a woody stem growing out from the main trunk of a tree **2.** a subdivision of something larger **3.** a smaller stream separating from but still forming part of a river

brass *noun* an alloy of copper and zinc

Brassicaceae *noun* a family of common plants, including cabbage, whose flowers have four petals. Former name **Cruciferae**

breakdown *noun* **1.** a failure of a system or organisation **2.** the separation of a substance into its component parts

breakthrough *noun* a situation occurring when sewage or other pollutants get into the main domestic water supply

breakwater *noun* a stone or wooden structure that is built out from the shore into the sea in order to block the force of waves and so prevent erosion

breccia *noun* a type of rough rock made of sharp fragments of other rocks fused together

breed *noun* a group of organisms of a specific species which have been developed by people over a period of time for desirable characteristics ○ *a hardy breed of sheep* ○ *Two new breeds of rice have been developed.* ■ *verb* **1.** (*of organisms*) to produce young ○ *Rabbits breed very rapidly.* **2.** to encourage something to develop ○ *Insanitary conditions help to breed disease.* **3.** to produce an improved animal or plant by crossing two parent animals or plants showing the desired characteristics ○ *Farmers have bred new hardy forms of sheep.* □ **to breed true** to reproduce all the

characteristics of the type in the next generation ○ *F₁ hybrids do not breed true.*

breeder *noun* a person who breeds new forms of animals or plants ○ *a cat breeder* ○ *a cattle breeder* ○ *a rose breeder* ○ *a plant breeder*

breeding *noun* the crossing of different plants or animals to produce offspring with desirable characteristics

breeding bird *noun* a bird that is actively reproducing in a specific place at a specific time

Breeding Bird Survey *noun* an ongoing assessment of breeding birds conducted by the British Trust for Ornithology, JNCC and RSPB

breeding ground *noun* an area where birds or animals come each year to breed

breeding pair *noun* two animals, especially birds, that have established a mating relationship with each other

breeding season *noun* the time of year when organisms produce offspring

breeze *noun* **1.** a light wind **2.** the solid waste of burnt coal or other material produced by a furnace

bridle path, **bridle way** *noun* a track along which a horse can be ridden

British thermal unit *noun* the amount of heat needed to raise the temperature of one pound of water by one degree Fahrenheit (NOTE: Its approximate SI equivalent is 1055 joules.)

British Trust for Ornithology *noun* an independent scientific research trust that investigates the populations, movements and ecology of wild birds in the British Isles. Abbr **BTO**

broad *noun* a river that has spreads to cover low-lying land

broadacre agriculture *noun* the large-scale cultivation of field crops

broadleaf, **broadleaf tree** *noun* a deciduous tree that has wide leaves, e.g. beech or oak. Compare **conifer**

broadleaved *adjective* (*of a tree*) having wide leaves rather than needles. Compare **coniferous**

broadleaved evergreen *noun* an evergreen tree or shrub with wide leaves, e.g. rhododendron or laurel

broadleaved forest, **broadleaved woodland** *noun* an area of wooded land consisting of more than 75% of broadleaved trees

broad-spectrum *adjective* referring to an antibiotic or pesticide which kills or controls many types of organism

'Broad-spectrum pesticides often control both pest and natural enemies removing the benefits of biological control. Often, pesticides are applied just after damage or infestations are identified. Such treatments will prevent beneficial pests from multiplying to populations that will significantly reduce pest numbers. (Pest Management in cereals and oilseed rape – a guide. HGCA 2003)'

bromine *noun* a chemical element. It is used in various industrial processes and in antiknock additives for petrol. (NOTE: The chemical symbol is **Br**; the atomic number is **35** and the atomic weight is **79.90**.)

brood *noun* a group of offspring produced at the same time, especially a group of young birds ○ *The territory provides enough food for two adults and a brood of six or eight young.*

brooding time *noun* the length of time a bird sits on its eggs to hatch them out

brook *noun* a little stream

brown *adjective* **1.** of a colour like the colour of earth or wood **2.** not produced from renewable sources

brown earth *noun* good fertile soil, slightly acid and containing humus

brownfields *plural noun* vacant industrial land that was formerly developed

brownfield site *noun* a development site that is in a town and formerly had buildings on it, preferred for building development to open fields. Compare **greenfield site**

brown fumes *plural noun* fumes from tarry substances produced by coal burning at low temperatures. Also called **brown smoke**

brownlands *plural noun* areas of land for development that have been previously developed but are currently unused

brown smoke *noun* ♦ **brown fumes**

browse *verb* to feed on plant material, especially the leaves of woody plants, which is not growing close to the ground. Compare **graze**

brucellosis *noun* a disease which can be caught from cattle or goats or from drinking infected milk, spread by a species of the bacterium *Brucella*

brushwood *noun* undergrowth with twigs and small branches

bryophyte *noun* a non-flowering plant, frequently growing in damp places, with separate gamete- and spore-bearing forms, e.g. moss. Division: *Bryophyta.*

BSE *noun* a fatal brain disease of cattle. Also called **mad cow disease**. Full form **bovine spongiform encephalopathy**

BTO *abbr* British Trust for Ornithology

bud *noun* a young shoot on a plant, which may later become a leaf or flower

budding *noun* a way of propagating plants in which a bud from one plant is grafted onto another plant

buffalo *noun* **1.** a common domestic animal in tropical countries, used for milk and also as a draught animal **2.** *US* same as **bison**

buffer *noun* a solution in which the pH is not changed by adding acid or alkali ■ *verb* to prevent a solution from becoming acid or alkaline ○ *If a lake is well buffered, it will not have a low pH factor, even if acid rain falls into it.* ○ *Bicarbonate is the main buffering factor in fresh water.*

buffer land, buffer zone *noun* land between a protected area such as a nature reserve and the surrounding countryside or town

bug *noun* **1.** an insect (*informal*) **2.** a winged insect belonging to the class Hemiptera

build *verb* to make a construction ○ *The developer is planning to build 2500 new houses on the greenfield site.* ○ *The female birds build nests of straw in holes in trees.*

building *noun* **1.** a construction such as a house, shop or office ○ *modern buildings with good insulation* **2.** the process of constructing something ○ *permission for building on the site*

building area *noun* an area of land on which building may take place or is taking place. Also called **building zone**

building certificate *noun* an official document allowing a person or company to build a property. Also called **building permit**

building control *noun* a system for regulating the design of buildings, especially for the safety and health of the occupants

building density *noun* a number of buildings allowed on a specific area of land, e.g. fifteen houses to the acre

building development *noun* an area of land on which building is taking or has taken place ○ *The company is planning a new building development of 1500 homes.*

building ground, building land *noun* an area of land suitable for or with permission for building on

building legislation *noun* the set of laws controlling all aspects of putting up new buildings or altering existing buildings

building permit *noun* same as **building certificate**

building-related illness *noun* an illness that can be traced to a specific pollutant or source within a building (NOTE: Legionnaires' disease is a building-related illness.)

building site *noun* an area of land on which building is taking place

building zone *noun* same as **building area**

build up *verb* 1. to form by accumulation ○ *The pesticide gradually built up in the food chain.* 2. to develop gradually ○ *Traffic has built up over the last five years.*

build-up *noun* a gradual accumulation ○ *a build-up of DDT in the food chain* ○ *a build-up of static electricity*

built environment *noun* the buildings, roads and other structures made by people and in which they live, work or travel. Compare **natural environment**

built heritage *noun* the part of a country's historic resources that consists of buildings and structures, as opposed to natural assets

built-up area *noun* an area which has many houses, shops, offices and other buildings, with very little open space

bulb *noun* an underground plant organ of fleshy scale leaves and buds. It can be planted and will produce flowers and seed.

bulk *noun* a large quantity of something □ **in bulk** in large quantities

bulking agent *noun* an additive which causes a substance to stick together as a mass

bulk plant *noun* a factory which produces something in large quantities

bund *noun* a soil wall built across a slope to retain water or to hold waste in a sloping landfill site

bunding *noun* the formation of bunds
'Farmers have traditionally relied on a system of bunding to grow sorghum in the area's semi-arid soil.' [*New Scientist*]

burial site *noun* 1. a place where nuclear waste is buried 2. a place where animals that have died from an infectious disease such as foot and mouth disease are buried

burn *noun* 1. an injury to skin and tissue caused by light, heat, radiation, electricity or a chemical 2. in Scotland, a small stream ■ *verb* 1. to destroy or damage something by fire ○ *Several hundred hectares of forest were burnt in the fire.* ◊ **slash and burn agriculture** 2. to use fuel or food to produce energy ○ *Swimming will help you burn calories.*

burner *noun* a device for burning something such as fuel or waste

burner reactor *noun* a type of nuclear reactor in which fuel such as uranium-239 is used to generate heat by fission

burning *noun* 1. the act or process of destroying or damaging something by fire 2. the process of burning something such as fuel or waste

burn-up *noun* the amount of fuel burnt in a nuclear reactor, shown as a proportion of the fuel originally used

bush *noun* 1. a plant with many woody stems ○ *a coffee bush* ○ *a rose bush* 2. in semiarid regions, natural land covered with bushes and small trees

bush-fallow *noun* a form of subsistence agriculture in which land is cultivated for a few years until its natural fertility is exhausted, then allowed to rest for a long period during which the natural vegetation regrows, after which the land is cleared and cultivated again

business park *noun* an area of land with buildings specially designed and constructed for business premises, light industries or science

butane *noun* a gas produced during petroleum distillation, used domestically for heating and sold in special containers as bottled gas. Formula: C_4H_{10}.

butterfly *noun* a flying insect with large, often colourful wings

butterwort *noun* an insectivorous plant that grows in bogs. Genus: *Pinguicula.*

butylated hydroxytoluene *noun* a common antioxidant additive (E321) used in processed foods containing fat. It may be carcinogenic. Abbr **BHT**

by-catch *noun* fish or sea mammals caught during fishing but not required and thrown back dead into the sea ○ *By-catch is a major environmental problem as it involves the uncontrolled destruction of populations.*

by-pass *noun* a road built around a town, to relieve traffic congestion ○ *Since the by-pass was built, traffic in the town has been reduced by half.*

by-product *noun* something additional produced during a process

byway *noun* a small country road or track

byway open to all traffic *noun* a road mainly used by the public as a footpath or bridleway on which vehicles are allowed. Abbr **BOAT**

C

C *symbol* **1.** carbon **2.** Celsius

C3 plant *noun* a plant found in temperate regions in which photosynthesis levels off at high light intensities

C4 plant *noun* a plant, usually found in hot dry regions, which is efficient at photosynthesis at high light intensities

Ca *symbol* calcium

CA *abbr* Countryside Agency

cactus *noun* a succulent plant with a fleshy stem often protected by spines, found in the deserts of North and Central America (NOTE: The plural is **cacti** or **cactuses**.)

cadmium *noun* a metallic element naturally present in soil and rock in association with zinc (NOTE: The chemical symbol is **Cd**; the atomic number is **48** and the atomic weight is **112.40**.)

caducous *adjective* referring to a part of a plant or animal which becomes detached during the organism's life

caesium *noun* a metallic alkali element which is one of the main radioactive pollutants taken up by fish (NOTE: The chemical symbol is **Cs**; the atomic number is **55** and the atomic weight is **132.91**.)

cal *symbol* calorie

calcareous *adjective* referring to a chalky soil that contains calcium or to a rock such as chalk or limestone that contains calcium

calcareous grassland *noun* the type of vegetation such as grasses that is typical on chalk soil. ◊ **acid grassland**

calcicole, calcicolous plant *noun* a plant which grows well on chalky or alkaline soils. Also called **calciphile**

calcification *noun* the process of hardening by forming deposits of calcium salts

calcified *adjective* made hard ○ *Bone is calcified connective tissue.*

calcifuge *noun* a plant which prefers acid soils and does not grow on chalky or alkaline soils. Also called **calciphobe**

calcimorphic soil *noun* soil which is rich in lime

calcination *noun* the heating of something such as a gas at high temperature in the production of metal oxides

calciphile *noun* same as **calcicole**

calciphobe *noun* same as **calcifuge**

calcium *noun* a metallic chemical element naturally present in limestone and chalk. It is essential for biological processes. (NOTE: The chemical symbol is **Ca**; the atomic number is **20** and atomic weight is **40.08**.)

calcium carbonate *noun* a white insoluble solid formed from animal organisms that is naturally abundant and is found in chalk, limestone and marble. It is used in the production of cement, paint and toothpaste. Formula: $CaCO_3$.

calcium phosphate *noun* the main constituent of bones and bone ash fertiliser. Formula: $(Ca_3(Po_4)_2$.

calibrate *verb* to make a scale on a measuring instrument

calm *noun* a period when there is no wind at all

caloric *adjective* referring to calories

calorie *noun* a unit of measurement of heat or energy. Symbol **cal** (NOTE: The **joule**, an SI measure, is now more usual: 1 calorie = 4.186 joules.)

calorific value *noun* same as **energy value**

calyx *noun* the part of a flower made up of green sepals which cover the flower when it is in bud (NOTE: The plural is **calyces**.)

camouflage *noun* the natural concealment of an animal's shape by colours or patterns ○ *The stripes on the zebra are a form of camouflage which makes the animal difficult to see in long grass.* ■ *verb* to hide the shape of an animal or object by using colours or patterns on the skin or exterior

canal *noun* **1.** a waterway made by people for boats to travel along **2.** a waterway made by people to take water to irrigate land

can bank *noun* a large container in a public place into which people can put their empty metal food containers for collection and recycling

candela *noun* an SI unit measuring the brightness of a light. Symbol **cd**

canker *noun* **1.** a disease causing lesions on a plant or on the skin of an animal ○ *a* *bacterial canker of fruit trees* **2.** an area of damage caused by canker ○ *cankers on the stem*

cankered *adjective* (*of skin or plant tissue*) having areas of damage caused by canker

canopy *noun* a layer of branches and leaves of trees which shade the ground underneath

'Trees that grow to form the tallest part of the canopy suffer more damage than the slower growing trees forming the understorey.' [*Guardian*]

canopy cover *noun* the percentage of the surface of the ground which is shaded by the leaves and branches of trees

canyon *noun* a deep valley with steep sides

cap *noun* a part of the dome-shaped structure of some fungi which bears spores on its lower surface

CAP *abbr* Common Agricultural Policy

capacity *noun* **1.** the ability to do something easily ○ *the capacity to conserve the woodland* **2.** the amount of something which a container can hold ○ *Each cylinder has a capacity of 0.5 litres.*

capillarity *noun* same as **capillary action**

capillary *noun* a narrow tube carrying a liquid

capillary action, capillary flow *noun* the movement of a liquid upwards inside a narrow tube or upwards through the soil

capillary pore *noun* a space in the soil through which water flows towards a root

capsid bug *noun* a tiny insect that sucks the sap of plants

capsular *adjective* referring to a capsule

capsule *noun* **1.** a dry structure which bursts open with force releasing the seeds of flowering plants or spores of mosses **2.** a membrane round an organ

captive breeding *noun* the breeding of threatened species in zoos, usually with the intention of later releasing them into the wild

carbamate *noun* a pesticide belonging to a large group used as insecticides, herbicides and fungicides

carbohydrate *noun* an organic compound composed of carbon, hydrogen and oxygen, e.g. sugars, cellulose and starch

carbon *noun* a common non-metallic element that is an essential component of living matter and organic chemical compounds (NOTE: The chemical symbol is **C**; the atomic number is **6** and the atomic weight is **12.01**.)

carbon-14 dating *noun* same as **carbon dating**

carbonaceous *adjective* referring to rock which is rich in hydrocarbons, e.g. coal

carbonate *noun* a compound formed from a base and carbonic acid ■ *verb* to add carbon dioxide to a drink to make it fizzy

carbonation *noun* the addition of carbon dioxide to a drink to make it fizzy

carbon cycle *noun* the circulation of carbon, by which carbon atoms from carbon dioxide are incorporated into organic compounds in plants during photosynthesis. They are then oxidised into carbon dioxide during respiration by plants or herbivores which eat them and by carnivores which eat the herbivores, thus releasing carbon to go round the cycle again.

carbon dating *noun* the process of finding out how old something is by analysing the amount of carbon, especially the radioactive isotope carbon-14, in it that has decayed. Also called **carbon-14 dating**

carbon dioxide *noun* a colourless odourless non-flammable atmospheric gas. It is used in photosynthesis and given off in aerobic respiration. Formula: CO_2.

COMMENT: Carbon dioxide exists naturally in air and is produced by burning or by decaying organic matter. In animals, the body's metabolism utilises carbon, which is then breathed out by the lungs as waste carbon dioxide. Carbon dioxide is removed from the atmosphere by plants when it is split by chlorophyll in photosynthesis to form carbon and oxygen. It is also dissolved from the atmosphere in water. The increasing release of carbon dioxide into the atmosphere, especially from burning fossil fuels, contributes to the greenhouse effect.

carbon dioxide equivalent *noun* a metric measure used in comparing emissions from different greenhouse gases to assess their global warming potential. Also called **CO₂ equivalent**

carbon dioxide tax *noun* same as **carbon tax**

carbon emissions *plural noun* the carbon dioxide and carbon monoxide produced by motor vehicles and industrial processes and regarded as atmospheric pollutants

carboniferous *adjective* containing coal or carbon ○ *carboniferous limestone*

Carboniferous period *noun* the period of geological time when reptiles first appeared and much of the Earth's surface was covered by forests

carbonisation *noun* the process by which fossil plants have become carbon

carbon monoxide *noun* a colourless, odourless and poisonous gas found in fumes from car engines, burning gas and cigarette smoke. Formula: CO.

carbon neutral *adjective* referring to the balance between producing and using carbon (NOTE: Renewable plant fuels are carbon neutral – if the same numbers of plants are replanted as are harvested the CO_2 levels in the air will remain about the same.)

carbon sequestration *noun* the uptake and storage of carbon by trees and other plants absorbing carbon dioxide and releasing oxygen

carbon sink *noun* a part of the ecosphere such as a tropical forest which absorbs carbon

carbon source *noun* a part of the ecosphere such as animals or an industrial or domestic process that releases carbon into the atmosphere in the form of carbon dioxide

carbon tax *noun* an amount of money added by a government to the price of fuel according to its carbon content, to encourage the use of fuels that contain less carbon and so reduce emissions of carbon dioxide. Also called **carbon dioxide tax**

carbon tetrachloride *noun* a dense non-flammable toxic liquid that is colourless with a sweetish smell, used as a solvent, refrigerant and dry-cleaning agent and in fire extinguishers. Formula: CCl_4.

carbon trading *noun* the system of one country using some of another country's permitted carbon dioxide output as well as its own. ◊ **emissions trading**

Carbon Trust *noun* a UK organisation supported by government grants that encourages and promotes the development of low-carbon technologies, both energy-efficient technologies and low-carbon energy supplies

carboxyhaemoglobin *noun* a compound of carbon monoxide and the blood pigment haemoglobin formed when a person breathes in carbon monoxide from car fumes or from ordinary cigarette smoke

carcin- *prefix* cancer

carcinogen *noun* a substance which causes cancer

carcinogenesis *noun* the formation of cancerous cells in tissue

carcinogenic *adjective* causing cancer

car lobby *noun* a group of people who try to persuade politicians that cars should be encouraged and not restricted

carnivore *noun* an animal that eats meat. ◊ **detritivore, frugivore, herbivore, omnivore**

carnivorous *adjective* **1.** referring to animals that eat meat ○ *a carnivorous animal* **2.** referring to plants which trap and digest insects ○ *Sundews are carnivorous plants.*

carotene *noun* an orange or red plant pigment (NOTE: Some carotenes are converted to vitamin A by animals.)

carpel *noun* a female part of a flower, formed of an ovary, style and stigma

carr *noun* an area of wetland which supports some trees ○ *fen carr* ○ *willow carr*

carrageen *noun* a purplish-brown seaweed that contains a mucilage. Genera: *Chondrus* or *Gigartina*. Also called **Irish moss**

carrageenan *noun* an extract of seaweed, used as an emulsifier. It may be carcinogenic.

carrier *noun* **1.** an organism that carries disease and infects other organisms, e.g. an insect that transmits the parasite causing malaria **2.** someone who has an infectious disease without showing symptoms, who may then infect other people **3.** a neutral substance to which an active ingredient is added

carrier bag *noun* a paper or plastic bag used for carrying goods bought in shops (NOTE: Plastic bags present a considerable problem in terms of waste disposal.)

carrier gas, carrier solvent *noun* a gas used in an aerosol can to make the spray come out

carrying capacity *noun* the maximum number of individuals of a species that can be supported in a given area

cascade *noun* **1.** a small waterfall **2.** a system for purifying substances, in which the substance passes through a series of identical processes, each stage increasing the purity ■ *verb* (*of liquid*) to fall down like a waterfall

case *noun* **1.** an outer covering ○ *A butterfly pupa is protected in a hard case or chrysalis.* **2.** same as **seedcase 3.** a single occurrence of a disease ○ *There were two hundred cases of cholera in the recent outbreak.*

cash crop *noun* a crop grown to be sold rather than eaten by the person who grows it, e.g. oil palm

cashew-nut shell liquor *noun* a highly corrosive substance produced from the shells of cashew nuts, used in paints for ships, heatproof materials and in ecocomposites to replace fossil oil. Abbr **CNSL**

caste *noun* a group with a particular function in a hierarchical society of social insects such as termites

CAT *abbr* control action threshold

catabolic *adjective* referring to catabolism

catabolism *noun* the breaking down of complex chemicals into simple chemicals

catadromous, katadromous *adjective* referring to fish that live in fresh water and go to the sea to spawn. Compare **anadromous**

catadromy, katadromy *noun* the migration of fish such as eels from fresh water to the sea for spawning. Compare **anadromy**

catalyse *verb* to act as a catalyst in helping to make a chemical process take place (NOTE: The US spelling is **catalyze**.)

catalysis *noun* a process in which a chemical reaction is helped by a substance, the catalyst, which does not change during the process

catalyst *noun* a substance which produces or helps a chemical reaction without itself changing ○ *an enzyme which acts as a catalyst in the digestive process.*

catalytic *adjective* referring to catalysis

catalytic converter, catalytic muffler *noun* a box filled with a catalyst such as platinum attached to the exhaust pipe of a motor vehicle burning unleaded petrol in order to reduce the emission of carbon monoxide

catch *noun* the amount of fish caught ○ *regulations to limit the herring catch*

catchment, catchment area *noun* **1.** an area of land, sometimes extremely large, that collects and drains the rainwater that falls on it, e.g. the area round a lake or the basin of a river. Also called **drainage area, drainage basin 2.** an area around a school, hospital, shopping centre, or other service from which its pupils, patients or customers come

catchment basin *noun* same as **catchment 1**

catchwater drain *noun* a type of drain designed to take rainwater from sloping ground

catena *noun* a diagram showing the differences in soil caused by drainage

cation *noun* an ion with a positive electric charge

catkin *noun* a long hanging structure consisting of many single-sex flowers on a thin stem, found on temperate trees such as hazel, birch and oak. They are pollinated by the wind.

cattle *plural noun* domestic farm animals raised for their milk, meat and hide. Class: Bovidae. ○ *herds of cattle* ○ *dairy cattle*

cattle identification document *noun* a document which identifies an animal and shows its movements from owner to owner. Abbr **CID**

caustic *adjective* acid

caustic soda *noun* same as **sodium hydroxide**

cave *noun* a large hole under the ground, usually in rock

cavern *noun* a very large cave, formed by water which has dissolved limestone or other calcareous rock

cavity *noun* a hole inside a solid substance

CB *abbr* cumulonimbus

CBD *abbr* Convention on Biological Diversity

CCW *abbr* Countryside Council for Wales

Cd *symbol* cadmium

CDM *abbr* Clean Development Mechanism

CE *abbr* consumption efficiency

cedar *noun* a large coniferous tree belonging to several genera, including *Thuya* and *Cedrus*

ceiling *noun* an upper limit or point that cannot be passed ○ *a ceiling on imports*

-cele, -coele *suffix* referring to a hollow

cell *noun* **1.** the basic independently functioning unit of all plant and animal tissue **2.** a separate unit or section of something larger **3.** a system of positive and negative plates for storage of electricity that form a battery **4.** the central part of a thunder cloud ○ *The life cycle of the thunderstorm cell ends when the downdraughts have spread throughout the cloud.*

cellular *adjective* **1.** referring to the cells of organisms **2.** made of many similar parts connected together

cellulose *noun* **1.** a carbohydrate which makes up a large percentage of plant matter, especially cell walls **2.** a chemical substance processed from wood, used for making paper, film and artificial fibres

Celsius *noun* a scale of temperature where the freezing and boiling points of water are, respectively, 0° and 100°. Symbol **C**. Former name **centigrade** (NOTE: It is used in many countries, except in the USA, where the Fahrenheit system is still commonly used.)

cement *noun* **1.** material which binds things together, such as that which binds minerals together to form sedimentary rocks **2.** a powder which, if mixed with water and then dried, sets hard like stone

census *noun* a survey of a specific population to assess numbers and other features

centigrade *noun* ♦ **Celsius**

centimetre *noun* a unit of measurement of length, equivalent to one hundredth of a metre. Symbol **cm**

centre *noun* **1.** a point in the middle of something ○ *a park in the centre of the town* ○ *The centre of the hurricane passed over the city.* **2.** a large building ○ *a conference centre* **3.** a focus for activity or attention, or where activities are coordinated ○ *a resource centre* (NOTE: The US spelling is **center**.)

Centre for Ecology and Hydrology *noun* a UK organisation that does research on and monitors terrestrial and freshwater environments

centre of gravity *noun* the point through which the resultant force of gravity acts

centre of origin, centre of origin and diversity *noun* a region where a species is thought to have originated and spread from

centrifugal *adjective* going away from the centre

centrifugation *noun* the separation of the components of a liquid in a centrifuge. Also called **centrifuging**

centrifuge *noun* a device which uses centrifugal force to separate or remove liquids

centrifuging *noun* same as **centrifugation**

centripetal *adjective* going towards the centre

cephal- *prefix* referring to the head

cephalic *adjective* referring to the head

cephalopod *noun* a marine invertebrate animal with a well-developed head and tentacles, e.g. an octopus, squid or cuttlefish. Class: Cephalopoda.

CERCLA *abbr* Comprehensive Environmental Response, Compensation, and Liability Act

cereal *noun* a type of grass which is cultivated for its grains. Cereals are used especially to make flour for breadmaking, for animal feed or for producing alcohol. (NOTE: The main cereals are wheat, rice, barley, maize and oats.)

certification *noun* the process of obtaining or giving approval for something such as carrying out specific tests, or confirmation for something such as the source from which something was obtained

certify *verb* to authorise or permit the use of something

cesspool, cesspit *noun* a tank for household sewage, constructed in the ground near a house which is not connected to the main drainage system, and in which the waste is stored before being pumped out for disposal somewhere else

Cetacea *noun* an order of mammals which live in the sea, e.g. dolphins, porpoises or whales

CFC *abbr* chlorofluorocarbon

CFM *abbr* chlorofluoromethane

CFP *abbr* Common Fisheries Policy

chain *noun* a number of components linked together, or a number of connected events

chalk *noun* a fine white limestone rock formed of calcium carbonate

chalkpit *noun* a hole in the ground from which chalk is extracted

chalky *adjective* referring to soil which is contains a lot of chalk

CHaMP *abbr* coastal habitat management plan

change *verb* to use one thing instead of another

channel *noun* **1.** a deep part of a harbour or sea passage where ships can pass, or a stretch of water between two seas **2.** a bed of a river or stream ■ *verb* to send water in a particular direction (NOTE: British English is **channelled – channelling**, but the US spelling is **channeled – channeling**.)

channelisation *noun* the process of straightening a stream which has many bends, in order to make the water flow faster

channelise *verb* to straighten a stream which has many bends, in order to make the water flow faster

chaos theory *noun* a theory stating that when a system is sensitive to small differences in initial values, the future behaviour of that system may be unpredictable

chaparral *noun* an area of temperate land covered with shrubs, found along the coast of California

character *noun* **1.** the way in which a person thinks and behaves **2.** the way in which an animal or plant is different from others **3.** a feature of an organism that can be inherited **4.** a graphical symbol which appears as a printed or displayed mark, e.g. one of the letters of the alphabet, a number or a punctuation mark

characterisation *noun* a description of the typical features of something ○ *ecological characterisation of the landscape*

characterise *verb* **1.** to be a characteristic of something or someone ○ *Deserts are characterised by little rainfall, arid soil and very little vegetation.* **2.** to describe the typical features of something

characteristic *noun* a property or feature of something ○ *inherited characteristics* ○ *One of the characteristics of an octopus is that it can send out a cloud of ink when attacked.* ■ *adjective* typical or special

characteristic species *noun* a species typical of and only occurring in a particular region

charcoal *noun* an impure form of carbon, formed when wood is burnt in the absence of oxygen

charge *noun* a quantity of electricity measured in coulombs

chart *noun* **1.** a diagram showing information as a series of lines or blocks **2.** a map of an area of water such as the sea or a large lake ■ *verb* to make a chart of something

chasm *noun* a deep hole in the earth or rock

chem- *prefix* referring to chemistry or chemicals

chemical *noun* a substance formed of chemical elements or produced by a chemical process ○ *the widespread use of chemicals in agriculture* ○ *The machine analyses the chemicals found in the collected samples.* ■ *adjective* **1.** referring to chemistry or chemicals **2.** not found in nature (*informal*) ○ *an unpleasant chemical taste*

chemical bond *noun* the force which links atoms to form molecules. Also called **bond**

chemical closet *noun* same as **chemical toilet**

chemical control *noun* the control of pests using chemicals

chemical element *noun* a substance which exists independently and cannot be broken down into simpler substances

chemical fertiliser *noun* same as **artificial fertiliser**

Chemical of Concern *noun* ◊ List of Chemicals of Concern

chemical oxygen demand *noun* the amount of oxygen taken up by organic matter in water used as a measurement of the amount of organic matter in sewage. Abbr **COD**

chemical toilet *noun* a toilet containing chemicals to neutralise the body's waste products. Also called **chemical closet**

chemical toxicity *noun* the poisonous nature of chemicals used in pest control

chemist *noun* a scientist who specialises in the study of chemistry

chemistry *noun* **1.** the study of substances, elements and compounds and their reactions with each other **2.** chemical substances existing together ○ *Human action has radically altered the chemistry of the atmosphere.*

chemo- *prefix* chemistry

chemoautotrophic *adjective* referring to the oxidation of nitrogen or other chemical elements to create a source of food. Compare **photoautotrophic**

chemolithotrophic *adjective* referring to organisms such as bacteria which obtain energy from inorganic substances

chemo-organotrophic *adjective* referring to an organism such as an animal which obtains its energy from organic sources

chemoreceptor *noun* a cell which responds to the presence of a chemical compound by activating a sensory nerve. ◊ **receptor**

chemosphere *noun* the zone in the Earth's atmosphere, above the upper part of the troposphere and within the stratosphere, where chemical changes take place under the influence of the Sun's radiation

chemosterilant *noun* a chemical substance which sterilises by microorganisms

chemosynthesis *noun* the production by bacteria of organic material using chemical reactions

chemotaxis *noun* a movement of a cell which is attracted to or repelled by a chemical substance

chemotroph *noun* an organism which converts the energy found in organic chemical compounds into more complex energy, without using sunlight. Compare **phototroph**

chemotrophic *adjective* obtaining energy from sources such as organic matter. Compare **phototrophic** (NOTE: Most animals are chemotrophic.)

chemotropism *noun* the movement or growth of an organism in response to a chemical stimulus

Chernobyl *noun* a town in the Ukraine where a large nuclear power station had a disastrous fire in 1986

chernozem *noun* a dark fertile soil, rich in organic matter, found in the temperate grass-covered plains of Russia and North and South America. Also called **black earth**

chickpea *noun* a legume crop, grown for its large round pale-yellow seeds. It is important in India and Pakistan as a source of protein. Genus: *Cicer arietinum*. Also called **gram**

chill *noun* coldness

chimney *noun* a tall tube, either inside a building or separate from it, which takes smoke and fumes away from a fire ○ *Smoke poured out of the factory chimneys.* ○ *Chimneys were built very tall, so that the polluting smoke would be carried a long way away by the wind.*

chimney stack *noun* a tall chimney, especially on an industrial building

china clay *noun* same as **kaolin**

China syndrome *noun* a potential disaster occurring when the core of a nuclear reactor overheats

chinook *noun* a warm wind that blows from the Rocky mountains down onto the Canadian plains in winter. Compare **föhn**

chitin *noun* a tough waterproof substance that forms part of the outer skeleton of insects and the cell walls of fungi

chlor- *prefix* same as **chloro-**

chlorella *noun* a very small green freshwater alga, occurring naturally or grown commercially for use in human food

chloride *noun* a salt of hydrochloric acid

chlorinate *verb* to treat something with chlorine, especially to sterilise drinking water or water in a swimming pool by adding chlorine

chlorinated *adjective* treated with chlorine

chlorinated hydrocarbon *noun* a compound containing chlorine, carbon and hydrogen that remains in the environment after use and may accumulate in the food chain, e.g. an organochlorine pesticide such as lindane or DDT, an industrial chemical such as a polychlorinated biphenyl (PCB), or a chlorine waste product such as a dioxin or furan

chlorination *noun* sterilisation by adding chlorine

chlorinator *noun* an apparatus for adding chlorine to water

chlorine *noun* a greenish chemical element. It is used to sterilise water and for bleaching. (NOTE: The chemical symbol is **Cl**; the atomic number is **17** and the atomic weight is **35.45**.)

chloro- *prefix* chlorine

chlorofluorocarbon *noun* a compound of fluorine and chlorine. It is used as a propellant in aerosol cans, in the manufacture of plastic foam boxes, as a refrigerant in refrigerators and air conditioners and as a cleaner of circuit boards for computers. Abbr **CFC**

COMMENT: Chlorofluorocarbons are classified by numbers: CFC-10 is used in aerosols; CFC-11 is used to make plastic foam; CFC-12 is a coolant for refrigerators; and CFC-13 is a cleaning substance used in the electronics industry. When CFCs are released into the atmosphere, they rise slowly, taking about seven years to reach the stratosphere. But once they are there, under the influence of the Sun's ultraviolet light they break down into chlorine atoms which destroy the ozone layer. This allows harmful solar UV radiation to pass through to the Earth's surface. Because it takes so long for the CFCs to reach the stratosphere, any reduction in their use on Earth does not have an immediate effect on the concentrations in the stratosphere. Replacements for CFCs are being developed.

chlorofluoromethane *noun* a gas that is a volatile organic compound, generated from landfill sites, petrol engine exhausts and other industrial processes. In the chemical industry, it is often manufactured from carbon tetrachloride. Formula: CH_2CHO. Abbr **CFM**

chloromethane *noun* a gas which is a compound of carbon and chlorine, formed by fungi as they rot wood (NOTE: It acts in a similar way to CFCs in depleting the ozone layer.)

chlorophyll *noun* a green pigment in plants and some algae

Chlorophyta *noun* a large group of algae that possess chlorophyll

chloroplast *noun* a tiny sac within the cells of plants and some algae which contains chlorophyll and other pigments and is the place where photosynthesis occurs (NOTE: The number of chloroplasts in a cell varies, but each consists of interconnected stacks of disc-shaped membranes in fluid, surrounded by a double membrane.)

chlorosis *noun* a reduction of chlorophyll in plants, making the leaves turn yellow

chlorpyrifos *noun* an organophosphate insecticide used on a wide range of crops

chlortoluron *noun* a herbicide applied as a spray, especially on cereals (NOTE: It is under review for withdrawal from use in the European Union.)

cholera *noun* a serious bacterial disease spread through food or water which has been infected by *Vibrio cholerae* ○ *A cholera epidemic broke out after the flood.*

cholesterol *noun* a fatty substance found in fats and oils. It is produced by the liver and forms an essential part of cells.

CHP plant *abbr* combined heat and power plant

chrom- *prefix* same as **chromo-**

chromatography *noun* a scientific method for separating and analysing chemicals through a porous medium

chromatophore *noun* a plant or animal cell which contains pigment, e.g. a cell in the eyes, hair and skin, or a similar cell in an alga (NOTE: Chromatophores enable chameleons to change colour.)

chromium *noun* a metallic trace element. It is used to make alloys. (NOTE: The chemical symbol is **Cr**; the atomic number is **24** and the atomic weight is **52.00**.)

chromo- *prefix* **1.** colour **2.** chromium

chromosomal *adjective* referring to chromosomes

chromosome *noun* a thin structure in the nucleus of a cell, formed of DNA which carries the genes (NOTE: Different types of organism have different numbers of chromosomes.)

chromosome number *noun* the number of chromosomes present in each cell nucleus of a specific animal or plant (NOTE: Each species has its own characteristic chromosome number, e.g. humans have 46 chromosomes, receiving 23 from each parent.)

chronic exposure *noun* exposure to a pollutant or radioactive substance for a long period, even for a whole lifetime

chronobiology *noun* the study of recurring cycles of events in the natural world

chrysalis *noun* **1.** a stage in the development of a butterfly or moth when the pupa is protected in a hard case **2.** the hard case in which a pupa is protected

Chrysophyta *noun* a group of golden-brown algae, which store oil in their cell walls

chute *noun* **1.** a sloping channel along which something such as water or rubbish may pass **2.** a waterfall

CID *abbr* cattle identification document

-cide *suffix* killing

cilia plural of **cilium**

ciliary *adjective* referring to cilia

ciliate, ciliated *adjective* having cilia

cilium *noun* one of many tiny projections resembling hairs which move backwards and forwards and drive particles or fluid along (NOTE: The plural is **cilia**.)

cinders *plural noun* **1.** hard pieces of material left when the flames from a burning substance have gone out **2.** the small pieces of lava and rock thrown up in a volcanic eruption

circadian rhythm *noun* a rhythm of daily activities in plants and animals, repeating every twenty-four hours

circuit breaker *noun* an electrical device used to interrupt an electrical supply when there is too much current flow

circulate *verb* to move round in such a way as to arrive at the point of departure ○ *Water circulates via the radiator and pump through to the engine block itself.*

circulation *noun* the act of moving round in such a way as to arrive at the point of departure ○ *the circulation of the blood* ○ *The general circulation is indicated by the arrows.*

circulatory *adjective* referring to circulation

circum- *prefix* around

circumpolar *adjective* around the North or South Pole

circumpolar vortex *noun* a circular movement of air around the North or South Pole. Also called **polar vortex**

cirque *noun* a hollow formed in mountains or high plateaux by small, separate glaciers. Also called **corrie, cwm**

cirrocumulus *noun* a form of high cloud, occurring above 5000 m, like altocumulus with little clouds

cirrostratus *noun* a high thin layer of cloud

cirrus *noun* a high cloud, occurring above 5000 m, forming a mass of separate clouds which look as if they are made of fibres, but which are formed of ice crystals

CITES *abbr* Convention on International Trade in Endangered Species of Wild Fauna and Flora

citric acid *noun* an acid found in fruit such as oranges, lemons and grapefruit

citric acid cycle *noun* same as **Krebs cycle**

Cl *symbol* chlorine

cladding *noun* a protective material surrounding something

clarification *noun* the process of removing solid waste matter from sewage

class *noun* one of the categories into which organisms are divided ○ *Groups of plant and animal families are classified into orders and groups of orders into classes.*

classification *noun* a system by which objects or organisms are put into order so as to be able to refer to them again and identify them ○ *the classification of plants and animals*

classify *verb* **1.** to allocate something to a category ○ *The area has been classified as an Area of Outstanding Natural Beauty.* ○ *The pollution records are classified under the name of the site which has been polluted.* **2.** to restrict the publication of ○ *The reports on the accident are classified and may not be consulted by the public.*

clay *noun* a type of heavy non-porous soil made of fine particles of silicate

clayey *adjective* containing clay ○ *These plants do best in clayey soils.*

claypan *noun* a hollow on the surface of clay land where rain collects

clean air *noun* air which does not contain impurities

Clean Development Mechanism *noun* a scheme by which an industrialised country can receive credit for emission reductions in a developing country which result from projects financed by the industrialised country. Abbr **CDM**

cleaner *noun* a fish or insect which cleans other animals by removing dirt or parasites

cleanse *verb* to make clean

cleanser *noun* a powder or liquid used for cleaning

clean up *verb* to remove refuse, waste substances or pollutants from a place ○ *They are working to clean up the beaches after the oil spill.*

clean-up, cleaning-up *noun* an act of removing refuse, waste substances or pollutants ○ *The local authorities have organised a large-scale clean-up of polluted beaches.*

clean-up costs *plural noun* the amount of money which has to be spent to remove pollutants, e.g. after an industrial process or an environmental disaster such as an oil spill

clear *verb* to remove something which is in the way ○ *They cleared hectares of jungle to make a new road to the capital.*

clear air *noun* an atmosphere with no mist or smoke

clearance *noun* the act of removing something which is in the way in order to make space for something else

clearcut *noun* the cutting down of all the trees in an area ■ *verb* to clear an area of forest by cutting down all the trees

clearcutting, clearfelling *noun* cutting down all the trees in an area at the same time ○ *The greatest threat to wildlife is the destruction of habitats by clearfelling the forest for paper pulp.*

clearfell *verb* to clear an area of forest by cutting down all the trees

clear sky *noun* a sky with no clouds

cliff *noun* the steep side of an area of high ground, often by the sea, usually rocky

climate *noun* the general weather patterns that a place has

climate change *noun* a long-term alteration in global weather patterns, occurring naturally, as in a glacial or post-glacial period, or as a likely result of atmospheric pollution (NOTE: Sometimes climate change is used interchangeably with 'global warming', but scientists tend to use the term in the wider sense to include natural changes in the climate.)

climatic *adjective* referring to climate

climatic factor *noun* a condition of climate which affects the organisms living in a specific area

climatic variation *noun* the differences between one type of climate and another, or within the same climate type on different occasions

climatic zone *noun* one of the eight areas of the Earth which have different climates

COMMENT: The climatic zones are: the two polar regions (the Arctic and Antarctic); the boreal in the northern hemisphere, south of the Arctic; two temperate zones, one in the northern hemisphere and one in the southern hemisphere; two subtropical zones, including the deserts; and the equatorial zone which has a damp tropical climate.

climatological *adjective* referring to climatology ○ *Scientists have gathered climatological statistics from weather stations all round the world.*

climatologist *noun* a scientist who specialises in the study of the climate

climatology *noun* the scientific study of climate

climax *noun* the final stage in the development of plant colonisation of a specific site, when changes occur within a mature and relatively stable community

climax community *noun* a plant community which has been stable for many years and which changes only as the environment or climate changes or there is human interference

cline *noun* the set of gradual changes which take place in a species according to geographical and climatic differences across the environment in which it lives. ◊ **ecocline, geocline**

clinker *noun* the lumps of ash and hard residue from furnaces, used to make road surfaces or breeze blocks

clisere *noun* the succession of communities influenced by the climate of an area

clog *verb* to prevent movement of fluid through a pipe, channel or filter because of a build-up of solid matter ○ *The stream was clogged with waterweed.*

clone *noun* 1. a group of cells derived from a single cell by asexual reproduction and therefore identical to the first cell 2. an organism produced asexually, either naturally or by means such as taking cuttings from a plant 3. a group of organisms all of which have been derived from a single individual by asexual means ■ *verb* to reproduce an individual organism by asexual means

cloning *noun* the reproduction of an individual organism by asexual means

Clostridium *noun* a type of bacterium (NOTE: Species of Clostridium cause botulism, tetanus and gas gangrene, but also increase the nitrogen content of soil.)

cloud *noun* 1. a mass of water vapour or ice particles in the sky which can produce rain or snow 2. a mass of particles suspended in the air ○ *Clouds of smoke poured out of the factory chimney.* ○ *Dust clouds swept across the plains.* (NOTE: As a plural, **clouds** means several separate clouds; otherwise the singular **cloud** can be used to refer to a large continuous mass: *There is a mass of cloud over the southern part of the country.*)

COMMENT: Clouds are formed as humid air rises and then cools, causing the water in it to condense. They are classified by meteorologists into ten categories: cirrus, cirrocumulus and cirrostratus (high-level clouds); altocumulus and altostratus (middle-level clouds); and stratocumulus, nimbostratus, cumulus, cumulonimbus and stratus (low-level clouds).

cloudbank *noun* a mass of low clouds

cloudbase *noun* the bottom part of a layer of cloud

cloudburst *noun* a sudden rainstorm

cloud chamber *noun* a piece of laboratory equipment in which clouds can be formed for the study of ionisation

cloud cover *noun* the amount of sky which is covered by clouds. ◊ **okta**

cloud forest *noun* a tropical forest growing at high altitude that is usually covered by cloud and where epiphytes such as orchids, mosses and ferns grow easily on the trees because of the constant moisture in the air

cloud formation *noun* a pattern of clouds in the sky

cloudlayer *noun* a mass of clouds at a specific height above the land

cloudless *adjective* without clouds

cloudy *adjective* 1. covered with clouds ○ *a cloudy sky* 2. not clear or transparent ○ *a cloudy liquid*

clump *noun* 1. a group of particles which stick together 2. a group of trees or plants growing together ○ *a clump of bushes* ○ *a clump of grass* 3. a group of items brought close together in a mass ○ *to form a clump* ■ *verb* to collect or stick together

clumping *noun* the formation of a mass of things in close association

cluster *noun* 1. a group of similar things that are close together ○ *a flower cluster* 2. a number of similar events happening at a similar time or in a similar place ○ *a cluster of leukaemia patients in the area of the nuclear power station*

cnidarian *noun* a marine invertebrate with tentacles surrounding its mouth, e.g. a sea anemone, coral and jellyfish. Phylum: Cnidaria.

CNSL *abbr* cashew-nut shell liquor

Co *symbol* cobalt

CO *symbol* carbon monoxide

CO₂, CO2 *symbol* carbon dioxide

coagulant *noun* a substance which can make blood coagulate

coagulate *verb* (*of a liquid*) to become semi-solid as suspended particles clump together

coagulation *noun* (*of a liquid*) the process of becoming semi-solid

coal *noun* a solid black organic substance found in layers underground in most parts of the world, burnt to provide heat or power

coal deposit *noun* a layer of coal in the rocks beneath the Earth's surface

coalescence *noun* the process of joining together to form a larger mass or number ○ *Coalescence of water vapour in the atmosphere forms larger droplets of water.*

coal-fired power station *noun* a power station which burns coal to produce electricity

coal measure *noun* a layer of rock containing coal that erodes very quickly and soon becomes covered in vegetation, therefore rarely seen exposed

coal mine *noun* a hole dug in the ground to extract coal

coarse *adjective* referring to a particle or feature which is larger than others ○ *Coarse sand fell to the bottom of the liquid as sediment, while the fine grains remained suspended.*

coarse fish *noun* freshwater fish other than salmon and trout

coarse fishing *noun* the leisure activity of catching freshwater fish other than salmon and trout

coast *noun* the zone where the land meets the sea

coastal *adjective* near the coast ○ *a plant found in coastal waters*

coastal area *noun* an area of land that is affected in various ways by its closeness to the sea together with the area of sea that is affected by being close to human activities on and from the land

coastal cell *noun* a specific area of coast within which sediments move

coastal defences *plural noun* structures such as sea walls or groynes built to protect the coast from erosion by the action of waves. Also called **sea defences**

coastal defence strategy *noun* an official plan for the protection of the coast

coastal erosion *noun* the loss of land from a coast as a result of the force of waves and currents

coastal fishery *noun* an area of sea near the coast where fish are caught

coastal fog *noun* a type of advection fog which forms along the coast

coastal habitat management plan *noun* an overview of the loss and gain of coastal habitats over 30–100 years and options for preventing, restoring or compensating for lost habitats. Abbr **CHaMP**

coastal lagoon *noun* a body of seawater near the coast, separated from the sea by a small strip of land and with only a small opening to the sea

coastal pelagic fish *noun* a fish which lives in the upper layer of the sea, close to land

coastal protection, coast protection work *noun* action to protect the coast from being eroded by the action of the sea such as building sea walls and projecting structures to break the force of the waves

coastal realignment *noun* the gradual change in a coastline, as land disappears into or is deposited from the sea, often as part of a policy to provide more effective sea defences or restore wetlands

coastal retreat *noun* serious erosion of a coastline

coastal squeeze *noun* the reduction of the area of land near a coast or the loss of its former use because of its position between rising sea levels and fixed sea defences or high ground

coastal waters *plural noun* the waters outside the low-water line or the outer limit of an estuary

coastline *noun* the outline of a coast as seen on a map or a high place, or the land as seen from the sea

cob *interjection* same as **corn cob**

cobalt *noun* a metallic element. It is used to make alloys. (NOTE: The chemical symbol is **Co**; the atomic number is **27** and the atomic weight is **58.93**.)

coccidioidomycosis *noun* a lung disease caused by inhaling spores of the fungus *Coccidioides immitis*

coccus *noun* a bacterium shaped like a ball (NOTE: The plural is **cocci**.)

cockroach *noun* a black beetle that is a common household pest. Order: Dyctyoptera.

coconut oil *noun* an oil extracted from dried coconut flesh or copra

coconut palm *noun* a palm tree with large hard-shelled edible nuts. Latin name: *Cocos nucifera.*

COD *abbr* chemical oxygen demand

code *verb* to convert instructions, information or data into another form

codisposal *noun* the final disposal of non-hazardous solid industrial waste that will not decompose together with hazardous waste in a managed site

codistillation *noun* the process by which molecules of toxic substances can be evaporated into clouds over land and then fall back into the sea as rain

codominant *adjective* **1.** referring to a species that is as abundant as another in a community ○ *There are three codominant* *tree species in this forest.* **2.** referring to alleles of a gene that are not fully dominant over other alleles in a heterozygous individual

coefficient *noun* a mathematical quantity placed before and multiplying another (NOTE: In $4xy$, 4 is the coefficient of x.)

coefficient of haze *noun* a number which shows the percentage of dust and smoke in the atmosphere

-coele *suffix* another spelling of **-cele**

coelom *noun* the body cavity in most many-celled animals including humans

coevolution *noun* the evolution of two species together such as parasite and host

coffee *noun* a bush or small tree widely grown in the tropics for its seeds, which are used to make a drink. Latin name: *Coffea arabica.*

cogeneration *noun* the production of heat and power, as in a combined heat and power installation

cohort *noun* a group of individuals sharing a common factor such as age or a set of circumstances

cohort study *noun* an investigation in which a group of people without a disease are classified according to their exposure to a risk and are studied over a period of time to see if they develop the disease, in order to study links between risk and disease

coir *noun* a rough fibre from the outer husk of coconuts

coke *noun* a fuel manufactured by heating coal to high temperatures without the presence of air

coke burner *noun* a device in which coal is heated to produce coke

col *noun* **1.** a high pass between two mountains **2.** a low pressure area between two anticyclones

cold-blooded *adjective* referring to an animal such as a reptile or fish whose body temperature is dependent on the temperature of its surroundings. Also called **ectotherm, poikilotherm**

coleopteran *noun* an insect such as a beetle with modified tough forewings that act as covers for the membranous hindwings. Order: Coleoptera.

coliform *adjective* referring to bacteria which are similar in shape to *Escherichia coli*

collection *noun* **1.** the process of gathering something together ○ *the regular collection of samples for analysis* **2.** a group of objects or organisms brought together ○ *a*

labelled collection of insects ○ *a living collection of plants*

collector panel *noun* same as **solar panel**

colloid *noun* a substance with very small particles that do not settle but remain in suspension in a liquid

colloidal *adjective* referring to a colloid

colonial *adjective* referring to a colony

colonial animal *noun* an animal which usually lives in colonies, e.g. an ant

colonisation *noun* the act of colonising a place ○ *Islands are particularly subject to colonisation by species of plants or animals introduced by people.*

colonise *verb* (*of plants and animals*) to become established in a new ecosystem ○ *Derelict city sites rapidly become colonised by plants.* ○ *Rats have colonised the sewers.*

coloniser, colonist *noun* an organism that moves into and establishes itself in a new ecosystem, e.g. a plant such as a weed

colony *noun* a group of animals, plants or microorganisms living together in a place ○ *a colony of ants*

coloration *noun* the colours or patterns of an animal ○ *protective coloration*

colour *noun* the set of differing wavelengths of light that are reflected from objects and sensed by the eyes ○ *Flower colour attracts insects.* ■ *verb* to give colour to something ○ *The chemical coloured the water blue.* (NOTE: [all senses] The US spelling is **color**.)

colouring *noun* **1.** the appearance of something in terms of its colour **2.** same as **food colouring**

colourless *adjective* with no colour ○ *Water is a colourless liquid.*

column *noun* **1.** a solid with a tall narrow shape ○ *Basalt rocks form columns in some parts of the world.* **2.** a body of fluid in a tall, narrow shape ○ *Torricelli first demonstrated that the atmosphere has weight by showing that it can support a column of liquid.* **3.** a vertical section of a table in a document ○ *Column four of the table shows the totals of the other three.*

columnar *adjective* in the form of a column ○ *Igneous rocks may have a columnar structure.*

combe, coombe *noun* a small valley with steep sides and usually no water flowing through it

combination *noun* **1.** two or more things together ○ *Lichens are a combination of a fungus and an alga.* **2.** the act of bringing two or more things together ○ *the successful combination of our ideas with their resources*

combine *verb* to bring two or more things together to make one, or to come together to make one

combined heat and power plant *noun* a power station that produces both electricity and hot water. Abbr **CHP plant** (NOTE: Such a plant may operate on almost any fuel, including refuse.)

combust *verb* to burn, or to burn something ○ *The region combusts 75% of its refuse for heat reclamation.*

combustion *noun* the burning of a substance with oxygen

command-and-control regulations *plural noun* rules that require polluters to meet specific emission-reduction targets, often using specific types of equipment

commensal *noun* an organism which lives on another plant or animal but does not harm it or influence it in any way. ◊ **parasite, symbiont** ■ *adjective* referring to a commensal

commensalism *noun* the state of organisms existing together as commensals

comminution *noun* the crushing or grinding of rock, ore or sewage into small particles

comminutor *noun* a crushing machine that makes particles smaller

committee *noun* a group of people dealing with a particular subject or problem

common *adjective* **1.** occurring frequently ○ *a common spelling error* **2.** used or done by several people ○ *a common ethical stance* **3.** ordinary ○ *common household chemicals* **4.** belonging to several different people or to everyone ○ *common land* ■ *noun* an area of land to which the public has access for walking

COMMENT: About 80% of common land is privately owned and, subject to the interests of any commoners, owners enjoy essentially the same rights as the owners of other land. Commoners have different types of 'rights of common', e.g. to graze animals, or to extract sand, gravel or peat.

Common Agricultural Policy *noun* a set of regulations and mechanisms agreed between members of the European Union to control the supply, marketing and pricing of farm produce. Abbr **CAP**

Common Birds Census *noun* an ongoing survey of commonly occurring birds, run by the British Trust for Ornithology

commoner *noun* someone with a right to use a common in a particular way, e.g. to graze animals on it

Common Fisheries Policy *noun* the legal framework which covers all fishing in the European Union. It aims to conserve fish stocks by regulating fish catches. Abbr **CFP**

common land *noun* same as **common**

common nuisance *noun* a criminal act which causes harm or danger to members of the public in general or to their rights

community *noun* **1.** a group of people who live and work in a district ○ *The health services serve the local community.* **2.** a group of different organisms which live together in an area ○ *the plant community on the sand dunes*

community architecture *noun* a way of designing new housing projects or adapting old buildings, in which the people living in the area as well as specialists are involved in the planning

community ecology *noun* the study of the processes that determine the composition and structure of the mixture of species found in a particular area

community forest *noun* a wooded landscape near an urban area, sometimes created on formerly derelict land, maintained for work, wildlife, recreation and education

community transport *noun* a bus or rail service which is available to the community

commute *verb* to travel regularly to and from home and a place of work ○ *Thousands of people commute long distances daily.*

commuter *noun* a person who travels regularly to and from his or her place of work, especially in a city

commuter belt *noun* an area around a big city, where commuters live

commuting *noun* the activity of travelling regularly to and from home and a place of work ○ *a huge increase in commuting from cheaper housing areas into the cities*

compact *verb* to compress the ground and make it hard, e.g. by driving over it with heavy machinery or as the result of a lot of people walking on it

compaction, compacting *noun* the compression of ground and making it hard, e.g. by driving over it with heavy machinery or as the result of a lot of people walking on it

compactor *noun* **1.** a machine which compresses the ground and makes it hard **2.** a machine that crushes refuse

companion animal *noun* an animal that is kept for company and enjoyable interaction, rather than for work or food

companion plant *noun* a plant which improves the growth of nearby plants (NOTE: Companion plants are often used by horticulturists and gardeners because they encourage growth or reduce pest infestation in an adjacent plant.)

companion planting *noun* the use of plants that encourage the growth of others nearby

comparative risk analysis *noun* the comparison of two types of risk

compartment *noun* a section of a managed plantation of trees

compensation depth *noun* the point in a lake or sea at which the rate of formation of organic matter by photosynthesis is the same as the rate of loss of matter by respiration

compensation point *noun* the point at which the rate of photosynthesis is the same as the rate of respiration (NOTE: It can be measured as the point at which the amount of carbon dioxide used by plants equals the amount of oxygen they release.)

compensatory habitat *noun* a habitat created because an existing protected natural area has been damaged or lost

compensatory measure *noun* a course of action that is taken to improve a situation when environmental damage cannot be directly restored

compete *verb* to try to obtain the same limited resources such as food, light or a mate as other organisms of the same or different species

competition *noun* the struggle for limited resources such as food, light or a mate, occurring between organisms of the same or different species

competitive exclusion principle *noun* the concept that two or more species with identical requirements will not be able to live on the same limited resources because one species will compete more successfully than the other (NOTE: The loser has to adapt its feeding habits or behaviour or migrate to another area, otherwise it will experience a decrease in population or even become extinct.)

competitive release *noun* the process by which a species may expand its niche if it has no competitors

complementarity *noun* nature conservation based on a balance between wild and domesticated species in an area

compliance *noun* the act of obeying a regulation or conforming to a set of standards

comply with *verb* to obey a regulation ○ *People importing plants have to comply with CITES regulations.*

compose *verb* to be made from a number of parts ○ *A carpel is composed of an ovary, a stigma and a style.*

Compositae *plural noun* former name for **Asteraceae**

composition *noun* the make-up or structure of something ○ *the composition of the atmosphere*

compost *noun* **1.** rotted vegetation, used as fertiliser or mulch **2.** a prepared soil or peat mixture in which plants are grown in horticulture ■ *verb* to form material resembling humus by the decomposition of organic waste, as in a compost heap

compost heap *noun* a pile of organic, especially plant, waste, usually kept in a container and left to decay gradually, being turned over occasionally. It is used as a fertiliser and soil improver.

composting *noun* the controlled decomposition of organic waste, especially used for the disposal for plant waste in gardens or domestic green waste such as vegetable peelings

compound *noun* a substance made up of two or more components

compound fertiliser *noun* a fertiliser that supplies two or more nutrients. Also called **mixed fertiliser**. Compare **straight fertiliser**

compulsory *adjective* forced or ordered by an authority ○ *the compulsory slaughter of infected animals*

concentrate *noun* **1.** the strength of a solution, or the quantity of a substance in a specific volume **2.** a strong solution which is to be diluted ○ *orange juice made from concentrate* ■ *verb* to reduce the volume of a solution and increase its strength by evaporation. Opposite **dilute**

concentration *noun* **1.** a collection in a particular place rather than spread around ○ *The maximum concentration of ozone is between 20 and 25km above the Earth's surface.* **2.** the amount of a substance in a given volume or mass of a solution

concentration peak *noun* the largest amount of a substance in a solution or in a given volume

concrete *noun* a hard stone-like substance made by mixing cement, sand, aggregate and water and letting it dry

concretion *noun* the formation of a solid mass of rock from pieces of stones and other sedimentary materials

concretionary *adjective* referring to stone which is formed by concretion

condensate *noun* 1. a substance formed by condensation, e.g. a liquid formed from a vapour 2. a substance that is a gas when occurring naturally underground but becomes liquid when brought to the surface

condensation *noun* 1. the action of making vapour into liquid 2. the water that forms when warm damp air meets a cold surface such as a wall or window

condense *verb* 1. to make something compact or more dense 2. to make a vapour become liquid

condensed *adjective* made compact or more dense

condenser *noun* a device that cools steam or other vapour and turns it back into liquid

condition *noun* 1. the present state of something 2. the physical state of a site of special scientific interest, according to whether or not conservation objectives are being achieved ○ *favourable condition* ○ *unfavourable condition* ■ *plural noun* **conditions** variable environmental factors such as temperature, salinity and acidity to which organisms respond ○ *in wet or dry conditions*

conditioned reflex *noun* 1. an automatic reaction by an animal to a stimulus, learned from past experience 2. a reaction to a stimulus learned from past experience

conditioner *noun* a substance that is used to make an improvement in something else ○ *mushroom compost used as a soil conditioner*

conditioning *noun* the act of improving the quality of something

conduct *verb* to carry out something such as an experiment, survey or review

conduction *noun* the process by which heat or electricity passes through a substance ○ *Heat is transferred to the layer of air next to the Earth's surface by conduction.*

conductive *adjective* having the ability to allow heat or electricity to pass through ○ *Steel is a conductive material.* ○ *Land masses are less conductive than water.*

conductivity *noun* the ability of a material to conduct heat or electricity ○ *Because* of the poor conductivity of air, heat is transferred from the Earth's surface upwards by convection.

conduit *noun* 1. a channel along which a fluid flows 2. a pipe or elongated box used to protect electrical cables

cone *noun* 1. a solid body with a base in the shape of a circle, and with sides that narrow to a point 2. a hard scaly structure containing seeds on such plants as conifers

Conference of the Parties *noun* the group of nations which have ratified the Framework Convention on Climate Change. Abbr **COP**

confluence *noun* a place where two rivers or streams of air join

congener *noun* 1. a species which belongs to the same genus as another 2. a chemical element which belongs to the same group as another

congenital *adjective* existing at or before birth

congested *adjective* blocked

congestion *noun* 1. the blocking of a tube or a passage 2. the situation that occurs when there is too much traffic to be able to flow freely in the streets of a town or city

congestion charge *noun* a sum of money paid by motorists to be allowed to drive a vehicle into a town or city centre

congestion charging *noun* a method of reducing congestion in a city by charging motorists a fee to drive within a certain area

conglomerate *noun* a sedimentary layer formed of small round stones

conifer *noun* a tree with long thin needle-shaped leaves and bearing seed in scaly cones. Most are evergreen.

coniferous *adjective* referring to conifers

coniferous forest, **coniferous woodland** *noun* an area of wooded land consisting of more than 75% conifers

coning *noun* the widening out of a column of smoke as it leaves a chimney

conjugation *noun* 1. a simple form of reproduction in single-celled organisms in which they join together, exchange genetic information and then separate 2. in algae and fungi, the fusion of male and female nuclei 3. the alternation in a molecule of two or more double or triple bonds with single bonds

connect *verb* to join or associate two or more objects, processes or ideas together ○ *Bones are connected to form a skeleton.*

connection *noun* a point at which things are joined or associated ○ *the connection* *between living things and their environment*

conservancy *noun* an official body which protects a part of the environment

conservation *noun* **1.** the process of protecting something from undesirable change **2.** the maintenance of environmental quality and resources by the use of ecological knowledge and principles

conservation area *noun* an area of special environmental or historical importance that is protected by law from changes that have not received official permission

conservation biology *noun* the study of how species and ecosystems can be maintained

conservation body *noun* a group of people or an organisation that promotes the conservation of species, habitats or an area of countryside and the careful management of natural resources

conservation headland *noun* an area between the edge of a crop and the first tractor tramline that is treated less intensively with pesticides so that a range of broadleaved weeds and beneficial insects survive, used as a method of encouraging biodiversity

conservationist *noun* a person who promotes, carries out or works for conservation

conservation measure *noun* a way in which environmental quality can be maintained

conservation of energy *noun* the process of making consumption of energy more efficient, preventing loss or waste of energy, e.g. by the loss of heat from buildings

conservation of resources *noun* the process of managing resources such as fossil fuels and other natural materials so as not to waste them, damage them or use them too quickly

conservation status *noun* the condition of a site of special scientific interest, according to whether or not conservation objectives are being achieved

conservation tillage *noun* a farming method which aims to plough the soil as little as possible, to prevent erosion, save energy and improve biodiversity. Also called **minimum tillage**

conserve *verb* **1.** to keep and not waste something □ **to conserve energy** to use only as much electricity or other fuel as is really needed, e.g. by keeping central heating a little lower than before **2.** to look after

and keep something in the same state ○ *to conserve tigers' habitat*

consociation, consocies *noun* an ecological community that has one main species, e.g. a wood consisting mostly of beech trees

conspecific *adjective* referring to an organism belonging to the same species as another organism ■ *noun* an organism belonging to the same species as another organism

constant *noun* an item of data whose value does not change. Opposite **variable** ■ *adjective* **1.** not changing □ **to remain constant** to stay the same ○ *The temperature of the gas remains constant.* **2.** continuous, not stopping ○ *The wardens complained about the constant stream of visitors to the reservation.*

constituent *noun* a substance or component which forms part of a whole ■ *adjective* forming part of a whole ○ *the constituent elements of air*

construction *noun* **1.** the building of something **2.** something built ○ *an elegant construction of steel*

construction industry *noun* the business or trade of constructing buildings

consultative body *noun* a group of people who can give their advice and opinion on a subject but who do not have the power to make laws

consumable *adjective* able to be consumed

consumable goods, consumables *plural noun* products that are used quickly and have to be bought often, e.g. food or stationery

consume *verb* **1.** to use up or burn fuel ○ *The new pump consumes only half the fuel which the other pump would use.* **2.** to eat foodstuffs ○ *The population consumes ten tonnes of foodstuffs per week.*

consumer *noun* **1.** a person or company which buys and uses goods and services ○ *Gas consumers are protesting at the increase in prices.* ○ *The factory is a heavy consumer of water.* **2.** an organism that eats other organisms. Compare **producer**

consumerism *noun* a movement for the protection of the rights of consumers

consumer panel *noun* a group of consumers who report on products they have used so that the manufacturers can improve them or use what the panel says about them in advertising

consumer protection *noun* protecting consumers against unfair or illegal traders

consumer research *noun* research into why consumers buy goods and what goods they really want to buy

consumption *noun* 1. the fact or process of using something ○ *a car with low petrol consumption* ○ *The country's consumption of wood has fallen by a quarter.* 2. the taking of food or liquid into the body ○ *Nearly 3% of all food samples were found to be unfit for human consumption through contamination by lead.*

consumption efficiency *noun* the percentage of the total available matter at one trophic level which is consumed by animals at the next trophic level, e.g. the percentage of plants eaten by herbivores. Abbr **CE**

contact *noun* a physical connection between two or more things

contact herbicide, contact weedkiller *noun* a substance which kills a plant whose leaves it touches, e.g. paraquat

contagion *noun* the spreading of a disease by touching an infected person, or objects which an infected person has touched. Compare **infection**

contagious *adjective* referring to a disease which can be transmitted by touching an infected person, or objects which an infected person has touched. Compare **infectious**

container *noun* 1. a box, case or bottle that holds something else 2. a large case, with internationally agreed measurements, that can be transported by truck and then easily loaded on a ship

containment *noun* the actions taken to stop the spread of something such as disease or contamination

contaminant *noun* a substance which causes contamination

contaminate *verb* to make something impure by touching it or by adding something, especially something harmful, to it ○ *Supplies of drinking water were contaminated by uncontrolled discharges from the factory.*

contaminated land, contaminated site *noun* an area which has been polluted as a result of human activities such as industrial processes, presenting a hazard to human health, and which needs cleaning before it can be used for other purposes

COMMENT: Contaminated land is a feature of most industrialised countries. Careless past management of waste, lack of pollution controls and many leaks and spills have left a legacy of land contaminated by a wide variety of substances. In some cases this presents unacceptable risks to human beings, ecosystems, water resources or property and has to be dealt with by formal remedial measures.

contamination *noun* 1. the action of making something impure ○ *the contamination of the water supply by runoff from the fields* □ **contamination of air** pollution in the atmosphere 2. the state of something such as water or food which has been contaminated and so is harmful to living organisms ○ *The level of contamination is dropping.*

content *noun* whatever is contained within something (NOTE: This is often expressed as a percentage.)

continent *noun* one of the seven large landmasses on the Earth's surface (NOTE: The continents are Asia, Africa, North America, South America, Australia, Europe and Antarctica.)

continental *adjective* referring to a continent

continental climate *noun* a type of climate found in the centre of a large continent away from the sea, with long dry summers, very cold winters and not much rainfall

continental crust *noun* the part of the Earth's crust under the continents and continental shelves, lying above the oceanic crust

continental drift *noun* a geological theory that the present continents were once part of a single landmass and have gradually drifted away from each other over a period of millions of years

continental shelf *noun* the sloping land surface of the seabed from the shore out to sea for an average distance of 70 km

contingent valuation method *noun* a survey-based economic method which is used to determine the monetary value of the benefits or costs of an environmental policy or feature

continuous *adjective* going on without stopping

contour *noun* 1. the shape of something 2. same as **contour line**

contour line *noun* a line drawn on a map to show ground of the same height above sea level

contour ploughing *noun* the practice of ploughing across the side of a hill so as to create ridges along the contours of the land which will hold water and prevent erosion

contract *noun* an agreement

control *noun* **1.** the action of directing or working in a specific way **2.** the process of restraining something or keeping something in order □ **to bring** *or* **keep something under control** to make sure that something is well regulated ○ *The authorities brought the epidemic under control.* □ **out of control** unregulated ○ *The epidemic appears to be out of control.* **3.** (*in experiments*) a sample used as a comparison with the one being tested ■ *verb* to direct or manage something

control action threshold *noun* the point at which the amount of pest infestation makes it necessary to start pest control. Abbr **CAT**

controlled atmosphere *noun* the conditions in which oxygen and carbon dioxide concentrations are regulated and monitored, e.g. to improve the storage of fruit and vegetables

controlled dumping *noun* the disposal of waste on special sites

controlled environment *noun* an environment in which conditions such as temperature, atmosphere and relative humidity are regulated and monitored

controlled experiment *noun* an experiment designed to test the effects of independent variables on a dependent variable by changing one independent variable at a time

controlled landfill *noun* the disposal of waste in a landfill carried out under a permit system according to the specific laws in force

controlled tipping *noun* the disposal of waste in special landfill sites. ◊ **fly-tipping**

conurbation *noun* a large area covered with buildings such as houses, factories or offices

convection *noun* the process by which hot air rises and cool air descends ○ *Heat is transferred from the Earth's surface upwards largely by convection.*

convention *noun* **1.** a meeting of large numbers of people ○ *a convention of environmentalists* **2.** a formal agreement ○ *Convention on Biological Diversity* □ **by convention** by general agreement or custom

conventional *adjective* usual, accepted and familiar to most people ○ *the conventional symbols used on weather charts*

conventional fuel *noun* a traditional means of providing energy, e.g. coal, wood or gas, as opposed to alternative energy sources such as solar power, tidal power or wind power

Convention on Biological Diversity *noun* an international agreement made at the Earth Summit in Rio de Janeiro in 1992 to conserve biological diversity, encourage sustainable use of natural resources and ensure that benefits from the use of genetic resources are shared in a fair way. Abbr **CBD**

Convention on International Trade in Endangered Species of Wild Fauna and Flora *noun* an international agreement between 123 countries to reduce or prevent the trade in endangered species of wild animals and plants. Abbr **CITES**

Convention on the Conservation of European Wildlife and Natural Habitats *noun* an agreement made in 1979 between 45 European and African states to conserve wild flora and fauna, especially endangered and vulnerable species, including migratory species, and their natural habitats. Also called **Bern Convention**

convergence *noun* **1.** the movement towards or the act of coming together or meeting at a point ○ *There is convergence of meridians of longitude at the North and South Poles.* **2.** a phenomenon that occurs whenever there is a net inflow of air into a region of the atmosphere, resulting in the accumulation of air and an increase in density. Compare **divergence 3.** the process that occurs in an ocean when warm surface water meets cold polar surface water and starts to cool and sink

convergence zone *noun* the area of an ocean in which convergence occurs

conversion *noun* a change from one system or set of beliefs to another

convert *verb* to change something to a different system, set of rules or state ○ *Photochemical reactions convert oxygen to ozone.* ○ *She has converted her car to take LPG.*

converter *noun* a device which alters the form of something ○ *A backup converter converts the alternating current power into direct current.*

cool *adjective* rather cold

coolant *noun* a substance used to cool something such as an engine

coombe *noun* another spelling of **combe**

cooperation *noun* the act of working together in harmony to achieve a common goal

COP *abbr* Conference of the Parties

copper *noun* a metallic trace element. It is essential to biological life and used in making alloys and in electric wiring. (NOTE: The chemical symbol is **Cu**; the atomic number is **29** and the atomic weight is **63.55**.)

coppice *noun* an area of trees which have been cut down to near the ground to allow shoots to grow which are then harvested. The shoots may be used as fuel or for making products such as baskets or fencing. ■ *verb* to cut trees down to near the ground to produce strong straight shoots ○ *Coppiced wood can be dried for use in wood-burning stoves.* Compare **pollard**

coppice forest, **coppice wood** *noun* woodland that has regrown from shoots formed on the stumps or roots of previously cut trees, usually cut again after a few years to provide small branches for uses such as fuel

coppicing *noun* the practice of regularly cutting down trees near to the ground to produce strong straight shoots for fuel or other uses ○ *Coppicing, a traditional method of woodland management, is now of interest for producing biofuel.*

COMMENT: The best trees for coppicing are those which naturally send up several tall straight stems from a bole, such as willow, alder or poplar. In coppice management, the normal cycle is about five to ten years of growth, after which the stems are cut back.

copra *noun* the dried pulp of a coconut, from which oil is extracted by pressing

coprolite *noun* fossilized dung of ancient animals, formerly mined and used as fertilizer

coprophilous *adjective* growing on dung ○ *coprophilous fungi*

copse *noun* an area of small trees

copy *noun* a duplicate of an original ○ *Make copies of the report for everyone.*

coral *noun* a rock-like substance composed of the skeletons of dead polyps

core *noun* the central part of something ○ *The Earth's core is believed to be formed of nickel and iron.*

Corinair *noun* a programme to establish an inventory of emissions of air pollutants in Europe

Corine *noun* a collection of information on important issues such as land cover, coastal erosion and biotopes for the major natural sites in Europe. Full form **Coordination of information on the environment**

cork *noun* a protective outer layer that forms part of the bark in woody plants, taking many years to regrow once stripped (NOTE: It is used, among other things, for bottle corks, fishing net floats and flooring, but cork oaks are now attracting conservation interest.)

cork oak, **cork tree** *noun* an evergreen tree from which cork is harvested. Latin name: *Quercus suber.*

corm *noun* a swollen underground plant stem with a terminal bud, e.g. a crocus corm

corn *noun* **1.** wheat or barley (*informal*) **2.** US maize

corn cob *noun* a seed head of maize. Also called **cob**

cornflour, **corn starch** *noun* a type of flour extracted from maize grain. It contains a high proportion of starch, and is used for thickening sauces.

corn on the cob *noun* a seed head of maize when used as food

corolla *noun* a set of petals in a flower

corona *noun* a trumpet-shaped, petal-like outgrowth in flowers such as narcissi

corrasion *noun* the wearing away of rock by material carried by ice, water or wind

correction *noun* the adjustment or changing of something to make it correct

correspond *verb* to write to someone ○ *She corresponded with several Russian scientists.*

corridor *noun* ♦ ecological corridor

corrie *noun* same as **cirque**

corrode *verb* to destroy something by a slow chemical process ○ *Turbine fuels tend to corrode the components of the fuel and combustion systems mainly as a result of the sulfur and water content of the fuel.*

corrosion *noun* **1.** a process in which the surface of a material, generally a metal, is changed by the action of moisture, air or a chemical **2.** erosion of rocks by the action of chemicals or the weather

corrosive *adjective* causing corrosion ○ *Sulfuric acid is very corrosive.*

cortex *noun* **1.** the tissue in plants between the outer layer (**epidermis**) and the central core (**stele**) of the stem or root **2.** an outer layer of tissue in the brain, glands or cells

COSHH *noun* UK regulations controlling substances with known health risks. Full form **Control of Substances Hazardous to Health (UK Regulations)**

cosmic *adjective* referring to the cosmos

cosmic radiation *noun* ♦ cosmic ray

cosmic ray *noun* a stream of high-energy particles entering Earth's atmosphere from space

COMMENT: Primary cosmic rays are of solar origin and their composition reflects the Sun's own, consisting mainly of **neutrons** and **alpha particles**, since the Sun consists mainly of hydrogen and helium. Other cosmic rays appear to come from deep space, especially from supernovae, which accounts for the appearance of heavier nuclei.

cosmopolitan *adjective* relating to plants or animals growing or occurring in many different parts of the world

cosmos *noun* the whole universe

cost-benefit analysis *noun* an economic examination of the advantages and disadvantages of a specific course of action

cost-benefit ratio *noun* a comparison of the cost to its benefits

cost-effectiveness *noun* the measurement of how cost-effective something is

cost of living *noun* the level of prices of the basic necessities of life such as food, clothing, shelter and fuel ○ *The cost of living has risen by 2% over the last year.*

cotton grass *noun* a plant with white fluffy flower heads that grows in boggy ground. Latin name: *Eriophorum angustifolium.*

cottonwood *noun* a kind of poplar tree. Genus: *Populus.*

cotyledon *noun* the green plant structure resembling a leaf that appears as a seed germinates and before the true leaves appear, developing from the embryo of the seed

count *noun* the process of totalling a number of items

countershading *noun* a type of animal coloration where the back is darker than the belly, making it more difficult to see the animal's shape clearly

country *noun* **1.** a politically independent nation or state **2.** same as **countryside**

country code *noun* a voluntary code of conduct for people spending leisure time in the countryside, which indicates how to respect the natural environment and avoid causing damage to it

country park *noun* an area in the countryside set aside for the public to visit and enjoy leisure activities. ◊ **national park**

country planning *noun* the activity of organising how land is to be used in the countryside and the amount and type of building there will be. Also called **rural planning**

countryside *noun* the land that surrounds towns and built-up areas

Countryside Agency *noun* a statutory body funded by Defra with the aim of making life better for people in the countryside. It is the statutory advisor on landscape issues and was formed by merging the Countryside Commission with parts of the Rural Development Commission, but is to be reorganised.

Countryside and Rights of Way Act *noun* legislation passed by the UK government in 2000 that gave the public greater freedom of access to privately owned areas of uncultivated land and strengthened legislation protecting wildlife. Abbr **CROW Act**

Countryside Commission *noun* a former organisation in the UK, which supervised countryside planning and recreation. It was particularly concerned with National Parks and Areas of Outstanding Natural Beauty.

Countryside Commission for Scotland *noun* an organisation in Scotland concerned with the protection of the countryside and with setting up country parks for public recreation. It is part of Scottish National Heritage.

Countryside Council for Wales *noun* a statutory advisory body of the UK government responsible for sustaining natural beauty, wildlife and outdoor leisure opportunities in Wales and its coastal areas. Abbr **CCW**

countryside management *noun* the study and practice of environmental conservation in association with rural enterprise, countryside access and recreational activities

Countryside Management Scheme *noun* in Northern Ireland, a system of payments designed to encourage landowners and farmers to adopt, or to continue with, environmentally sensitive farming practices

countryside recreation *noun* leisure activities that take place in the countryside. Also called **rural recreation**

countryside recreation site *noun* a location visited or used by tourists in the countryside, e.g. a national park, heritage coast, cycle path or watersports facility

countryside stewardship *noun* the practice of altering farming practices to benefit wildlife and retain natural diversity. Abbr **CSS**

Countryside Stewardship Scheme
noun in England and Wales, a system of payments made to landowners and farmers who alter their farming practices to benefit the natural environment and maintain biodiversity
'The Defra-funded Countryside Stewardship and Environmentally Sensitive Areas schemes help to maintain and enhance the biodiversity and landscape value of farmed land, protect historic features and promote public access. (Delivering the evidence. Defra's Science and Innovation Strategy, 2003–06)'

Countryside Vegetation System
noun a standard classification of common vegetation types in Britain into 8 major and ultimately 100 smaller vegetation classes. Abbr **CVS** (NOTE: The major classes are: crops and weeds, tall grass and herb, fertile grassland, infertile grassland, lowland wooded, upland wooded, moorland grass, and heath and bog.)

country stewardship *noun* ♦ **countryside stewardship**

coupe *noun* an area of a forest in which trees have been cut down

course *noun* **1.** a set of actions taken in a particular situation ○ *What course of action do you recommend?* **2.** the development of events over a period of time ○ *the usual course of the disease* □ **in the normal course of events** usually

cover *noun* **1.** something that goes over something else completely **2.** the amount of soil surface covered with plants. ◊ **ground cover**

cover crop *noun* **1.** a crop sown to cover the soil and prevent it from drying out and being eroded (NOTE: When the cover crop has served its purpose, it is usually ploughed in, so leguminous plants which are able to enrich the soil are often used as cover crops.) **2.** a crop grown to give protection to another crop that is sown with it ○ *In the tropics, bananas can be used as a cover crop for cocoa.* **3.** a crop grown to give cover to game birds

CPRE *noun* a UK charity that campaigns for rural areas to be protected. Full form **Campaign to Protect Rural England**

Cr *symbol* chromium

CR *abbr* critically endangered

craft *noun* a practical skill ○ *a revival of country crafts such as basket-making*

crater *noun* a round depression at the top of a volcano

creek *noun* a narrow tidal inlet on a sea coast

creep *noun* **1.** gradual change **2.** a slow movement of soil down a slope ■ *verb* to move slowly or without being noticed

creeper *noun* **1.** a plant that spread or climbs by clinging to a surface, forming roots at each node of long shoots **2.** a small insectivorous bird of the northern hemisphere that climbs in trees. Family: Certhidae.

creosote *noun* a yellowish brown oily substance with a characteristic smell, derived from wood tar and formerly used as a wood preservative (NOTE: It is now banned in the European Union.)

crest *noun* **1.** the highest point on the top of an object **2.** the highest point of a hill or mountain ridge **3.** a growth on the head of a bird or other animal **4.** the white top of a wave

crested *adjective* referring to a bird or other animal with a crest ○ *a crested newt*

crevasse *noun* a large crack in a glacier

crevice *noun* a crack or little hole in rock

crisis *noun* a time when things are in a very bad state ○ *a crisis caused by drought* (NOTE: The plural is **crises**)

criterion *noun* a standard by which something is defined, decided or judged (NOTE: The plural is **criteria**.)

critical *adjective* referring to a crisis ○ *critical conditions*

critical factor *noun* something in the environment which causes a sudden change to occur, e.g. the introduction of a pollutant or a drop in temperature

critical link *noun* an organism in a food chain which is responsible for taking up and storing nutrients which are then passed on down the chain

critical load *noun* the highest level of pollution which will not cause permanent harm to the environment

critically endangered *adjective* referring to a species facing a high risk of becoming extinct, usually taken to be when there are fewer than 50 mature individuals. Abbr **CR**

critical point, critical state *noun* a moment at which a substance undergoes a change in temperature, volume or pressure

critical threshold *noun* the point at which a species is likely to become extinct

criticise *verb* to say what is wrong with something ○ *The report criticised the safety procedures.*

crocoite *noun* an orange mineral containing lead chromate. Formula: $PbCrO_4$.

crop *noun* **1.** a plant grown for food **2.** a yield of produce from plants ○ *The tree has produced a heavy crop of apples.* ○ *The first crop was a failure.* ○ *The rice crop has failed.* **3.** the bag-shaped part of a bird's throat where food is stored before digestion ■ *verb* (*of plants*) to produce fruit ○ *a new strain of rice which crops heavily*

crop breeding *noun* the development of new varieties of crops

crop dusting *noun* the practice of applying insecticide, herbicide or fungicide to crops in the form of a fine dust or spray. Also called **crop spraying**

cropland *noun* agricultural land which is used for growing crops

crop relative *noun* a wild plant that is genetically related to a crop plant

crop rotation *noun* a system of cultivation where crops such as cereals and oilseed rape that need different nutrients and/or management are grown one after the other

crop spraying *noun* same as **crop dusting**

cross *verb* to produce a new form of plant or animal from two different breeds, varieties or species ○ *They crossed two strains of rice to produce a new strain which is highly resistant to disease.* ■ *noun* **1.** an act of crossing two plants or animals ○ *made a cross between two strains of cattle* **2.** a new form of plant or animal bred from two different breeds, varieties or species

crossbred *adjective* having been bred from two parents with different characteristics ○ *a herd of crossbred sheep*

crossbreed *noun* an animal bred from two different pure breeds ■ *verb* to produce new breeds of animals by mating animals of different pure breeds

cross-compliance *noun* the setting of environmental conditions that must be met when developing agricultural support policies, especially in the European Union. Also called **environmental conditionality**

cross-fertilisation *noun* the fertilising of one individual plant by another of the same species

crossing *noun* the breeding of plants or animals from two different breeds or varieties

cross-pollination *noun* the pollination of a flower with pollen from another plant of the same species. Compare **self-pollination** (NOTE: The pollen goes from the anther of one plant to the stigma of another.)

cross-section *noun* **1.** a typical representative range ○ *The group included a cross-section of backgrounds and age groups.* **2.** a view of an object seen as if cut through ○ *a cross-section of a leaf*

CROW Act *abbr* Countryside and Rights of Way Act

crown *noun* the top part of a plant where the main growing point is ○ *protecting the crowns from frost* ○ *The disease first affects the lower branches, leaving the crowns still growing.*

crown cover *noun* the area of land shaded by the branches and leaves of a tree

crown-of-thorns *noun* **1.** a large starfish which lives on coral and destroys reefs **2.** one of various thorny plants

Cruciferae *noun* former name for **Brassicaceae**

crude *adjective* in a natural or original state and not treated or improved in any way ○ *crude results* ○ *crude products*

crude oil *noun* oil before it is refined and processed into petrol and other products

crusher *noun* a machine for breaking down material such as rock, ore or seed into smaller pieces

crust *noun* **1.** a hard top layer **2.** the top layer of the surface of the Earth, which is formed of rock

Crustacea *noun* a class of animals which have hard shells which are shed periodically as the animals grow

crustacean *noun* an invertebrate animal with a hard chalky outer shell, several pairs of jointed legs and eyes on stalks. Subphylum: Crustacea. (NOTE: Crabs, lobsters, barnacles and woodlice are all crustaceans.)

crustaceous *adjective* referring to crustaceans

cryogenic *adjective* referring to very low temperatures

cryophilous *adjective* referring to a plant that needs a period of cold weather to grow properly

cryophyte *noun* a plant which lives in cold conditions, such as in snow

cryopreservation *noun* the storage of biological material at very low temperatures

cryosphere *noun* the frozen part of the Earth's surface

cryptic coloration *noun* a pattern of colouring which makes an animal less easy to see, e.g. stripes on a zebra

crypto- *prefix* hidden

cryptobiosis *noun* a form of dormancy where the animal remains dormant for a very long period, found in animals which live in moss

cryptogam *noun* an organism that reproduces by means of spores, e.g. mosses or fungi

cryptogamic *adjective* referring to cryptogams

cryptosporidium *noun* a single-celled organism that can infect humans, usually found in contaminated water

cryptozoic *adjective* referring to animals which live hidden in holes in rocks or trees or under stones

crystal *noun* a regular geometric shape formed by minerals, or as water freezes

crystalline *adjective* formed of crystals

Cs *symbol* caesium

CSS *abbr* Countryside Stewardship Scheme

Cu *symbol* copper

cubic centimetre, cubic foot, cubic inch, cubic metre, cubic yard *noun* the volume of a cube whose edge measures one centimetre, foot, inch, metre or yard, respectively

cull *verb* to reduce the numbers of wild animals by killing them in a controlled way ○ *Deer may have to be culled each year to control the numbers on the hills.*

cullet *noun* broken glass collected for recycling

culm *noun* **1.** the stem of a grass which bears flowers **2.** a type of waste from an anthracite processing plant

cultch *noun* waste material placed in the sea to act as a breeding ground for oysters

cultivar *noun* a variety of a plant that has been developed under cultivation and that does not occur naturally in the wild

cultivate *verb* **1.** to grow crops ○ *Potatoes are cultivated as the main crop.* **2.** to dig and manure the soil ready for growing crops ○ *The fields are cultivated in the autumn, ready for sowing wheat.*

cultivated land *noun* land that has been dug or prepared for growing crops

cultivation *noun* the action of cultivating land or plants □ **to take land out of cultivation** to stop cultivating land or growing crops on it and allow it to lie fallow

cultivator *noun* **1.** a person who cultivates land **2.** an instrument or small machine for cultivating small areas of land

cultural *adjective* referring to agricultural techniques

cultural control *noun* the control of pests using various agricultural techniques such as crop rotation

culture *noun* a microorganism or tissues grown in a culture medium ■ *verb* to grow a microorganism or tissue in a culture medium. ◊ **subculture**

culvert *noun* a covered drain for water

cumulative *adjective* produced by being added in small, regular amounts ○ *The cumulative effect of these chemicals is considerable over time.*

cumulative impacts *plural noun* the effects of a group of activities throughout an area or region, although each individual effect may not be significant on its own, including the effects of any future activities that may reasonably be expected to take place

cumulonimbus *noun* a dark low cumulus cloud associated with thunderstorms ○ *A cumulonimbus has a characteristic anvil shape.* Abbr **CB**

cumulus *noun* a quantity of big, fluffy, white or grey clouds heaped or piled up, which develop at low altitude ○ *Grey cumulus often develop into cumulonimbus.* ○ *Cumulus clouds may develop because of thermal activity resulting from the warming of the surface.*

curie *noun* a former unit of measurement of radioactivity, now replaced by the becquerel. Symbol **Ci**

current *noun* a flow of water, air or electricity ○ *Dangerous currents make fishing difficult near the coast.* ○ *A warm westerly current of air is blowing across the country.*

Curry Report *noun* a UK government report published in 2002 after a major outbreak of foot and mouth disease. It recommended radical changes to the agriculture and food industries, looking forward to a profitable sustainable future for farming in providing good food for consumers who place increasing emphasis on a healthy diet as well as caring for the environment.

curvature of the earth *noun* the visible curving of the horizon, seen most clearly at sea

curve *noun* a smoothly bending line, as on a graph

cusp *noun* the point where two arcs of a curve meet

cuspate foreland *noun* a large triangular area of deposits made by the sea on a coast

cuticle *noun* **1.** a thin waxy protective layer on plants **2.** the outer layer of skin in animals

cutting *noun* a small piece of a plant from which a new plant will grow

CVS *abbr* Countryside Vegetation System

cwm *noun* ♦ **cirque**

cyanide *noun* a salt of hydrocyanic acid

cyanobacterium *noun* a bacterium of a large group that carry out photosynthesis. Family: Cyanophyta. Former name **blue-green alga**

cyanocobalamin *noun* vitamin B_{12}

Cyanophyta *noun* a group of blue-green algae, usually found in fresh water, which store starch in the form of glycogen

cycad *noun* a tropical plant that has an unbranched trunk with large divided leaves growing from the top and cones

cycle *noun* **1.** a series of actions which end at the same point as they begin ○ *the life cycle of a moth* ○ *A biennial plant completes its life cycle within two years.* **2.** a series of events which recur regularly ○ *Industrial waste upsets the natural nutrient cycle.*

cycle path *noun* a track alongside a road, or a marked strip at the side of a road, along which only bicycles may be ridden

cyclical *adjective* occurring in cycles ○ *Off-shore and on-shore wind patterns are cyclical.*

cyclo- *prefix* cyclic

cyclone *noun* **1.** an area of low pressure around which the air turns in the same direction as the Earth. ◊ **anticyclone 2.** a device which removes solid particles from waste gases produced during industrial processes

cyclonic *adjective* referring to a cyclone □ **in a cyclonic direction** flowing in the same direction as the rotation of the Earth

cyclonically *adverb* in a cyclonic direction ○ *Waterspouts rotate cyclonically, that is anticlockwise in the northern hemisphere and clockwise in the southern hemisphere.*

cyto- *prefix* cell

cytochemistry *noun* the study of the chemical activity of living cells

cytogenetics *noun* a branch of genetics which studies the structure and function of cells, especially chromosomes

cytology *noun* the study of the structure and function of cells

cytolysis *noun* the breaking down of cells

cytoplasm *noun* a jelly-like substance inside the cell membrane which surrounds the nucleus of a cell

cytoplasmic *adjective* referring to the cytoplasm of a cell

cytotoxic *adjective* harmful or fatal to living cells (NOTE: Cells that kill other cells as part of the immune response are described as cytotoxic.)

cytotoxin *noun* a substance which has a toxic effect on living cells

D

DACTARI *noun* a pilot scheme set up to assess the implications of exotic diseases in dogs and cats travelling into the UK. Full form **Dog and Cat Travel and Risk Information**

dam *noun* **1.** a construction built to block a river in order to channel the flow of water into a hydroelectric power station or to regulate the water supply to an irrigation scheme **2.** the female parent of an animal, usually a domestic animal

COMMENT: Dams are constructed either to channel the flow of water into hydroelectric power stations or to regulate the water supply to irrigation schemes. Dams can have serious environmental effects: the large lake behind the dam may alter the whole climate of a region; the large heavy mass of water in the lake may trigger earth movements if the rock beneath is unstable; in tropical areas, dams encourage the spread of bacteria, insects and parasites, leading to an increase in diseases; dams may increase salinity in watercourses and retain silt which otherwise would be carried down the river and be deposited as fertile soil in the plain below; dams may also deprive downstream communities or countries of water, leading to regional tensions.

damage *noun* the harm done to something ○ *environmental damage*

damp off *verb* to die from a fungus infection which spreads in warm damp conditions and attacks the roots and lower stems of seedlings

dangerous substance *noun* a substance which is particularly hazardous because of any of 14 features such as toxicity, flammability, bioaccumulation potential or persistence

DARDNI *abbr* Department of Agriculture and Rural Development, Northern Ireland

Darrius Rotator *noun* a type of vertical-axis wind turbine that has thin blades

Darwin, Charles (1809–92) a scientist known for the theory of evolution proposed in his book *On the Origin of Species* that described how species gradually change and evolve to succeed in their environment

Darwinian fitness *noun* a measure of the success of organisms at passing on their genes to subsequent generations

Darwinism, Darwinian theory *noun* the theory of evolution, formulated by Charles Darwin, which states that species of organisms arose by natural selection. ◊ **neo-Darwinism**

data *plural noun* factual information ○ *The data show that a chemical change takes place.* ○ *The data show that the number of plants in the population has increased.* (NOTE: The singular is **datum**)

data analysis *noun* the extraction of information and results from data

database *noun* an integrated collection of files of data stored in a structured form in a large memory, which can be accessed by one or more users at different terminals

daylength *noun* ◆ **photoperiod**

daylight *noun* the light of the sun during the day

dB *abbr* decibel

dBA scale *abbr* decibel A scale

DC *abbr* direct current

DDT *noun* an insecticide that was formerly used especially against malaria-carrying mosquitoes. It is now banned in many countries because of its toxicity and ability to accumulate in the environment. Formula: $C_{14}H_9Cl_5$. Full form **dichlorodiphenyltrichloroethane**

DDT-resistant insect *noun* an insect that has developed resistance to DDT

DE *abbr* diatomaceous earth

deactivate *verb* to turn off a system or a piece of equipment, stopping it from being ready to operate

de-aerator *noun* a device to remove gas from a liquid

death rate *noun* the number of deaths per year, shown per 1000 of a population ○ *a death rate of 15 per 1000* ○ *an increase in the death rate* Also called **mortality rate**

debacle *noun* the breaking up of ice on a large river as it melts in spring

debris *noun* rubbish or waste matter ○ *volcanic debris from the eruption* ○ *Check that the area is free of stones and other debris.*

decay *noun* a process by which tissues become rotten and decompose, caused by the action of microorganisms and oxygen ○ *The soft leaves will gradually decay on the* compost heap ■ *verb* **1.** (*of organic matter*) to rot or decompose **2.** (*of radioactive matter*) to disintegrate

dechannelise, dechannelize *verb* to make a river return to its original place and pattern of flow

dechlorination *noun* removal of chlorine and its replacement with hydrogen or with hydroxide ions to detoxify a substance

decibel *noun* a unit for measuring the power of a sound or the strength of a signal. The decibel scale is logarithmic. Abbr **dB**

decibel A scale *noun* an international scale of noise level

deciduous *adjective* referring to trees that shed all their leaves in one season ○ *beech, oak and other deciduous trees* ○ *deciduous woodlands*

deciduous forest *noun* a wooded area composed mainly of broadleaved trees that lose all their leaves during one season. Such forests are found in regions with a temperate climate that have a winter and rainfall throughout the year.

decimate *verb* **1.** to reduce something severely ○ *Overfishing has decimated the herring population in the North Sea.* **2.** to reduce by one in ten

decision framework *noun* a method of organising and evaluating information, leading eventually to the making of a decision

decline *noun* a process of becoming less ○ *The decline in the number of cases of pollution is due to better policing of factory emissions.* ○ *The population of these birds now seems to be on the decline.* ○ *Ecologists are working to diagnose forest decline in its early stages.* □ **decline in population** reduction in the number of organisms living in one place ■ *verb* to become less ○ *The fish population declined sharply as the water became more acid.*

decommission *verb* to shut down a nuclear reactor or a power station

decommissioning *noun* the process of shutting down a power station

decommissioning waste *noun* radioactive material no longer needed as a result of the shutting down of a nuclear reactor or a nuclear power station

decomposable *adjective* referring to a substance which can be broken down into simple chemical compounds

decompose *verb* (*of organic material*) to break down into simple chemical compounds by the action of sunlight, water or bacteria and fungi

decomposer *noun* an organism which feeds on dead organic matter and breaks it down into simple chemicals, e.g. a fungus or bacterium

decomposition *noun* the process of breaking down into simple chemical compounds

decontaminate *verb* to remove a harmful substance such as poison or radioactive material from a building, a watercourse, a person's clothes or some other place

decontamination *noun* the removal of a harmful substance such as poison or radioactive material from a building, a watercourse, a person's clothes or some other place

decrease *noun* a lessening or reduction ○ *a decrease in power* □ **on the decrease** becoming less ■ *verb* to become less ○ *Air density and pressure decrease with an increase in altitude.* Opposite **increase**

deductive reasoning *noun* the process of drawing conclusions from observations of the natural world by using logical reasoning. Compare **inductive reasoning**

deep ecology *noun* an extreme form of ecological thinking in which humans are considered as only one species among many in the environment and large numbers of humans are seen as harmful to the environment in which they live

deep-freezing *noun* long-term storage at temperatures below freezing point (NOTE: Many crops such as peas and beans are grown specifically for commercial deep-freezing.)

deep-litter *noun* a system of using straw, wood shavings, sawdust or peat moss for bedding poultry or cattle

deep-sea *adjective* referring to the deepest part of the sea a long way from land

defensive mutualism *noun* a relationship between two species in which one protects the other from a predator

deficiency *noun* a lack of something

deficiency disease *noun* a disease caused by the lack of an essential element in the diet, e.g. vitamins or essential amino acids and fatty acids

deficient *adjective* lacking something essential ○ *The soil is deficient in important nutrients.* ○ *Scrub plants are well adapted to this moisture-deficient habitat.* ○ *She has a calcium-deficient diet.*

deficit *noun* a situation in which the amount going out is larger than the amount coming in

definitive host *noun* a host on which a parasite settles permanently

deflate *verb* to allow air to escape from something such as a tyre or balloon so that it becomes smaller or collapses ○ *To deflate a tyre, remove or depress the valve and allow the air to escape.* Opposite **inflate**

defoliant *noun* a type of herbicide which makes the leaves fall off plants

defoliate *verb* to make the leaves fall off a plant, especially by using a herbicide or as the result of disease or other stress

defoliation *noun* the loss of leaves from a plant, especially as the result of using a herbicide or because of disease or other stress

deforest *verb* to cut down forest trees from an area for commercial purposes or to make arable land ○ *Timber companies have helped to deforest the tropical regions.* ○ *About 40 000 square miles are deforested each year.*

deforestation *noun* the cutting down of forest trees for commercial purposes or to make arable or pasture land

Defra *abbr* Department for Environment, Food and Rural Affairs

degas *verb* to remove gas from something such as a borehole

degassing *noun* the removal of gas from something such as a borehole

degradable *adjective* referring to a substance which can be broken down into its separate elements. ◊ **biodegradable**

degradation *noun* **1.** a reduction in the quality of something ○ *Chemical degradation of the land can be caused by overuse of fertilisers and by pollutants from industrial processes.* □ **degradation of air** the pollution of the air **2.** the decomposition of a chemical compound into its elements

degradative succession *noun* the colonisation and subsequent decomposition of dead organic matter by fungi and microorganisms

degrade *verb* **1.** to reduce the quality of something ○ *The land has been degraded through overgrazing.* ○ *Ozone may worsen nutrient leaching by degrading the water-resistant coating on pine needles.* **2.** to make a chemical compound decompose into its elements

degreaser *noun* a device for removing grease and oil

degree *noun* **1.** a level, amount or quantity ○ *The degree of compression is insufficient.* ○ *Manufacturers aim for a high de-gree of safety.* □ **to a certain degree, to some degree** partly □ **to a minor degree** in a small way **2.** a unit of temperature ○ *twenty degrees Centigrade (20°C)* Symbol ° □ **degree Celsius** unit of measurement on a scale of temperature where the freezing and boiling points of water are 0° and 100°, respectively. ◊ **Celsius** □ **degree Fahrenheit** unit of measurement on a scale of temperature where the freezing and boiling points of water are 32° and 212°, respectively **3.** a unit of measurement of an angle equal to 1/360th of a circle. Symbol ° (NOTE: Each degree is divided into 60 minutes and each minute into 60 seconds.)

dehisce *verb* (*of a ripe seed pod, fruit or capsule*) to burst open to allow seeds or spores to scatter

dehiscence *noun* the sudden bursting of a seed pod, fruit or capsule when it is ripe, allowing the seeds or spores to scatter

dehiscent *adjective* referring to seed pods, fruit or capsules which burst open to allow the seeds or spores to scatter. Compare **indehiscent**

dehumidifier *noun* a machine which removes the moisture from air, often part of an air-conditioning system

dehydrate *verb* **1.** to lose water, or to make something lose water ○ *dehydrated foods* **2.** to lose water from the body ○ *After two days without food or drink, he became severely dehydrated.*

dehydration *noun* **1.** loss of water, or the removal of water from something ○ *preservation of food by dehydration* **2.** loss of water from the body

deinking *noun* the process of removing the ink from waste newspaper to allow it to be recycled

deinking unit *noun* a factory or machine which removes the ink from waste newspaper

deintensified farming *noun* farming which was formerly intensive, using chemical fertilisers to increase production, but has now become extensive

delta *noun* a triangular piece of land at the mouth of a large river formed of silt carried by the river ○ *the Nile Delta* ○ *the Mississippi Delta*

deltaic deposit *noun* a deposit of silt in a river delta

deme *noun* a population of organisms in a small area

-deme *suffix* a section of a population which has distinctive characteristics

demersal *adjective* referring to fish which live on or near the seabed. Compare **pelagic**

demineralisation, **demineralization** *noun* the removal of salts which are dissolved in water

demineralise, demineralize *verb* to remove dissolved salts from water

demographic *adjective* referring to demography

demographic transition *noun* the pattern of change of population growth from high birth and death rates to low birth and death rates

demography *noun* the study of human populations and their development

denaturation *noun* 1. making something change its nature 2. converting a protein into an amino acid

denature *verb* 1. to add a poisonous substance to alcohol to make it unsuitable for humans to drink 2. to change the natural structure of a protein or nucleic acid by high temperature, chemicals or extremes of pH 3. to add an isotope to fissile material to make it unsuitable for use in nuclear weapons 4. to make something change its nature 5. to convert a protein into an amino acid

dendrite *noun* a crystal that has branched in two as it grows

dendritic *adjective* with branched parts

dendrochronology *noun* a scientific method of finding the age of wood by the study of tree rings

dendroclimatology *noun* the study of climate over many centuries, as shown in tree rings

COMMENT: Because tree rings vary in width depending on the weather during a specific year, it has been possible to show a pattern of yearly growth which applies to all wood from the same region. This method allows old structures to be dated even more accurately than with carbon-dating systems. It is also possible to chart past changes in climate in the same way, as rings vary in thickness according to climatic conditions, allowing scientists to compare the climatic changes in various parts of the world over a very long period of time.

dendrological *adjective* referring to dendrology

dendrology *noun* the study of trees

denitrification *noun* the releasing of nitrogen from nitrates in the soil by the action of bacteria

denizen *noun* a non-native plant or animal that grows or lives in a specific area

dense *adjective* referring to a substance which is closely pressed together

densely populated *adjective* having many humans or other organisms inhabiting the same area

density *noun* 1. the quantity of mass per unit of volume ○ *air density* 2. the number of individuals in a specific area

density dependence *noun* a situation in which an aspect or feature of a population varies with population density

density-dependent *adjective* referring to a situation where an aspect or feature of a population varies with population density ○ *density-dependent population regulation*

density-independent *adjective* referring to a situation where an aspect or feature of a population does not vary with population density ○ *density-independent mortality*

dentate *adjective* same as **toothed**

denudation *noun* the process of making land or rock bare by cutting down trees or by erosion

denude *verb* to make land or rock bare by cutting down trees and other plants or by erosion ○ *The timber companies have denuded the mountains.*

deoxygenate *verb* to remove oxygen from water or air ○ *The weed rapidly deoxygenates watercourses, killing fish and other aquatic life.*

deoxygenation *noun* the removal of oxygen from water or air

deoxyribonucleic acid *noun* ♦ RNA. Full form of **DNA**

Department for Environment, Food and Rural Affairs *noun* the UK government department responsible for rural affairs in England and Wales. Abbr **Defra**

'Defra was created to focus and lead the Government's wider approach to sustainable development and specifically to address this aim for the environment, the food industry and rural economies and communities. (Delivering the evidence. Defra's Science and Innovation Strategy, 2003–06)'

dependency ratio *noun* a measure of the number of children and old people that each 100 people of working age have to support

dependent *adjective* affected by or varying with something else ○ *The output is dependent on the physical state of the link.*

deplete *verb* to remove a resource from something

depletion *noun* the removal of a resource from something ○ *a study of atmospheric* *ozone depletion* ○ *Production of ice crystals from methane can deplete ozone still further.*

deploy *verb* to use something ○ *They needed to deploy more resources to complete the review on time.*

depollution *noun* the removal of pollution from a contaminated area

deposit *noun* **1.** a layer of metal, coal or other substance that occurs in the ground ○ *Deposits of coal have been found in the north of the country.* **2.** a quantity of material moved from one place on the Earth's surface to another by natural agents such as wind or water ○ *deposits of silt* ○ *glacial deposits* **3.** a thin layer or coating on an inner or outer surface ○ *deposits of red dust* ○ *fatty deposits in the arteries* **4.** a fee that is added to the price of a product and refunded when the used product is returned for recycling ■ *verb* to coat a surface with a thin layer of a substance

depository *noun* a place where something is stored, e.g. refuse or nuclear waste ○ *They carried out tests to establish the suitability of the rock formation as a waste depository.*

depot *noun* a place or building where something is stored ○ *There has been a fire at the oil depot.*

depression *noun* **1.** an area of low atmospheric pressure. Also called **low 2.** a lower area on a surface that is often difficult to see ○ *A depression on the wing surface must be investigated in case it is an indication of more serious structural damage.*

depth *noun* the distance from the top surface of something to the bottom ○ *The troposphere's depth is variable in temperate latitudes.* □ **the water is two metres in depth** the water is two metres deep

depth of rainfall *noun* a measurement of the amount of rain which has fallen

derelict *adjective* **1.** referring to land which has been damaged and made ugly by mining or other industrial processes, or which has been neglected and is not used for anything ○ *a plan to reclaim derelict inner city sites* **2.** referring to a building which is neglected and in ruins ○ *derelict factories*

dereliction *noun* **1.** a state of being damaged or neglected **2.** a failure to do what you ought to do ○ *dereliction of duty*

derivative *noun* a substance or product which is formed from something else

dermal *adjective* referring to the skin

derris *noun* a powdered insecticide extracted from the root of a tropical plant, used against fleas, lice and aphids

desalinate *verb* to remove salt from a substance such as sea water or soil

desalination *noun* the removal of salt from a substance such as sea water or soil

COMMENT: Desalination may be used to removing salt from sea water to make it drinkable. Desalination plants work by distillation, dialysis or by freeze drying. The process is only cost-effective where the supplies of fresh water are very small.

desert *noun* an area of land with very little rainfall, arid soil and little or no vegetation

COMMENT: A desert will be formed in areas where rainfall is less than 25 cm per annum whether the region is hot or cold. About 30% of all the land surface of the Earth is desert or in the process of becoming desert. The spread of desert conditions in arid and semi-arid regions is caused not only by climatic conditions, but also by human pressures. So overgrazing of pasture and the clearing of forest for fuel and for cultivation both lead to the loss of organic material, a reduction in rainfall by evaporation and soil erosion.

desert formation *noun* same as **desertification**

desertification *noun* the process by which an area of land becomes a desert because of a change of climate or because of the action of humans, e.g. through intensive farming ○ *Changes in the amount of sunlight reflected by different vegetation may contribute to desertification.* ○ *Increased tilling of the soil, together with long periods of drought, have brought about the desertification of the area.*

'Desertification, broadly defined, is one of the principal barriers to sustainable food security and sustainable livelihoods in our world today' [*Environmental Conservation*]

desertify *verb* to make land into a desert ○ *It is predicted that half the country will be desertified by the end of the century.*

desiccant *noun* **1.** a substance which dries something **2.** a type of herbicide which makes leaves wither and die

desiccate *verb* to dry out

desiccation *noun* **1.** the act or process of removing water **2.** the act of drying out the soil ○ *The greenhouse effect may lead to climatic changes such as the desiccation of large areas.*

design *noun* the planning or drawing of something before it is constructed or manufactured ○ *product design and develop-*

ment ○ *a creative garden design* ○ *She works in design.*

designate *verb* to name something officially or appoint someone to a position officially ○ *The city centre has been designated a traffic-free zone.*

desk study *noun* an investigation of relevant available facts and figures, often before starting practical study of a problem

destroy *verb* to damage something so severely that it cannot recover ○ *At this rate, all virgin rainforests will have been destroyed by the year 2020.* ○ *The building of the motorway will destroy several areas of scientific importance.*

destruction *noun* the act of severely damaging something ○ *The destruction of the habitat has led to the almost complete extinction of the species.*

desulfurisation, **desulphurisation** *noun* the process of removing sulfur from a substance such as oil, iron ore or coal

detect *verb* 1. to notice something that is not obvious ○ *She detected a slight smell of gas.* 2. to discover the existence of something using scientific methods and equipment ○ *The equipment can detect very faint signals.*

detectable *adjective* which can be detected ○ *The increase in the amount of carbon dioxide, together with trace gases such as methane and nitrogen oxide, is likely to cause a detectable global warming.*

detection *noun* the discovery of the presence of something

detection limit *noun* the smallest amount of a substance, noise, etc., that can be detected

detergent *noun* a cleaning substance which removes grease and bacteria from the surface of something (NOTE: The first detergents contained alkyl benzenesulfonate which does not degrade on contact with bacteria and so passed into sewage, creating large amounts of foam in sewers and rivers.)

detergent foam *noun* a large mass of froth on the surface of rivers, canals and sewers, caused by detergent in effluent

detergent swans *plural noun* ▸ **detergent foam**

deteriorate *verb* to become worse ○ *The quality of the water in the river has deteriorated since the construction of factories on its banks.* ○ *The electrolyte in the cells of a nickel-cadmium battery does not chemically react with the plates and so the plates do not deteriorate.*

deterioration *noun* the process of becoming worse ○ *The rapid deterioration of the peri-urban environment gives cause for concern.*

determine *verb* 1. to discover something by observation, calculation or experiment ○ *To determine the average age, divide the total number of years by the number of people.* 2. to control or have an effect on something ○ *These characteristics are genetically determined.* ○ *Health is significantly determined by diet.*

detinning *noun* the removal of a coating of tin from something

detoxication, **detoxification** *noun* the removal of harmful or poisonous substances

detoxify *verb* to remove harmful or poisonous substances from something

detrimental *adjective* harmful ○ *Conservation groups have criticised the introduction of red deer, a species which is highly detrimental to local flora.*

detrital *adjective* 1. formed from detritus 2. referring to a crystal which has been uncovered from weathered rock

detrital food chain *noun* the link between green plants and the decomposer organisms which feed on them

detritivore *noun* an organism which feeds on dead organic matter and breaks it down into simple chemicals, e.g. a fungus or bacterium. Also called **detrivore, scavenger**

detritivorous *adjective* referring to an organism which feeds on dead organic matter and breaks it down into simple chemicals

detritus *noun* waste matter which may be either organic or mineral

detrivore *noun* same as **detritivore**

deuterium oxide *noun* water containing deuterium instead of the hydrogen atom, used as a coolant or moderator in some types of nuclear reactor. Formula: D_2O.

develop *verb* 1. to come into being, or cause something to come into being ○ *The plant soon develops branches.* 2. to grow and change ○ *During the day, light breezes may develop into strong winds.* ○ *The plants develop quickly in the right conditions.* 3. to plan and produce something ○ *The company is trying to develop a new pesticide to deal with the problem.* 4. to plan and build on an area of land ○ *They are planning to develop the site as an industrial estate.*

developed country *noun* a country which has a high state of industrialisation

developer *noun* a person or company that plans and builds structures such as roads, airports, houses, factories or office buildings ○ *The land has been acquired by developers for an industrial park.*

developing country *noun* a country which is not fully industrialised

development *noun* **1.** growth and change ○ *To study weather and its development, the meteorologist has to be aware of the horizontal changes in atmospheric pressure both in space and time.* **2.** something new, made as an improvement on something older ○ *Satellite navigation aids are a useful development.* **3.** planning and building on an area of land ○ *They are planning large-scale development of the docklands area.*

development area *noun* an area which has been given special help from a government to encourage business and factories to be set up there. Also called **development zone**

development rate *noun* the rate at which a plant or animal grows

development zone *noun* same as **development area**

deviate *verb* to be different from the usual or expected pattern or to do something that is different from the usual or expected pattern

deviation *noun* **1.** a difference from what is usual or expected **2.** the difference between one value in a series and the average of all the values

device *noun* a machine or piece of equipment ○ *a device for controlling humidity*

dew *noun* drops of condensed moisture left on surfaces overnight in cool places

dewater *verb* to remove or reduce the water content of something such as sludge

dew pond *noun* a small pond of rainwater which forms on high ground in chalky soil

DHW *abbr* domestic hot water

diagnose *verb* **1.** to identify a disease from symptoms **2.** to use scientific methods to discover the cause of a problem or fault

diagnosis *noun* the identification of a disease or problem

diagram *noun* an often simplified drawing showing the structure or workings of something ○ *a diagram illustrating a food web* ○ *The diagram shows the life cycle of a fern.*

dialysis *noun* the use of a semi-permeable membrane as a filter to separate soluble waste substances from a liquid

diameter *noun* the distance across the widest part of a circle or a tube (NOTE: The diameter passes through the centre.) □ **less than 0.5mm in diameter** measuring less than 0.5 mm across the widest part

diapause *noun* a period of reduced metabolic rate in some animals or insects during which growth and development are temporarily suspended, often linked to seasonal or environmental changes

diatom *noun* a type of single-celled alga found in fresh and sea water that has a cell wall containing silica which forms two overlapping halves

diatomaceous earth *noun* a mineral deposit formed from the bodies of diatoms, used in filters and in the manufacture of polishes. Also called **kieselguhr**. Abbr **DE**

diatomist *noun* a scientist who studies diatoms

dichlorodiphenyltrichloroethane *noun* full form of **DDT**

dichotomous branching *noun* a pattern of plant growth that develops when a growing point forks into two points that later divide into two

dichotomous key *noun* a series of questions leading to other questions used as part of the process of identifying an organism

dicot *noun* same as **dicotyledon** (*informal*)

dicotyledenous *adjective* referring to dicotyledons

dicotyledon *noun* a plant with seeds that have a cotyledon with two parts ○ *Dicotyledons form the largest group of plants.* Compare **monocotyledon**. ◊ **cotyledon**

die *verb* to stop living ○ *The fish in the lake died, poisoned by chemical discharge from the factory.* ○ *Scientists are trying to find out what is making the trees die.* ○ *Several people died after eating the contaminated shellfish.*

die back *verb* (*of plants*) to be affected by the death of a branch or shoot ○ *Roses may die back after pruning in frosty weather.*

dieback *noun* **1.** a fungal disease of some plants which kills shoots or branches **2.** a gradual dying of trees starting at the ends of branches ○ *Half the trees in the forest are showing signs of dieback.*

die down *verb* **1.** to become less strong ○ *The strong winds eventually died down.* ○ *The food safety controversy shows no sign* *of dying down.* **2.** to stop growing before the winter and keep only the parts below ground until spring (*of a plant*) ○ *Herbaceous plants die down in autumn.*

diel *adjective* referring to a period of 24 hours ○ *The diel cycle was due to the interaction of damage and repair processes.*

dieldrin *noun* an organochlorine insecticide which kills on contact (NOTE: It is very persistent and can kill fish, birds and small mammals when it enters the food chain. It is banned in the European Union.)

die off *verb* to die one by one over a period

die out *verb* to become fewer in numbers and eventually cease to exist

diesel *noun* same as **diesel oil**

diesel engine *noun* an engine in which air is compressed in a cylinder causing a rise in temperature before the introduction of oil which ignites on contact with the hot air

COMMENT: In a diesel engine, a quantity of oil is pumped to each cylinder in turn. Diesel-engined cars are usually more economical to run, but cause more pollution, especially particulates, than petrol-engined cars.

diesel-engined *adjective* using a diesel engine to provide power. Also called **diesel-powered**

diesel oil, diesel fuel *noun* oil used as fuel in a diesel engine. Also called **diesel**

diesel-powered *adjective* same as **diesel-engined**

diet *noun* **1.** the amount and type of food eaten □ **to live on a diet of** to eat ○ *It lives on a diet of insects and roots.* **2.** a measured amount of food eaten to maintain, gain or lose weight □ **to be** *or* **go on a diet** Same as **diet** ■ *verb* to reduce the quantity or change the type of food eaten in order to maintain a sensible weight and become healthier

dietary *adjective* referring to diet

dietary fibre *noun* same as **roughage**

COMMENT: Dietary fibre is found in cereals, nuts, fruit and some green vegetables. It is believed to be necessary to help digestion and to avoid developing constipation, obesity and appendicitis.

dietary reference values *plural noun* the nutrients that are essential for health, published as a list by the UK government

dietetic *adjective* referring to diet

dietetics *noun* the study of food, nutrition and health, especially when applied to food intake

difference *noun* the way in which two things are not the same ○ *Describe the major differences between plants and animals.*

different *adjective* not the same ○ *Living in the country is very different from living in town.* ○ *The landscape looks quite different since the mine was opened.*

differential *adjective* referring to things which react differently when measured against a norm or standard

differential reproduction *noun* the ability to produce more offspring with the same adaptations as the parents, allowing the species to survive under changed environmental conditions

diffuse *adjective* **1.** spread out in every direction **2.** widespread in effect and without a single identifiable source ○ *diffuse pollution* ◊ **non-point source**

diffusion *noun* **1.** the process of spreading out ○ *Gas from the turbine enters the exhaust system at high velocities but, because of high friction losses, the speed of flow is decreased by diffusion.* **2.** the mixing of a liquid with another liquid, or of a gas with another gas **3.** the passing of a liquid or gas through a membrane

digest *verb* **1.** to break down food and convert it into elements which can be absorbed by the body **2.** to use bacteria to process waste, especially organic waste such as manure, in order to produce biogas ○ *55% of UK sewage sludge is digested.* ○ *Wastes from food processing plants can be anaerobically digested.*

digester *noun* a device that produces gas such as methane from refuse

digestible organic matter *noun* an organic substance which can be processed to produce biogas, e.g. manure. Abbr **DOM**

digestion *noun* **1.** the process by which food is broken down and converted into elements which can be absorbed by the body **2.** the conversion of organic matter into simpler chemical compounds, as in the production of biogas from manure

digit *noun* a finger or toe, or a similar body part

digitate *adjective* **1.** having fingers or toes, or body parts like fingers or toes **2.** same as **palmate**

dilation *noun* an increase in volume

diluent *noun* a substance which is used to dilute a liquid

dilute *verb* to add water or solvent to a liquid to make it weaker. Opposite **concentrate** ■ *adjective* with water or solvent added

dilute and disperse *noun* a method of using landfill sites in which the waste is allowed to leak gradually into the surrounding soil

dilution *noun* **1.** the action of diluting a liquid **2.** a liquid which has been diluted

dilution effect *noun* a strategy adopted by prey to reduce the effect of predators, by which the prey congregates in large numbers so that a predator can only remove a small proportion of the total

dimethyl sulfide, dimethyl sulphide *noun* a gas given off by water which is rich in sewage pollution

diminished *adjective* reduced ○ *At higher altitudes, ground objects are less easily seen because of diminished size.*

diode *noun* an electronic component that allows an electrical current to pass in one direction and not the other

dioecious *adjective* referring to a plant species in which male and female flowers occur on different individuals. ◊ **monoecious**

dioxin *noun* an extremely poisonous gas. It is formed as a product of waste incineration and some other combustion processes and is also a by-product of the manufacture of the herbicide 2,4,5-T. (NOTE: It is the gas that escaped in the disaster at Seveso in 1976.)

diploid *adjective* referring to an organism that has two matched sets of chromosomes in a cell nucleus, one set from each parent (NOTE: Each species has a characteristic diploid number of chromosomes.)

direct current *noun* an electric current of constant value that flows in one direction. Abbr **DC**

disaster *noun* a serious event causing deaths and/or great damage to the environment. Disasters are often classified as either natural, e.g. earthquakes, or manmade, e.g. oil spills.

disaster management *noun* the policies developed and the actions undertaken to deal with a disaster

disc floret *noun* a small tubular part among those on the central rounded part of the flower head of a plant belonging to the Compositae, such as a daisy or sunflower. Compare **ray floret**

discharge *noun* **1.** the action of releasing waste material into the environment **2.** waste material, such as that from an industrial process or in the form of sewage, that is passed into the environment **3.** the rate of flow of a liquid in a channel ■ *verb* **1.** (*of a river*) to flow into a lake or the sea ○ *The river Rhine discharges into the North Sea.* **2.** to pass waste material into the environment ○ *The factory discharges ten tonnes of toxic effluent per day into the river.*

disclimax *noun* a stable ecological state which has been caused by human intervention, e.g. a desert caused by deforestation

disclimax community *noun* a stable plant community which is caused by human action, e.g. felling a rainforest for timber. Compare **climax**

discoloration, discolouration *noun* a change of colour, especially one caused by deterioration

discolour *verb* to change the colour of something, especially through deterioration, usually making it paler (NOTE: The US spelling is **discolor**.)

discoloured *adjective* with a changed colour, especially through deterioration

discontinuity *noun* **1.** a break in a layer of rock, caused by a fault or erosion **2.** a band in the interior of the Earth which separates two layers and through which seismic shocks do not pass

discounting *noun* a method used by economists to calculate the cost in current value of a project's future costs and benefits

disease *noun* an illness of people, animals or plants ○ *He caught a disease in the tropics.* ○ *He is a specialist in occupational diseases.*

diseased *adjective* affected by a disease and so not functioning as usual or not whole ○ *To treat dieback, diseased branches should be cut back to healthy wood.*

disinfect *verb* to make something or somewhere free from microorganisms such as bacteria ○ *All utensils must be thoroughly disinfected.* (NOTE: **Disinfect, disinfection** and **disinfectant** are used for substances which destroy germs on instruments, objects or the skin.)

disinfectant *noun* a substance used to kill microorganisms such as bacteria

disinfection *noun* the process of making something or somewhere free from microorganisms such as bacteria

disinfest *verb* to remove insect or animal pests from a place

disintegrate *verb* to break into pieces ○ *In holocrine glands the cells disintegrate as they secrete.*

disintegration *noun* the process of breaking into pieces ○ *Electromagnetic radiations resulting from the disintegration of* radioactive materials are known as gamma rays.

disjunct *noun* a distribution area for an animal or plant which is split into geographically different regions

disorder *noun* a disruption of a system or balanced state

dispersal *noun* the moving of individual plants or animals into or from an area ○ *seed dispersal by wind* ○ *Aphids breed in large numbers and spread by dispersal in wind currents.*

disperse *verb* 1. (*of organisms*) to separate and move away over a wide area 2. to send something out over a wide area ○ *Some seeds are dispersed by birds.* ○ *Power stations have tall chimneys to disperse the emissions of pollutants.*

dispersing agent *noun* a chemical substance sprayed onto an oil slick to break up the oil into smaller particles

dispersion *noun* the pattern in which animals or plants are found over a wide area

dispersion model *noun* a mathematical prediction of how pollutants from a source will be distributed in the surrounding area under specific conditions of wind, temperature, humidity and other environmental factors

disposable *adjective* thrown away after use ○ *disposable syringes*

disposal *noun* the process of getting rid of something ○ *The disposal of raw sewage into the sea contaminates shellfish.* ◊ **final disposal**

disposal site *noun* same as **landfill site**

dispose of *verb* to get rid of something ○ *The problem with nuclear reactors is how to dispose of the radioactive waste.*

disrupt *verb* to upset a system or balanced state ○ *The storm disrupted the electricity supply.*

disruption *noun* the process of upsetting a system or balanced state

disseminate *verb* to make information or knowledge available ○ *The information was disseminated widely throughout the organisation.*

dissemination *noun* the process of making information about something available ○ *the dissemination of new technology*

dissolvable, dissoluable *adjective* able to be dissolved

dissolve *verb* to become part of a liquid and form a solution ○ *Sugar dissolves in water.* ○ *There is a possibility that gas may be dissolved into the fluid and thus introduced into the system.*

dissolved oxygen *noun* the amount of gaseous oxygen present in water, expressed as either its presence in a volume of water (in milligrams per litre) or its percentage in saturated water. Abbr **DO**

distal *adjective* away from the centre or point of attachment. Compare **proximal**

distil *verb* 1. to produce a pure liquid by heating a liquid and condensing the vapour, as in the production of alcohol or essential oils 2. to produce by-products from coal

distillate *noun* a substance produced by distillation

distillation *noun* the process of producing a pure liquid by heating a liquid and condensing the vapour, as in the production of alcohol or essential oils

distributary *noun* a stream or river flowing out from a larger river, as in a delta

distribute *verb* to give something or send something out ○ *distribute electrical power*

distribution *noun* 1. the process of giving or sending something out ○ *power distribution systems* 2. the pattern in which something is found in various areas, depending on factors such as climate or altitude ○ *The distribution of crops in various regions of the world is a result of thousands of years of breeding and testing.*

distributional effects *plural noun* the net costs and benefits of a policy across the population and economy

distribution area *noun* a number of places in which a species is found

district *noun* a part of an area, especially for administrative purposes

disturb *verb* to alter the usual condition of something ○ *Small hills can disturb the flow of air.* ○ *The building of the road has disturbed the balance of the ecosystem.*

disturbance *noun* 1. an alteration in the usual condition of something ○ *In general, the higher the mountain and the faster the air flow the greater is the resulting disturbance.* 2. a change in an ecosystem caused by an alteration of the environmental conditions, by a process such as drought, pollution or felling of woodland

disturbance threshold *noun* the point at which an alteration of the environmental conditions causes change in an ecosystem

ditch *noun* a channel to take away rainwater

dithiocarbamates *plural noun* fungicides widely used on fruit, vegetables and arable crops

diurnal *adjective* **1.** referring to the 24-hour cycle of day and night ○ *Diurnal changes in surface temperature over the sea are small.* **2.** happening every day **3.** happening in the daytime

diurnal jet *noun* a current of water in the ocean created by the heat of the sun during the daytime

diuron *noun* a herbicide used as a ground spray around trees and bushes (NOTE: It is under review for withdrawal from use in the European Union.)

divergence *noun* a difference ○ *a divergence of opinion on the cloning issue* ○ *a divergence between the preliminary report and the final results*

divergent *adjective* different

diversification *noun* changing to a different way of working

diversify *verb* **1.** to develop in different ways **2.** to start doing several different things ○ *Farmers are encouraged to diversify land use by using it for woodlands or for recreational facilities.*

diversity *noun* the richness of the number of species

divide *verb* to separate something into parts, or become separated into parts ○ *Air masses are divided into two types according to source region and these are known as polar and tropical air masses.*

division *noun* **1.** a separation into parts **2.** a traditional category in the scientific classification of plants, now replaced by **phylum**

DM *abbr* dry matter

DNA *noun* a nucleic acid chain carrying genetic information that is a major constituent of chromosomes. Full form **deoxyribonucleic acid.** ◊ **RNA**

DO *abbr* dissolved oxygen

Dobson unit *noun* a unit used in measuring the total amount of ozone present in a vertical column of air above the surface of the Earth (NOTE: In a layer of ozone at atmospheric pressure of 1013 hPa and temperature of 298 K which measures 1 mm in thickness, the ozone present is equivalent to 100 Dobson units.)

doline, dolina *noun* a round or oval depression in the ground, found in limestone regions

dolomite *noun* an alkaline carbonate of magnesium or calcium rock

dolphin *noun* a marine mammal belonging to the family which also includes killer whales and pilot whales. Family: Delphinidae.

DOM *abbr* **1.** digestible organic matter **2.** dry organic matter

domain *noun* a particular area of activity ○ *The subject is controversial outside the scientific domain.*

domestic *adjective* **1.** referring to the home ○ *domestic waste* **2.** not foreign ○ *domestic politics* **3.** kept as a farm animal or pet

domestic animal *noun* **1.** an animal such as a dog or cat which lives with human beings as a pet **2.** an animal such as a pig or goat which is kept by human beings for food or other uses

domesticated *adjective* **1.** referring to a wild animal which has been trained to live near a house and not be frightened of human beings **2.** referring to a species which was formerly wild but has been selectively bred to fill human needs

domestication *noun* the action of domesticating wild animals or plants

domestic consumption *noun* same as **home consumption**

domestic green waste *noun* the waste produced by a household that is from plants or other materials that can be composted

domestic hot water *noun* hot water used for washing in a house. Abbr **DHW**

domestic refuse *noun* waste material from houses. Also called **domestic waste, household refuse**

domestic sewage *noun* the sewage from houses

domestic waste *noun* same as **domestic refuse**

dominance *noun* **1.** a state where one species in a community is more abundant than others **2.** the priority for food and reproductive mates that one animal has over another in a group **3.** the characteristic of a gene form (**allele**) that leads to the trait which it controls being shown in any individual carrying it. Compare **recessiveness**

dominance hierarchy *noun* the system of priority given to specific individuals in terms of access to food and reproductive mates ○ *In many species a male is at the top of the dominance hierarchy.*

dominant *adjective* **1.** important or powerful **2.** (*of an allele*) having the characteristic that leads to the trait which it controls being shown in any individual carrying it. Compare **recessive 3.** (*of a species*) being more abundant than others in a community ■ *noun* a plant or species which has most influence on the composition and distribution of other species. ◊ **codominant, subdominant**

dominant species *noun* species which has most influence on the composition and distribution of other species

dormancy *noun* an inactive period ○ *seed dormancy*

dormant *adjective* **1.** not active or developing ○ *Some seeds lie dormant in the soil for many years.* **2.** referring to a volcano which is not erupting but is still able to erupt. Compare **extinct**

dormitory suburb, dormitory town *noun* a suburb or town from which the residents travel to work somewhere else

dorsal *adjective* referring to the back of a structure such as the body of a leaf. Opposite **ventral**

dose *noun* the amount of a drug or of ionising radiation received by an organism ○ *The patients received more than the permitted dose of radiation.*

dosimeter, dosemeter *noun* an instrument for measuring the amount of radiation

double hulled tanker *noun* an oil tanker made with two hulls, one inside the other, so as to prevent oil from spilling out if there is an accident

doubling time *noun* the time a population takes to double in numbers

Douglas fir *noun* a North American softwood tree widely planted throughout the world, and producing strong timber. Latin name: *Pseudotsuga menziesii.*

down *noun* **1.** the small soft feathers of a young bird, or soft feathers below the outer feathers in some adult birds **2.** a grass-covered chalky hill with low bushes and few trees ■ *plural noun* **downs** an area of grass-covered chalky hills with low bushes and few trees

down draught *noun* **1.** the cool air which flows downwards as a rainstorm approaches **2.** the air which flows rapidly down the lee side of a building or mountain **3.** the air which blows down a chimney

downland *noun* an area of grassy treeless hills

downpipe *noun* a pipe carrying rainwater from a roof into a drain or soakaway

downstream *adverb, adjective* towards the mouth of a river ○ *The silt is carried downstream and deposited in the delta.* ○ *Pollution is spreading downstream from the factory.* ○ *Downstream communities have not yet been affected.* Compare **upstream**

down-the-drain chemical *noun* a household chemical such as a product used

for cleaning that is disposed of through the public drains

downwash *noun* the action which brings smoke from a chimney down to the ground as it is caught in a downward moving current of air

drain *noun* **1.** an underground pipe which takes waste water from buildings or from farmland **2.** an open channel for taking away waste water ■ *verb* **1.** to remove liquid from somewhere **2.** (*of liquid*) to flow into something ○ *The stream drains into the main river.*

drainage *noun* **1.** the removal of liquid from somewhere **2.** the removal of liquid waste and sewage from a building

drainage area, drainage basin *noun* same as **catchment 1**

drainpipe *noun* a pipe carrying rainwater, sewage or other liquid into a drain or soakaway

draught animal *noun* an animal used to pull vehicles or carry heavy loads

dredge *verb* to remove silt and alluvial deposits from a river bed or other water course or channel

drift *noun* a slow movement or change

drift mine *noun* a mine used when the material to be extracted is visible on the side of a hill or mountain and can be dug into directly

driftnet *noun* a very wide long net for catching fish that a fishing boat allows to drift in the sea

drill *verb* to bore a hole or an oil well ○ *They are hoping to start drilling for oil by the end of the year.*

drilling *noun* the process of boring a hole or an oil well

drilling rig, drilling platform *noun* a large metal construction containing the drilling and pumping equipment for extracting oil or gas

drinkable *adjective* referring to water or another liquid that is safe to drink

drinking water *noun* water for drinking, especially water that is safe to drink

drizzle *noun* a light persistent rain with drops of less than 0.5 mm in diameter

drizzly *adjective* referring to weather with a lot of drizzle

drop *noun* **1.** a small amount of liquid that falls ○ *a drop of water* ○ *a few drops of rain* **2.** a lowering or reduction ○ *The passage of a cold front is usually followed by a drop in temperature.* ○ *A sudden drop in oil pressure is usually an indication of serious en-*

gine trouble. **3.** a fall of immature fruit ■ *verb* to fall or let something fall

droplet *noun* a small drop of liquid ○ *Experiments show that smaller droplets of rain can remain supercooled to much lower temperatures than large droplets.*

droppings *plural noun* excreta from animals ○ *The grass was covered with rabbit and sheep droppings.*

drought *noun* a long period without rain at a time when rain usually falls

drought stress *noun* a lack of growth caused by drought

drowned valley *noun* a valley which has been submerged by the advance of the sea or a lake

drumlin *noun* a small oval hill formed by the movement of a glacier, with one end steep and the other sloping

drupe *noun* a fruit with a single seed and a fleshy body (NOTE: Stone fruits such as cherries or plums are drupes.)

dry *adjective* with very little moisture ■ *verb* to remove moisture from something

dry deposition *noun* the fall of dry particles from polluted air forming a harmful deposit on surfaces such as buildings or the leaves of trees

dryfall *noun* the fall of polluting substances as particulates. Compare **wetfall**

drying *noun* removing moisture from something

drying out *noun* a process whereby water is drained away from wetlands

dry land *noun* **1.** land contrasted with the sea or other body of water **2. dryland** an area that often has no rain for long periods (*often plural*) ■ *adjective* referring to areas where there is little rain

dry matter *noun* the matter remaining in a biological sample or in animal feed after the water content has been removed. Abbr **DM**

dryness *noun* a state of not being wet ○ *the dryness of the atmosphere on very high mountains*

dry organic matter *noun* organic matter such as sewage sludge or manure which has been dried out and may be used as a fertiliser. Abbr **DOM**

dry season *noun* the time of year in some countries when very little rain falls

dry-stone wall *noun* a wall made of stones carefully placed one on top of the other without using any mortar

dry up *verb* (*of a river or lake*) to become dry ○ *The river dries up completely in summer.*

duct *noun* a channel or tube through which things such as fluids or cables can pass ○ *Air-conditioning ducts need regular cleaning.*

dump *noun* a place where waste, especially solid waste, is thrown away ○ *The mine is surrounded with dumps of excavated waste.* ■ *verb* to throw away waste, especially without being subject to environmental controls

dumping *noun* **1.** the disposal of waste ○ *the dumping of nuclear waste into the sea* ○ *illegal dumping* **2.** the sale of agricultural products at a price below the true cost, to get rid of excess produce cheaply, usually in an overseas market

dumping ground *noun* a place where waste is thrown away, especially casually

dumpsite *noun* a place on land or at sea where waste is dumped ○ *Sludge bacteria can survive in seawater for long periods and are widely dispersed from dumpsites.*

dunes *plural noun* an area of sand blown by the wind into small hills and ridges which may have plants growing on them ○ *The village was threatened by encroaching dunes.* ○ *The dunes were colonised by marram grass.*

dung *noun* solid waste excreta from animals, especially cattle, often used as fertiliser

duplication *noun* a situation where two or more things have the same purpose

duramen *noun* same as **heartwood**

durum *noun* a type of wheat grown in southern Europe and the USA and used in making semolina for processing into pasta. Latin name: *Triticum durum.*

dust *noun* a fine powder made of particles, e.g. dry dirt or sand

dustbin *noun* a container into which household rubbish is placed to be collected by municipal refuse collectors

dustcart *noun* a large vehicle that is used for collecting household waste

dust devil *noun* a rapidly turning column of air which picks up sand over a desert or beach, and things such as dust, leaves and litter elsewhere

dust discharge *noun* a release of dust into the atmosphere, especially from an industrial process

dust storm *noun* a storm of wind which blows dust and sand with it, common in North Africa

dust veil *noun* a mass of dust in the atmosphere created by volcanic eruptions, storms and burning fossil fuels, which cuts off solar radiation and so reduces the temperature of the Earth's surface. Compare **greenhouse effect**

Dutch elm disease *noun* a fungal disease that kills elm trees, caused by *Ceratocystis ulmi* and spread by a bark beetle

duty of care *noun* a duty which every citizen and organisation has not to act negligently, especially the system for the safe handling of waste, introduced by the UK Environmental Protection Act 1990

dwelling *noun* a place where a person lives, e.g. a house, apartment or flat

dye *noun* a substance used to change the colour of something ○ *Minute surface cracks which are difficult to detect by visual means may be highlighted by using penetrant dyes.*

dyke *noun* **1.** a long wall of earth built to keep water out **2.** a ditch for drainage ■ *verb* to build walls of earth to help prevent water from flooding land

dynamic coastline *noun* a coastline that is changing naturally through wind and wave action and may be increasing or eroding, either rapidly over a longer period

dynamic equilibrium *noun* a situation which is fluctuating around an apparent average state, where that average state is also changing through time

dynamometer *noun* a machine that measures the output of an engine

dysphotic *adjective* referring to the area of water in a lake or the sea between the aphotic zone at the bottom of the water and the euphotic zone which sunlight can reach

dystrophic *adjective* referring to a pond or lake that contains very acidic brown water, lacks oxygen, and is unable to support much plant or animal life because of excessive humus content. ◊ **eutrophic, mesotrophic, oligotrophic**

dystrophy *noun* a condition in which pond or lake water is unable to support much plant or animal life because of excessive humus content. The dead vegetation does not decompose but settles at the bottom forming a peat bog.

E

EA *abbr* Environment Agency

ear *noun* **1.** an organ which is used for hearing **2.** the flower head of a cereal plant such as wheat or maize where the grains develop

early successional plant *noun* a plant which grows rapidly and produces many seeds, often not tolerating shade. Such plants are the first to colonise new areas.

earth *noun* **1.** soil **2.** the ground or land surface ■ *verb* to connect an electrical device to the ground ○ *All appliances must be earthed.* (NOTE: The US term is **ground**.)

Earth *noun* the planet on which human beings developed and live

COMMENT: Earth is the third planet of the solar system and the only one known to support life. Earth is also remarkable for its seas of liquid water, for its oxygen-containing atmosphere and for being geologically very active. Earth rotates on its axis in a day, orbits the Sun in a year and has a satellite, the Moon, which orbits it once per lunar month. Earth can be divided into various zones: the lithosphere (solid rock and molten interior), the hydrosphere (the water covering the surface), the atmosphere (the gaseous zone rising above Earth's surface) and the biosphere (those parts of the other zones in which living organisms exist).

earth closet *noun* a toilet in which the excreta are covered with earth instead of being flushed away with water or treated with chemicals

earth dam *noun* a dam made of piled earth

earth flow *noun* the sliding of wet earth and rocks down the side of a slope or mountain, often after heavy rainfall or sometimes caused by excavation

earthquake *noun* a phenomenon in which the Earth's crust or the mantle beneath it shakes and the surface of the ground moves because of movement inside the crust along fault lines, often causing damage to buildings. ◊ **epicentre, Modified Mercalli scale, Richter scale, seismic**

earth science *noun* any science concerned with the physical aspects of the planet Earth, e.g. geochemistry, geodesy, geography, geology, geomorphology, geophysics or meteorology,

Earth Summit *noun* the United Nations Conference on Environment and Development held in Rio de Janeiro, Brazil, in June 1992

earthworks *plural noun* constructions such as walls or banks made from soil

earthworm *noun* an invertebrate animal with a long thin body divided into many segments, living in large numbers in the soil

COMMENT: Earthworms aerate the soil as they tunnel. They also eat organic matter and help increase the soil's fertility. They help stabilise the soil structure by compressing material and mixing it with organic matter and calcium. It is believed that they also secrete a hormone which encourages rooting by plants.

ebb *verb* (*of the sea or water affected by tides*) to move away from a shore, as the tide falls ■ *noun* the movement of the sea or water affected by tides away from a shore as the tide falls. Compare **flow**

ebb tide *noun* a tide which is going down or which is at its lowest ○ *The plan is to build a barrage to generate electricity on the ebb tide.* Compare **flood tide**

ebony *noun* a black tropical hardwood tree, now becoming scarce. Genus: *Diospyros.*

ecdysis *noun* the regular shedding of the hard outer layer (**cuticle**) of arthropods or the skin of reptiles

ecesis *noun* the successful establishment of a plant or animal species in a new environment

echinoderm *noun* a marine invertebrate animal with a radially symmetrical body, tube feet, and an internal skeleton of calcareous plates, e.g. a starfish, sea urchin, sea lily or sea cucumber. Phylum: Echinodermata.

echo *noun* the repetition of a sound by reflection of sound waves from a surface

echolocation *noun* the technique of finding the location of something by sending out a sound signal and listening to the reflection of the sound (NOTE: Bats and whales navigate and find their food by using echolocation.)

echosounder *noun* a device used to find the depth of water by sending a sound signal down to the bottom and calculating the distance from the time taken for the reflected sound to reach the surface again

echosounding *noun* the process of finding the depth of water using an echosounder

eclipse *noun* a situation when the Moon passes between the Sun and the Earth or when the Earth passes between the Sun and the Moon, in both cases cutting off the light visible from Earth. ◊ **solar eclipse, lunar eclipse**

eco- *prefix* ecology, ecological

ecoagriculture *noun* the practice of productive agriculture using methods designed to maintain natural resources, biodiversity and the landscape

eco-audit *noun* same as **environmental audit**

ecocatastrophe *noun* an event that results in very severe damage to the environment, especially one caused by human action

ecoclimate *noun* the climate of a specific habitat, regarded as an ecological factor

ecocline *noun* the changes which take place in a species as individuals live in different habitats

ecocomposite *noun* a material made from a plant fibre such as hemp fixed in a resin based on a plant extract such as cashew-nut shell liquor

eco-efficiency *noun* the efficient manufacture of goods at competitive prices without harm to the environment

eco-engineering *noun* the use of trees and traditional materials to protect areas of land likely to suffer erosion or landslips, keeping hard construction to a minimum

ecol. *abbr* 1. ecological 2. ecology

ecolabelling *noun* the identification and labelling of products and services that are considered less harmful to the environment than other similar products or services

E. coli *abbr* Escherichia coli

ecological *adjective* referring to ecology

ecological balance *noun* the theoretical concept of stability occurring when relative numbers of different organisms living in the same ecosystem remain more or less constant, although in practice there is always fluctuation

ecological corridor *noun* a strip of vegetation allowing the movement of wildlife or other organisms between two areas

ecological damage *noun* the harm done to an ecosystem

ecological disaster *noun* an event which seriously disturbs the balance of the environment

ecological diversity *noun* a variety of biological communities that interact with one another and with their physical and chemical environments

ecological efficiency *noun* a measurement of how much energy is used at different stages in the food chain or at different trophic levels

ecological engineering *noun* a design process that aims to integrate human activities with the natural environment for the benefit of both, taking ecological impact into account in the construction of roads or harbours, the introduction of new plants or animals, or other actions

ecological factor *noun* a factor which influences the growth and distribution of a plant species in a habitat

ecological fitness *noun* the number of offspring that survive to maturity and themselves reproduce

ecological footprint *noun* an area of the Earth that supplies the ecosystem resources for an organism to exist ○ *Ecological footprints enable people to visualise the impact of their consumption patterns and activities on ecosystems.* ○ *You can alter the size of your ecological footprint by modifying your actions.*

ecological indicator *noun* a species that has particular nutritional or climatic requirements and whose presence in an area indicates that those requirements are satisfied

ecological justification *noun* the reasoning for nature conservation based on the idea that the environment provides specific functions necessary for human life

ecologically *adverb* in an ecological way

ecologically sustainable development *noun* development which limits the size of the human population and the use of resources, so as to protect the existing natural resources for future generations

ecological niche *noun* the chemical, physical or biological characters that determine the position of an organism or species in an ecosystem (NOTE: This is also referred to as the 'role' or 'profession' of an organism, which may be described in terms of its environment and type, e.g. as an aquatic predator or a terrestrial herbivore.)

ecological pyramid *noun* same as **biotic pyramid**

ecological recovery *noun* the return of an ecosystem to its former favourable condition

ecological restoration *noun* the process of renewing and maintaining the health of an ecosystem

ecological structure *noun* the spatial and other arrangements of species in an ecosystem

ecological succession *noun* the series of stages by which a group of organisms living in a community reaches its final stable state or climax

ecologist *noun* **1.** a scientist who studies ecology **2.** a person who is in favour of maintaining a balance between living things and the environment in which they live in order to improve the life of all organisms

ecology *noun* the study of the relationships among organisms as well as the relationships between them and their physical environment

Eco-Management and Audit Scheme *noun* full form of **EMAS**

ecomovement *noun* a grouping of people and organisations dedicated to the protection of the environment

economic conservation *noun* the management of the natural environment to maintain a regular yield of natural resources

economic development *noun* the process of change from an economy based on agriculture to one based on industry

economic injury level *noun* the level of an activity such as pest control at which it is not longer profitable to continue. Abbr **EIL**

ecoparasite *noun* a parasite which is adapted to a specific host. Compare **ectoparasite, endoparasite**

ecophysiology *noun* the study of organisms and their functions and how they exist in their environment

ecosphere *noun* the part of the Earth and its atmosphere where living organisms exist, including parts of the lithosphere, the hydrosphere and the atmosphere. Also called **biosphere**

ecosystem *noun* a complex of plant, animal and microorganism communities and their interactions with the environment in which they live ○ *European wetlands are classic examples of ecosystems that have been shaped by humans.*

ecosystem approach *noun* a set of internationally agreed principles guiding the way in which the natural environment and wildlife should be managed

ecosystem diversity *noun* the variety of habitats that exist in the biosphere

ecosystem services *plural noun* services provided naturally by the ecosystem, which help humans to exist, e.g. reduction in atmospheric carbon dioxide levels, stabilising the climate and maintenance of the ozone layer

ecotax *noun* a tax that is used to encourage people to change from an activity that damages the environment or to encourage activities with beneficial environmental effects. Also called **environmental tax**

ecotone *noun* an area between two different types of vegetation which may share the characteristics of both, e.g. the border between forest and moorland

ecotourism *noun* a form of tourism that increases people's understanding of natural areas, without adversely affecting the environment, and gives local people financial benefits from conserving natural resources

ecotoxic *adjective* likely to cause severe damage to organisms and their environment

ecotoxicity *noun* the degree to which a chemical released into an environment by human activities affects the organisms that live or grow there

ecotoxicology *noun* the study of how chemicals associated with human activities affect organisms and their environment

ecotype *noun* a form within a species that has special characteristics which allow it to live in a specific habitat

ecowarrior *noun* an activist who is prepared to take direct, sometimes illegal, action on environmental issues rather than just campaign

ecto- *prefix* outside. Compare **endo-**

ectoparasite *noun* a parasite which lives on the skin or outer surface of its host but feeds by piercing the skin. Compare **endoparasite**

ectotherm *noun* an organism which is largely reliant on external sources of heat to raise its body temperature ○ *Plants and reptiles are ectotherms.* Compare **endotherm**. Also called **poikilotherm**

edaphic *adjective* referring to soil

edaphic climax *noun* a climax community caused by the type of soil in an area

edaphic factors *plural noun* the soil conditions that affect the organisms living in a specific area

edaphon *noun* an organism living in soil

eddy *noun* a whirlpool of air or of water in a current

Eden Project *noun* a development by a conservation charity in a large disused clay pit in Cornwall that explores human dependence on plants in a global context, illustrating economic, social and environmental impacts. Plants from tropical and other climates are housed in extremely large, domed glasshouses.

edgeland *noun* land at the edge of a field or wood, or on the edge of an urban area (*often plural*) ○ *The edgelands around big cities often have blossoming wildlife.*

edible *adjective* referring to something that can be eaten

EEA *abbr* European Environment Agency

EER *abbr* energy efficiency ratio

EFA *abbr* essential fatty acid

effect *noun* something which happens as the result of an action ○ *Pressure patterns have an effect on weather.* Compare **affect**

effective *adjective* having an expected and satisfactory result ○ *effective control measures*

effective height *noun* the height above the ground when a column of smoke from a factory chimney becomes horizontal

effectiveness *noun* an assessment of how effective an action is ○ *Ice covering reduces the effectiveness of an aerial.*

efficiency *noun* the ability to act or produce something with a minimum of waste, expense or unnecessary effort

efficient *adjective* referring to the ability to act or produce something with a minimum of waste, expense or unnecessary effort ○ *Composting is an efficient method of recycling organic matter.*

effluent *noun* liquid, semisolid or gas waste from industrial processes or material such as slurry or silage effluent from a farm

effluent standard *noun* the amount of sewage allowed to be discharged into a river or the sea

egg *noun* **1.** a reproductive cell produced in a female mammal by the ovary which, if fertilised by male sperm, becomes an embryo **2.** a fertilised ovum of an animal such as a bird, fish, reptile, amphibian or insect, protected by a membrane layer in which the embryo continues developing outside the mother's body until it hatches

EHO *abbr* Environmental Health Officer

EIA *abbr* environmental impact assessment

EIL *abbr* economic injury level

EINECS *abbr* European Inventory of Existing Commercial Chemical Substances

EIS *abbr* environmental impact statement

ejecta *plural noun* the ash and lava thrown up by an erupting volcano

electric *adjective* worked by, charged with or producing electricity

electrical *adjective* referring to electricity ○ *an electrical fault*

electrical conductivity *noun* a measurement of salt concentration in soils

electric car *noun* a car that is propelled by an electric battery so that it produces no harmful emissions

electric generator *noun* a device which produces electricity

electricity *noun* an electric current used to provide light, heat or power

electricity grid *noun* a system for carrying electricity round a country, using power lines from power stations. Also called **national grid** (NOTE: The electricity is at a high voltage, which is reduced by transformers to low voltage by the time the electricity is brought into use.)

electric meter, electricity meter *noun* a device which records how much electricity has been used

electric storm *noun* a storm with thunder and lightning

electrodialysis *noun* the process by which ions dissolved in sea water are removed, making the water fit to drink

electrolysis *noun* a chemical reaction caused by the passage of electricity from one electrode to another

electrolyte *noun* a chemical solution of a substance which can conduct electricity

electromagnet *noun* a magnet made from a coil of wire through which an electric current is passed

electromagnetic *adjective* **1.** having magnetic properties caused by a flow of electricity **2.** containing or worked by an electromagnet

electromotive force *noun* a source of electrical energy, from the movement of electrons, required to produce an electric current, produced by devices such as batteries or generators and measured in volts. Abbr **emf**

electron *noun* a negatively charged subatomic particle within an atom

electronegative *adjective* (*of atoms*) having negative electric charge and therefore tending to move towards a positive electric pole

electronic *adjective* referring to, based on, operated by or involving the controlled conduction of electrons, especially in a vacuum, gas or semi-conducting material

electron microscope *noun* a microscope that uses a beam of electrons instead of light. Abbr **EM**

electrostatic *adjective* referring to devices using the properties of static electrical charge

electrostatic precipitator *noun* a device for collecting minute particles of dust suspended in gas by charging the particles as they pass through an electrostatic field

element *noun* a chemical substance that cannot be broken down to a simpler substance (NOTE: There are 110 named elements.)

elemental *adjective* in the form of a pure element

elementary particle *noun* a particle that is smaller than an atom or forms part of an atom, e.g. an electron. Also called **fundamental particle, subatomic particle**

elements *plural noun* the weather ○ *protected from the elements*

elephant grass *noun* same as **miscanthus**

elevated *adjective* **1.** raised to a higher place or position **2.** increased ○ *elevated concentrations of particles in the air*

eliminate *verb* **1.** to get rid of or remove something that is not wanted ○ *Mosquitoes were eliminated by spraying breeding grounds with oil.* **2.** to rule out a possibility ○ *Bacteria were eliminated as a possible cause of the illness.*

elimination *noun* **1.** the removal of a problem **2.** the removal of waste matter from the body **3.** the process of ruling out a possibility ○ *the elimination of possible sources of contamination* □ **by a process of elimination** by removing possibilities one by one until only the most likely cause or answer is left

ELINCS *abbr* European List of Notified Chemical Substances

elm *noun* a large hardwood tree that grows in temperate areas. Genus: *Ulmus.* ◊ **Dutch elm disease**

El Niño *noun* a phenomenon occurring every few years in the Pacific Ocean, where a mass of warm water moves from west to east, rising as it moves, giving very high tides along the Pacific coast of South America and affecting the climate

eluviation *noun* the action of particles and chemicals leaching from the topsoil down into the subsoil

eluvium *noun* gravel formed as rocks are broken down into fragments where they are lying. Compare **alluvium**

ELV *abbr* end-of-life vehicle

EM *abbr* electron microscope

EMAS *noun* a voluntary scheme of the European Union in which commercial and other organisations are encouraged to assess their approach to environmental matters against a given set of criteria. Full form **Eco-Management and Audit Scheme**

embankment *noun* a wall made along a river bank to prevent a river from overflowing

embryo *noun* an organism that develops from a fertilised egg or seed, e.g. an animal in the first weeks of gestation or a seedling plant with cotyledons and a root (NOTE: After eight weeks an unborn baby is called a **fetus.**)

embryonic *adjective* **1.** referring to an embryo **2.** in the first stages of development

emergence *noun* **1.** a gradual upward movement of a land mass **2.** the germination of a seed

emergency *noun* a dangerous situation in which immediate action needs to be taken ○ *You should know the safety procedures to be taken in case of emergency.* ○ *After the earthquake, an emergency was declared.*

emergent *adjective* **1.** referring to a plant that is just starting to grow **2.** referring to a country that is starting to become developed industrially

emerging disease *noun* a new disease which is beginning to appear and affect human beings or wildlife

emf *abbr* electromotive force

emigration *noun* the movement of an individual out of an area. Opposite **immigration**

emission *noun* **1.** the sending out of matter, energy or signals ○ *light emissions* ○ *One factor on which the operational range of a radio emission depends is the transmitted power.* **2.** a substance discharged into the air by an internal combustion engine or other device ○ *Exhaust emissions contain pollutants.* ○ *Gas emissions can cause acid rain.*

emission charge *noun* a fee paid by a company to be allowed to discharge waste into the environment

emission credit *noun* the amount by which an industrialised country can buy emission reductions in a less developed country, under the Kyoto agreement of 1997. ◊ **Kyoto Protocol**

emission factor *noun* the ratio between the pollution produced and the amount of fuel burnt

emission rate *noun* the amount of pollutant produced over a specific period

emission standard *noun* the amount of an effluent or pollutant that can legally be released into the environment, e.g. the amount of sewage which can be discharged into a river or the sea, or the amount of carbon monoxide that can legally be released into the atmosphere by petrol and diesel engines

emissions trading *noun* the system of one country using some of another country's permitted emission amount as well as its own, as a result of the rule that any new source of pollution must be offset by the reduction of pollution from existing sources

emission tax *noun* a tax levied on air or water emissions

emit *verb* to send out matter, energy or a signal ○ *radiation emitted by the sun* ○ *An X-ray tube emits radiation.* (NOTE: **emitting – emitted**)

emulsifier *noun* a substance added to mixtures of food such as water and oil to hold them together. ◊ **stabiliser**. Also called **emulsifying agent** (NOTE: Emulsifiers are used in sauces and added to meat to increase the water content so that the meat is heavier. In the European Union, emulsifiers and stabilisers have E numbers E322 to E495.)

emulsify *verb* to mix two liquids so thoroughly that they will not separate

emulsifying agent *noun* same as **emulsifier**

EN *abbr* **1.** endangered species **2.** English Nature

encapsulation *noun* the enclosure of something inside something else, especially for protection

enclosure *noun* an area surrounded by a fence, often to contain animals. Compare **exclosure**

encroach on *verb* to come close to and gradually cover something ○ *The town is spreading beyond the by-pass, encroaching on farming land.* ○ *Trees are spreading*

down the mountain and encroaching on the lower more fertile land in the valleys.

endanger *verb* to put something in danger ○ *Pollution from the factory is endangering the aquatic life in the lakes.*

endangered species *noun* a species that is facing a risk of extinction in the wild, usually taken to be when fewer than 250 mature individuals exist. Abbr **EN** (NOTE: The plural is **endangered species**.)

endemic *adjective* **1.** referring to an organism that exists or originated from a specific area ○ *The isolation of the islands has led to the evolution of endemic forms.* ○ *The northern part of the island is inhabited by many endemic mammals and birds.* **2.** referring to a disease that occurs within a specific area ○ *This disease is endemic to Mediterranean countries.* ◊ **epidemic, pandemic**

endemic population *noun* a group of organisms existing in a specific geographic area

endemic species *noun* a species that is native to a specific geographic area

endo- *prefix* inside or within. Compare **ecto-**

endocarp *noun* the innermost of the layers of the wall (**pericarp**) of a fruit (NOTE: Sometimes it is toughened or hardened, as in a cherry stone or peach stone.)

endocrine disrupter, endocrine inhibitor *noun* a substance that damages the activity of the endocrine system, sometimes causing reproductive or developmental problems, sometimes because it has a similar action to a natural hormone

end-of-life directive *noun* a set of regulations about the disposal of something such as a vehicle or appliance at the end of its useful service

end-of-life vehicle *noun* a vehicle that has reached the end of its useful service and is subject to regulations for its disposal in order to avoid pollution

endoparasite *noun* a parasite that lives inside its host. Compare **ectoparasite**

endosperm *noun* a storage tissue in plant seeds that provides nourishment for the developing embryo

endotherm *noun* an organism that is able to generate heat internally in order to raise its body temperature ○ *Birds and mammals are endotherms.* Compare **ectotherm**. Also called **homoiotherm**

endothermic reaction *noun* a chemical reaction in which heat is removed from the surroundings. Compare **exothermic reaction**

endotoxin *noun* a poison from bacteria which passes into the body when contaminated food is eaten

enemy-free space *noun* an area into which a prey can escape from a predator, especially where two species of prey live in the same environment

energise *verb* to supply energy such as electricity to a machine or system to make it work

energostasis *noun* energy balance

energy *noun* **1.** the force or strength to carry out activities ○ *You need to eat carbohydrates to give you energy.* **2.** electricity or other fuel ○ *We have to review our energy requirements regularly.*

energy balance *noun* a series of measurements showing the movement of energy between organisms and their environment

energy budget *noun* the level of energy at different points in an ecosystem or an industrial process

energy conservation *noun* the avoidance of wasting energy

COMMENT: Energy conservation is widely practised to reduce excessive and costly consumption of energy. Reduction of heating levels in houses and offices, insulating buildings against loss of heat, using solar power instead of fossil fuels and increasing the efficiency of car engines are all examples of energy conservation.

energy conservation law *noun* a law which makes it illegal to waste energy

energy content *noun* the amount of energy available in a specific amount of fuel

energy crop *noun* a crop which is grown to be used to provide energy, e.g. a fast-growing tree

energy efficiency ratio *noun* a measure of the efficiency of a heating or cooling system such as a heat pump or an air-conditioning system, shown as the ratio of the output in Btu per hour to the input in watts. Abbr **EER**

energy-efficient *adjective* referring to the careful use of energy with minimum waste ○ *energy-efficient manufacturing processes*

energy flow *noun* the flow of energy from one trophic level to another in a food chain

energy gain *noun* an increase in the amount of energy or heat. Also called **heat gain**

energy recovery *noun* the production of energy from synthetic materials, e.g. using the heat from incineration of solid waste to generate electricity

energy tax *noun* a tax on an energy source intended to discourage the use of environmentally damaging sources and encourage energy conservation or use of alternative sources

energy value *noun* the heat value of a substance measured in joules. Also called **calorific value**

engineer *noun* a person who works in engineering ■ *verb* to design and make something

engineering *noun* the application of the principles of science to the design, construction and use of machines or buildings

English Nature *noun* the UK government agency that is responsible for nature conservation in England. Abbr **EN** (NOTE: It was formerly part of the Nature Conservancy Council and is about to undergo another reorganisation.)

enhanced greenhouse effect *noun* the warming influence on the climate produced as human emissions of greenhouse gases increase the natural greenhouse effect

enhancer *noun* an artificial substance that increases the flavour of food or of artificial flavouring that has been added to food (NOTE: In the European Union, flavour enhancers added to food have the E numbers E620 to E637.)

enquire, inquire *verb* to ask questions about something

enquiry, inquiry *noun* **1.** a question, or the process of asking a question. ◊ **public enquiry** (NOTE: The plural is **enquiries**.) **2.** a request for data or information from a device or database

enrich *verb* **1.** to make something richer or stronger, e.g. adding humus to enrich the soil **2.** to improve the nutritional quality of food ○ *enrich with vitamins* **3.** to increase the amount of uranium-235 in the fuel of a nuclear reactor ○ *Fuel is enriched to 15% with fissile material.*

enrichment *noun* the increase in nitrogen, phosphorous and carbon compounds or other nutrients in water, especially as a result of a sewage flow or agricultural run-off, which encourages the growth of algae and other water plants

ensilage, ensiling *noun* the process of making silage for cattle by cutting grass and other green plants and storing it in silos

enteric *adjective* referring to the intestine

entero- *prefix* referring to the intestine

Enterobacteria *plural noun* a family of bacteria, including *Salmonella* and *Escherichia*

entire *adjective* referring to leaves that are not divided into parts

entity *noun* something which is distinct and separate from something else ○ *The institutes are closely connected but are separate legal entities.*

entomological *adjective* referring to insects

entomologist *noun* a scientist who specialises in the study of insects

entomology *noun* the study of insects

entrap *verb* **1.** to catch an animal by means of a trap **2.** to catch and retain something ○ *Moisture is entrapped in the layers.* ○ *Up to 90% of sulfur emissions can be entrapped.*

entropy *noun* a measure of the degree of disorder in a closed system

entry point *noun* a place where people can enter or by which something can be accessed

environment *noun* the surroundings of any organism, including the physical world and other organisms. ◊ **built environment, natural environment**

COMMENT: The environment is anything outside an organism in which the organism lives. It can be a geographical region, a climatic condition, a pollutant or the noises which surround an organism. The human environment includes the country or region or town or house or room in which a person lives. A parasite's environment includes the body of the host. A plant's environment includes the type of soil at a specific altitude.

Environment Act *noun* a piece of UK legislation passed in 1995 that created the Environment Agency and set out measures for dealing with contaminated land

Environment Agency *noun* in England and Wales, the government agency responsible for protection of the environment, including flood and sea defences. Abbr **EA**

environmental *adjective* referring to the environment

environmental accounting *noun* same as **full-cost accounting**

environmental assessment *noun* the identification of the expected environmental effects of a proposed action

environmental audit *noun* an assessment made by a company or organisation of the financial benefits and disadvantages of adopting an environmentally sound policy. Also called **eco-audit**

'Environmental audits can alert an organisation to areas in which it does not meet current or proposed legislative requirements. Such audits can also encourage more efficient techniques and waste reduction measures.' [*Environmental Conservation*]

environmental biology *noun* the study of living organisms in relationship to their environment

environmental conditionality *noun* same as **cross-compliance**

environmental control *noun* the means of maintaining an environment

environmental damage *noun* harm done to the environment, e.g. pollution of rivers

environmental degradation *noun* a reduction in the quality of the environment

environmental directive *noun* an EU policy statement on the appropriate ways of dealing with a specific environmental issue

environmental disorder *noun* a disruption of the usual condition of an environment

environmental equity *noun* the principle that no section of the population receives a greater effect of environmental pollution or disruption than any other. Also called **environmental justice**

environmental ethics *noun* the examination and discussion of people's obligations towards the environment

environmental fluctuation *noun* a long- or short-term change in the environment, which may have a large effect on the populations living there

environmental forecasting *noun* the prediction of the effects on the surrounding environment of new construction programmes

environmental health *noun* the local government functions concerned with minimising risks to public health and the local environment, including water and air quality, hygiene in restaurants and shops, and pest control

Environmental Health Officer *noun* an official of a local authority who examines the environment and tests for hazards such as bad sanitation or noise pollution. Abbr **EHO**

environmental hygiene *noun* the measures undertaken to keep the human environment safe and healthy to live in, including waste disposal, clean water supplies, food safety controls and good housing

environmental impact *noun* the effect upon the environment of actions or events such as large construction programmes or the draining of marshes

environmental impact assessment *noun* an evaluation of the effect upon the environment of an action such as a large construction programme. Abbr **EIA**

environmental impact statement *noun* a statement required under US law for any major federal project, evaluating the effect of the project on the environment. Abbr **EIS**

environmental indicator *noun* an organism that increases or decreases in specific environmental conditions and whose presence indicates the state of an environment or a change in an environment, e.g. a lichen sensitive to industrial pollution becoming rare in a polluted area, or a species of fish returning to a formerly polluted river

environmentalism *noun* concern for the protection of the environment

environmentalist *noun* a person who is concerned with protecting the environment

environmentalist group *noun* an association or society concerned with the protection of the environment and increasing awareness of environmental issues

environmentalist lobby *noun* a group of people who try to persuade politicians that the environment must be protected and that pollution must be controlled

environmental justice *noun* same as **environmental equity**

environmental labelling *noun* same as **ecolabelling**

environmentally *adverb* with regard to the natural world and its vulnerability to damage

environmentally friendly *adjective* intended to minimise harm to the environment, e.g. by using biodegradable ingredients. Also called **environment-friendly**

Environmentally Sensitive Area *noun* in the UK, a rural area designated by Defra as needing special protection from modern farming practices. Abbr **ESA**

'The Defra-funded Countryside Stewardship and Environmentally Sensitive Areas schemes help to maintain and enhance the biodiversity and landscape value of farmed land, protect historic features and promote public access. (Delivering the evidence. Defra's Science and Innovation Strategy, 2003–06)'

environmental policy *noun* a plan for dealing with all matters affecting the environment on a national or local scale

environmental pollution *noun* the pollution of the environment by human activities

environmental protection *noun* the activity of protecting the environment by regulating the discharge of waste, the emission of pollutants and other human activities. Also called **environment protection**

Environmental Protection Act 1990 *noun* a UK regulation to allow the introduction of integrated pollution control, regulations for the disposal of waste and other provisions. Abbr **EPA**

Environmental Protection Agency *noun US* an administrative body in the USA which deals with pollution. Abbr **EPA**

environmental protection association *noun* an organisation concerned with protecting the environment from damage and pollution

environmental quality standard *noun* a limit for the concentration of an effluent or pollutant which is accepted in a specific environment, e.g. the concentration of trace elements in drinking water or of additives in food

environmental radioactivity *noun* the energy in the form of radiation that is emitted into the environment by radioactive substances

environmental resistance *noun* the ability to withstand pressures such as competition, weather conditions or food availability, which restrict the potential growth of a population

environmental science *noun* the study of the relationship between humans and the environment, the problems caused by pollution or loss of habitats, and proposed solutions

environmental set-aside *noun* a scheme of suspending cultivation of food crops for a period with clearly defined environmental aims and designed appropriately for local conditions

environmental studies *noun* a course of study that includes a range of disciplines focusing on the natural environment

environmental tax *noun* same as **eco-tax**

environmental variation *noun* the continual changes in the environment over a period

Environment Council *noun* the forum of environment ministers of member countries of the European Union that agrees legislation on environmental matters

environment-friendly *adjective* same as **environmentally friendly**

environment protection *noun* same as **environmental protection**

Envirowise *noun* a government programme providing advice to businesses in industry and commerce on improving efficiency in the use of resources and reducing waste

enzymatic *adjective* referring to enzymes

enzyme *noun* a protein substance produced by living cells which promotes a biochemical reaction in living organisms (NOTE: The names of enzymes mostly end with the suffix **-ase**.)

eolian *adjective* caused by wind ○ *eolian deposits*

EPA *abbr* **1.** Environmental Protection Act 1990 **2.** Environmental Protection Agency

ephemeral *noun* a plant or insect that has a short life cycle and may complete several life cycles within a year ○ *Many weeds are ephemerals.*

epibiont *noun* an organism that lives on the surface of another without being a parasite

epibiosis *noun* a state where an organism lives on the surface of another, but is not a parasite

epicentre *noun* a point on the surface of the Earth above the focus of an earthquake or in the centre of a nuclear explosion. Also called **focus**

epidemic *noun* a rapidly spreading infection or disease. ◊ **endemic, pandemic**

epidemiological *adjective* referring to epidemiology

epidemiologist *noun* a person who studies the factors involved in the incidence, distribution and control of disease in a population

epidemiology *noun* the study of diseases in a population, how they spread and how they can be controlled

epidermis *noun* an outer layer of cells of a plant or animal

epigeal *adjective* occurring or developing above ground ○ *epigeal germination* Compare **hypogeal**

epigenous *adjective* developing or growing on a surface

epilimnion *noun* the top layer of water in a lake, which contains more oxygen and is warmer than the water below. ◊ **hypolimnion, metalimnion**

epilithic *adjective* growing on or attached to the surface of rocks or stones

epiphyte *noun* a plant that lives on another plant for physical support, but is not a parasite of it (NOTE: Many orchids are epiphytes.)

epiphytic *adjective* attached to another plant for support, but not parasitic

episode *noun* an event, or a group of related events

episodic *adjective* happening sometimes but not regularly

epithelial *adjective* referring to the epithelium

epixylous *adjective* growing on wood

epizoite *noun* an animal that lives on the surface of another, without being a parasite

epoch *noun* ◆ **geological epoch**

equator *noun* an imaginary circle around the Earth's surface, equidistant from the poles and perpendicular to the axis of rotation, which divides the Earth into the northern and southern hemispheres ○ *Every point on the equator is equidistant from the poles.*

equatorial *adjective* referring to the equator

equilibrium *noun* a state of balance

equine *adjective* relating to horses

equinox *noun* either of the two occasions in the year, spring and autumn, when the sun crosses the celestial equator and night and day are each 12 hours long

equip *verb* to provide a person, organisation or place with machinery or equipment ○ *The laboratory has been recently equipped with new microscopes.*

equipment *noun* the devices, systems or machines that are needed for a particular purpose ○ *drilling equipment* (NOTE: no plural: for one item say a **piece of equipment**.)

equivalent *adjective* being the same, or effectively the same ○ *A metal part could be as much as 25 times heavier than an equivalent plastic part.* ○ *The electricity it uses is equivalent to the amount needed to power a small radio.*

era *noun* ◆ **geological era**

eradicate *verb* to remove something completely ○ *action to eradicate an infestation of woodworm*

eradication *noun* **1.** the complete removal of something **2.** the total extinction of a species

ergot *noun* a fungus that grows on cereals, especially rye, producing a mycotoxin which causes hallucinations and sometimes death if eaten. Genus: *Claviceps.*

ergotamine *noun* the toxin that causes ergotism

ergotism *noun* poisoning by eating cereals or bread contaminated by ergot

ericaceous *adjective* belonging to the group of plants such as heather and azalea that grow on acid soils

erode *verb* to wear away gradually, or to wear something away ○ *The hills have been eroded by wind and rain.*

erosion *noun* the wearing away of soil or rock by rain, wind, sea or rivers or by the action of toxic substances ○ *Grass cover provides some protection against soil erosion.*

COMMENT: Accelerated erosion is caused by human activity in addition to the natural rate of erosion. Cleared land in drought-stricken areas can produce dry soil which may blow away. Felling trees removes the roots which bind the soil particles together and so exposes the soil to erosion by rainwater. Ploughing up and down slopes as opposed to contour ploughing, can lead to the formation of rills and serious soil erosion.

erupt *verb* (*of a volcano*) to become active and produce lava, smoke and hot ash

eruption *noun* a sudden violent ejection of lava, smoke and ash by a volcano ○ *Several villages were destroyed in the recent volcanic eruption.*

eruptive *adjective* **1.** referring to a volcano that produces lava, smoke and hot ash **2.** referring to rock formed by the solidification of magma

ESA *abbr* Environmentally Sensitive Area

escape *noun* **1.** the action of allowing toxic substances to leave a container ○ *The area around the reprocessing plant was evacuated because of an escape of radioactive coolant.* **2.** a cultivated plant that now reproduces in the wild. Compare **feral 3.** a domesticated animal that has become wild. Compare **feral** ■ *verb* **1.** to move out of a container ○ *Steam was escaping from holes in the pipes.* **2.** to move from a domestic or cultivated area and live or grow wild **3.** to get out of captivity ○ *The monkey had escaped from a wildlife park.*

escarpment *noun* a steep slope at the edge of a plateau

Escherichia coli *noun* a Gram-negative bacterium commonly found in faeces and associated with acute gastroenteritis if it enters the digestive system

esker *noun* a long winding ridge formed of gravel

essence *noun* a concentrated oil extracted from a plant, used in food, cosmetics, analgesics and antiseptics ○ *vanilla essence*

essential *adjective* extremely important or necessary

essential fatty acid *noun* an unsaturated fatty acid essential for growth but which cannot be synthesised by the body and has to be obtained from the food supply. Abbr **EFA** (NOTE: The two essential fatty acids are linoleic acid and linolenic acid.)

essential oil *noun* an oil from a plant, used in cosmetics, analgesics or antiseptics, e.g. peppermint oil. Also called **volatile oil**

establish *verb* **1.** to work out or calculate something □ **to establish a position** to find out where something is **2.** to start or set up something ○ *We established routine procedures very quickly.* □ **to establish communication** to make contact □ **to establish control** to get control **3.** to settle or grow permanently ○ *The starling has become established in all parts of the USA.* ○ *Even established trees have been attacked by the disease.*

estate *noun* **1.** a rural property consisting of a large area of land and a big house **2.** same as **plantation** ○ *a tea estate* **3.** an area specially designed and constructed for residential or industrial use ○ *a housing estate*

estimate *noun* an approximate calculation of size, weight or extent ■ *verb* to make an approximate calculation of size, weight or extent

estivation *noun* US spelling of **aestivation**

estrogen *noun* US spelling of **oestrogen**

estuarine *adjective* referring to estuaries

estuarine plant *noun* a plant which lives in an estuary, where the water is alternately fresh and salty as the tide comes in and goes out

estuary *noun* a part of a river where it meets the sea and is partly composed of salt water

ethanol *noun* a colourless inflammable liquid, produced by the fermentation of sugars. It is used as an ingredient of organic chemicals, intoxicating drinks and medicines. Formula: C_2H_5OH. Also called **ethyl alcohol**

ethene *noun* same as **ethylene**

ethical *adjective* concerning accepted standards of behaviour and practice

ethics *noun* **1.** a set of moral standards by which people behave **2.** a code of practice which shows how a group of professionals should interact with each other

Ethiopian Region *noun* a biogeographical region, part of Arctogea, comprising Africa south of the Sahara

ethno- *prefix* human

ethnobotany *noun* the study of the way plants are used by humans

ethnopharmacology *noun* the study of the medicines used by people in traditional communities

ethology *noun* the study of the behaviour of living organisms

ethyl alcohol *noun* same as **ethanol**

ethylene *noun* a hydrocarbon occurring in natural gas and ripening fruits. It is used in the production of polythene and as an anaesthetic. Also called **ethene**

etiolation *noun* the process by which a green plant grown in insufficient light becomes yellow and grows long shoots

etiology *noun* another spelling of **aetiology**

-etum *suffix* area containing a particular type of plant ○ *arboretum* ○ *pinetum*

EU *abbr* European Union

eucalypt, eucalyptus *noun* a quick-growing Australian hardwood tree with strong-smelling resin. Genus: *Eucalyptus.*

Euglenophyta *noun* a division of unicellular algae

eukaryote, eucaryote *noun* an organism that has a cell or cells with nuclei and organelles. Compare **prokaryote**

eukaryotic, eucaryotic *adjective* referring to eukaryotes. Compare **prokaryotic**

EUNIS *noun* a database of publicly available data on species, habitat types and designated sites in Europe, maintained by the European Union Nature Information System

euphotic *adjective* relating to the upper layer of a body of water that allows the penetration of enough light to support plants which photosynthesise

euphotic zone *noun* the top layer of water in the sea or a lake, which sunlight can penetrate and in which photosynthesis takes place. Also called **photic zone**. Compare **aphotic zone**

Eurobeach *noun* a beach in any of the countries of the European Union that meets the EU regulations on the content of bacteria in the water, making it safe for swimming

Europarc *noun* a group of government and non-government organisations concerned with the management of protected areas

European Environment Agency *noun* an EU organisation with responsibility for environmental matters. Abbr **EEA**

European Union *noun* an alliance of 25 European countries, originally established with six members in 1957 by the Treaty of Rome. Among its powers are those for environmental and agricultural policy in its member states. Abbr **EU** (NOTE: formerly called the **European Community** or **European Economic Community**)

'NOTE: formerly called the European Commission or European Economic Community or common market; in 2004 there will be ? States in the EU…???'

European Union Nature Information Service *noun* a source of information on environmentally important matters in Europe, which also aims to encourage the use of terms referring to the environment in a standard way

Eurosite *noun* a group of European government and non-government organisations concerned with the management of wildlife sites, currently with 75 members in 17 countries

euryhaline *adjective* referring to an organism which can survive a wide range of salt concentrations in its environment. Compare **stenohaline**

euryphagous *adjective* referring to organisms that consume a variety of different foods

eurythermous *adjective* referring to an organism which can survive a wide range of temperatures in its environment. Compare **stenothermous**

eurytopic *adjective* referring to organisms that tolerate a wide range of environmental conditions

eusociality *noun* a situation in which a eusocial society exists

eusocial society *noun* a group of animals such as ants, bees and wasps in which some individuals are workers and do not reproduce, while others are fertile

eustatic change *noun* a change resulting from worldwide variations in sea level, as distinct from regional change caused by ground movements in a particular area

eutectic point *noun* the temperature at which a eutectic mixture freezes, which is the lowest freezing point of any constituent of the mixture

eutherian *noun* a mammal whose young develop within the womb attached to maternal tissues by a placenta. Subclass: Eutheria. Also called **placental mammal**

eutrophic *adjective* referring to water which is high in dissolved mineral nutrients. ◊ **dystrophic, mesotrophic, oligotrophic**

eutrophication, eutrophy *noun* the process by which water becomes full of phosphates and other mineral nutrients which encourage the growth of algae and kill other organisms

evaporate *verb* to change from being a liquid to being a vapour, or to change a liquid into a vapour ○ *In the heat of the day, water evaporates from the surface of the earth.* ○ *The sun evaporated all the water in the puddle.* Opposite **condense**

evaporation *noun* the process of changing from a liquid into a vapour

evaporative *adjective* able to evaporate

evaporative emission *noun* a pollutant emitted through the evaporation of a substance, e.g. from petrol when filling a tank

evapotranspiration *noun* the movement of water from soil through a plant until it is released into the atmosphere from leaf surfaces

evapotranspire *verb* to lose water into the atmosphere by evaporation and transpiration

event *noun* **1.** an action or activity **2.** a catastrophic event such as an earthquake or eruption

evergreen *adjective* referring to a plant which has leaves all year round ■ *noun* a tree or shrub which has leaves all year round (NOTE: Yew trees and holly are evergreens.) ▶ compare (all senses) **deciduous**

evolution *noun* heritable changes in organisms which take place over a period of time involving several generations (NOTE: Significant evolutionary changes can occur in a species in relatively few generations.)

evolutionary *adjective* referring to evolution ○ *Evolutionary changes have taken place over millions of years.*

evolutionary ecology *noun* the study of the impact of evolution on current ecological patterns

evolve *verb* **1.** to develop gradually ○ *The strategy is still evolving.* **2.** to change and develop gradually over millions of years from primitive forms into the range of plant and animal species known on Earth

examination *noun* the activity of looking at someone or something carefully ○ *They carried out an examination of the problem.*

exceed *verb* to be more than expected, needed or allowed ○ *The concentration of radioactive material in the waste exceeded the government limits.*

exceedance *noun* the degree to which the concentration of a pollutant is more than a standard or permissible limit ○ *exposure of the population to exceedances of air quality standards*

excess *noun* an amount or quantity greater than what is expected, needed or allowed ■ *adjective* more than is expected, needed or allowed

excessive *adjective* more than expected, needed or allowed ○ *Excessive ultraviolet radiation can cause skin cancer.*

exchange *noun* the act of taking one thing and putting another in its place ○ *gas exchange*

exclosure *noun* an area fenced to prevent animals from entering. Compare **enclosure**

exclusion zone *noun* an area that people may not enter because a hazardous substance has been released

excrement *noun* faeces

excreta *plural noun* the waste material excreted from the body of an animal, e.g. faeces, urine, droppings or sweat

excrete *verb* to pass waste matter out of the body ○ *The urinary system separates waste liquids from the blood and excretes them as urine.* Compare **secrete**

excretion *noun* the passing of the waste products of metabolism such as faeces, urine, sweat or carbon dioxide out of the body. Compare **secretion**

exhaust *verb* to use something up completely ○ *The supplies are exhausted.* ■ *noun* **1.** waste gases from an engine **2.** the part of an engine through which waste gases pass ○ *Fumes from vehicle exhausts contribute a large percentage of air pollution in towns.*

exhaustion *noun* the complete using up of something ○ *the exhaustion of the area's natural resources*

exhaustive *adjective* complete and thorough ○ *an exhaustive reply to the safety concerns* ○ *an exhaustive search for the information*

existing chemicals *plural noun* the chemicals listed in the European Inventory of Existing Commercial Chemical Substances between January 1971 and September 1981, a total of over 100,000. Compare **new chemicals**

exosphere *noun* the highest layers of Earth's atmosphere, more than 650km above the surface and composed almost entirely of hydrogen

exothermic reaction *noun* a chemical reaction in which heat is given out to the surroundings. Compare **endothermic reaction**

exotic *adjective* referring to an organism or species that is not native and has been introduced from another place or region ■ *noun* an organism or species that is not native to its current environment ▶ also called (all senses) **alien**

exotoxin *noun* a poison produced by bacteria which affects parts of the body away from the place of infection

expanded *adjective* referring to plastic or polystyrene made into a hard lightweight foam by blowing air or gas into it

expenditure *noun* **1.** the spending of money ○ *agreed the expenditure of public funds for this project* **2.** the amount of money spent

experiment *noun* a scientific test under controlled conditions that is made to demonstrate or discover something ○ *Experiments have shown that time to flowering is affected by daylength.* ■ *verb* to carry out a scientific test under controlled conditions in order to demonstrate or discover something □ **to experiment with something** to try something to see how it performs or affects you ○ *experimenting with planting density* □ **to experiment on someone or something** to use someone or something in an experiment ○ *experimented on laboratory mice*

experimental *adjective* referring to something still at an early stage of development ○ *the experimental and testing stages of a new technique*

experimentally *adverb* by carrying out experiments

explode *verb* **1.** to burst, or to make something burst, violently **2.** to increase rapidly ○ *Population numbers have exploded.*

exploit *verb* **1.** to take advantage of something ○ *Ladybirds have exploited the sudden increase in the numbers of insects.* **2.** to use a natural resource ○ *exploiting the natural wealth of the forest* **3.** to treat something or someone unfairly for personal benefit

exploitation *noun* **1.** the action of taking advantage of something **2.** the utilisation of natural resources ○ *Further exploitation of the coal deposits is not economic.* **3.** the unfair use of something or treatment of someone for personal benefit

explosion *noun* **1.** a release of energy in a sudden and often violent way ○ *an explosion caused by a bomb* **2.** a sudden increase ○ *An explosion in cases of the virus disease is predicted.*

explosive *adjective* **1.** able to or designed to burst or explode ○ *an explosive device* ○ *an explosive mechanism of seed dispersal* **2.** causing a rapid increase ○ *explosive growth*

exponential *adjective* increasing more and more rapidly

exponential growth *noun* a type of growth rate of a population which varies in proportion to the number of individuals present: at first the growth rate is slow, then it rapidly increases, theoretically to infinity, but in practice it falls off as the population exhausts its food, accumulates poisonous waste, etc.

exponentially *adverb* more and more rapidly ○ *We can expect this population to increase exponentially over the next few years.*

expose *verb* to subject something or someone to an action or an effect ○ *When the slope of a hill is exposed to solar radiation, wind currents are set up.* ○ *She had been exposed to the contaminant at work.*

exposed *adjective* **1.** referring to something or someone not covered or hidden ○ *painted all the exposed surfaces* **2.** not protected from environmental effects ○ *left in an exposed position on the hillside*

exposure *noun* **1.** the act or process of being exposed to an agent ○ *exposure to radiation* **2.** the harmful effect of having no protection from the weather ○ *suffering from exposure after spending a night in the snow*

exposure assessment *noun* an assessment of the amount of exposure to a chemical or other hazard to which a population has been subjected

exposure dose *noun* the amount of radiation to which someone has been exposed

ex-situ *adjective* referring to the study, maintenance or conservation of an organism away from its natural surroundings. Compare **in-situ**

extant species *noun* a species which still exists and is not extinct

extensification *noun* the use of less intensive farming methods. Compare **intensification**

extensive agriculture, extensive farming *noun* a way of farming which is characterised by a low level of inputs per unit of land. Compare **intensive agriculture**

extensive system *noun* a farming system which uses a large amount of land per unit of stock or output ○ *an extensive system of pig farming*

external *adjective* referring to the outside of something ○ *external appearance* Opposite **internal**

extinct *adjective* **1.** referring to a species which has died out and no longer exists ○ *Several native species have become extinct since sailors in the nineteenth century introduced dogs to the island.* **2.** referring to a volcano which is no longer erupts. Compare **dormant**

extinction *noun* the process of a species dying out

extinction rate *noun* the rate at which species become extinct

extinction vortex *noun* a situation where genetic traits and environmental conditions combine to make a species gradually become extinct

extinguishing agent *noun* **1.** a chemical substance which makes another substance react **2.** a substance or organism which causes a disease or condition

extract *noun* a preparation made by removing water or alcohol from a substance, leaving only the essence ■ *verb* **1.** to take something out of somewhere ○ *Vanilla essence is extracted from an orchid.* **2.** to obtain something such as information or data from a source **3.** to take something such as a mineral out of the ground

extraction *noun* the act or process of removing something ○ *The extraction of coal from the mine is becoming too costly.*

extractor *noun* a device that extracts something, e.g. a machine which removes fumes or gas

extrusive *adjective* referring to rock formed from molten lava which has pushed up through the Earth's crust

exurbia *noun* the area outside a city or town

eye *noun* **1.** a sense organ that is used for seeing **2.** the central point of a tropical storm, where pressure is lowest (NOTE: The eye can be several kilometres wide and may take some minutes to pass.)

eyesore *noun* something which is unpleasant to look at ○ *The lake full of old bottles and cans is an eyesore.*

F

F *symbol* **1.** Fahrenheit **2.** fluorine

F₁ *noun* (*in breeding experiments*) the first generation of offspring from a cross between two plants or animals

F₁ hybrid *noun* an animal or plant that is the result of a cross between two different plants or animals (NOTE: F₁ hybrids can be crossbred to produce F₂ hybrids and the process can be continued for many generations.)

facies *noun* the characteristic appearance of something such as an animal or plant

facilitation *noun* a situation in which a developing community changes an environment allowing other species to invade

facility *noun* a building or site with a particular function ○ *a processing facility* ○ *a recycling facility* ■ *plural noun* **facilities** the building, equipment or resources which can be used to do something ○ *laboratory facilities* ○ *leisure facilities*

factor *noun* **1.** something that has an influence on something else ○ *Annual rainfall is an important factor in affecting plant growth.* **2.** the amount by which something is multiplied □ **by a factor of** indicating a quantity by which a stated quantity is multiplied or divided, so as to indicate an increase or decrease in a measurement ○ *The number of plants in the quadrat had increased by a factor of 10.*

factory *noun* a building where products are manufactured ○ *a chemical factory*

factory farm *noun* a farm that uses intensive methods of rearing animals

factory farming *noun* a highly intensive method of rearing animals characterised by keeping large numbers of animals indoors in confined spaces and feeding them processed foods, with the use of drugs to control diseases

facultative *adjective* describing an organism that usually exists in a particular set of circumstances but is also able to do so in different circumstances ○ *a facultative anaerobe* ○ *A facultative parasite can also live as a saprophyte.* Compare **obligate**

faecal *adjective* referring to faeces (NOTE: The US spelling is **fecal**.)

faeces *plural noun* solid waste matter passed from the bowels of a human or other animal after food has been eaten and digested (NOTE: The US spelling is **feces**.)

Fahrenheit *noun* a scale of temperatures on which the freezing and boiling points of water are 32° and 212°, respectively. Compare **Celsius**. Symbol **F** (NOTE: The Fahrenheit scale is still commonly used in the USA.)

fail *verb* to be unsuccessful ○ *Attempts to reach agreement on the environmental agenda failed.*

fall *noun* **1.** a reduction ○ *a fall in pressure* **2.** the amount of rain or snow which comes down at any one time ○ *an overnight fall of snow* **3.** *US* autumn ■ *verb* **1.** to become less in amount ○ *atmospheric pressure is falling* **2.** to be included within the range of something ○ *Design methods fall into four groups.* **3.** to come down freely because of gravity ○ *Light rain may fall occasionally.* **4.** to occur at a particular time ○ *The vernal equinox falls in March.* (NOTE: **falling – fell – fallen**)

fallout *noun* the radioactive matter which falls from the atmosphere as particles, either in rain or as dust

fallout shelter *noun* a building where people are protected from radioactive material which falls from the atmosphere after a nuclear explosion

fallow *noun* a period when land is not being used for growing crops for a period so that nutrients can build up again in the soil or to control weeds ○ *Shifting cultivation is characterised by short cropping periods and long fallows.* ■ *adjective* referring to land that is not being used for growing crops for a period □ **to let land lie fallow** to allow land to remain without being cultivated for a period

falls *plural noun* a large waterfall (NOTE: often used in names: *Niagara Falls, Victoria Falls*)

fallspeed *noun* the speed at which raindrops or dry particles fall through the air

fallstreak *noun* a column of ice particles which are falling through a cloud

family *noun* **1.** a group of people, or of some other animals, composed of parents and offspring **2.** a group of genera which have some characteristics in common ○ *the* *plant family Orchidaceae* ○ *Tigers and leopards are members of the cat family.* (NOTE: Scientific names of families of animals end in **-idae** and those of families of plants end in **-ae**.)

famine *noun* a period of severe shortage of food ○ *When the monsoon failed for the second year, the threat of famine became more likely.*

famine food *noun* a plant that is regarded as suitable for eating only when other food is scarce

famine relief *noun* the supplies of basic food sent to help people who are starving

fanning *noun* the spreading out of a horizontal layer of smoke and other pollutants from a chimney

fan out *verb* to spread out from a central point

FAO *abbr* Food and Agriculture Organization

farm *noun* an area of land used for growing crops and keeping animals to provide food and the buildings associated with it ■ *verb* to run a farm

Farm Assured *noun* a UK government scheme to inform the public that farm produce is of good quality according to a set of standards. It is symbolised by a little red tractor on the packaging.

farmed *adjective* grown or produced commercially and not in the wild ○ *farmed salmon*

farmer *noun* someone who runs or owns a farm

farming *noun* running a farm, including activities such as keeping animals for sale or for their products and growing crops

farming community *noun* a group of families living near to each other and having farming as their main source of income

farmland *noun* land on a farm which is used for growing crops or rearing animals for food

farmland bird *noun* a bird that nests in an agricultural environment. Many are declining in numbers because of changes in agricultural practices.

farmland bird indicator *noun* a standard way of measuring the frequency of birds found in agricultural areas

'The farmland bird indicator is calculated on the breeding populations of 20 species (including skylark, grey partridge and goldfinch), which have collectively declined by 40% since the mid-1970s. (Delivering the evidence. Defra's Science and Innovation Strategy 2003–06)'

farmstead *noun* a farmhouse and the farm buildings around it

farmworker *noun* a person who works on a farm

farmyard *noun* the area around farm buildings

farmyard manure *noun* manure formed of cattle excreta mixed with straw, used as a fertiliser. Abbr **FYM**

fast breeder reactor, fast breeder *noun* a nuclear reactor which produces more fissile material than it consumes, using fast-moving neutrons and making plutonium-239 from uranium-238, thereby increasing the reactor's efficiency. Abbr **FBR**

fat *noun* **1.** a compound of fatty acids and glycerol. ◊ **lipid 2.** a white oily substance in the body of mammals, which stores energy and protects the body against cold (NOTE: Fat has no plural when it means the substance in the body of mammals; the plural **fats** is used to mean different types of fat.) ■ *adjective* **1.** describing the body of a large person or animal (NOTE: **fat – fatter – fattest**) **2.** referring to an animal which has been reared for meat production and which has reached the correct standard for sale in a market

fatal *adjective* causing death ○ *a fatal accident* ○ *a fatal dose*

fat-soluble *adjective* referring to a substance that can be dissolved in fat ○ *Vitamin D is fat-soluble.* ○ *Polychlorinated biphenyls are fat-soluble and collect in the blubber of seals.*

fatstock *noun* livestock which has been fattened for meat production

fatten *verb* to give animals food so as to prepare them for slaughter

fatty *adjective* containing a lot of fat ○ *Fatty foods contribute to the risk of obesity.*

fault *noun* **1.** a feature that spoils the overall quality of something ○ *a design fault* **2.** an error, especially in a calculation **3.** a change in the position of the rock layers of the Earth's crust in response to stress, leading to earthquakes

fault line *noun* a line of cracks in the Earth's crust occurring where changes in the position of rock layers have taken place and along which earthquakes are likely to occur

fault plane *noun* the face of the rock at a fault where one mass of rock has slipped against another

fauna *noun* the wild animals and birds which live naturally in a specific area. Compare **flora**

favourable condition *noun* a category indicating a good state of conservation of an area of the environment

FBC *abbr* fluidised-bed combustion

FBR *abbr* fast breeder reactor

FDA *abbr* Food and Drug Administration

Fe *symbol* iron

feasibility *noun* the practical likelihood of being able to do something ○ *a report on the feasibility of introducing restricted car access*

fecal *adjective* US spelling of **faecal**

feces *plural noun* US spelling of **faeces**

fecundity *noun* the fertility of a plant or animal

fecundity schedule *noun* a chart showing the number of eggs or offspring produced by a group during a specific period, indicating whether the population of the group has increased or decreased

feed *verb* **1.** to take food ○ *The herd feeds here at dusk.* **2.** to give food to a person or an animal **3.** to provide fertiliser for plants or soil **4.** to supply or add to something **5.** to lead into and so make larger ○ *Several small streams feed into the river.* ■ *noun* **1.** food given to animals and birds ○ *Traces of pesticide were found in the cattle feed.* **2.** fertiliser for plants or soil ○ *Tomato plants need liquid feed twice a week at this time of year.*

feed additive *noun* a supplement added to the feed of farm livestock, particularly pigs and poultry, to promote growth, e.g. an antibiotic or hormone

feed concentrate *noun* an animal feed which has a high food value relative to volume

feeder *noun* **1.** an animal that eats particular food or eats in a particular way ○ *a night feeder* **2.** a device which supplies something ○ *a bird feeder* **3.** something which supplies or adds to something else of the same type

feed grain *noun* a cereal which is fed to animals and birds, e.g. wheat or maize

feeding ground *noun* an area where animals come to feed ○ *Estuaries are the winter feeding grounds for thousands of migratory birds.*

feeding strategy *noun* the tactics used by an animal to obtain food

feedingstuff *noun* same as **feedstuff**

feedlot *noun* a field with small pens in which cattle are fattened

feedstuff *noun* food for farm animals. Also called **feedingstuff**

feldspar, feldspath *noun* a common type of crystal rock formed of silicates

fell *noun* a high area of open moorland in the north of England ■ *verb* to cut down a tree. ◊ **clearfell**

female *adjective* **1.** referring to an animal that produces ova and bears young **2.** referring to a flower which has carpels but not stamens, or a plant that produces such flowers

fen *noun* an area of flat marshy land, with plants such as reeds and mosses growing in alkaline water

fence *noun* a barrier put round a field, either to mark the boundary or to prevent animals entering or leaving ■ *verb* to put a fence round an area of land

fenland *noun* a large area of flat marshy land with alkaline water

feral *adjective* referring to an animal which was formerly domesticated and has since reverted to living wild ○ *The native population of rabbits was exterminated by feral cats.*

fermentation *noun* the process by which organic compounds such as carbohydrates are broken down by enzymes from microorganisms such as yeasts to produce energy

fern *noun* a type of green flowerless plant with large leaves (**fronds**) that propagates by spores. ◊ **pteridophyte** (NOTE: Ferns grow in damp rocky places and woodlands.)

ferric oxide *noun* a red insoluble oxide of iron. Formula: Fe_2O_3.

ferro- *prefix* referring to or containing iron

ferrous *adjective* referring to or containing iron

ferruginous *adjective* referring to rock or water which contains iron

fertile *adjective* **1.** referring to an animal or plant that is able to produce offspring by sexual reproduction. Opposite **sterile 2.** referring to soil with a high concentration of nutrients that is able to produce good crops

fertilisation *noun* the joining of an ovum and a sperm to form a zygote and so start the development of an embryo

fertilise *verb* **1.** (*of a sperm*) to join with an ovum **2.** (*of a male*) to make a female pregnant **3.** to put fertiliser on crops or soil

fertiliser *noun* a chemical or natural substance spread and mixed with soil to stimulate plant growth

COMMENT: Organic materials used as fertilisers include manure, slurry, rotted vegetable waste, bonemeal, fishmeal and seaweed. Inorganic fertilisers such as powdered lime or sulfur are also used. In commercial agriculture, artificially prepared fertilisers (manufactured compounds containing nitrogen, potassium and other chemicals) are most often used, but if excessive use of them is made, all the chemicals are not taken up by plants and the excess is leached out of the soil into ground water or rivers where it may cause algal bloom.

fertility *noun* **1.** the state of being fertile **2.** the proportion of eggs which develop into young

fertility rate *noun* the number of births per year, shown, in humans, per thousand females aged between 15 and 44

fetus, foetus *noun* an unborn animal in the womb at the stage when all the structural features are visible, i.e. after eight weeks in humans (NOTE: The usual scientific spelling is 'fetus', although 'foetus' is common in non-technical British English usage.)

fibre *noun* **1.** a natural filament such as cotton or a synthetic filament such as nylon **2.** a long narrow plant cell with thickened walls that forms part of a plant's supporting tissue, especially in the outer region of a stem (NOTE: [all senses] The US spelling is **fiber**.)

fibrous *adjective* made of a mass of fibres

field *noun* **1.** an area of land, usually surrounded by a fence or hedge, used for growing crops or for pasture **2.** an area over which something such as snow, ice or lava is found **3.** an area of natural resources, e.g. an oilfield or coalfield **4.** an area of interest or activity ○ *He specialises in the field of environmental health.*

field margin *noun* the edge of a field

field observation *noun* an examination made in the open air, looking at organisms in their natural habitat, as opposed to in a laboratory

field research *noun* a programme of scientific studies carried out at a geographical location as opposed to in a laboratory

field station *noun* a scientific research centre located in the area being researched

field study *noun* an investigation carried out at a geographical location as opposed to in a laboratory

field trial *noun* a trial that tests the ability of a crop variety to perform under normal cultivation conditions

fieldwork *noun* scientific studies carried out somewhere other than in a laboratory

filament *noun* the stalk of a stamen, carrying an anther

film *noun* a thin layer, covering or coating ○ *a thin film of oil on the surface of the lake* ○ *An electrical element made of gold film is sandwiched between the layers of glass.*

filter *noun* a material or device through which a liquid or a gas is passed in order to separate the fluid from solid matter or to remove unwanted substances ○ *a fuel filter* ○ *an oil filter*

filter basin *noun* a large tank through which drinking water is passed to be filtered

filter bed *noun* a layer of charcoal, gravel or similar material through which liquid sewage is passed to clean it

filter cake *noun* a deposit of semisolids or solids that separates out between layers of filtering material

filter feeder *noun* an animal that lives in water and feeds on small particles that it filters out of the water it takes in, e.g. a clam, sponge, or baleen whale

filtrate *noun* a liquid which has passed through a filter

filtration *noun* the process of passing a liquid through a filter to remove solid substances

fin *noun* a thin flat projection on the body of a fish

final disposal *noun* the last stage in getting rid of waste, e.g. incineration or placing in a landfill

fine *adjective* **1.** describing something that is very small in size, thickness or weight **2.** referring to weather that is warm and sunny, with few clouds and no rain or fog

finite *adjective* referring to something that has an end ○ *Coal supplies are finite and are forecast to run out in 2020.*

finite resource *plural noun* a natural resource that is does not renew itself and which will potentially be completely used up, e.g. coal or oil. Opposite **renewable resource**

fiord *noun* another spelling of **fjord**

fir *noun* a common evergreen coniferous tree. Genus: *Abies*.

fir cone *noun* a hard oval or round structure on a fir tree containing the seeds (NOTE: The term is sometimes applied to the cones of other trees such as pines.)

fire *noun* the process, or an area, of burning

firebreak *noun* an area kept free of vegetation, so that a fire cannot pass across and spread to other parts of the forest or heath

fire climax *noun* the condition by which an ecosystem is maintained by fire

-fired *suffix* burning as a fuel ○ *coal-fired power station* ○ *gas-fired central heating*

firedamp *noun* same as **methane**

fire hazard *noun* something that increases the risk of fire ○ *These piles of paper are a fire hazard.*

fire management *noun* the practice of burning in a controlled and selective way grasses, brush, undergrowth and trees in an area, to maintain an ecological balance of species and prevent uncontrolled fires

fire-prone *adjective* liable to catch fire

fire-prone ecosystem *noun* an ecosystem such as fynbos or a eucalypt forest that is likely to be frequently affected by fires

fireproof *adjective* referring to a material or structure designed to resist the effect of fire ○ *A fireproof fence surrounds the forest.*

fire-retardant *adjective* referring to a substance which slows down the rate at which a material burns

firewood *noun* wood which is burnt to provide heat

firn *noun* the spring snow on high mountains which becomes harder during the summer

fish *noun* a cold-blooded vertebrate that lives in water (NOTE: Some species are eaten for food. Fish are high in protein, phosphorus, iodine and vitamins A and D. White fish have very little oil.) ■ *verb* to try to catch fish

fisherman *noun* a man who catches fish as an occupation or as a leisure activity

fishery *noun* 1. the commercial activity of catching fish 2. an area of sea where fish are caught ○ *The boats go each year to the rich fisheries off the north coast.*

fish farm *noun* a place where edible fish are bred or reared in special pools for sale as food

fish farming *noun* the commercial activity of keeping fish in ponds or fenced areas of the sea for sale as food. Also called **aquaculture, aquafarming, aquiculture**

fishing *noun* the activity of catching fish as an occupation or as a leisure activity ○ *He enjoys fishing in trout streams.*

fishing quota *noun* the amount of a species of fish that it is permitted to catch within a period of time

fish kill *noun* an instance of a lot of fish being killed ○ *Aluminium is a critical factor in fish kills.*

fish ladder *noun* a series of pools at different levels, specially built to allow fish

such as salmon to swim up or down a river on migration

fishless lake *noun* a lake containing no fish

fishmeal *noun* a powder of dried fish, used as an animal feed or as a fertiliser

fish pass *noun* a channel near a dam, built to allow migrating fish to swim past the dam. Also called **fishway**. ◊ **fish ladder**

fish stock *noun* the fish population from which catches are taken, usually within a specific fishery

fishway *noun* same as **fish pass**

fissile *adjective* 1. referring to rock which can split or be split 2. referring to an isotope which can split on impact with a neutron

fission *noun* 1. ♦ **atomic fission** 2. the process of splitting 3. a process of reproduction, in which an organism splits in two and two complete new organisms grow, as in corals ■ *verb* (*in nuclear fission*) to split an atomic nucleus ○ *When the plutonium is fissioned, fast neutrons are produced.*

fissure *noun* a crack or groove

fit *adjective* 1. referring to something that is suitable for its purpose ○ *This food is fit to eat.* □ **fit-for-purpose** a standard for assessing the suitability of something for a particular use 2. referring to an organism that is well adapted or evolutionarily successful ○ *survival of the fittest* ○ *Only the fit individuals will survive.* (NOTE: **fitter-fittest**)

fitness *noun* a measure of the evolutionary success of genes, traits, organisms or populations

fixation *noun* the act of fixing something. ◊ **nitrogen fixation**

fjord, fiord *noun* a long inlet of the sea among mountains in temperate or arctic regions

flagellum *noun* a long thin tapering outgrowth of some cells that waves or rotates to propel the cell (NOTE: Flagella are found in some bacteria and protozoa, and in sperm cells.)

flake *noun* 1. a small piece of a solid ○ *a flake of rock* 2. a small piece of snow which falls from the sky. Also called **snowflake**

flammability *noun* the ability of a material to catch fire

flammable *adjective* easily set on fire and capable of burning fiercely and rapidly ○ *Aviation gasoline is a flammable liquid.* (NOTE: **Flammable** and **inflammable** mean the same thing. To avoid confusion, it is recommended to use **flammable**.)

flare *noun* a device that burns surplus gases to prevent them from being released into the environment, usually found on top of tall chimneys

flash *noun* a sudden or periodic burst of light ○ *Lightning is accompanied by a brilliant flash.* ■ *verb* to switch a light on and off ○ *He flashed his torch as a signal.*

flash flood *noun* a sudden rush of water in a stream or narrow river, often causing damage

flashy *adjective* referring to a river whose water level is rising rapidly after it has rained a lot

flatfish *noun* a type of fish with a flattened back that lives on the bed of the sea or of a lake and has both eyes on the top of its body, e.g. plaice (NOTE: The body of a flatfish is flattened in such a way that the fish is lying on its side. As the young fish grows, the eye underneath moves round its head to join the one on top.)

flatworm *noun* a worm with a flat body, a single gut opening, and no circulatory system. Phylum: Platyhelminthes. (NOTE: Flatworms include both free-living species and parasites such as flukes and tapeworms.)

flaw *noun* a fault or error

flea *noun* a small jumping insect which lives as a parasite on animals, sucking their blood and possibly spreading disease. Order: Siphonaptera. (NOTE: Historically, bubonic plague was spread by fleas.)

flexible *adjective* **1.** not rigid or stiff **2.** capable of responding to a variety of conditions or situations ○ *AC electrical energy is more flexible and more efficient than DC.*

flightless bird *noun* a bird which has small wings and cannot fly, e.g. an ostrich or a penguin

flocculant *noun* a substance added to water as it is treated to encourage impurities to settle

flocculation *noun* the gathering together of particles into lumps ○ *flocculation of yeast in brewing* ○ *The flocculation of particles is very important in making clay soils easy to work.*

flock *noun* a large group of birds or some farm animals such as sheep and goats ○ *a flock of geese* ○ *a flock of sheep* (NOTE: The word used for a group of cattle, deer or pigs is **herd**.)

flood *noun* a large amount of water covering land that is usually dry, caused by phenomena such as melting snow, heavy rain, high tides or storms ■ *verb* to cover dry land with a large amount of water ○ *The river bursts its banks and floods the whole valley twice a year in the rainy season.*

flood alleviation, flood control *noun* the avoidance of the possibility of flooding by controlling the flow of water in rivers with structures such as dams and embankments

flood control measures *noun* ways of managing water flow to reduce the possibility of flooding by rivers or the sea

flood damage *noun* the damage caused by floodwater

flood defence *noun* the measures taken to protect low-lying areas from flooding by rivers or the sea

flood forecasting *noun* the process of establishing when an area is at risk of being flooded, taking into account local features, climate change, the likelihood of extreme weather, and socio-economic factors

floodgate *noun* a gate in a weir or dyke, designed to control water flow

flooding *noun* the uncontrolled spread of a large amount of water onto land that is usually dry ○ *Severe flooding has been reported after the heavy rain overnight.* (NOTE: About 10% of the land area of England is at risk of flooding.)

flood plain *noun* a wide flat part of the bottom of a valley which is usually covered with water when the river floods

flood storage *noun* the measures taken to control and retain the large amount of water produced in a flood until it can disperse naturally

flood tide *noun* a tide that is rising. Compare **ebb tide**

flood warning *noun* an alert that there is likely to be a flood

floodwater *noun* water that spreads uncontrolled onto land that is usually dry ○ *After the floodwater receded the centre of the town was left buried in mud.*

floor *noun* the ground beneath something ○ *fish that live on the floor of the ocean* ○ *The forest floor is covered with decaying vegetation.*

flora *noun* the wild plants that grow naturally in a specific area. Compare **fauna**

Flora, flora *noun* a book or list describing the plants of a specific area ○ *a Flora of the British Isles*

floral *adjective* referring to plants or flowers

floret *noun* a little flower that forms part of a larger flower head

flourish *verb* to live or grow well and increase in numbers ○ *The colony of rabbits flourished in the absence of any predators.*

flow *verb* to move or run smoothly with continuity ○ *Water flows down the outer surface, cooling the interior.* ■ *noun* **1.** continuous movement of a fluid in a particular direction ○ *the flow of water downstream* **2.** the rate at which a substance is moving ○ *The meter measures the flow of water through the pipe.* **3.** the movement of the sea or water affected by tides towards a shore as the tide rises. Compare **ebb 4.** an area of peat bog, especially in Scotland ○ *the flow country*

flower *noun* the reproductive part of a seed-bearing plant (NOTE: Some flowers are brightly coloured to attract pollinating insects and birds and usually consist of protective sepals and bright petals surrounding the stamens and stigma. Many are cultivated for their colour and perfume.)

flowerless *adjective* without flowers

flowmeter *noun* a meter attached to a pipe to measure the speed at which a liquid or gas moves through the pipe

fluctuate *verb* to vary or change irregularly ○ *The magnetic field will fluctuate at the supply frequency.*

fluctuation *noun* an irregular variation or change ○ *Fluctuations in the water table affect the growth of plants.*

flue *noun* a chimney or other structure through which gas or smoke is released from a furnace or stove ○ *Gases are passed directly from the flue into the atmosphere.*

flue gas *noun* a gas produced by a burning substance that is released into the atmosphere from a chimney

fluid *noun* a substance whose molecules move freely past one another and that takes the shape of its container (NOTE: Both liquids and gases are fluids.)

fluidise *verb* to make a solid move in the manner of a fluid (NOTE: One way to do this is by pulverising it into a fine powder and passing a gas through to induce flow.)

fluidised-bed combustion *noun* a method of burning fluidised low-grade fuel while keeping the emission of pollutant gases to a minimum. Abbr **FBC**

fluke *noun* a parasitic flatworm (NOTE: Flukes may settle inside the liver, bloodstream or in other parts of the body.)

fluoridate *verb* to add sodium fluoride to drinking water to help prevent tooth decay

fluoridation *noun* the addition of sodium fluoride to drinking water to help prevent tooth decay

fluoride *noun* a chemical compound of fluorine, usually with sodium, potassium or tin

fluorine *noun* a yellowish gas (NOTE: The chemical symbol is **F**; the atomic number is **9** and the atomic weight is **19.00**.)

fluorocarbon *noun* an inert compound of fluorine and carbon, with high temperature stability. ◊ **chlorofluorocarbon**

fluorosis *noun* a condition caused by excessive fluoride in drinking water or food (NOTE: It causes discoloration of teeth and affects the milk yields of cattle.)

flush *verb* **1.** to clear a tube such as a sewer by sending water through it **2.** to pass water through a tube or system in order to remove something and clean it

flush toilet *noun* a toilet in which the excreta are washed into the sewage system by a flow of water. Compare **chemical toilet, earth closet**

fluvial, fluviatile *adjective* referring to rivers

flux *noun* the rate at which heat, energy or radiation flows

fly *noun* a small insect with two wings. Order: Diptera. ■ *verb* to move through the air (NOTE: **fly – flew – flown**)

fly ash *noun* solid particles in the air that have come from burning coal or another solid fuel ○ *The cloud contained particles of fly ash.* (NOTE: Fly ash can be collected and used to make bricks.)

fly-tipper *noun* a person who dumps rubbish somewhere other than at an official rubbish dump

fly-tipping *noun* the dumping of rubbish somewhere other than at an official site

'A quarter of all farms in England and Wales have experienced fly-tipping on their land in recent years. The total quantity of waste tipped in 2001 was estimated at 600000 tons. (Agricultural Waste: Opportunities for Change. Information from the Agricultural Waste Stakeholders' Forum)'

foam *noun* a mass of bubbles of air or gas in a liquid film ○ *detergent foam on the river* ○ *foam fire extinguishers*

foam plastic *noun* plastic with bubbles blown into it to make a light material used for packing. Also called **plastic foam**

fodder, fodder crop *noun* plant material or a crop which is grown to give to animals as food, e.g. grass or clover ○ *winter fodder*

FoE *abbr* Friends of the Earth

foehn *noun* another spelling of **föhn**

foetus *noun* another spelling of **fetus** (NOTE: The usual scientific spelling is 'fetus', although 'foetus' is common in non-technical British English usage.)

fog *noun* a thick mist made up of tiny drops of water

foggy *adjective* referring to weather conditions when there is fog

föhn, foehn *noun* a warm dry wind which blows down the side of a mountain away from the prevailing wind. It occurs when moist air rises up the mountain on the windward side, loses its moisture as rain or snow and then flows down the other side as a dry wind. Compare **chinook**

foliage *noun* the leaves on plants ○ *In a forest, animals are hard to see through the thick foliage on the trees.*

foliar *adjective* referring to leaves

foliar spray *noun* **1.** a method of applying pesticides or liquid nutrients as droplets to plant leaves ○ *needs weekly foliar sprays* **2.** a pesticide or liquid nutrient applied to plant leaves as droplets

folic acid *noun* a vitamin in the vitamin B complex found in milk, liver, yeast and green plants such as spinach

follicle *noun* **1.** a fruit in the form of a dry case that splits along one side to release the seeds **2.** the small structure in the skin from which each hair develops **3.** one of many small structures in the ovaries where egg cells develop

food *noun* **1.** the nutrient material eaten by animals for energy and growth **2.** the nutrient material applied to plants as fertiliser

Food and Agriculture Organization *noun* an international organisation that is an agency of the United Nations established with the purpose of improving standards of nutrition and eradicating malnutrition and hunger. Abbr **FAO**

Food and Drug Administration *noun* a US government department that protects the public against unsafe foods, drugs and cosmetics. Abbr **FDA**

food balance *noun* the balance between food supply and the demand for food from a population

food chain *noun* a series of organisms that pass energy and minerals from one to another as each provides food for the next (NOTE: The first organism in the food chain is the producer and the rest are consumers.)

COMMENT: Two basic types of food chain exist: the grazing food chain and the detrital food chain, based on plant-eaters and detritus-eaters respectively. In practice, food chains are interconnected, making up food webs.

food colouring *noun* a substance used to colour food

food grain *noun* a cereal crop used as food for humans, e.g. wheat, barley or rye

food mile *noun* a measure of the distance that food is transported from its place of origin to the consumer

food pyramid *noun* a chart of a food chain showing the number of organisms at each level

food safety *noun* the issues surrounding the production, handling, storage and cooking of food that determine whether or not it is safe to eat

food scare *noun* a situation when food is believed to be unsafe or contaminated, often leading to many people refusing to buy it

food security *noun* the situation that exists when people have both physical access to, and the economic means to buy, sufficient food of a quality that meets their nutritional needs and food preferences

Food Standards Agency *noun* a British government agency set up in 2000 to offer advice on food safety and quality. Abbr **FSA**

foodstuff *noun* something that can be used as food ○ *cereals, vegetables and other foodstuffs*

food supply *noun* **1.** the production of food and the way in which it gets to the consumer **2.** a stock of food ○ *The ants will vigorously defend their food supply.*

food web *noun* a series of food chains that are linked together in an ecosystem

footpath *noun* a route along which people walk on foot but along which vehicles are not permitted ○ *Long-distance footpaths have been created through the mountain regions.*

footprint *noun* the resources that an individual or organisation consumes ○ *the ecological footprint of the building*

forage *noun* a crop planted for animals to eat in the field ■ *verb* to look for food ○ *The woodpecker forages in the forest canopy for insects.*

force of gravity *noun* same as **gravity**

forecast *noun* a description of what it is thought will happen in the future on the basis of current knowledge ○ *the weather forecast* ○ *population forecasts* ○ *a forecast of the requirements for new homes*

forecasting *noun* the activity of using current knowledge to describe what might happen in the future

foreign *adjective* belonging to or coming from another country

foreshock *noun* a small shock that comes before a main earthquake. ◊ **aftershock**

foreshore *noun* an area of sand or pebbles which is only covered by the sea when there are very high tides

forest *noun* **1.** an area of land (more than 0.5 ha), 10% of which is occupied by trees **2.** same as **plantation** ■ *verb* to manage a forest, by cutting wood as necessary, and planting new trees

forest conservation *noun* the active maintenance of forests by controlled felling and planting

forest degradation *noun* the loss of the natural resources in areas covered by forests, whether permanent or reversible

forest dieback *noun* a disease affecting pine trees in which the pine needles turn yellow. Also called **Waldsterben**

forester *noun* a person who manages woodland and plantations of trees

forest fire *noun* a sudden intense fire that spreads rapidly and often destroys a very large wooded area (NOTE: Some trees such as eucalyptus grow again from their blackened stumps and some seeds only germinate after experiencing the intense heat of such a fire.)

forest floor *noun* the ground at the base of the trees in a forest

forest management *noun* the conservation and regeneration of the ecological resources of a forest while maintaining its productivity

forest regeneration *noun* the process of new trees growing again on land that was formerly wooded, whether naturally or as a result of planting schemes

forestry *noun* the management of forests, woodlands and plantations of trees

Forest Stewardship Certification *noun* a mark of recognition by the Forest Stewardship Council, based in the USA, that a forest is being managed in an environmentally responsible, socially beneficial and economically viable way. Abbr **FSC**

forest tree *noun* a large tree of the type that grows in a forest

formation *noun* **1.** the way in which something is formed, shaped or arranged ○ *a formation of flower buds* **2.** the shape or structure that something has ○ *The geese flew in a V formation.* **3.** a structure formed of layers of rock ○ *an unusual rock formation*

forward *verb* to improve or send on something

fossil *noun* the remains of an ancient animal or plant found preserved in rock

fossil fuel *noun* a substance containing carbon formed from the decomposed remains of prehistoric plants, e.g. oil, natural gas or peat

fossilised *adjective* referring to an animal or plant that has become a fossil

fossil record *noun* the information about ancient climate and species preserved in fossils

fossil water *noun* water that has accumulated in underground strata over millions of years and is therefore not a renewable resource

foul water *noun* water containing waste or sewage

founder crop *noun* a crop that was one of the earliest to be used and developed by humans, e.g. wheat, barley, lentils and chickpeas

founder effect *noun* the existence of low levels of genetic variation due to a new population being established by only a few original individuals. ◊ **genetic bottleneck**

fowl *noun* a bird, especially a hen, raised on a farm for food. ◊ **waterfowl**

Fr *symbol* francium

fraction *noun* a part of a whole unit, expressed as one figure above another, e.g. ¼ or ½

fractional distillation *noun* a distillation process in which different fractions of a mixture of liquids are collected at different points during the process

fractional process *noun* a process that separates out the components of a mixture

fragile *adjective* referring to something that is easily broken or damaged ○ *a fragile glass tube* ○ *The desert is a fragile environment.*

fragment *noun* **1.** a small piece of something ○ *a fragment of rock* **2.** a piece of DNA, especially one cut by an enzyme ○ *a restriction fragment* ■ *verb* to break into pieces

framework *noun* **1.** the supporting structure round which something is made or built ○ *This house has a timber framework.* **2.** a set of ideas or principles that form the basis of something that will be developed more at a later stage ○ *The draft report will provide a framework for our discussions.*

Framework Convention on Climate Change *noun* a treaty agreed at the Earth Summit requiring states to take steps to limit the emission of greenhouse gases, especially carbon dioxide, believed to be responsible for global warming

francium *noun* a naturally radioactive element (NOTE: The chemical symbol is **Fr**; the atomic number is **87** and the atomic weight is **223**.)

free *adjective* **1.** not attached, confined or controlled **2.** chemically uncombined ■ *verb* to release something or someone from constraint

freedom to roam *phrase* ♦ **Countryside and Rights of Way Act**

free-living animal *noun* an animal that exists in its environment without being a parasite on another

free radical *noun* an atom or group of atoms that is highly reactive due to the presence of an unpaired electron

free-range eggs *noun* eggs from hens that are allowed to run about in the open and eat more natural food

free-swimming *adjective* same as **pelagic**

free temperature rise *noun* the difference between the temperature outside a building and the free heat inside it (NOTE: If a building is well insulated, the difference can be as much as 10K.)

freeze *verb* **1.** (*of liquid*) to become solid as a result of a drop in temperature **2.** to preserve something such as food by keeping it at a very low temperature **3.** (*of weather*) to be so cold that water turns to ice ○ *It will freeze tomorrow.* Opposite **melt 4.** to become or remain motionless to avoid the attention of predators ○ *These small birds freeze if a hawk passes overhead.* (NOTE: **freeze – froze – frozen**)

freeze drying *noun* a method of preserving food or tissue specimens by freezing rapidly and drying in a vacuum

freezer *noun* an appliance for preserving perishable items by keeping them at a very low temperature

frequency *noun* **1.** the number of times something happens in a given period of time **2.** the probability of a item occurring in a sample **3.** the percentage occurrence of a single species in a set of samples

fresh *adjective* **1.** not used, not dirty **2.** not tinned or frozen ○ *Fresh fish is less fatty than tinned fish.* ○ *Fresh vegetables are expensive in winter.*

fresh air *noun* the air outside buildings or other structures ○ *They came out of the office into the fresh air.*

fresh water *noun* water in rivers and lakes which contains almost no salt. Compare **salt water**

freshwater *adjective* **1.** containing fresh water ○ *freshwater lakes* **2.** living in fresh water ○ *freshwater fish such as pike*

friable *adjective* referring to soil which is light and crumbles easily into fragments

fridge mountain *noun* the unexpected result of an EU decision that required CFCs to be recovered from fridges that were being thrown away, because there was not enough special equipment to do the job and the fridges had to be stored

Friends of the Earth *noun* a pressure group formed to influence local and central governments on environmental matters. Abbr **FoE**

frond *noun* a large compound leaf, divided into many sections, such as that found on ferns and palm trees

front *noun* **1.** the forward part or surface ○ *The entrance is at the front.* **2.** same as **weather front**

frontal *adjective* referring to the forward part or surface area of something ○ *the frontal area*

frost *noun* the deposit of ice that forms on surfaces when the temperature is below the freezing point of water ○ *frost on the windowpanes*

frosty *adjective* referring to an air temperature below 0°C ○ *a frosty night*

fructose *noun* a sugar with six carbon atoms, which together with glucose forms sucrose. Also called **fruit sugar**

frugivore *noun* an animal that mainly eats fruit (NOTE: Many bats and birds are frugivores.)

fruit *noun* the structure of a plant formed after flowering and usually containing seeds. Many fruits are eaten as food. ○ *a diet of fresh fruit and vegetables* ○ *A peach is a fleshy fruit.* ■ *verb* (*of a plant*) to produce fruit ○ *Some varieties of apple fruit very early.*

fruit farming *noun* the activity of growing fruit for sale

fruit sugar *noun* same as **fructose**

fruitwood *noun* the wood from a fruit tree such as apple or cherry, which may be used to make furniture

fruticose *adjective* (*of some lichens*) with upright branches, like a small shrubby plant

FSA *abbr* Food Standards Agency

FSC *abbr* Forest Stewardship Certificate

fuel *noun* a substance that can be burnt to provide heat or power, e.g. wood, gas or oil

fuel efficiency *noun* the percentage of the heat from burning a fuel that is converted into energy

fuel-efficient *adjective* referring to an engine or process that uses fuel efficiently

fuel-saving *adjective* using less fuel than others of the same type

fuel switching *noun* the act of changing from a fuel with a high sulfur content to one such as natural gas that contains a relatively low amount of sulfur

fuelwood *noun* wood that is grown to be used as fuel

fugitive dust *noun* dust caused by an activity that makes it blow in the air, as occurs when tractors are ploughing dry fields

fugitive emissions *plural noun* polluting substances released into the atmosphere as a result of leaks, evaporation or wind effects

full-cost accounting *noun* the practice of including the less obvious costs of a product or activity, such as its effects on the environment or health, together with its direct costs when making decisions. Also called **green accounting, environmental accounting**

fumarole *noun* a small hole in the Earth's crust near a volcano from which gases, smoke or steam are released

fumes *plural noun* **1.** gas or vapour **2.** the solid particles produced by a chemical reaction which pass into the air as smoke

fumigant *noun* a chemical compound that becomes a gas or smoke when heated and is used to kill insects

fumigate *verb* to kill microorganisms or insects by using a fumigant

fumigation *noun* **1.** the use of a fumigant to kill microorganisms or insects **2.** a high amount of air pollution near the ground, caused when the morning sun heats the air and forces polluted air down from higher levels

function *noun* the use or purpose of something or how it works ○ *The function of a wing is to provide lift.*

functional food *noun* a food designed to be medically beneficial, helping to protect against serious conditions such as diabetes, cancer or heart disease

functionality *noun* the purpose that something is designed to fulfil, or the range of functions that something has

functional response *noun* the response of a predator to an increase in population of its prey. Either the predator increases its consumption as the population of the prey increases, or it reduces its consumption because it has enough to eat.

fundamental *adjective* referring to or forming the foundation or base ○ *the fundamental characteristics of cells*

fundamental niche *noun* the full range of physical, chemical and biological factors each species could use if there were no competition from other species. ◊ **interspecific competition**

fundamental particle *noun* same as **elementary particle**

fungal *adjective* referring to fungi ○ *Powdery mildew is a fungal disease.*

fungi plural of **fungus**

fungicidal *adjective* referring to a substance which kills fungi ○ *fungicidal properties*

fungicide *noun* a substance used to kill fungi

fungoid *adjective* referring to something shaped like a fungus ○ *a fungoid growth on the skin*

fungus *noun* an organism that has thread-like cells with walls made of chitin and no green chlorophyll (NOTE: The plural is **fungi**. For other terms referring to fungi, see words beginning with **myc-**.)

COMMENT: Fungi grow in almost every environment and are vital in nutrient cycling as they can digest the cellulose in dead plants. Mushrooms are the spore-producing structures of a large group of otherwise threadlike fungi; many are edible although some are deadly poisonous. Fungi are used in brewing, cheese-making and the production of antibiotics such as penicillin. Some fungi can cause diseases of animals and plants.

funnel cloud *noun* a rotating, visible extension of a cloud, with the top attached to the cloud but without the bottom tip touching the ground ○ *When a funnel cloud touches the ground it becomes a tornado.*

fur *noun* **1.** a coat of hair covering an animal ○ *The rabbit has a thick coat of winter fur.* **2.** skin and hair removed from an animal, used to make clothes

furling *noun* a way of preventing damage to horizontal-axis wind turbines by automatically turning them out of the wind

furrow *noun* a long trench cut in the soil by a plough

FYM *abbr* farmyard manure

fynbos *noun* the scrubland typical of the Western Cape area of South America, consisting of low bushes with hard leaves

G

g *symbol* gram

Ga *symbol* gallium

Gaia hypothesis, Gaia theory *noun* a theory that the biosphere is like a single organism where the living fauna and flora of Earth, its climate and geology, all function together and are interrelated, influencing the development of the whole environment

gain *noun* an increase ○ *a gain in altitude* ○ *There is a gain of heat by the Earth due to solar radiation.*

gale *noun* a very strong wind usually blowing from a single direction (NOTE: A gale is force 8 on the Beaufort scale.)

galena *noun* a shiny blue-grey mineral consisting of lead sulfide. Symbol **PbS** (NOTE: It is a source of lead and silver.)

gall *noun* a hard growth on a plant caused by a parasitic insect

gallium *noun* a rare blue-grey metal element used in semiconductors, high-temperature thermometers and alloys (NOTE: The chemical symbol is **Ga**; the atomic number is **31** and the atomic weight is **69.72**.)

gallon *noun* a unit of liquid volume in the Imperial System, approximately equal to 4.5 litres

galvanised iron *noun* iron that has been coated with zinc to prevent it from rusting (NOTE: Sheets of galvanised iron are widely used for roofs.)

game *noun* animals that are hunted and killed for sport or food or both

game reserve *noun* an area of land where wild animals are kept to be hunted and killed for sport

gamete *noun* a sex cell (NOTE: In animals the male and female gametes are a spermatozoon and an ovum respectively, in plants they are a pollen grain and an ovule.)

gametocide *noun* a drug that kills gametocytes

gametocyte *noun* a cell that develops into a gamete

gametophyte *noun* the part of a plant's life cycle when sex organs and sex cells (**gametes**) are produced

garden *noun* an area of land cultivated as a hobby or for pleasure, rather than to produce an income. ◊ **market garden**

garden city *noun* a large town planned in the early 20th century on farmland near a large town, with both public parks and a private garden for each house. The aim was to mix the urban and rural environments. ◊ **garden suburb**

gardener *noun* a person who looks after a garden

gardening *noun* the activity of looking after a garden

garden suburb *noun* an area of a city planned in the early 20th century to include large open public spaces and many private gardens. ◊ **garden city**

garrigue, garigue *noun* in the Mediterranean area, low-growing vegetation of drought-resistant prickly shrubs and herbs

gas *noun* **1.** a substance that is not a liquid or a solid, which will completely fill the container it occupies, and which becomes liquid when it is cooled ○ *Heating turned the liquid into a gas.* **2.** a substance found underground, or produced from coal, and used to cook or heat ○ *gas central heating* ○ *We heat our house by gas.* **3.** *US* same as **gasoline** (NOTE: The UK term is **petrol**.)

gas cleaning *noun* the removal of pollutants from gas, especially from emissions from factories and power stations

gaseous *adjective* referring to a substance formed or in the form of gas □ **water in the gaseous state** steam

gaseous pollutant *noun* a pollutant in the form of a gas

gas exchange *noun* the transfer of gases between an organism and its environment

gasoline *noun US* a liquid made from petroleum, used as a fuel in internal combustion engines (NOTE: The UK term is **petrol**.)

gastropod *noun* a mollusc that has a head with eyes, tongue and tentacles, a large flattened muscular foot and often a single shell. Class: Gastropoda. (NOTE: Limpets, snails and slugs are gastropods.)

gather *verb* to collect things together ○ *The children gathered sea shells on the beach.* ○ *We gathered information from several reports and reviews.*

gatherers *plural noun* people who collect their food and materials, rather than growing them

Gause's principle *noun* a theory that suggests that two similar and competitive species cannot occupy the same ecological niche at the same time

GCV *abbr* gross calorific value

GE *abbr* genetic engineering

Geiger counter, Geiger-Muller detector *noun* an instrument for the detection and measurement of radiation

gene *noun* a unit of DNA on a chromosome which governs the synthesis of one protein and may combine with other genes to determine a particular characteristic

gene bank *noun* a collection of seeds from potentially useful wild plants, which may be used in the future for breeding new varieties

gene flow *noun* a movement of genes among populations through interbreeding, dispersal and migration

gene frequency *noun* the ratio of a specific variant form (**allele**) of a gene to the total number of alleles in a specific population

gene mutation *noun* a change in a single base or base pair in the DNA sequence of a gene

gene pool *noun* the total of all the genes carried by the individual organisms in a population

genera plural of **genus**

general circulation model *noun* a complex computer simulation of climate and its various components ○ *General circulation models are used by researchers and policy analysts to predict climate change.*

generalist *noun* **1.** a species which can live in many different environments **2.** a person who studies many different subjects, rather than specialising in one

generate *verb* to make something exist ○ *Carbon monoxide is generated by car engines.* ○ *The nuclear reaction generates a huge amount of heat.*

generation *noun* **1.** the act or process of making or creating something ○ *the generation of electricity* ○ *the generation of ideas* **2.** a group of individual organisms derived from the same parents

generator *noun* a device that generates electricity ○ *The centre has its own independent generator, in case of mains power failure.*

generic *adjective* **1.** relating to or suitable for a broad range of things or situations **2.** referring to a genus

generic name *noun* the scientific name of a genus. Compare **specific name** (NOTE: It is the first name in the binomial classification system, the second being the name which identifies the species. It is written with a capital letter.)

genet *noun* **1.** an individual organism which is genetically different from others **2.** a clone from a genetically distinct organism

genetic, genetical *adjective* referring to genes or genetics

genetically modified *adjective* referring to an organism that has received genetic material from another in a laboratory procedure, leading to a permanent change in one or more of its characteristics. Abbr **GM**

genetically modified organism *noun* a plant or animal produced by the technique of genetic modification. Abbr **GMO**

genetic bottleneck *noun* a change in gene frequencies and decline in total genetic variation where there is a sharp decrease in population numbers

genetic code *noun* the information carried by an organism's DNA which determines the synthesis of proteins by cells and which is passed on when the cell divides. Also called **genetic information**

genetic damage *noun* damage to an organism's genes by external agents such as radiation or chemicals

genetic diversity *noun* the richness of the variety and range of genes

genetic drift *noun* a random change in gene frequency

genetic engineering *noun* same as **genetic modification**. Abbr **GE**

genetic information *noun* same as **genetic code**

genetic manipulation *noun* same as **genetic modification**

genetic marker *noun* a known, usually dominant, gene that is used in the identification of genes, chromosomes and characteristics already known to be associated with that gene

genetic material *noun* the parts of a cell that carry information that can be inherited, e.g. DNA, genes or chromosomes

genetic materials *plural noun* same as **germplasm**

genetic modification *noun* the alteration and recombination of genetic material under laboratory conditions, resulting in transgenic organisms. Abbr **GM**. Also called **genetic manipulation, genetic engineering**

genetic resources *plural noun* the genes found in plants and animals that have value to humans ○ *Modern plant varieties have been developed from genetic resources from South America.*

genetics *noun* the study of the way in which the characteristics of an organism are inherited

genetic variation *noun* the inherited differences between the members of a species

-genic *suffix* produced by or producing

genome *noun* **1.** the set of all the genes in an individual **2.** all the genes in a species

genomic *adjective* relating to a genome

genotype *noun* **1.** the genetic constitution of an organism. ◊ **phenotype 2.** an individual organism

genotypic *adjective* relating to a genotype

genus *noun* a group of closely related species (NOTE: The plural is **genera**.)

geo- *prefix* Earth

geochemical *adjective* relating to geochemistry

geochemist *noun* a scientist who specialises in the study of geochemistry

geochemistry *noun* the scientific study of the chemical composition of the Earth

geocline *noun* the set of changes that take place in a species across different geographical environments

geodesy *noun* the science of the measurement of the Earth or of very large sections of it to determine the exact location of points on the Earth's surface through precise observation of distances and angles

geodetic, geodesic *adjective* referring to geodesy

geographer *noun* a person who specialises in the study of geography

geographic, geographical *adjective* referring to geography ○ *a specific geographical area* ○ *the north geographic pole*

geographical barrier *noun* a natural feature such as a mountain range or a wide river that prevents easy movement from one area to another and separates different habitats

geographic information system *noun* a computer system for capturing, manipulating, analysing and displaying all forms of geographic information. Abbr **GIS**

geographic isolation *noun* the state of being separated from other members of the same species by the sea or a range of mountains

geography *noun* the scientific study of the Earth's surface, climate and physical features

geological *adjective* referring to geology

geological aeon *noun* a unit of geological time, lasting millions of years and containing several eras, during which Earth's surface and its underlying strata underwent particular changes

geological epoch *noun* a unit of geological time, a subdivision of a geological period

geological era *noun* a unit of geological time containing several geological periods

geological period *noun* a unit of geological time, shorter than an era and longer than an epoch

geological timescale *noun* the time during which the Earth has existed, i.e. many millions of years

geologist *noun* a scientist who specialises in the study of geology

geology *noun* the scientific study of the composition of the Earth's surface and its underlying strata

geomagnetic *adjective* referring to the Earth's magnetic field

geomagnetic pole *noun* same as **magnetic pole**

geomagnetism *noun* the study of the Earth's magnetic field

geomorphology *noun* the study of the physical features of the Earth's surface, their development and how they are related to the core beneath

geophone *noun* a sensitive device which records sounds of seismic movements below the Earth's surface

geophysicist *noun* a scientist who specialises in the study of geophysics

geophysics *noun* the scientific study of the physical properties of the Earth

geophyte *noun* a perennial herbaceous plant that lives through the winter as an underground structure such as a bulb or corm

geopolitics *noun* the influence of geographical factors on the politics of a country

geoscience *noun* a science concerned with the physical aspects of the Earth, e.g. geochemistry, geodesy, geography, geology, geomorphology, geophysics or meteorology

geoscientist *noun* a person who specialises in one or several of the geosciences

geosphere *noun* the central part of the Earth, which contains no living organisms

geostrophic wind *noun* a wind which blows horizontally along the isobars, across the surface of the Earth

geosyncline *noun* a long fold in the Earth's crust, forming a basin filled with a sediment of volcanic rocks

geothermal *adjective* referring to heat from the interior of the Earth

geothermal deposit *noun* the heat-producing matter inside the Earth

geothermal energy *noun* the energy or electricity generated from the heat inside the Earth, e.g. in hot springs. Also called **geothermal power**

COMMENT: Apart from channelling water from hot springs, geothermal energy can also be created by pumping cold water into deep holes in the ground at points where hot rocks lie close to the surface. The water is heated and becomes steam which returns to the surface and is used for domestic heating.

geothermally *adverb* from geothermal sources ○ *Geothermally heated water can be used for domestic heating.*

geothermal power *noun* same as **geothermal energy**

geotropism *noun* the growth or movement of a plant in response to gravity (NOTE: Stems and other parts that grow upwards against gravity show negative geotropism. The downwards growth of roots is positive geotropism.)

germ *noun* **1.** a microorganism that causes a disease, e.g. a virus or bacterium (*informal*) **2.** a part of an organism that develops into a new organism

germ cell *noun* a cell which is capable of developing into a spermatozoon or ovum

germicide *adjective, noun* a substance that can kill germs

germinate *verb* (*of a seed or spore*) to start to grow

germination *noun* the process of a seed or spore developing into a plant

germplasm *noun* the genetic material that is transmitted from one generation of an organism to another

geyser *noun* a natural feature occurring when hot water and steam rise out of a hole in the ground at regular intervals

GHG *abbr* greenhouse gas

gibberellin *noun* a plant hormone that stimulates growth and seed germination

giga- *prefix* one thousand million, or 10^9. Symbol **G**

gigawatt *noun* a unit of one thousand million watts ○ *Air-conditioning accounts for one-third of the 500 gigawatt peak demand in the USA.* Abbr **GW**

gigawatt-hour *noun* a unit of one thousand million watts of electricity used for one hour. Abbr **GWh**

gillnet *noun* a type of net which is attached to the seabed, in which fish are caught by their gills

gills *plural noun* **1.** the breathing apparatus of fish and other animals living in water, consisting of a series of layers of tissue which extract oxygen from water as it passes over them **2.** a series of thin structures on the underside of the cap of a fungus, carrying the spores

GIS *abbr* geographic information system

glabrous *adjective* smooth and without hairs

glacial *adjective* referring to a glacier ○ *The rocks are marked by glacial action.*

glacial drift *noun* the material left behind by a glacier, e.g. sand, soil or gravel

glaciation *noun* **1.** the formation of glaciers **2.** the formation of ice crystals at the top of a rain cloud

glacier *noun* **1.** a mass of ice moving slowly across land, like a frozen river **2.** a large amount of stationary ice covering land in the Arctic regions

COMMENT: During the Ice Ages, glaciers covered large parts of the northern hemisphere, depositing sand in the form of glacial moraines and boulder clay. Glaciers are still found in the highest mountain areas and in the Arctic and Antarctic regions.

glaciologist *noun* a scientist who specialises in the study of glaciers

glaciology *noun* the study of glaciers

gland *noun* (*in animals and plants*) a cell or group of cells that secrete a specific substance

glandular *adjective* referring to glands

glass *noun* a substance made from sand and soda or lime, usually transparent and used for making windows, bottles and other objects

glasshouse *noun* a large structure made of glass inside which plants are grown, especially commercially or for scientific purposes

glauconite *noun* a green mineral composed of iron, potassium, aluminium and magnesium

glaucous *adjective* blue-green, or with a waxy blue-green covering

glen noun (*in Scotland*) a long narrow mountain valley with a stream running along it

gley noun a thick rich soil found in water-logged ground

gleyed soil noun soil which is water-logged

gleying noun a set of properties of soil which indicate poor drainage and lack of oxygen (NOTE: The signs are a blue-grey colour, rusty patches and standing surface water.)

global adjective referring to the whole Earth ○ *global biodiversity* ○ *Global temperatures will rise over the next fifty years.*

global distillation noun the movement of persistent organic pollutants from warm tropical and subtropical regions to cooler higher latitudes via evaporation and condensation

global ecology noun the study of the relationship of organisms to each other and to their environment throughout the world

globalisation noun the development of a similar culture and economy across the whole world as a result of technological advances in communications

global positioning system noun an extremely accurate method of locating a position using satellite signals. Abbr **GPS**

global solar radiation noun the rays emitted by the Sun which fall on the Earth. Abbr **GSR**

global stability noun the ability of an ecological or taxonomic unit to be unaffected by large disturbances

global temperature noun the temperature over the Earth as a whole

global warming noun a gradual rise in temperature over the whole of the Earth's surface, caused by the greenhouse effect

global warming potential noun a concept that takes into account the differing times that gases remain in the atmosphere, in order to find out the potential climate effects of equal emissions of each of the greenhouse gases. Abbr **GWP**

globe noun **1.** a spherical object **2.** the Earth

globule noun a round drop of liquid

gloom noun **1.** low light intensity **2.** dark and miserable weather

glowworm noun a beetle of which the females and larvae produce a greenish light

glucose noun a simple sugar found in some fruit

glufosinate ammonium noun a systemic herbicide acting against a wide range of species. Some crops have been genetically modified to tolerate it.

glume noun one of a pair of dry leaves (**bracts**) that occur at the base of a spikelet in grasses and cereals or at the base of an inflorescence in reeds

gluten noun a protein found in some cereals which makes a sticky paste when water is added (NOTE: The gluten content of flour affects the quality of the bread made from it.)

glycogen noun a type of starch that is converted from glucose by the action of insulin and stored in the liver as a source of energy

glycoprotein noun a protein that is linked to a carbohydrate

glyphosate noun a systemic herbicide acting against a wide range of species. Some crops have been genetically modified to tolerate it.

GM abbr **1.** genetically modified **2.** genetic modification

GMO abbr genetically modified organism

gneiss noun a rough rock with layers of different minerals

goat noun a small animal with horns, kept for its milk and meat

gold noun a heavy yellow metal that is relatively rare. It is used to make jewellery and precious objects. (NOTE: The chemical symbol is **Au**; the atomic number is **79** and the atomic weight is **196.97**.)

gold mine noun a hole dug in the ground to extract gold

gorge noun a narrow valley with steep sides

government agency, **government body** noun an organisation set up by a government to deal with a specific area of specialist responsibility

GPS abbr global positioning system

graben noun a type of rift valley, formed where land between fault lines has sunk

grab sample noun a single sample of soil or water taken without considering factors such as time or flow

gradient noun **1.** the angle of a slope ○ *Plant roots cannot retain the soil on very steep gradients.* **2.** the rate of increase or decrease of a measurement

graft noun a piece of plant or animal tissue transferred onto another plant or animal and growing there ■ verb to transfer a piece of tissue from one plant or animal to another

grain *noun* **1.** the seed (technically a fruit) of a cereal crop such as wheat or maize **2.** a cereal crop such as wheat of which the seeds are dried and eaten ○ *grain farmers* **3.** the size of crystals in a rock or the size of particles of sand

grain crop *noun* a cereal crop such as wheat of which the seeds are dried and eaten

grain reserves *plural noun* the amount of cereal grain held in a store by a country which is estimated to be above the country's requirements for one year

gram *noun* **1.** a metric measure of weight equal to one thousandth of a kilogram. Abbr **g 2.** same as **chickpea**

-gram *suffix* a record of information in the form of a picture

Gramineae *plural noun* former name for **Poaceae**

Gram's stain, Gram's method *noun* a method of staining bacteria that allows two main types to be distinguished

granite *noun* a hard grey rock with pieces of quartz, feldspar and other minerals in it

grant *noun* an amount of money given to support a specific person or project

granular *adjective* in the form of granules

granule *noun* **1.** a small particle ○ *granules of sand* **2.** a small artificially made particle of a substance ○ *Fertilisers are produced in granule form, which is easier to handle and distribute than powder.*

graph *noun* a diagram that shows a relationship between two sets of numbers as a series of points often joined by a line ○ *The graph shows the relationship between sulfur in the atmosphere and lichen numbers.*

-graph *suffix* a machine which records by drawing

-grapher *suffix* **1.** a person skilled in a subject **2.** a technician who operates a machine which records information

graphite *noun* a mineral form of carbon occurring naturally as crystals or as a soft black deposit (NOTE: It is used as a moderator in some types of nuclear reactor and is mixed with clay to make lead pencils.)

-graphy *suffix* the process of making an image

grass *noun* a monocotyledonous plant in the Poaceae family. There are many genera. (NOTE: Grasses include cereals and are important as food for herbivores and humans.)

grassland *noun* land covered mainly by grasses. ◊ **acid grassland, calcareous grassland** ■ *plural noun* **grasslands** wide areas of land covered mainly by grasses, e.g. the prairies of North America and the pampas of South America

gravel *noun* sand and small pebbles occurring as deposits (NOTE: On the Wentworth-Udden scale, gravel has a diameter of 2–4 millimetres.)

graveyard *noun* a place where nuclear waste is buried, or where unwanted machines or vehicles are left (*informal*)

gravitational *adjective* referring to gravity

gravity *noun* a natural force of attraction which pulls bodies towards each other and which pulls objects on the Earth towards its centre ○ *In order for a bird to fly, lift must overcome gravity.* Also called **force of gravity**

gray *noun* an SI unit of measurement of absorbed radiation equal to 100 rads. Symbol **Gy**

graze *verb* (*of animals*) to feed on low-growing plants

grazer *noun* a grazing animal

grazer system *noun* the section of a community where animals feed on plants

grazier *noun* a farmer who looks after grazing animals

grazing *noun* **1.** the action of animals feeding on growing grass, legumes or other plants ○ *Spine on plants may be a protection against grazing.* **2.** the action of animals eating plankton or other very small animals **3.** an area of land covered with low-growing plants suitable for animals to feed on ○ *There is good grazing on the mountain pastures.*

grazing food chain *noun* a cycle in which vegetation is eaten by animals, digested, then passed into the soil as dung and so taken up again by plants which are eaten by animals

Great Barrier Reef *noun* a coral reef about 200km long that lies parallel to the coast of north-east Australia

green *adjective* **1.** referring to a colour like that of grass ○ *The green colour in plants is provided by chlorophyll.* **2.** referring to an interest in ecological and environmental problems ○ *green policies* ■ *noun* **1.** a colour like that of grass **2.** *also* **Green** a person with a concern for ecological and environmental problems

green accounting *noun* same as **full-cost accounting**

green area index *noun* the total area of leaves, green fruits and green stems per unit of ground area covered by a plant. Abbr **GAI**

green audit *noun* same as **environmental audit**

Green Belt *noun* an area of agricultural land, woodland or parkland which surrounds an urban area

green burial *noun* an act of burial designed to have low environmental impact, typically placing a corpse that has not been embalmed in a biodegradable coffin or bag and burying it in a grave marked with a sapling. ◊ **woodland burial**

green certificate *noun* a official record confirming that a specific percentage of electricity has been produced from renewable energy sources

green chemistry *noun* the development of chemical products that do not cause pollution or environmental and human health risks

green consumerism *noun* a movement to encourage people to buy food and other products such as organic foods or lead-free petrol which are regarded as environmentally good

green electricity *noun* same as **green tariff electricity**

greenfield site *noun* a place in the countryside, not previously built on, that is chosen as the site for a new housing development or factory ○ *Urban fringe sites are less attractive to developers than greenfield sites.* Compare **brownfield site**

greenhouse *noun* a structure made of glass inside which plants are grown

greenhouse effect *noun* the effect produced by the accumulation of carbon dioxide crystals and water vapour in the upper atmosphere, which insulates the Earth and raises the atmospheric temperature by preventing heat loss

COMMENT: Carbon dioxide particles allow solar radiation to pass through and reach the Earth, but prevent heat from radiating back into the atmosphere. This results in a rise in the Earth's atmospheric temperature, as if the atmosphere were a greenhouse protecting the Earth. Even a small rise of less than 1°C in the atmospheric temperature could have serious effects on the climate of the Earth as a whole. The polar ice caps would melt, causing sea levels to rise everywhere with consequent flooding. Temperate areas in Asia and America would experience hotter and drier conditions, causing crop failures. Carbon dioxide is largely formed from burning fossil fuels. Other gases contribute to the greenhouse effect, for instance methane is increasingly produced by rotting vegeta-

tion in swamps, from paddy fields, from termites' excreta and even from the stomachs of cows. Chlorofluorocarbons also help create the greenhouse effect.

greenhouse gas *noun* a gas that occurs naturally in the atmosphere or is produced by burning fossil fuels and rises into the atmosphere, forming a barrier which prevents heat loss ○ *planning to introduce a tax to inhibit greenhouse gas emissions.* Abbr **GHG**

COMMENT: The six greenhouse gases with a direct effect are carbon dioxide, methane, nitrous oxide (all of which occur naturally), hydrofluorocarbons and perfluorocarbons, and sulfur hexafluoride. Indirect greenhouses gases are nitrogen oxides, which produce ozone during their breakdown in the atmosphere, carbon monoxide and non-methane volatile compounds.

greening *noun* **1.** the process of planting trees and other vegetation in an area **2.** the process of becoming more aware, or increasing others' awareness, of the environment and environmental issues

green manure *noun* fast-growing green vegetation such as mustard or rape which is grown and ploughed into the soil to rot and act as manure

Green Party *noun* a political party which is mainly concerned with environmental issues

Greenpeace *noun* an international pressure group that takes action to publicise environmental issues

green petrol *noun* a type of petrol containing fewer pollutants than ordinary petrol

green politics *noun* the kind of political proposals put forward by environmentalists

green pricing *noun* the choice offered to customers of energy companies to pay extra on their bills to cover the costs of researching and using renewable resources

Green Revolution *noun* the development in the 1960s of new forms of widely grown cereal plants such as wheat and rice, which gave high yields and increased food production especially in tropical countries

green space *noun* an area of land which has not been built on, containing grass, plants and trees

greenstrip *noun* a firebreak on open grassland, planted with vegetation that does not burn easily

green tariff electricity *noun* electricity produced from renewable resources such as wind. Also called **green electricity**

greenwash *noun* a public relations initiative such as advertising or public consultation, that is designed to show the concern of a business or organisation for the environmental impact of its activities but which is often regarded as propaganda

green waste noun leaves, grass cuttings and other plant material that is to be disposed of

greenway noun 1. a grass track 2. a system of linked open spaces such as parks and privately owned natural areas, often in an urban area

green wood noun new shoots on a tree, which have not ripened fully

grey water, greywater noun the relatively clean waste water from sinks, baths, and kitchen appliances

grid noun a pattern of equally spaced vertical and horizontal lines

grid reference noun a set of numbers which refer to a point on a map, used for accurate location of a place

grind verb to reduce a substance to fine particles by crushing

grinder noun a device or machine which reduces a substance to fine particles by crushing

grinding noun the process of reducing of a substance to fine particles by crushing

grit noun 1. sharp-grained sand 2. a tiny solid particle in the air, larger than dust

groove noun a long shallow depression in a surface

gross calorific value noun the total number of calories which a specific amount of a substance contains. Abbr **GCV**

gross primary production noun the rate at which a biomass assimilates organic matter

gross primary productivity noun the rate at which producers in an ecosystem capture and store chemical energy as biomass. ◊ **net primary productivity**

ground noun 1. the solid surface of the Earth 2. a surface layer of soil or earth ○ *stony ground* 3. an area of land ○ *a stretch of open ground before you reach the trees*

ground clearance noun the removal of trees and undergrowth in preparation for an activity such as ploughing or building

ground cover noun plants that grow densely close to the ground, either in natural conditions or planted to prevent soil erosion or the spread of weeds

ground-level concentration noun the amount of a pollutant measured at the height of the ground, just above it or just below it

ground-nesting adjective (*of birds*) building nests on the ground

ground pollution noun the presence of unusually high concentrations of harmful substances in the soil

ground source heat pump noun a heat pump used to extract heat from the ground at several metres deep and transfer it to a building where heat is required

ground water noun water that stays in the top layers of soil or in porous rocks and can collect pollution. Compare **surface water**

groundwater recharge noun the process by which water from above the surface is added to the saturated zone of an aquifer, either directly or indirectly

group noun a number of individual items or people brought together ■ verb to bring several things together

grove noun a small group of trees

grow verb 1. (*of plants*) to exist and develop well ○ *Bananas grow only in warm humid conditions.* 2. (*of plants and animals*) to increase in size ○ *The tree grows slowly.* ○ *A sunflower can grow 3 cm in one day.* 3. to cultivate plants ○ *Farmers here grow two crops in a year.* ○ *He grows peas for the local canning factory.* 4. to become ○ *It's growing colder at night now.* ○ *She grew weak with hunger.*

growth noun 1. an increase in size ○ *the growth in the population since 1960* ○ *The disease stunts the conifers' growth.* 2. the amount by which something increases in size ○ *The rings show the annual growth of the tree.*

growth hormone noun a natural or artificial chemical that makes an organism grow

growth rate noun the amount or speed of increase in size

growth ring noun same as **annual ring**

groyne noun a structure that is built out from the shore into the sea to help hold back material moving along the shoreline by the force of waves and so prevent erosion

grub noun a small caterpillar or larva ■ verb □ **to grub up** to dig up a plant with its roots ○ *Miles of hedgerows have been grubbed up to make larger fields.*

GSR abbr global solar radiation

guano noun a mass of accumulated bird droppings, found especially on small islands and used as organic fertiliser

guard cell noun either of a pair of cells that border a leaf pore and control its size

(NOTE: The guard cells and pore are called a stoma, and are most common on the underside of leaves.)

guerrilla *noun* a plant species that invades a community as isolated individuals. Compare **phalanx**

guideline *noun* a piece of advice that suggests the best way for something to be done ○ *guidelines for the conduct of experiments*

guild *noun* a group of plants or animals of different species which live in the same type of environment

gulf *noun* a very large area of sea enclosed partly by land

Gulf Stream *noun* a current of warm water in the Atlantic Ocean, which flows north along the east coast of the USA, then crosses the Atlantic to northern Europe, passing close to the west coast of Scotland and giving the British Isles and European coast a mild winter climate compared with countries at the same latitude such as eastern Canada

gulfweed *noun* floating seaweed that grows in the Sargasso Sea

gull *noun* a seabird, with a large body, usually white or grey feathers, a hooked beak and webbed feet. There are several different species.

gully *noun* **1.** a deep channel formed by soil erosion and unable to be filled in by cultivation **2.** a small channel for water, e.g. an artificial channel dug at the edge of a field or a natural channel in rock

gully cleaning *noun* the clearance of rubbish from drainage gullies at the edge of roads

gum *noun* a liquid substance in the trunks and branches of some trees, which hardens on contact with air. It is used in confectionery, pharmacy and stationery.

gust *noun* a strong sudden rush of wind ○ *Strong gusts blew dust off the fields into the air.*

gusty *adjective* referring to wind blowing in sudden strong bursts

GW, gW *abbr* gigawatt

GWh *abbr* gigawatt-hour

GWP *abbr* global warming potential

Gy *abbr* gray

gymnosperm *noun* a seed-bearing plant in which the seeds are carried naked on the scales of a cone rather than being inside a fruit, e.g. a conifer, cycad or ginkgo. ◊ **angiosperm**

gynoecium *noun* the female sex organs (**carpels**) of a plant

gyre *noun* a circular or spiral motion of ocean water

H

ha *symbol* hectare

haar *noun* a sea mist occurring during the summer in the north of the British Isles

habit *noun* the characteristic way in which a specific plant grows ○ *a bush with an erect habit* ○ *a plant with a creeping habit*

habitat *noun* the type of environment in which a specific organism lives

habitat action plan *noun* a detailed description of a specific habitat together with the detailed actions and targets proposed for conserving it. Abbr **HAP**

habitat diversity *noun* a variety of habitats within an area. The larger the area, the more diverse the habitats.

habitat island *noun* an area suitable for a species that is surrounded by other less suitable areas such as urban areas

habitat loss *noun* a permanent disappearance of or decrease in the amount of suitable environment available to an organism. Also called **habitat reduction**

habitat management *noun* same as **nature management**

habitat reduction *noun* same as **habitat loss**

habitat restoration *noun* activity carried out to return an area to a former more favourable condition for wildlife

haboob *noun* a violent dust storm or sand storm of a type found in North Africa, especially in Sudan (NOTE: Such dust storms are associated with cumulonimbus clouds.)

HACCP *noun* a process for identifying and controlling hazards within a process, e.g. in the food industry. Full form **Hazard Analysis Critical Control Points**

hadal zone *noun* a zone of the ocean at depths greater than the abyssal zone, i.e. below 6 000 m

haematite *noun* iron oxide, the most common form of iron ore. Formula: Fe_2O_3.

hail *noun* water falling from clouds in the form of small round pieces of ice ■ *verb* to fall as small pieces of ice

hailstone *noun* a piece of ice which falls from clouds like rain

hailstorm *noun* a storm in which the precipitation is hail and not rain

hair *noun* **1.** a slender outgrowth on the surface of a plant or animal **2.** a mass of outgrowths on an animal's skin or a person's head or body

half-hardy *adjective* referring to a plant that is able to tolerate cold weather down to about 5C. ◊ **hardy**

half-life, half-life period *noun* **1.** the time taken for half the atoms in a radioactive isotope to decay. Also called **half-value period 2.** the time required for an organism to eliminate naturally half the amount of a substance that has entered its body

halo- *prefix* salt

halobiotic *adjective* referring to organisms which live in salt water

halocarbon *noun* a chemical consisting of carbon, sometimes hydrogen, and a halogen such as chlorine, fluorine, bromine or iodine. Also called **halogenated carbon**

halocline *noun* a salinity gradient where two masses of water such as fresh water and the sea meet

halogen *noun* a non-metallic element belonging to a series of chemically related non-metallic elements that includes fluorine, chlorine, iodine, bromine and astatine

halogenated *adjective* referring to a chemical compound that contains one of the halogens

halogenated carbon *noun* same as **halocarbon**

halogen lamp *noun* a light bulb containing a halogen that runs at a much higher temperature than a conventional incandescent lamp

halogenous *adjective* referring to or containing a halogen

halomorphic soil *noun* soil that contains large amounts of salt

halon *noun* a chemical compound that contains bromine and resembles a chlorofluorocarbon

halophile *noun* a species that can live in salty conditions

halophyte *noun* a plant that is able to grow in salty soil, as in estuaries

hands-on *adjective* referring to being actively involved in something ○ *hands-on experience*

hanging valley *noun* a valley high above the side of another valley, formed when the main valley was cut deeper by a larger glacier, leaving the smaller valley to join it at a cliff (NOTE: This is one of the ways in which waterfalls are formed.)

HAP *abbr* Habitat Action Plan

hard *adjective* (*of water*) containing calcium and magnesium in solution

harden *verb* to make something hard, or become hard □ **to harden off** to make plants become gradually more used to cold ○ *After seedlings have been grown in the greenhouse, they need to be hardened off before planting outside in the open ground.*

hardness *noun* **1.** an indication of the percentage of calcium in water **2.** a measurement of how hard a mineral is

hardpan *noun* a hard soil surface, usually formed of dried clay

hardwood *noun* **1.** a slow-growing broad-leaved tree, e.g. oak, teak or mahogany **2.** the fine-grained, dense wood produced by a tree such as oak, teak or mahogany. Compare **softwood**

hardy *adjective* referring to a plant able to tolerate cold weather, especially below 5 °C. ◊ **half-hardy**

harmattan *noun* a hot dry winter wind that blows from the northeast and causes dust storms in the Sahara

harness *verb* to control a natural phenomenon and make it produce energy ○ *A tidal power station harnesses the power of the tides.*

harvest *noun* **1.** the time when a crop is gathered **2.** a crop that is gathered ■ *verb* **1.** to gather a crop that is ripe ○ *They are harvesting the rice crop.* **2.** to gather a natural resource

hatch *verb* (*of an animal*) to break out of an egg

hatchery *noun* a place where eggs are kept warm artificially until the animal inside becomes mature enough to break out

hay *noun* grass mowed and dried before it has flowered, used for feeding animals

hay fever *noun* same as **pollinosis**

haymaking *noun* the cutting of grass in fields to make hay

hazard *noun* something with the potential to cause injury, damage or loss ○ *a fire hazard* ○ *a health hazard* ○ *Thunderclouds may pose hazards to aircraft.* Compare **risk**

hazard assessment *noun* a formal assessment of the potential of something to harm humans or the environment

hazardous *adjective* referring to the danger that something might present ○ *hazardous chemicals* ○ *Climbing mountains can be hazardous.*

hazardous substance *noun* a substance that is toxic, persistent and likely to accumulate in organisms

hazardous waste *noun* a by-product of manufacturing processes or nuclear processing that is toxic and can damage people's health or the environment if not treated correctly

hazard profile *noun* data on the physical and chemical characteristics, toxicity, bioaccumulation, persistence and mobility in environmental media and other properties of a chemical, used together with information on exposure to assess risk

haze *noun* dust or smoke in the atmosphere ○ *Haze can seriously reduce air-to-ground visibility.*

HD polythene *noun* same as **high-density polythene**

He *symbol* helium

head *noun* **1.** a point where a river starts to flow **2.** pressure shown as the vertical distance that water falls from the inlet of the collection pipe to the water turbine in a hydroelectric power system **3.** pressure shown as the vertical distance of a water tank above the taps in a house ■ *verb* **1.** to be in charge of an organisation or group of people **2.** to move or move something in a particular direction

headland *noun* **1.** a high mass of land protruding into the sea **2.** an uncultivated area of soil at the edge of a field, where a tractor turns when ploughing. ◊ **conservation headland**

headstream *noun* a stream that flows into a river near the river's source

headwaters *plural noun* the area in which tributary streams feed into a river near the river's source

health *noun* the state of a plant, animal or person being well and free from disease ○ *Fumes from the factory were a danger to public health.* ◊ **plant health**

Health and Safety at Work Act *noun* an Act of Parliament which indicates how the health of workers should be protected by the companies they work for

Health and Safety Executive *noun* a UK government organisation responsible for checking people's working environment. Abbr **HSE**

health assessment *noun* an assessment of the dangers to the health of the population involved in a contaminated area

health food *noun* a food that is regarded as contributing to good health, especially one with no artificial additives (NOTE: Health foods include natural cereals, dried fruit and nuts.)

health hazard *noun* something that is likely to harm someone's health

health risk assessment *noun* a prediction of the potential health effects of being exposed to hazardous substances

healthy *adjective* **1.** not ill, or not showing signs of diseases or disorders **2.** likely to keep or make you well ○ *a healthy diet*

heart *noun* the compact central part of a vegetable such as lettuce, cabbage or celery, where new leaves or stalks form

heartwood *noun* the hard dead wood in the centre of a tree trunk which helps support the tree. Compare **sapwood**. Also called **duramen**

heat *noun* **1.** energy that is moving from a source to another point ○ *The heat of the Sun made the surface of the road melt.* **2.** the period when a female animal will allow mating □ **an animal on heat** a female animal in the period when she will accept a mate ■ *verb* to make something hot ○ *The solution should be heated to 25 °C.*

heat accumulator *noun* a vessel for storing hot liquid, allowing even heat distribution or distribution over a period of time. Also called **thermal accumulator**

heat discharge *noun* a release of waste heat into the atmosphere, especially from an industrial process. Also called **thermal discharge**

heat engine *noun* a phenomenon that produces the Earth's climatic pattern, caused by the difference in temperature between the hot equatorial zone and the cold polar regions, making warm water and air from the tropics move towards the poles

heat gain *noun* same as **energy gain**

heath *noun* an area of acid soil where low shrubs such as heather and gorse grow and which are treeless as a result of grazing by animals

COMMENT: Lowland heaths are found on dry sandy soils or gravel below 300 m. Upland heaths are found on mineral soils or shallow peat and may be dry or wet, with mosses growing in wetter conditions.

heathland *noun* a wide area of heath

heating *noun* **1.** the process of making something hot **2.** a system that supplies heat

heat island *noun* an increase in temperature experienced in the centre of a large urban area, caused by the release of heat from buildings

heat-proof *adjective* referring to a material or something made from a material through which heat cannot pass

heat reclamation, heat recovery *noun* the process of collecting heat from substances heated during a process and using it to heat further substances, so as to avoid heat loss

heat storage *noun* the storage of heat produced during a period of low consumption until a peak period when it is needed. Also called **thermal storage**

heavy *adjective* **1.** weighing a lot **2.** severe, difficult or unpleasant **3.** involving a lot of effort

heavy industry *noun* an industry that extracts raw materials such as coal

hectare *noun* an area of land measuring 100 by 100 metres, i.e. 10000 square metres or 2.47 acres. Symbol **ha**

hedge *noun* a row of bushes planted and regularly cut to provide a barrier around a field or garden

hedgebank *noun* a raised strip of earth on which a hedge is planted ○ *primroses growing on the hedgebank*

hedgelaying *noun* a traditional method of cultivating hedges, where tall saplings are cut through halfway and then bent over so that they lie horizontally and make a thick barrier

hedgerow *noun* a line of bushes forming a hedge

hedging *noun* the skill of cultivating hedges

helio- *prefix* Sun

heliophyte *noun* a plant that is adapted to grow in strong light

heliotropic *adjective* referring to a plant that grows or turns towards a light source

helium *noun* a light inert gas, used in balloons and as a coolant in some types of nuclear reactor (NOTE: The chemical symbol is **He**; the atomic number is **2** and the atomic weight is **4.00**.)

helophyte *noun* a plant that typically grows in marshy or lake-edge environments

hemisphere *noun* **1.** one half of a sphere **2.** one half of the Earth north or south of the equator ○ *the northern hemisphere*

hemlock *noun* **1.** a North American softwood tree. Genus: *Tsuga*. **2.** a poisonous plant. Latin name: *Conium maculatum*.

herb *noun* **1.** a plant that is used to add flavour in cooking **2.** a plant that has medicinal properties **3.** a non-woody flowering plant that has no perennial stem above the ground in winter

herb- *prefix* referring to plants or vegetation

herbaceous *adjective* referring to plants with soft non-woody tissue that die down above ground to survive through the winter

herbage *noun* the green plants, especially grass, eaten by grazing animals

herbal *adjective* referring to plants

herbalism *noun* the treatment of illnesses or disorders by the use of herbs or by medicines extracted from herbs

herbarium *noun* a collection of preserved plant or fungal specimens, especially one that is used for scientific study and classification

herbicide *noun* a chemical that kills plants, especially used to control weeds

herbivore *noun* an animal that feeds only on plants. ◊ **carnivore, detritivore, frugivore, omnivore**

herbivorous *adjective* referring to an animal that feeds only on plants

herd *noun* a group of herbivorous animals that live together ○ *a herd of cows* (NOTE: The word **herd** is usually used for cattle; for sheep, goats, and birds such as hens or geese, the word to use is **flock**.) ■ *verb* **1.** to tend a herd of animals **2.** to gather animals together ○ *herding the cows into the yard*

herdsman *noun* someone who looks after a herd of animals

hereditary *adjective* referring to a genetically controlled characteristic that is passed from parent to offspring

hereditary factor *noun* a genetically controlled characteristic that is passed from parent to offspring

heredity *noun* the transfer of genetically controlled characteristics from parent to offspring

heritable *adjective* able to be passed from parent to offspring

heritage *noun* the environment, including the countryside, biodiversity of species, and historic buildings and sites, seen as something to be passed on in good condition to future generations

heritage coast *noun* an area of coastline that is protected because of its special scenic or environmental value

hermaphrodite *noun* an animal, plant or flower that has both male and female sexual organs

hertz *noun* the SI unit of frequency. Symbol **Hz** (NOTE: One hertz is equal to one cycle per second.)

hetero- *prefix* different. Compare **homo-**

heterogeneous *adjective* having different characteristics or qualities (NOTE: Do not confuse with **heterogenous**.)

heterogenous *adjective* coming from a different source (NOTE: Do not confuse with **heterogeneous**.)

heterologous *adjective* differing in structural features or origin

heterophyte *noun* **1.** a plant that grows in a wide range of habitats **2.** a plant that lacks chlorophyll and is parasitic

heterosis *noun* an increase in size or rate of growth, fertility or resistance to disease found in offspring of a cross between organisms with different genotypes. Also called **hybrid vigour**. Compare **inbreeding depression**

heterotroph *noun* an organism that requires carbon in organic form and cannot manufacture it (NOTE: Animals, fungi and some algae and bacteria are heterotrophs.)

heterotrophic *adjective* referring to a heterotroph ○ *a heterotrophic organism*

heterozygosity *noun* the state of being heterozygous

heterozygous *adjective* relating to a cell or organism that has two or more variant forms (**alleles**) of at least one of its genes (NOTE: The offspring of such an organism may differ with regard to the characteristics determined by the gene or genes involved, depending on which version of the gene they inherit.)

hexachlorocyclohexane *noun* same as **lindane**

HFC *abbr* hydrofluorocarbon

Hg *symbol* mercury

HGCA *noun* an organisation established to improve the production and marketing of UK cereal crops and oilseeds, and to promote research. Full form **Home-Grown Cereals Authority**

hibernaculum *noun* a place where an animal hibernates, e.g. a nest (NOTE: The plural is **hibernacula**.)

hibernate *verb* (*of an animal*) to survive the cold winter months by a big reduction in metabolic rate and activity, and by using up stored body fat for food

hibernation *noun* a big reduction in metabolic rate and activity, and the using up of stored body fat to survive the cold winter months. Compare **aestivation**

hickory *noun* a North American hardwood tree. Genus: *Carya*.

hide *noun* **1.** the skin of a large animal **2.** a shelter where humans can stay hidden while watching birds or animals

high *adjective* **1.** reaching far from ground level ○ *Altocumulus clouds form at higher levels than cumulus.* **2.** of greater than average amount ○ *The sample gave a high reading of radioactivity.* ○ *The soil is red and high in aluminium and iron oxide.* ■ *noun* an area of high atmospheric pressure

high-density *adjective* **1.** having a large mass per unit of volume **2.** having a lot of people or organisms living closely together ○ *high-density housing*

high-density polythene *noun* very thick strong plastic. Abbr **HD polythene**

high-energy food *noun* a kind of food which gives a lot of energy when broken down by the digestive system, e.g. fats or carbohydrates

higher plants *plural noun* plants that have a vascular system. Compare **lower plants**

high-grade *adjective* of very high quality

highland *noun* an area of high land or mountains. Opposite **lowland** ■ *adjective* referring to a hilly or mountainous area ○ *Highland vegetation is mainly grass, heather and herbs.*

high-level waste, high-level nuclear waste, high-level radioactive waste *noun* waste that is hot and emits strong radiation

high-performance *adjective* designed to operate very efficiently

high production volume chemical *noun* a chemical of which more than 1000 tonnes is sold per year per manufacturer or importer

high-risk *adjective* having a strong likelihood of damage or injury ○ *high-risk occupations*

high-tech *adjective* technologically advanced (*informal*)

high-tension *adjective* (*of electricity cable*) carrying a high voltage

Highways Department *noun* a local government office dealing with all matters affecting the planning, construction and maintenance of roads in an area

high-yielding *adjective* producing a large crop ○ *They have started to grow high-yielding varieties of wheat.*

hill *noun* an area of ground higher than the surrounding areas but not as high as a mountain

hill farm *noun* a farm in mountainous country, with 95% or more of its land classified as rough grazing, mainly for sheep

hillside *noun* the sloping side of a hill

hinterland *noun* an area of land lying behind the shore of the sea or of a river

histaminic *adjective* referring to histamine

histo- *prefix* biological tissue

histochemistry *noun* the study of the chemical constituents of cells and tissues and their function and distribution

histology *noun* the study of the anatomy of tissue cells and minute cellular structures, using a microscope after the cells have been stained

history *noun* **1.** the study of what happened in the past ○ *the history of science* **2.** a record of past events and experiences ○ *the history of the discovery of DNA* ○ *the life history of a frog*

hoar frost *noun* the frozen dew that forms on outside surfaces when the temperature falls below freezing point

hoe *noun* a garden implement, with a small sharp blade, used to break up the surface of soil or cut off weeds ■ *verb* to cultivate land with a hoe

Holarctic region *noun* a biogeographical region which includes the Nearctic, i.e. North America, and the Palaearctic, i.e. Europe, North Africa and North Asia

holiday home *noun* a house where a person only lives for part of the time, such as at weekends or during a holiday. Also called **second home**

holistic *adjective* referring to an approach that deals with a subject as a whole rather than looking at just one aspect

hollow *adjective* referring to an object with a space inside it ○ *hollow plant stems*

holophytic *adjective* referring to organisms such as plants that can make complex organic molecules by photosynthesis

holoplankton *plural noun* organisms which remain as plankton throughout their entire life cycle, e.g. algae

holozoic *adjective* referring to organisms such as animals that feed on other organisms or organic matter

home noun **1.** a place where a person or animal lives **2.** an environment or habitat

home consumption noun the eating, drinking or use of something in the home rather than in a public place ○ *Home consumption of alcohol has increased greatly over the last twenty years.*

Home Grown Cereals Authority noun full form of **HGCA**

homeo- prefix similar

homeostasis noun **1.** the tendency of a system to resist change and maintain itself in a state of equilibrium **2.** the process by which the functions and chemistry of a cell or organism are kept stable, even when external conditions vary greatly

homeotherm noun another spelling of **homoiotherm**

home range noun the area that an animal moves about in during its day-to-day activities (NOTE: Do not confuse with territory, which is a defended area and may be part or all of the home range.)

home zone noun a street or group of streets organised to be suitable for the needs of pedestrians and cyclists rather than motorists (NOTE: There are traffic-calming measure to encourage motorists to drive slowly and sometimes play areas or sitting areas.)

homing noun an animal's return to a specific site which is used for sleeping or breeding

hominid noun any member of the family of humans, especially humans early in their history

homo- prefix same. Compare **hetero-**

homoeo- prefix same as **homeo-**

homoiotherm, homoeotherm noun same as **endotherm**

homologous adjective having the same structural features

homologous pair noun a pair of chromosomes in a diploid organism that are structurally similar and have the same arrangement of genes, although they may carry different alleles (NOTE: One member of each pair is inherited from each parent.)

homosphere noun the zone of the Earth's atmosphere, including the troposphere, the stratosphere and the mesosphere, where the composition of the atmosphere remains relatively constant

homozygosity noun the state of being homozygous

homozygous adjective relating to a cell or organism that has two identical forms (**alleles**) of a gene

honeypot site noun a place that attracts large numbers of visitors because of its reputation or position

hookworm noun a parasitic worm in the intestine which holds onto the wall of the intestine with its teeth and lives on the blood and protein of the carrier

horizon noun **1.** the line where the sky and the ground appear to join **2.** a layer of soil which is of a different colour or texture from the rest

horizontal-axis wind turbine noun a wind turbine with two or three blades attached to a central hub that drives a generator and where the main shaft is parallel with the surface of the ground ○ *Horizontal-axis wind turbines are the most common form of wind turbine.*

hormonal adjective referring to hormones

hormone noun **1.** a substance produced in animals in one part of the body which has a particular effect in another part of the body **2.** a plant growth factor

horticultural adjective referring to horticulture

horticulture noun the cultivation of flowers, fruit and vegetables in gardens, nurseries or glasshouses, as a science, occupation or leisure activity. ◊ **botanical horticulture**

horticulturist noun a person who specialises in horticulture

host noun a plant or animal on which a parasite lives ■ adjective referring to a plant or animal on which a parasite lives

host–parasite interaction noun a relationship between a host and a parasite

hot adjective **1.** having a high temperature ○ *hot weather* ○ *hot water* **2.** dangerously radioactive (*informal*) **3.** electrically charged **4.** extremely infectious

hot desert noun a desert situated in the tropics, e.g. the Sahara Desert or the Arabian Desert. Also called **tropical desert**

hot rock noun a rock with a high temperature beneath the Earth's surface (NOTE: Hot rocks can be used to create geothermal energy by pumping down cold water and making use of the rising hot water which the rocks have heated.)

hotspot noun a place where background radiation is particularly high

house noun **1.** a building where a person lives **2.** a structure where animals or machinery are kept ○ *the reptile house* ○ *the engine house*

housefly *noun* a common fly living in houses, which can spread disease by laying its eggs in decaying meat and vegetables

household *noun* a group of people living together in a single home ■ *adjective* **1.** referring to or used in houses where people live ○ *household appliances such as fridges and ovens* **2.** familiar ○ *household knowledge*

household refuse, household waste *noun* same as **domestic refuse**

housing *noun* the buildings where people live

housing estate *noun* an area of land with buildings specially designed and constructed for residential use

HSE *abbr* Health and Safety Executive

human *adjective* referring to a man, woman or child ■ *noun* same as **human being** ○ *Most animals are afraid of humans.*

human being *noun* a man, woman or child

human capital *noun* the information and skills of individual people which form the basis of knowledge can be increased by training

human-caused *adjective* referring to a disaster or event which has been brought about by human beings

human ecology *noun* the study of communities of people, the place that they occupy in the natural world and the ways in which they adapt to or change the environment

human geography *noun* the study of the distribution of human populations with reference to their geographical environment

human-induced stress *noun* stress in animals caused by interactions with humans

humankind *noun* all human beings considered as a whole

human race *noun* same as **humankind**

human settlement *noun* a place such as a village or city where humans live

human timescale *noun* the time during which humans have existed on earth, i.e. several thousand years

humate *noun* a salt that is derived from humus

humid *adjective* relating to air that contains moisture vapour ○ *Decomposition of organic matter is rapid in hot and humid conditions.*

humidifier *noun* a device for making dry air moist, especially in air conditioning or heating systems

humidify *noun* to make something moist

humidity *noun* a measurement of how much water vapour is contained in the air

humification *noun* the breakdown of rotting organic waste to form humus

humify *verb* to break down rotting organic waste to form humus

humus *noun* **1.** the fibrous organic matter in soil, formed from decomposed plants and animal remains, which makes the soil dark and binds it together **2.** a dark organic residue left after sewage has been treated in sewage works

hunt *verb* to follow and kill wild animals for sport ■ *noun* **1.** an organised event during which a group of people and often dogs hunt a wild animal for sport ○ *a fox hunt* ○ *a deer hunt* **2.** *also* **Hunt** a group of people who regularly hunt together

hunter *noun* a person who follows and kills wild animals for sport ■ *plural noun* **hunters** people who kill wild animals for food. Compare **gatherers**

hunting *noun* the activity of following and killing wild animals for sport

hunting season *noun* the time of year when people hunt animals for sport

hunt saboteur *noun* a person who objects to hunting and tries to prevent hunts taking place

hurricane *noun* a tropical storm with extremely strong winds

husband *verb* to use a resource carefully

husbanding *noun* the activity of using a resource carefully ○ *a policy of husbanding scarce natural resources*

husbandry *noun* the activity of looking after farm animals and crops ○ *a new system of intensive cattle husbandry*

hybrid *noun* a new form of plant or animal resulting from a cross between organisms that have different genotypes ○ *high-yielding maize hybrids* ■ *adjective* being the result of a cross between organisms that have different genotypes

hybridisation, hybridization *noun* the production of hybrids

hybrid vigour *noun* same as **heterosis**

hydr- *prefix* same as **hydro-** (NOTE: used before vowels)

hydrarch *adjective* relating to the sequence of ecological stages that begins in a freshwater habitat such as a pond

hydraulic gradient *noun* the direction of ground water flow due to changes in the depth of the water table

hydric *adjective* referring to an environment that is wet. Compare **xeric**

hydro- *prefix* water

hydrocarbon *noun* a compound formed of hydrogen and carbon

COMMENT: Hydrocarbons are found in fossil fuels such as coal, oil, petroleum and natural gas. They form a large part of exhaust fumes from cars and contribute to the formation of smog. When released into the air from burning coal or oil they react in the sunlight with nitrogen dioxide to form ozone. Hydrocarbons are divided into aliphatic hydrocarbons (paraffins, acetylenes and olefins) and aromatic hydrocarbons (benzenes).

hydroelectric *adjective* relating to hydroelectricity ○ *The valley was flooded to construct the hydroelectric scheme.*

hydroelectricity *noun* the electricity produced by water power

hydroelectric power *noun* the electricity produced by using a flow of water to drive turbines. Also called **hydropower**

hydrofluorocarbon *noun* a chemical that is emitted as a by-product of industrial processes and contributes to global warming, although it does not damage the ozone layer. Abbr **HFC**

hydrogen *noun* a gaseous chemical element that combines with oxygen to form water, with other elements to form acids, and is present in all animal tissue (NOTE: Hydrogen is also used as a moderator to show the speed of neutrons in some nuclear reactors. The chemical symbol is **H**; the atomic number is **1** and the atomic weight is **1.01**.)

hydrogen carbonate *noun* a salt of carbonic acid in which one hydrogen atom has been replaced, usually by a metal. Also called **bicarbonate**

hydrogen cyanide *noun* a poisonous liquid or gas with a smell of almonds, which is found naturally in some plants such as cassava or almond nuts. Formula: HCN.

hydrograph *noun* a graph showing the level or flow of water in a river or lake

hydrography *noun* the science of measuring and charting rivers, lakes and seas

hydrological *adjective* referring to hydrology

hydrology *noun* the study of water, its composition and properties and in particular the place of water in the environment

hydrometer *noun* an instrument that measures the density of a liquid

hydromorphic soil *noun* waterlogged soil found in bogs and marshes

hydrophyte *noun* a plant that lives in water or in marshy conditions

hydroponics *noun* the practice of growing plants in a nutrient liquid with or without sand, vermiculite or other granular material

hydropower *noun* same as **hydroelectric power**

hydrosere *noun* a series of plant communities growing in water or in wet conditions. ◊ **clisere, lithosere, xerosere**

hydrosphere *noun* all the water on the Earth, in the atmosphere, the sea and on land

hydrostatic *adjective* referring to water that is not moving

hydrothermal *adjective* referring to water and heat under the Earth's crust

hydroxide *noun* a metallic compound containing inorganic OH- groups giving it basic properties

hygiene *noun* **1.** the state or practice of being clean and keeping healthy conditions **2.** the science of health

hygienic *adjective* referring to the state or practice of being clean ○ *hygienic conditions* ○ *Don't touch the food with dirty hands – it isn't hygienic.*

hygro- *prefix* wet

hygrometer *noun* an instrument used for the measurement of humidity ○ *The most common type of hygrometer is the wet and dry bulb thermometer arrangement.*

hygrometry *noun* the scientific measurement of humidity

hygroscope *noun* a device or substance which gives an indication of humidity, often by changing colour

hygroscopic *adjective* referring to a substance which absorbs moisture from the atmosphere

hyp- *prefix* same as **hypo-** (NOTE: used before vowels)

hyper- *prefix* over, above, higher or too much. Opposite **hypo-**

hyperaccumulate *verb* to take up and retain an unusually high concentration of metal from the environment

hyperactive *adjective* being unusually active and restless

hyperparasite *noun* a parasite which is a parasite on other parasites

hypersensitive *adjective* reacting more strongly than usual to a factor such as stress, an antigen, an event or a disease agent

hypersensitivity *noun* a condition in which an organism reacts unusually strongly to a factor such as stress, an antigen, an event or a disease agent

hypertonic *adjective* referring to a solution with a higher osmotic pressure than that of another solution to which it is compared

hypha *noun* a long thin structure containing cytoplasm that is part of the network forming the vegetative body of a fungus (NOTE: The plural is **hyphae**.)

hypo- *prefix* under, less, too little or too small. Opposite **hyper-**

hypogeal *adjective* occurring or developing below ground. Compare **epigeal**

hypolimnion *noun* the lowest layer of water in a lake, which is cold and stationary and contains less oxygen than upper layers. ◊ **epilimnion, metalimnion**

hypothesis *noun* a suggestion that something may account for observed facts, though without proof, used as a basis for reasoning (NOTE: The plural is **hypotheses**.)

hypotonic *adjective* referring to a solution with lower osmotic pressure than that of another solution to which it is compared

hypoxia *noun* the depletion of oxygen in water caused by too great a supply of nutrients stimulating the growth of algae which use large amounts of oxygen as they decompose

hypoxic water *noun* water containing very little oxygen

Hz *abbr* hertz

I *symbol* iodine

IAEA *abbr* International Atomic Energy Authority

ice *noun* frozen water

COMMENT: Ice is formed when water freezes at 0°C. Ice is less dense than water and so floats. Because the ice in the polar ice caps is very thick and has been formed over many thousands of years, scientists are able to discover information about the climate over a very long period of time by examining core samples obtained by drilling into the ice.

Ice Age *noun* a long period of time when Earth's temperature was cool and large areas of the surface were covered with ice

iceberg *noun* a very large block of ice floating in the sea, formed when ice breaks away from an Arctic glacier or ice sheet

ice cap *noun* same as **polar ice cap**

ice floe *noun* a block of ice floating in the sea

ice sheet *noun* a large area of thick ice in the north or south polar regions

ice shelf *noun* an outer margin of an ice cap or ice sheet that extends into and over the sea

-icide *suffix* substance which destroys a particular organism

ICRP *abbr* International Commission on Radiological Protection

identical *adjective* exactly the same as something else

identification *noun* the action or process of recognising or establishing the nature of something ○ *keys for the identification of plants* ○ *the identification of our priorities*

identify *verb* **1.** to recognise somebody or something as different from somebody or something else ○ *The team has identified a new species.* **2.** to understand the nature of something ○ *We soon identified the problem.*

igneous *adjective* referring to rock such as basalt and granite, formed from molten lava. ◊ **metamorphic, sedimentary**

illegal *adjective* referring to an action not permitted by the criminal law

illegally *adverb* in a way that is not according to the law ○ *The company was accused of illegally felling protected forest.*

illuviation *noun* the movement of particles and chemicals from the topsoil into the subsoil

imago *noun* an insect in the final adult stage after metamorphosis

imbalance *noun* a situation where the balance between a set of things is unequal

○ Lack of vitamins A and E creates hormonal imbalances in farm animals.

imbricate *adjective* on top of and partially covering something

immature *adjective* referring to an organism or part that is still developing *○ an immature duck ○ an immature fruit*

immigrant species *noun* a species that migrates into or is introduced into an ecosystem, deliberately or accidentally

immigration *noun* the movement of an individual into a new area. Opposite **emigration**

immune *adjective* referring to a person, other animal or plant that is not affected by a specific microorganism *○ This barley strain is not immune to the virus.*

immunisation *noun* the production of immunity to a specific disease, either by injecting an antiserum or by giving an individual the disease in such a small dose that the body does not develop the disease, but produces antibodies to counteract it

immunity *noun* **1.** the natural or acquired ability of a person or other animal to resist a microorganism and the disease it causes *○ The vaccine gives immunity to tuberculosis.* **2.** the ability of a plant to resist disease through a protective covering on leaves, through the formation of protoplasts or through the development of inactive forms of viruses

immunological *adjective* referring to immunology

immunological response *noun* the response of an animal to an attack by parasites by the production of antibodies

immunology *noun* the study of immunity and immunisation

impact *noun* **1.** a collision of one object against another **2.** the effect that something or someone has

impact assessment *noun* an evaluation of the effect upon the environment of an activity such as a large construction programme or the draining of marshes. Also called **impact study**

impacted area *noun* an area of land affected by something such as a large-scale building project

impact study *noun* same as **impact assessment**

impair *verb* to cause something to become less effective *○ An unfortunate legacy of past contamination still impairs the ecosystem.*

impairment *noun* **1.** the inability of something to function effectively **2.** the

process of damaging something so that it does not function effectively

imperial unit *noun* a unit in a system measuring weight, distance and volume in pounds, yards and gallons and their subunits, now generally replaced by SI units

impermeable *adjective* **1.** referring to a substance which does not allow a liquid or gas to pass through *○ rocks which are impermeable to water* **2.** referring to a membrane which allows a liquid to pass through, but not solid particles suspended in the liquid

impervious *adjective* not allowing a liquid to enter

implementation *noun* the process of carrying out a plan *○ the rapid implementation of flood defence plans*

implication *noun* **1.** a suggestion rather than a direct statement *○ There was an implication that the method was unsound.* **2.** the effect that one thing has on another *○ The recent cuts in funding carry serious implications for research.*

import *verb* **1.** to bring something into a country from abroad **2.** to introduce new things from elsewhere ■ *noun* **1.** the action of bringing something into a country from abroad **2.** something brought into a country from abroad

Important Plant Area *noun* a natural or semi-natural site supporting an exceptionally rich range of plants or populations of species that are of concern, or is a threatened habitat. Abbr **IPA**

impoundment *noun* a body of water or sludge confined by a barrier such as a dam, dyke or floodgate

impoverish *verb* to reduce the quality of something □ **to impoverish the soil** to make soil less fertile *○ Overcultivation has impoverished the soil.*

impoverished *adjective* referring to something with reduced quality *○ If impoverished soil is left fallow for some years, nutrients may build up in the soil again.*

impoverishment *noun* a reduction in quality

impregnate *verb* **1.** to fill something with a substance by passing it inside through the outer surface *○ Fruits on sale may be impregnated with pesticides even if they have been washed. ○ They impregnated the wooden posts with creosote.* **2.** to fertilise a female, by introducing male spermatozoa into the female's body so that they fuse with the female's ova

imprint *verb* (*of young animals*) to learn from a source, usually the mother, by imitation at a very early age, usually occurring during a very brief period such as the first few hours after a bird has hatched

improvement grant *noun* a grant available to improve the standard of a building or an area. Grants are available for a variety of purposes, such as putting in domestic drainage and bathrooms, the eradication of bracken on pasture land, or providing a water supply to fields.

impulse *noun* **1.** a force of short duration **2.** a sudden strong feeling

impulse turbine *noun* a turbine where jets of water are directed at bucket-shaped blades which catch the water

impulsive *adjective* **1.** propelling or having the power to propel **2.** done suddenly

impure *adjective* not pure

impurity *plural noun* a substance that makes another substance not pure or clean ○ *impurities in drinking water* (NOTE: The plural is **impurities**.)

in. *abbr* inch

inactivate *verb* to make something unable to act ○ *The ultraviolet component of sunlight inactivates some herbicides.*

inactive *adjective* **1.** not doing anything **2.** (*of a volcano*) not erupting or likely to erupt, though not necessarily extinct **3.** (*of a chemical*) not reacting with other substances **4.** (*of a disease*) not producing symptoms **5.** biologically inert

inactivity *noun* the state of not being active

inbred *adjective* resulting from inbreeding

inbreeding *noun* the process of mating or crossing between closely related individuals, leading to a reduction in variation. Compare **outbreeding** (NOTE: Inbreeding as a result of self-fertilisation occurs naturally in many plants)

inbreeding depression *noun* a reduction in variation and vigour arising in an outbreeding population that is repeatedly inbred. Compare **heterosis**

incapacity *noun* not having the necessary power to do something

incentive *noun* something which encourages someone to do something

incentive-based regulation *noun* the use of official measures to affect the economic behaviour of companies and households to achieve environmental goals ○ *Emission taxes are a form of incentive-based regulation.*

inch *noun* a British Imperial System unit of length, also used in the USA, equal to 25.4 millimetres or 2.54 centimetres or 1/12 of a foot. Abbr **in.** (NOTE: The plural is **inches**.)

incidence *noun* the frequency of occurrence of something ○ *the incidence of flooding*

incident *noun* an event or happening which interrupts usual activities □ **without incident** without any problems occurring ○ *The research review passed without incident.*

incinerate *verb* to burn a substance such as waste

incineration *noun* the burning of a substance such as waste ○ *Uncontrolled incineration can contribute to atmospheric pollution.* ○ *Controlled incineration of waste is an effective method of disposal.*

incineration ash *noun* a powder left after a substance has been burnt

incineration plant *noun* an industrial site which has furnaces for burning waste

incinerator *noun* a device in which a substance such as waste is burnt

incipient *adjective* in the early stages of development

incipient lethal level *noun* the concentration of toxic substances at which 50% of affected organisms will die

include *verb* to add as a part with others ○ *Please include full bibliographical details in your report.*

inclusion *noun* the state of having or an act of adding something as a part ○ *the inclusion of checks at each stage*

inclusive fitness *noun* the sum of an organism's Darwinian fitness with the fitness of its relatives

incompatibility *noun* the state of being incompatible

incompatible *adjective* **1.** having basic differences that prevent effective joint working ○ *Our ideas were incompatible with their outline plans.* **2.** unable to cross-fertilize and produce offspring

increase *noun* the act or an instance of becoming greater or more ○ *Decreasing engine rpm results in an increase in the rate of descent.* Opposite **reduction** ■ *verb* to become greater or more or make something greater or more ○ *As you increase in height, the countryside below you appears to flatten out.* ○ *Efforts are being made to increase productivity.* Opposite **reduce** ▶ opposite (all senses) **decrease**

incubate *verb* **1.** to keep eggs warm until the young birds come out, either by an adult bird sitting on them or in an incubator **2.** to keep microorganisms at a temperature that promotes their growth

incubation *noun* **1.** the process of keeping eggs warm until the young birds come out, either by an adult bird sitting on them or by artificial means **2.** the process of keeping microorganisms at a temperature that matures their growth

incubator *noun* a container that keeps a constant temperature and controls other environmental conditions (NOTE: Incubators are used for allowing premature babies to grow, hen's eggs to hatch, or microorganisms to develop.)

indefinite *adjective* without a clear end or purpose ○ *an indefinite period* ○ *indefinite plans*

indehiscent *adjective* referring to seed pods, fruit or capsules that do not open to release seeds when ripe. Compare **dehiscent**

indentation *noun* a gap in the edge of something ○ *The indentations of the leaves were typical of the species.*

independent *adjective* free from the influence or effects of other people or things ○ *an independent existence*

indeterminate waste *noun* waste which is more radioactive than low-level waste, but not as dangerous as high-level waste

indicator *noun* **1.** something which shows the state of something else **2.** a substance which shows that another substance is present **3.** an organism whose presence or absence in an environment indicates conditions such as oxygen level or the presence of a contaminating substance ○ *Lichens act as indicators for atmospheric pollution.* Also called **indicator organism**

indicator organism *noun* same as **indicator**

indicator species *noun* a species which is very sensitive to particular changes in the environment and can show that environmental changes are taking place

indigenous *adjective* native to a place ○ *There are six indigenous species of monkey on the island.* ○ *Bluebells are indigenous to the British Isles.*

individual *noun* a single organism or item considered as one rather than as a member of a group

individual variation *noun* the range of differences found between individuals within a population

indoor air pollution *noun* the pollution inside a building, caused by something such as smoke or carbon monoxide

indoor air quality *noun* the condition of the air inside buildings, including the extent of pollution caused by smoking, dust, mites, mould spores, radon, as well as gases and chemicals from materials and appliances

induce *verb* to cause something to happen ○ *an animal induced to live in the reserve*

inductive reasoning *noun* the drawing of a general conclusion based on a limited set of observations. Compare **deductive reasoning**

indumentum *noun* a covering of hairs on plant leaves or stems, or of hairs or feathers on an animal

industrial *adjective* referring to industries or factories

industrial crop *noun* a crop grown for purposes other than food, e.g. flax grown for fibre

industrial dereliction *noun* the ugly and neglected condition of a landscape or environment that has been damaged by industrial processes

industrial development *noun* the planning of new industries and the construction of new factories and production facilities

industrial effluent *noun* the liquid waste produced by industrial processes. Also called **industrial sewage**

industrial estate *noun* an area of land with buildings specially designed and constructed for light industries

industrialisation, industrialization *noun* the process of developing industry in a country

industrialise, industrialize *verb* to develop industry in a country, by building factories and encouraging new processes and methods of production

industrialist *noun* a person who owns or manages an industrial business

industrial melanism *noun* the increase in the numbers of animals such as moths with dark coloration in places where industries create a lot of black smoke, causing discoloration of surfaces and allowing predators to see and feed on lighter-coloured individuals more easily

industrial park *noun* same as **industrial estate**

industrial sewage *noun* same as **industrial effluent**

industrial waste *noun* the waste produced by industrial processes. Compare **post-consumer waste**

industry *noun* the factories, companies or processes involved in the manufacturing of products

inert *adjective* referring to a chemical substance or gas that does not react with other chemicals

inert gas *noun* same as **noble gas** ○ *Inert gases, dust, smoke, salt, volcanic ash, oxygen and nitrogen together constitute 99% of the atmosphere.*

infect *verb* **1.** (*of an organism*) to enter a host organism and cause disease ○ *The new strain has infected many people and the disease is spreading fast.* ○ *All these plants have been infected by a virus.* **2.** to contaminate something with a microorganism that causes disease

infection *noun* **1.** the process of a microorganism entering a host organism and causing disease ○ *As a carrier he was spreading infection to other people in the office.* **2.** a disease caused by a microorganism ○ *West Nile fever is a virus infection transmitted by mosquitoes.* ○ *Coral spot is a fungal infection that affects woody plants.*

infectious *adjective* referring to a disease that is caused by microorganisms and can be transmitted to other individuals by direct means ○ *This strain of flu is highly infectious.* Compare **contagious**

infective *adjective* referring to a disease caused by a microorganism, which can be caught from another person but which cannot always be directly transmitted

infectivity *noun* the state of being infective

inference *noun* a deduction of results from data according to specific rules

infertile *adjective* **1.** referring to any organism that is not able to reproduce or produce offspring **2.** referring to trees and plants that are not able to produce fruit or seeds **3.** referring to soil that is not able to produce good crops

infertility *noun* the inability to reproduce or have offspring

infest *verb* (*of pests*) to be present somewhere in large numbers ○ *Pine forests are infested with these beetles.* ○ *Plants that have been infested should be dug up and burnt.*

infestation *noun* the presence of large numbers of pests ○ *The crop showed a serious infestation of greenfly.*

infiltration *noun* the passing of water into the soil or into a drainage system

infiltration water *noun* the water which passes into the soil or into a drainage system

inflammable *adjective* easily set on fire ○ *Petrol is an inflammable liquid.* Opposite **non-flammable** (NOTE: **Flammable** and **inflammable** mean the same thing. To avoid confusion, it is recommended to use **flammable**.)

inflate *verb* to blow air into something and thereby increase its size ○ *A sharp pull on the cord will discharge the gas bottle and inflate the life jacket.* Opposite **deflate**

inflorescence *noun* a flower or a group of flowers on a stem

inflow *noun* the action of flowing in ○ *an inflow of effluent into a river*

influent *noun* **1.** a stream or river flowing into a larger river **2.** an organism which has an important effect on the balance of its community

infrared radiation *noun* long invisible rays, below the visible red end of the colour spectrum, which form part of the warming radiation which the Earth receives from the Sun

infrared rays *plural noun* ♦ **infrared radiation**

infrastructure *noun* **1.** the basic framework of a system or organisation **2.** the basic facilities and systems of a country or city, e.g. roads, pipelines, electricity and telecommunications networks, schools or hospitals

ingest *verb* to take in or absorb food

ingestion *noun* the process of taking in or absorbing food

inhabit *verb* to live in a place

inhabitant *noun* an animal or plant which lives or grows in a place

inherit *verb* to receive a genetically controlled characteristic from a parent ○ *Flower colour is inherited.*

inheritance *noun* the transfer of genetically controlled characteristics from parent to offspring

inhibit *verb* to prevent or limit the effect of something ○ *Cloud cover inhibits cooling of the Earth's surface at night.*

inhibition *noun* the prevention or limitation of the effect of something ○ *Fuel contains chemicals for the inhibition of fungal growth.*

inject *verb* **1.** to force or drive a fluid into something **2.** to inject a liquid into a body using a syringe **3.** to introduce something new or stimulating

injection *noun* **1.** the forcing of fluid into something **2.** the act of injecting a liquid into a body using a syringe **3.** the introduction of something new or stimulating

inland *adjective* not near a sea coast

inland water *noun* a body of water away from a sea coast, e.g. a river, canal or lake

inlet *noun* **1.** an opening which allows an intake of something ○ *an air inlet* **2.** the mouth of a small river in a coast or lake

inner *adjective* being further inside or further towards the centre of something ○ *the inner ear*

inner city *noun* a part of a city at or near the centre, especially an area where there is high-density housing and sometimes a poorly maintained environment

innovative technology *noun* new or inventive methods to treat hazardous waste, prevent pollution or conserve energy

inoculate *verb* **1.** to introduce vaccine into a body in order to stimulate the production of antibodies to a particular organism, giving rise to immunity to the disease ○ *The baby was inoculated against diphtheria.* **2.** to introduce a microorganism into a plant or a growth medium

inorganic *adjective* **1.** referring to a substance which does not come from an animal or a plant ○ *Inorganic substances include acids, alkalis and metals.* **2.** referring to a substance that does not contain carbon

inorganic acid *noun* an acid which comes from a mineral

inorganic fertiliser *noun* an artificially synthesised fertiliser

inorganic matter *noun* a substance which does not contain carbon

inorganic pesticide *noun* a pesticide made from inorganic substances such as sulfur

inorganic waste *noun* substances such as glass, metals, dust or synthetic products disposed of as waste. Compare **organic waste**

input *noun* something such as energy, electrical power, fertilisers or information, put into a system to achieve a specific result ○ *inputs and outputs of nutrients to ecosystems*

inquiry *noun* another spelling of **enquiry** (NOTE: The plural is **inquiries**.)

insanitary *adjective* unhygienic ○ *Cholera spread rapidly because of the insanitary conditions in the town.*

insect *noun* a small animal with six legs and a body in three parts

insect-borne *adjective* referring to infection which is carried and transmitted by insects ○ *insect-borne viruses* ○ *Malaria is an insect-borne disease.*

insecticide *noun* a substance which is used to kill insects

insectivore *noun* an animal that feeds mainly on insects

insectivorous *adjective* referring to an animal or plant that feeds mainly on insects (NOTE: Pitcher plants and sundews are insectivorous.)

inselberg *noun* a steep-sided isolated hill that stands above nearby hills

inshore *adjective* referring to an area of sea near the coast

inshore waters *plural noun* the parts of the sea that are near a coast

in-situ *adjective, adverb* referring to the study, maintenance or conservation of an organism within its natural surroundings. Compare **ex-situ**

insolation *noun* the radiation from the Sun

insoluble *adjective* referring to a substance that cannot be dissolved in liquid

inspect *verb* to look at something closely to see if it is in the correct condition or if there are problems

inspection *noun* a careful check to see if something is in the correct condition or if there are problems ○ *The officials have carried out an inspection of the factory to see if waste is being properly managed.*

installation *noun* the act of putting equipment or devices into the position and condition in which they will be used ○ *the installation of an irrigation system*

instar *noun* a developmental stage of insects and other arthropods between two moults

instinct *noun* a pattern of behaviour particular to a species and developed in response to priorities such as survival and reproduction

insulate *verb* to prevent the passing of heat, cold or sound into or out of an area

insulation *noun* the act of preventing the passing of heat, cold, sound or electricity from one area to another

insulation material *noun* material used to insulate something, especially a building

intake *noun* an opening through which a fluid is allowed into a container or tube

integrated crop management *noun* an approach to growing crops that combines traditional good farm husbandry with reduction in the use of agrochemicals and takes into consideration the impact of farming practices on the environment

integrated farm management, integrated farming *noun* an approach to farming that combines the best of traditional methods with modern technology, to achieve high productivity with a low environmental impact

integrated pest management *noun* an appropriate combination of different methods of pest control, involving good cultivation practices, use of chemical pesticides, resistant crop varieties and biological control. Abbr **IPM**

integrated pollution control, integrated pollution prevention and control *noun* an approach which looks at all inputs and outputs from a process that is likely to cause pollution and regulates other factors as well as emissions. Abbr **IPC, IPPC**

intensification *noun* **1.** the process of becoming stronger or greater **2.** the use of intensive farming methods ○ *Intensification of farming has contributed to soil erosion.* Compare **extensification**

intensify *verb* **1.** to become stronger or greater **2.** to use intensive farming methods

intensity *noun* the degree or strength of something ○ *high intensity of land use in a small country with a large population* ○ *These plants grow well in low light intensity.*

intensive *adjective* achieving maximum production from land or animals ○ *intensive agriculture*

intensive agriculture, intensive farming, intensive cultivation *noun* a method of farming in which as much use is made of the land as possible by growing crops close together, growing several crops in a year or using large amounts of fertiliser. Opposite **extensive agriculture**. Also called **productive agriculture**

intensive animal breeding *noun* a system of raising animals in which livestock are kept indoors and fed on concentrated foodstuffs, with frequent use of drugs to control the diseases which tend to occur under these conditions

intensively *adverb* using intensive farming methods

inter- *prefix* between

interaction *noun* a relationship between two or more organisms or things

interactive *adjective* referring to a process involving people reacting to and communicating with other people or situations ○ *an interactive display describing the process of river pollution*

interbreed *verb* **1.** to mate and have offspring **2.** to cross animals or plants with different characteristics to produce offspring with distinctive features. (NOTE: Individuals from the same species can interbreed, those from different species cannot.)

intercropping *noun* the growing of crops with different characteristics and requirements on the same area of land at the same time ○ *intercropping beans with maize*

interdependence *noun* a state of two or more organisms or processes depending on each other

interdependent *adjective* referring to organisms or things being dependent on each other

interest group *noun* a group of people who are all concerned about the same issue. They may try to influence the opinions of politicians, local officials and business people on this issue.

interfluve *noun* the area of land between two rivers

intergenerational equity *noun* the fairness of the distribution of the costs and benefits of an environmental policy when they are experienced by different generations

intergeneric *adjective* involving two or more genera

interglacial period, interglacial *noun* the period between two Ice Ages when the climate becomes warmer

intergovernmental *adjective* involving the governments of several countries

Intergovernmental Panel on Climate Change *noun* an international group of expert scientists who assess information on climate change

intermediate *adjective* referring to a state or a stage between two others

intermediate host *noun* a host on which a parasite lives for a time before passing on to another host

internal *adjective* on or from the inside of something. Opposite **external**

internal combustion engine *noun* a type of engine used in motor vehicles, where the fuel is a mixture of petrol and air burnt in a closed chamber to give energy to the pistons

international *adjective* referring to more than one country

International Atomic Energy Agency *noun* the agency of the United Nations Organization dealing with all aspects of nuclear energy. Abbr **IAEA**

International Commission on Radiological Protection *noun* a group of scientists who try to decide on worldwide safety standards for the nuclear industry by fixing a maximum allowable dose of radiation. Abbr **ICRP**

International Council of Chemical Associations *noun* a group of trade associations representing chemical manufacturers worldwide

International Whaling Commission *noun* an international body set up under an agreement signed in 1946 to control the commercial killing of whales

internode *noun* the part of a plant stem between two adjacent nodes

interpretation *noun* an explanation of the meaning or importance of something

intersexual selection *noun* the selection of a mate where an individual looks for special traits in the opposite sex

interspecific *adjective* involving two or more species

interspecific competition *noun* the competition between species for one or more of the same limited resources of food, sunlight, water, soil, nutrients or space. ◊ **fundamental niche**

intertidal *adjective* relating to land that is covered by the sea at high tide and exposed at low tide ○ *intertidal communities* Also called **littoral**

intertidal zone *noun* an area of sea water and shore between the high and low water marks ○ *seaweeds of the intertidal zone*

intertropical convergence zone *noun* the boundary between the trade winds and tropical air masses of the northern and southern hemispheres. Abbr **ITCZ**

intervention *noun* the act of making a change in a system

intra- *prefix* inside or within

intrasexual selection *noun* the selection of a mate where several individuals compete with each other

intraspecific *adjective* occurring within a species ○ *an intraspecific cross between two cultivars*

intraspecific competition *noun* competition from other members of the same species for the same resources of food, sunlight, water, soil, nutrients or space

intrinsic value *noun* the value placed on the inherent qualities of a species, as opposed to its value to humans

introduce *verb* **1.** to bring something into being or start to use something new ○ *The lab introduced a new rapid method of testing.* **2.** to bring something to a new place ○ *Several of the species of plant now common in Britain were introduced by the Romans.* ○ *Starlings were introduced to the USA in 1891.*

introduced species *noun* a species that has been brought to an area by humans and did not occur there naturally

introduction *noun* **1.** the process of bringing something into being or using something new ○ *the introduction of a new rapid testing method* ○ *The death rate from malaria was very high before the introduction of new anti-malarial techniques.* **2.** the bringing of something to a new place ○ *Before the introduction of grey squirrels, the red squirrel was widespread.* **3.** a plant or animal that has been brought to a new place ○ *It is not an indigenous species but a 19th-century introduction.*

introgression *noun* the transfer of genes from one species into the gene pool of another as a result of hybridisation

intrusion *noun* an area of rock which has pushed into other rocks

invade *verb* to arrive in an area in large unwanted numbers ○ *These introduced pests could cause serious problems if they invaded our marine environment.*

invasion *noun* the arrival of large numbers of unwanted organisms into an area ○ *an invasion of weeds*

invasive *adjective* referring to an organism that enters an area in large numbers, especially a non-native species that threatens an ecosystem, habitat or other species ○ *invasive weeds* ○ *Giant hogweed is a non-native invasive species in the British Isles.*

inventory *noun* a list of items existing in a place

inversion *noun* **1.** an atmospheric phenomenon in which cold air is nearer the ground than warm air ○ *Smog is smoke or pollution trapped on the surface by an inversion of temperature with little or no wind.* **2.** the act of turning something upside down ○ *Inversion of soil by ploughing buries weeds and weed seeds.*

invertebrate *noun* an animal that has no backbone. Compare **vertebrate** ■ *adjec-*

tive referring to animals that have no backbone ○ *marine invertebrate animals*

in vitro *adjective, adverb* occurring outside a living organism, in laboratory conditions ○ *in vitro experiments* ○ *The tissue was cultured in vitro.*

in vivo *adjective, adverb* occurring within or taking place on a living organism ○ *in vivo experiments* ○ *The experiments were carried out in vivo.*

involucre *noun* a ring of modified leaves (**bracts**) at the base of a flower or flower head

iodine *noun* a chemical element. It is essential to the body, especially to the functioning of the thyroid gland, and is found in seaweed. (NOTE: The chemical symbol is **I**; the atomic number is **53** and the atomic weight is **126.90**.)

iodise, iodize *verb* to treat or impregnate something with iodine

ion *noun* an atom or a group of atoms that has obtained an electric charge by gaining or losing one or more electrons (NOTE: Ions with a positive charge are called cations and those with a negative charge are anions.)

ion-exchange filter *noun* a water-softening device attached to a water supply to remove nitrates or calcium from the water

ionisation, ionization *noun* the production of atoms with electric charges

ionise, ionize *verb* to give an atom an electric charge

ioniser, ionizer *noun* a machine that increases the concentration of negative ions in the atmosphere of a room, so counteracting the effect of positive ions. Also called **negative ion generator**

ionising radiation *noun* the radiation that produces atoms with electrical charges as it passes through a medium, e.g. alpha particles or X-rays

ionosphere *noun* the part of the atmosphere 50km above the Earth's surface (NOTE: Because the strength of the Sun's radiation varies with latitude, the structure of the ionosphere varies over the surface of the Earth. It is composed of 70% nitrogen, 15% oxygen and 15% helium, in which atoms are ionised by solar radiation.)

COMMENT: The uppermost layer of Earth's atmosphere is where most of the atoms are ionised. Some 350 km above sea level, the ionosphere has high temperatures because high-energy solar photons are captured there, including those in X-ray wavelengths. This prevents radiation which would otherwise be fatal to human

and other life from reaching sea level, so that without the ionosphere any life on Earth would have evolved very differently. The ionosphere is also useful for communications and radar, since it is possible to bounce radio signals off it for transmission beyond the visible horizon.

IPA *abbr* Important Plant Area

IPC ⬧ **IPPC** ■ *abbr* integrated pollution control

IPCC *abbr* Intergovernmental Panel on Climate Change

IPM *abbr* integrated pest management

IPPC *abbr* Integrated Pollution Prevention and Control

iris *noun* a plant with coloured flowers and sword-shaped leaves. Genus: *Iris*.

Irish moss *noun* same as **carrageen**

iroko *noun* an African hardwood tree, formerly widely used but becoming rarer. Latin name: *Milicia excelsa*.

iron *noun* a metallic element. It is essential to biological life. (NOTE: The chemical symbol is **Fe**; the atomic number is **26** and atomic weight is **55.85**.)

iron oxide *noun* same as **ferric oxide**

iron pan *noun* a layer of deposition in podzol soils

iron pyrites *noun* same as **pyrite**

irradiance *noun* the amount of radiation received in a specific area

irradiate *verb* to subject something to radiation

irradiation *noun* **1.** the spread of something from a centre **2.** exposure to radiation, especially ionising radiation

irradiation dose *noun* the amount of radiation to which an organism is exposed

irreversibility *noun* the inability to change something back to its earlier state, resulting in its permanent loss

irreversible *adjective* referring to a process that cannot be turned back to its original state ○ *an irreversible change*

irrigate *verb* to supply water to land to allow plants to grow, by channels, pipes, sprays or other means

irrigation *noun* the process of supplying of water to land to allow plants to grow ○ *irrigation channels* ○ *New areas of land must be brought under irrigation to meet the rising demand for food.*

COMMENT: Irrigation can be carried out using sprinklers or by channelling water along small irrigation canals from reservoirs or rivers. Irrigation can cause salinisation of the soil, as the soil becomes waterlogged and salts rise to the surface. At the surface, the irrigated water rapidly evaporates, leaving the salts behind as a saline crust. Irrigation can also increase the spread of disease. Water insects are easily spread through irrigation canals and reservoirs.

irritability *noun* same as **sensitivity**

irritant *noun* a substance or object that can cause irritation (NOTE: An irritant can have an acute effect on respiration from a single high-level exposure, or chronic effects from repeated low-level exposures.)

island *noun* a piece of land surrounded by water, in a sea, river or lake

island biogeography *noun* a theory stating that the number of species on an island or other area results from a dynamic equilibrium between colonisation and extinction

iso- *prefix* equal

isobar *noun* a line on a map linking points which are of equal barometric pressure at a given time

isobaric chart *noun* a weather map showing the isobars at a given time

isohaline *noun* a line on a map linking areas of equal salt content

isohyet *noun* a line on a map linking points of equal rainfall

isolate *verb* **1.** to separate and keep objects or organisms apart from others ○ *isolated the sick animals in a separate enclosure* ○ *Organisms that are isolated may evolve into new species.* **2.** to separate a microorganism from its host or the material on which it grows ○ *Scientists have isolated the bacterium which lives in air-conditioning systems and causes legionnaires' disease.* ■ *noun* a pure culture of a microorganism

isolated *adjective* separate from others ○ *an isolated incident*

isolation *noun* a state or the process of being separated and kept apart from other objects or organisms

isoproturon *noun* a herbicide used on cereals that is found as a contaminant of surface water (NOTE: It is commonly used in the UK but it is under review for withdrawal from use in the European Union.)

isotach *noun* a line on a map linking points where the wind is blowing at the same speed

isotherm *noun* a line on a map linking points of equal temperature

isotope *noun* a form of a chemical element which has the same chemical properties as other forms, but a different atomic mass

isotropic *adjective* referring to something that has physical properties that do not differ according to direction

isthmus *noun* a narrow piece of land linking two larger areas of land

ITCZ *abbr* intertropical convergence zone

iteration *noun* a repetition

IUCN *noun* a union of 140 countries that generates scientific knowledge, advice and standards on environmental subjects and monitors the status of species, publishing findings in its Red Lists. Full form **IUCN - The World Conservation Union**

ivory *noun* a smooth whitish substance forming the tusks of animals such as elephants and walruses, formerly used to make piano keys and ornaments (NOTE: The ban on the trade in ivory was confirmed at the 50th Meeting (2004) of the Standing Committee of CITES (Convention on International Trade in Endangered Species of Wild Fauna and Flora) when it was declared that there would be no sale of ivory until further notice.)

JK

jet *noun* a strong fast stream of fluid forced out of an opening ○ *a jet of water from a pipe*

jet fuel *noun* same as **kerosene**

JNCC *abbr* Joint Nature Conservation Committee

join *noun* a place at which two or more things are connected

joint *noun* a place at which two bones are connected

Joint Implementation *noun* a set of agreements made between two or more nations under the Framework Convention on Climate Change to help reduce greenhouse gas emissions

Joint Nature Conservation Committee *noun* a UK government advisory body on conservation. Abbr **JNCC**

joule *noun* an SI unit of measurement of energy. Symbol **J**

journal *noun* a scientific publication

jungle *noun* a tropical rainforest (*informal*)

juvenile *noun* a young animal or plant ■ *adjective* referring to an animal, plant, organ or type of behaviour that is not yet adult ○ *The juvenile foliage of eucalyptus is different from its adult foliage.*

K *symbol* potassium

kaolin *noun* a fine white clay used for making china, for coating shiny paper and in medicines ○ *Spoil heaps from kaolin workings are bright white.* Also called **china clay**

karst *noun* ground typical of limestone country, with an uneven surface and holes and cracks due to weathering

katabatic wind *noun* a cold wind which blows downhill as the ground surface cools at night. Compare **anabatic wind**

katadromous *adjective* another spelling of **catadromous**

katadromy *noun* another spelling of **catadromy**

kelp *noun* a brown seaweed with large leathery fronds. It is a source of iodine and potash.

kelp forest *noun* a large area of kelp found in cold and temperate seawater, especially on the western coasts of continents

kelvin *noun* a base SI unit of measurement of thermodynamic temperature. Symbol **K** (NOTE: 0°C is equal to 273.15 K. Temperatures are shown in kelvin without a degree sign: *20 K*.)

kernel *noun* **1.** the soft edible part of a nut **2.** the seed and husk of a cereal grain

kerosene, kerosine *noun* a thin fuel oil made from petroleum. Also called **jet fuel**

ketose *noun* a simple sugar

key *noun* a set of questions to enable something to be identified or classified ○ *a key for identifying lichens*

keystone species *noun* a species that plays a significant role in helping to maintain the ecosystems that it is part of

kg *symbol* kilogram

kG *symbol* kilogray

khamsin *noun* a hot wind that brings dust storms in North Africa

kieselguhr *noun* same as **diatomaceous earth**

kill *verb* to make someone or something die ■ *noun* **1.** an act of making someone or something die ○ *Pollutants in water are one of the main causes of fish kills.* **2.** prey which has been killed ○ *The vultures surrounded the remains of the lion's kill.*

kill off *verb* to kill all the individual members of a species, usually one by one ○ *Dodos were killed off by 18th-century sailors.*

kiln *noun* a furnace used for making something such as pottery or bricks ○ *The smoke from the brick kilns was dispersed by the prevailing winds.*

kilo *noun* same as **kilogram**

kilo- *prefix* one thousand, 10^3. Symbol **K**

kilocalorie *noun* a unit of measurement of heat equal to 1000 calories (NOTE: In scientific use, the SI unit **joule** is now more usual. 1 calorie = 4.186 joules.)

kilogram *noun* the base unit of mass in the SI system, equal to 1000 grams or 2.2046 pounds. Symbol **kg**. Also called **kilo**

kilogray *noun* an SI unit of measurement of absorbed radiation equal to 1000 grays. Symbol **kG**

kilojoule *noun* an SI unit of measurement of energy or heat equal to 1000 joules. Symbol **kJ**

kilometre *noun* a measure of length equal to 1000 metres or 0.621 miles. Symbol **km** (NOTE: The US spelling is **kilometer**.)

kilowatt *noun* a unit of measurement of electricity equal to 1000 watts. Symbol **kW**

kinesis *noun* the movement of a cell or organism in response to the intensity of a stimulus rather than its direction

kinetic *adjective* referring to motion or something produced by motion

kinetics *noun* the scientific study of bodies in motion

kingdom *noun* the largest category in the classification of organisms ○ *The largest species in the animal kingdom is the whale.*

kJ *abbr* kilojoule

knock *verb* to make a loud noise as the mixture of petrol and air in a petrol engine explodes, caused when the mixture is not rich enough in petrol

knot *noun* **1.** a structure formed when several strands are joined together or a single strand is looped on itself **2.** a dark area in a piece of wood where a branch formerly grew

Köppen classification *noun* a standard classification of climate

COMMENT: The classification of climate types was drawn up by Wladimir Köppen in 1900 and has been much modified since then. The classification divides the Earth into five climate types: A, B, C, D and E, according to temperature and rainfall.

Kr *symbol* krypton

Krebs cycle *noun* a series of reactions in which pyruvic acid is broken down in the presence of oxygen to carbon dioxide. It is the final step in the oxidation of carbohydrates and fats, and occurs in mitochondria. Also called **citric acid cycle**

krill *noun* a mass of tiny shrimps that live in the cold seas of the Antarctic and form the basic diet of many sea animals including whales

krotovina *noun* an animal burrow that has been filled with organic or mineral material from another soil horizon

krummholz *noun* **1.** the stunted trees that grow just above the timberline on a mountain **2.** a high-altitude zone in which krummholz grows

krypton *noun* an inert gas found in very small quantities in the atmosphere (NOTE: The chemical symbol is **Kr**; the atomic number is **36** and atomic weight is **83.80**.)

K selection *noun* a process of natural selection that leads to a reduction in births when the population of a species approaches the maximum number that its environment can sustain

K strategy *noun* a form of reproduction in which a mother produces a few large offspring which need constant care and attention over a long period of time. Compare **R strategy**

kW *abbr* kilowatt

Kyoto Protocol *noun* an international agreement on strategies for coping with climate change signed in December 1997 by the United Nations Framework Convention on Climate Change (UNFCCC)

L

lab *noun* same as **laboratory** (*informal*) ○ *The samples have been returned by the lab.*

label *noun* a piece of information attached to something that gives information about it ○ *pesticide labels* ■ *verb* **1.** to identify something by using a label ○ *Parts are labelled with the manufacturer's name.* **2.** to add identifying words and numbers to a diagram ○ *There is a standard way of labelling the navigation vector.*

labelling *noun* the presentation of information about a product on a label ○ *regulations for food labelling*

laboratory *noun* a room with equipment for scientists to do experimental research and testing ○ *The samples of water have been sent to the laboratory for testing.* ■ *adjective* referring to laboratories ○ *The new drug has passed its laboratory tests.*

laboratory technique *noun* a method or skill needed to perform experiments in a laboratory

lactation *noun* the production of milk as food for young

lacustrine *adjective* referring to a lake or pond

lag *verb* **1.** to cover something with an insulating material to protect against cold or to stop heat escaping ○ *Boilers and pipes should be carefully lagged to prevent heat loss.* **2.** to be slower or not as advanced ○ *Public opinion sometimes lags behind scientific discoveries.* ■ *noun* a delay ○ *a time lag* ○ *a lag in supply*

lagging *noun* the material used to insulate pipes

lagoon *noun* a shallow part of the sea in the tropics, surrounded or almost surrounded by reefs. ◊ **saline lagoon, sewage lagoon**

lagoonal *adjective* referring to lagoons

lagooning *noun* the creation of artificial lakes for purifying sewage

lake *noun* **1.** a large area of fresh water surrounded by land **2.** a large quantity of liquid produce stored because of overproduction (*informal*) ○ *a wine lake* ○ *a milk lake* ◊ **mountain**

lake bloom *noun* a mass of algae which develops rapidly in a lake due to eutrophication

land *noun* the solid part of the Earth's surface □ **back to the land** encouragement given to people who once lived in the country and moved to urban areas to return to the countryside □ **land under cultivation** land which is being cultivated or which has crops growing on it ○ *The area under rice cultivation has grown steadily in the past 40–50 years.*

land burial *noun* same as **land disposal**

land clearance *noun* the removal of trees or undergrowth in preparation for ploughing or building

land disposal *noun* the act of depositing waste in a hole in the ground. Also called **land burial**

land erosion control *noun* a method of preventing the soil from being worn away by irrigation, planting or mulching

landfill *noun* **1.** the disposal of waste by putting it into holes in the ground and covering it with earth **2.** same as **landfill site**

landfill gas *noun* a gas produced by the decomposition of rubbish in a landfill site, e.g. methane

landfilling *noun* the practice of disposing of waste by putting it into holes in the ground and covering it with earth

landfill site *noun* an area of land where waste is put into holes in the ground and covered with earth ○ *The council has decided to use the old gravel pits as a landfill site.* ○ *Landfill sites can leak pollutants into the ground water.* ○ *Landfill sites, if properly constructed, can be used to provide gas for fuel.* Also called **landfill**

landfill tax *noun* a tax on every metric ton of waste put in a landfill site instead of being recycled that is paid by companies and local councils

landlocked *adjective* referring to a place that has no sea coast ○ *a landlocked country in central Africa*

land management *noun* the use and maintenance of land according to a set of principles for a particular purpose such as the cultivation of crops or recreational activities

land manager *noun* someone who is responsible for the condition of land, e.g. a farmer or landowner

landmass *noun* a large area of land ○ *the continental landmass of the USA*

landrace *noun* a local variety of plant or animal developed over many thousands of years by farmers selecting for favourable characteristics within a species

land reclamation, land restoration *noun* the process of bringing back into productive use a piece of land such as a site that was formerly used for an industrial process

Landsat *noun* a US satellite belonging to a set which scan the land surface of the Earth, particularly the vegetation cover

landscape *noun* the scenery, general shape, structure and features of the surface of an area of land

landscape assessment, landscape character assessment *noun* the analysis, description and classification of an area of land, noting the features that contribute to its special character and developing appropriate proposals for its future conservation and management

landscape design, landscape planning, landscaping *noun* a plan of how to lay out an artificial landscape, including where to plant trees and shrubs

landscape ecology *noun* the study of the ecology of an area and how it affects the landscape

landscape manager *noun* somebody such as a farmer or landowner who is responsible for the way land is used and looked after

landscape value *noun* the degree to which an area is seen as attractive and of benefit to society in general ○ *The landscape value of new woodlands is high in areas where loss of hedges and trees by disease or deliberate policy took place in the past.*

landslide, landslip *noun* a sudden fall of large amounts of soil and rocks down the side of a mountain or of waste matter down the side of a spoil heap

land use *noun* the way in which land is used for different purposes such as farming or recreation ○ *a survey of current land use*

lapse *noun* a short period of time which separates two events

lapse rate *noun* the rate at which temperature changes according to altitude

larch *noun* a deciduous European softwood tree that has cones. It is fast-growing and used as a timber crop. Genus: *Larix*.

large-scale *adjective* big in size or extensive in scope. Compare **small-scale**

larva *noun* the form of an insect or other animal in the stage of development after the egg has hatched but before the animal becomes adult (NOTE: The plural is **larvae**.)

larval *adjective* referring to larvae ○ *the larval stage*

latent *adjective* present but not yet developed

lateral *adjective* referring to the side ○ *lateral buds* ○ *Drift is lateral movement caused by wind.*

laterisation, laterization *noun* the process of weathering tropical soil into hard laterite

laterise, laterize *verb* to weather tropical soil into hard laterite

laterite *noun* a hard rock-like clay found in the tropics, formed when latosol dries out (NOTE: When tropical rainforests are cleared, the soil beneath rapidly turns to laterite as nutrients are leached out by rain and the land cannot be cultivated.)

lateritic *adjective* referring to soil that contains laterite

late successional plant *noun* a plant that grows slowly to a large size, tolerates shade and is competitive towards other plants, e.g. a hardwood tree (NOTE: Such trees form a **climax community**.)

latex *noun* a white fluid from a plant such as poppy, dandelion or rubber tree

latitude *noun* an angular distance north or south of the Earth's equator, measured in degrees, minutes and seconds, along a meridian ○ *Parallels of latitude are imaginary circles on the surface of the Earth, their planes being parallel to the plane of the equator.* □ **at a latitude of 46°N** at a position on the Earth's surface which is 46 degrees north of the equator

latosol *noun* a type of reddish soft soil found in tropical areas that is characterised by deep weathering and hydrous oxide material

launch *noun* the start of a planned activity ○ *the launch of their public awareness campaign* ■ *verb* to begin a planned activity, especially by announcing it publicly ○ *to launch a new research initiative*

lava *noun* molten rock and minerals which flow from an erupting volcano and solidify into various types of igneous rock

law *noun* **1.** a rule or set of rules by which a country is governed □ **under British, French, etc., law** according to British, French, etc., law **2.** a basic principle of science or mathematics

lawrencium *noun* a chemical element (NOTE: The chemical symbol is **Lr**; the atomic number is **103** and the atomic weight is **256**.)

layer *noun* **1.** a flat area of a substance under or over another area (NOTE: In geological formations, layers of rock are called **strata**; layers of soil are called **horizons**.) **2.** a stem of a plant which has made roots where it touches the soil ■ *verb* to propagate a plant by bending a stem down until it touches the soil and letting it form roots there

LC$_{50}$ *abbr* lethal concentration 50

LD$_{50}$ *abbr* lethal dose 50%

leach *verb* to be washed out of the soil by water ○ *Excess chemical fertilisers on the surface of the soil leach into rivers and cause pollution.* ○ *Nitrates have leached into ground water and contaminated the water supply.*

leachate *noun* **1.** a substance which is washed out of the soil **2.** a liquid which forms at the bottom of a landfill site

leaching *noun* the process by which a substance is washed out of the soil by water passing through it

lead^1 *noun* a very heavy soft metallic element (NOTE: The chemical symbol is **Pb**; the atomic number is **82** and the atomic weight is **207.20**.)

lead^2 *noun* an electrical wire or narrow cable ○ *A lead connects the monitor to the computer.*

lead-acid battery, lead-acid accumulator *noun* a type of battery consisting of lead and lead-oxide plates, surrounded by a sulfuric acid electrolyte

leaded petrol *noun* petrol to which a fuel additive such as tetraethyl lead has been added to prevent knocking

lead-free *adjective* referring to something such as paint or fuel which has no lead in it ○ *lead-free petrol* ○ *Lead-free fuel is used in most modern piston engines.*

lead poisoning *noun* poisoning caused by taking in lead salts

lead replacement petrol *noun* a lead-free petrol for compulsory use in vehicles that were designed to be used with leaded petrol, introduced as a way of improving air quality and protecting the environment

leaf *noun* a structure growing from a plant stem, with a stalk and a flat blade. It is usually green and carries out photosynthesis. (NOTE: A leaf stalk is called a **petiole**, and a leaf blade is called a **lamina**.)

LEAF *noun* an independent organisation that promotes better understanding of farming by the public and helps farmers improve the environment by combining the best traditional farming methods with modern technology. Full form **Linking Environment and Farming**

leaf cutting *noun* a piece of a leaf, root or stem cut from a living plant and put in soil where it will sprout

leaf litter *noun* dead leaves lying on the floor of a forest. Also called **litter**

leaf mould *noun* a soft fibrous material formed of decomposed leaves

leak *noun* an escape of liquid or gas from a sealed container ○ *a gas leak* ■ *verb* (of liquid or gas) to escape from a sealed container ○ *Fuel may leak from a fuel tank if the drain plug is not seated correctly.*

leakage *noun* the process of a gas or liquid leaking out of a container ○ *Any internal or external leakage of fuel will cause a reduction in the operating period.*

leak rate *noun* the speed at which a liquid or gas escapes from a sealed container

lean-burn engine *noun* a type of internal combustion engine adapted to use less fuel than other engines, and so release less carbon monoxide and nitrogen oxide into the atmosphere

LED *abbr* light-emitting diode

lee *noun* the side of something which is protected from the wind ○ *The trees in the lee of the hill grow better than those on the windward side.* □ **on the lee side** on the side away from the wind

leeward *adjective* protected from the wind

leg *noun* a part of the body with which a person or animal walks and stands

legionnaires' disease *noun* a bacterial disease similar to pneumonia (NOTE: The bacteria develop in warm, moist areas such as air-conditioning systems and are transmitted through droplets of moisture in the air, often affecting many people at once.)

legislation *noun* the laws by which a country is governed

legislative body *noun* a group of people who make laws for a country

legume *noun* a member of the plant family that produces seeds in pods, e.g. peas and beans. Family: Leguminosae.

COMMENT: There are many species of legume, including trees, and some are particularly valuable because they have root nodules that contain nitrogen-fixing bacteria. Such legumes have special value in maintaining soil fertility and are used in crop rotation. Peas, beans, clover and vetch are all legumes.

Leguminosae *noun* a family of plants including peas and beans, that produce seeds in pods

leguminous *adjective* referring to a legume

leguminous plant *noun* a plant that is a legume

leisure *noun* free time that can be used for relaxation, entertainment or sport

leisure centre *noun* a place that provides equipment and resources for activities such as swimming or sport

leisure facilities *plural noun* equipment and resources such as sports centres, swimming pools, parks or cinemas which can be used during free time

leisure visitor *noun* someone who visits a place for pleasure ○ *The number of leisure visitors to the area has increased.*

lek *noun* a small territory established by a male for breeding purposes

lentic *adjective* referring to stagnant water

Lepidoptera *noun* an order of insects that includes butterflies and moths

lessen *verb* to make something less or to become less ○ *Clean filters lessen the possibility of blockage.*

lethal *adjective* causing death ○ *These fumes are lethal if inhaled.*

lethal concentration 50 *noun* the concentration of a pollutant or effluent at which 50% of the test organisms die. Abbr **LC$_{50}$**

lethal dose 50% *noun* the dose of a substance which will kill half the organisms which absorb it. Abbr **LD$_{50}$**

LEV *abbr* low-emission vehicle

levee *noun* (*in the USA*) an embankment built up along the bank of a river to prevent flooding

level *adjective* having a flat, smooth surface ■ *noun* a relative amount, intensity or concentration ○ *an unsafe level of contamination* ○ *reduced noise levels* ■ *verb* **1.** to make something become flat ○ *levelling the ground* **2.** to knock down and destroy something ○ *The developers levelled the derelict buildings.*

ley *noun* a field in which crops are grown in rotation with periods when the field is sown with grass for pasture (NOTE: Leys are an essential part of organic farming.)

LH2 *abbr* liquid hydrogen

Li *symbol* lithium

liana *noun* a climbing plant found in tropical rainforests

lias *noun* a type of rock formation consisting of shale and limestone

lice plural of **louse**

lichen *noun* a complex of two organisms growing in symbiosis, a fungus providing the outer shell and an alga or a cyanobacterium giving the organism its colour. Lichens are often found on the surface of stones or trunks of trees. (NOTE: As they are able to survive in cold or exposed conditions, they provide food for many arctic animals. Many lichens are very sensitive to pollution, especially sulfur dioxide, and act as indicators for atmospheric pollution.)

lidar *noun* a device that uses pulses of laser light to measure the distance between an aircraft and the ground, used to produce many reference points over an area of land and allow the mapping of large areas such as marshes and river networks to which access might be difficult. Full form **Light Detection and Ranging**

life *noun* **1.** the time from birth to death □ **adult life** the time period during which a person or other organism is an adult **2.** a state of active metabolism **3.** the state or experience of being alive. ○ *Their lives were put at risk by the contamination.* **3.** living organisms ○ *bird life* ○ *plant life*

life cycle *noun* **1.** all the changes an organism goes through between a specific stage in its development and the same stage in the next generation **2.** the process that a product undergoes from manufacture to disposal

life cycle analysis *noun* a review of a product from manufacture to final disposal in order to assess its full impact on the environment

life form *noun* a living thing, e.g. a plant, animal or microorganism

life span *noun* the length of time that an organism lives or a product is useful ○ *Some insects have a life span of only one day.*

lifestyle *noun* the way in which a person or group of people live their daily lives, including habits, behaviour and activities

lifestyle farmland buyer *noun* a purchaser of farmland for leisure or investment purposes rather than as a working farmer

life system *noun* a part of an ecosystem which is formed of a living organism and the parts of the environment which support it

lifetime *noun* **1.** the time during which an organism is alive ○ *Humans consume tons of sugar in a lifetime.* **2.** the approximate time it would take for the part of an atmospheric pollutant concentration created by humans to return to its natural level assuming emissions cease ○ *Average lifetimes range from about a week for products such as sulfate aerosols to more than a century for CFCs and carbon dioxide.* Also called **atmospheric lifetime 3.** a period of time during which a device is useful or not outdated ○ *This new computer has a four-year lifetime.*

life zone *noun* a place or area in which the type and number of organisms differ slightly from neighbouring areas because of variations in environmental conditions

light *noun* **1.** brightness produced by the Sun, the Moon or a lamp **2.** electromagnetic radiation which can be sensed by the eyes ■ *adjective* **1.** bright because the sun is shining ○ *a light room* ○ *At six o'clock in the morning it was just getting light.* **2.** without much weight ○ *Aluminium is a light metal.*

light-emitting diode *noun* a semiconductor diode that emits light when a current is applied, used in clock and calculator displays and as an indicator. Abbr **LED**

lightning *noun* a discharge of electricity between clouds and the Earth, seen as a bright flash and accompanied by the sound of thunder which is heard after a short delay

light pollution *noun* the effect of street or other artificial lighting which makes the sky red or orange at night, and so reduces the visibility of stars

light water reactor *noun* a nuclear reactor which uses ordinary water as a coolant. Abbr **LWR**

light wave *noun* **1.** a visible wave of electromagnetic radiation that travels from a source of light and is capable of stimulating the retina **2.** any wave of electromagnetic radiation, including ultraviolet and infrared

lignin *noun* the material in plant cell walls that makes plants woody and gives them rigidity and strength

lignite *noun* a type of soft coal with a low carbon content

limb *noun* **1.** a leg or arm □ **lower limbs** legs □ **upper limbs** arms **2.** a main branch of a tree

lime *noun* **1.** calcium oxide made from burnt limestone, used to spread on soil to reduce acidity and add calcium **2.** a hardwood tree. Genus: *Tilia.* **3.** a citrus fruit tree, with green fruit similar to, but smaller than, lemons. Latin name: *Citrus aurantifo-*

lia. ■ *verb* to treat acid soil by spreading lime on it

limestone *noun* a common sedimentary rock, formed of calcium minerals and often containing fossilised shells of sea animals. It is porous in its natural state and may form large caves by being weathered by water. It is used in agriculture and building. ○ *carboniferous limestone*

limestone pavement *noun* an area of outcrops of rock where the surface has been dissolved by water over millions of years into blocks, giving it the appearance of a street pavement. Some rare plants live on limestone pavements.

lime treatment *noun* same as **liming**

limewater *noun* a solution of calcium hydroxide in water

liming *noun* the spreading of lime on soil to reduce acidity and add calcium. Also called **lime treatment**

limit *noun* a furthest point or place beyond which you cannot go ○ *They have set a strict limit on the amount of fish which foreign fishing boats are allowed to catch.* ■ *verb* to set a limit on something ○ *The government has limited the number of barrels of oil to be extracted each day.*

limiting factor *noun* something that is essential for a chemical reaction to take place and which prevents the reaction or limits its rate of occurrence if it is not present ○ *Oxygen is a limiting factor for combustion.*

limiting factor principle *noun* a general rule that too much or too little of any abiotic factor can limit or prevent the growth of a population

limiting similarity *noun* the extent of niche differentiation required for species to coexist

limn- *prefix* fresh water

limnetic *adjective* referring to deep fresh water

limnic *adjective* referring to deposits in fresh water

limnology *noun* the study of river systems and their ecology

lindane *noun* an organochlorine pesticide. It is a persistent organic pollutant and has been banned for all agricultural uses in the European Union. Formula: $C_6H_6Cl_6$.

line *verb* to cover the inside of a container to prevent the contents escaping ○ *Landfill sites may be lined with nylon to prevent leaks of dangerous liquids.*

lined landfill *noun* a hole in the ground covered on the inside with nylon sheets to prevent leaks of dangerous liquids from waste deposited there

line of latitude *noun* an imaginary line running round the Earth, linking points at an equal distance from the equator

liner *noun* material used to line something, e.g. a sheet or bag of nylon or plastic

line squall *noun* a series of thunderstorms advancing in a line

link *noun* a connection between two things ○ *proved a link between smoking and lung cancer* ■ *verb* to be related to or associated with something ○ *Health is linked to diet* or *Health and diet are linked.*

linkage *noun* the process of two or more genes situated close together on a chromosome being inherited together

Linnaean system *noun* the scientific system of naming organisms devised by the Swedish scientist Carolus Linnaeus (1707–78). See Comment at **binomial classification** (NOTE: Carl von Linné is another form of his name.)

linoleic acid *noun* one of the two essential fatty acids which cannot be produced in the body by humans and has to be taken in from food such as vegetable oil. Formula: $C_{18}H_{32}O_2$.

linolenic acid *noun* one of the two essential fatty acids which cannot be produced in the body by humans and has to be taken in from food such as vegetable oil. Formula: $C_{25}H_{30}O_2$. (NOTE: Linolenic acid is also used in paints and in synthetic resin manufacture.)

lipid *noun* an organic compound belonging to a group of compounds that are not water-soluble and include animal fat, plant oils and waxes

liposoluble *adjective* referring to a substance that can be dissolved in fat

liquefaction *noun* the process of making a solid or gas into liquid

liquefied natural gas *noun* a natural gas, extracted from under ground, that is cooled and transported in containers. Abbr **LNG**

liquefied petroleum gas *noun* propane or butane or a combination of both produced by refining crude petroleum oil. Abbr **LPG** (NOTE: Liquefied petroleum gas is used for domestic heating and cooking and for powering vehicles.)

liquefy *verb* to make a gas into liquid or to become liquid

liquid *noun* a substance with a consistency like water ○ *Water is a liquid, ice is a solid.*

liquid fertiliser *noun* a solution of a solid fertiliser

liquid hydrogen *noun* an alternative fuel proposed for use in cars and aircraft. Abbr **LH2**

list *noun* a set of short pieces of information, each one given on a separate line ○ *a list of endangered species*

listeria *noun* a bacterium found in human and animal faeces, one species of which can cause meningitis if ingested in contaminated food. Genus: *Listeria.*

List of Chemicals of Concern *noun* a list of chemicals believed to be produced or used in the UK in substantial amounts which meet specific criteria for concern relating to risks to the environment and human health on the basis of information currently available. The list is drawn up by the UK Chemicals Stakeholder Forum and is intended for discussion and input.

liter *noun* US spelling of **litre**

lith- *prefix* stone

lithium *noun* a soft silvery metallic element, the lightest known metal, used in batteries (NOTE: The chemical symbol is **Li**; the atomic number is **3** and the atomic weight is **6.94**.)

lithosere *noun* a succession of communities growing on rock

lithosol *noun* soil which forms on the surface of rock, with no clearly different layers

lithosphere *noun* **1.** the Earth's solid surface, together with the molten interior above the core **2.** the solid surface of the Earth which lies above the asthenosphere

lithospheric *adjective* referring to the lithosphere

litmus *noun* a dye obtained from lichens which is used to make litmus paper

litmus paper *noun* paper treated with litmus, used in tests for acidity (NOTE: The paper becomes red when the pH falls below 7, indicating acid, and becomes blue when the pH is above 7, indicating alkaline.)

litre *noun* a measure of capacity equal to 1000cc or 1.76 pints. Symbol **l**, **L** (NOTE: It is the volume of one kilogram of water at 4°C.)

litter *noun* **1.** rubbish left by people **2.** a group of young mammals born to one mother at the same time ○ *The sow had a litter of ten piglets.* **3.** bedding for livestock ○ *Straw is the best type of litter.* **4.** same as **leaf litter** ■ *verb* **1.** to lie all over the place ○ *The valley is littered with huge boulders.* **2.** to leave rubbish in a place **3.** to give birth ○ *Bears litter in early spring.*

litter basket, litter bin *noun* a container in a public place in which rubbish is thrown away

littoral *adjective* **1.** referring to a coast **2.** same as **intertidal** ■ *noun* a coast

littoral zone *noun* **1.** an area of water at the edge of a lake where plants grow **2.** an area of the sea and shore between the high and low water marks

live *adjective* **1.** (*of an organism*) carrying out metabolism **2.** (*of cables*) carrying electricity **3.** (*of a volcano*) erupting from time to time **4.** in active use ■ *verb* to be or remain alive

live off *verb* to exist by eating something ○ *These fish live off the debris which sinks to the bottom of the lake.*

live on *verb* **1.** to exist by eating something ○ *Most apes live on berries and roots.* **2.** to exist on the surface of something ○ *Lice live on the skin of their host.*

livestock *noun* cattle and other farm animals which are reared to produce meat, milk or other products ○ *Livestock production has increased by 5%.*

living environment *noun* the part of the environment made up of living organisms

LLW *abbr* low-level waste

LNG *abbr* liquefied natural gas

load *noun* **1.** something that is loaded or transported **2.** the power output of an electrical generator or power plant **3.** the amount of something that a vehicle can carry or a machine can deal with at one time ■ *verb* **1.** to put something that is to be transported onto a vehicle or other means of transport **2.** to put something into a container or piece of equipment ready for use

load up *verb* same as **load**

loam *noun* dark soil, with medium-sized grains of sand, which crumbles easily and is very fertile

loamy *adjective* referring to soil that is dark, crumbly and fertile

lobby *noun* a group of people trying to influence the opinions of politicians, local officials and businessmen on a particular issue ○ *the road lobby* ○ *a green lobby group* ■ *verb* to ask someone such as a politician or local official to do something on somebody's behalf ○ *They lobbied their MP about the plan to build houses on the Green Belt.*

lobby group *noun* same as **lobby**

lobbyist *noun* a person who is paid by a lobby group to act on the group's behalf

lobe *noun* a rounded part of a divided leaf

local *adjective* referring to a particular area

local authority *noun* an official body that is responsible for public services in a specific area of a country

local government *noun* government of a specific area of a country by locally elected politicians

location *noun* **1.** a place where something can be found **2.** the process of finding where something is

loch *noun* (*in Scotland*) a lake

locomotion *noun* movement or travel from one place to another

locus *noun* the position of a gene on a chromosome (NOTE: The plural is **loci**.)

locust *noun* a flying insect which occurs in subtropical areas, flies in large groups and eats large amounts of vegetation

lode *noun* a deposit of metallic ore

loess *noun* a fine fertile soil formed of tiny clay and silt particles deposited by the wind

log *noun* **1.** a full record of a set of actions or events **2.** a large piece of wood cut from the trunk or from a main branch of a tree ■ *verb* **1.** to keep a full record of a set of actions or events **2.** to cut down trees for their wood as a commercial activity

logger *noun* a person whose job is to cut down trees

logging *noun* the commercial activity of cutting down trees

long-day plant *noun* a plant that flowers as the days get longer in the spring. Compare **short-day plant**

long-grass prairie *noun* an area in the east of the North American prairies where mainly varieties of tall grasses grow. Also called **tall-grass prairie**

longitude *noun* an angular distance on the Earth's surface, measured east or west from the prime meridian to the meridian passing through a position, expressed in degrees, minutes and seconds

COMMENT: Longitude is measured from Greenwich, just east of London, and, together with latitude, is used to indicate an exact position on the Earth's surface. Longitude is measured in degrees, minutes and seconds. The centre of London is latitude 51°30'N, longitude 0°5'W

longline *noun* a very long fishing line, which stretches for miles and is baited with many hooks (NOTE: Longlines are a problem in that they catch all types of fish, some of which are not of commercial interest, and even dolphins)

long-lived *adjective* referring to an animal or plant that lives for a long time

long-range *adjective* referring to a weather forecast that covers a period more than five days ahead

longshore *adjective* referring to a current which flows along the length of a shore

long-term *adjective* lasting for a long time ○ *the long-term effects of grazing*

long ton *noun* same as **ton 1**

looping *noun* a situation in which a column of smoke from a tall chimney is brought down to ground level by air currents and then rises again

loss *noun* the state of not having something any more, or of having less of something ○ *loss of control* ○ *the loss of natural habitats* ○ *loss of amenity value* ○ *hearing loss from noisy working conditions*

lotic *adjective* referring to ecological communities that live in water that flows quickly

Lotka-Volterra predator-prey model *noun* a simple mathematical model representing the interaction between predators and their prey

lough *noun* (*in Ireland*) a lake

louse *noun* a small wingless insect that sucks blood and lives on the skin as a parasite on animals and humans. There are several types, the commonest being body louse, crab louse and head louse. Some diseases can be transmitted by lice. Genus: *Pediculus*. (NOTE: The plural is **lice**.)

low *adjective* near the bottom or towards the bottom ■ *noun* same as **depression 1** ○ *A series of lows are crossing the North Atlantic towards Ireland.*

low-emission vehicle *noun* a vehicle which does not emit much pollution when compared to vehicles with conventional internal combustion engines. Abbr **LEV**

lower *verb* **1.** to put something in a lower position ○ *lower the barrier* **2.** to reduce something in amount or intensity ○ *lowered the temperature* ○ *lower the pressure*

lower plants *plural noun* organisms traditionally classed as plants but which do not have a vascular system, e.g. mosses

low-grade *adjective* not of high quality

low input farming, lower input farming *noun* a system of farming based on restricted use of chemical fertilisers, pesticides and herbicides

lowland *noun* an area of low-lying land as opposed to hills and mountains or highlands

low-level radioactive waste, low-level waste *noun* waste which is only slightly radioactive and does not cause problems for disposal

low production volume chemical *noun* a chemical of which 10–1000 tonnes is sold per year per manufacturer or importer

low tide *noun* the point when the sea level at the coast is lowest

low-waste technology *noun* efficient technology which produces little waste

LPG *abbr* liquefied petroleum gas

LPV chemical *abbr* low production volume chemical

Lr *symbol* lawrencium

lucerne *noun* a perennial, drought-resistant, leguminous plant that is rich in protein. It is mainly used either for green feed for animals or for hay or silage. Latin name: *Medicago sativa*. (NOTE: The US name is **alfalfa**.)

lumber *noun* (*in the USA and Canada*) trees which have been cut down

lumberjack *noun* (*in the USA and Canada*) a person whose job is to cut down trees

lunar *adjective* referring to the moon

lunar eclipse *noun* a situation when the Earth passes between the Sun and the Moon causing the shadow of the Earth to fall across the Moon, so cutting off its light. Compare **solar eclipse**

lunar phase *noun* a change in the appearance of the Moon as it moves from new to full and back again every 29 days (NOTE: The phases are: new moon, first quarter, full moon and last quarter.)

lung *noun* the organ of respiration of vertebrates that breathe air

lush *adjective* referring to vegetation which is thick and green ○ *Lush tropical vegetation rapidly covered the clearing.*

lux *noun* an SI unit of brightness of light shining on a surface. Symbol **lx**

LWR *abbr* light water reactor

lyophilise *verb* to preserve food by freezing it rapidly and drying in a vacuum

lysimeter *noun* a device used for measuring the rate of drainage of water through soil and the soluble particles removed in the process

lysis *noun* the destruction of a cell by disrupting its outer membrane, allowing the cell contents to escape

M

m *symbol* milli-

M *symbol* mega-

MAB *abbr* Man and the Biosphere Programme

MAC *abbr* maximum allowable concentration

mackerel sky *noun* a pattern of wavy cirrocumulus or altocumulus cloud with holes which looks like the body markings of mackerel fish

macro- *prefix* large. Opposite **micro-**

macrobenthos *noun* plants or animals living at the bottom of a lake or the sea whose shortest dimension is equal to or more than 0.5 mm

macrobiotic *adjective* referring to a vegetarian diet without artificial additives or preservatives ○ *a macrobiotic diet*

macrobiotics *noun* a dietary system based on vegetarian foods without artificial additives or preservatives, especially organically grown whole grains, fruit and vegetables

macroclimate *noun* the climate over a large area such as a region or country. ◊ **mesoclimate, microclimate**

macronutrient *noun* a nutrient that an organism uses in very large quantities, e.g. oxygen, carbon, hydrogen, nitrogen, phosphorus, potassium, calcium, magnesium and iron

macroparasite *noun* a parasite which lives on or inside the body of the host but does not multiply, e.g. a worm or insect larva

macrophyte *noun* a plant that is large enough to be studied without the aid of a microscope

macroplankton *plural noun* plankton of about 1 mm in length

macroscopic *adjective* referring to an object or organism that can be seen without the aid of a microscope

mad cow disease same as **BSE** (*informal*)

magma *noun* a molten substance in the Earth's mantle, which escapes as lava during volcanic eruptions and solidifies to form igneous rocks

magmatic *adjective* referring to magma

magnesium *noun* a light, silvery-white metallic element that burns with a brilliant white flame (NOTE: It is also found in green vegetables and is essential especially for the correct functioning of human muscles. The chemical symbol is **Mg**; the atomic number is **12** and the atomic weight is **24.31**.)

magnet *noun* an object that produces a magnetic field and attracts iron and steel

magnetic *adjective* referring to a magnet or a magnetic field

magnetic field *noun* an area round an object that is under the influence of its magnetic effect ○ *The Earth's magnetic field is concentrated round the two magnetic poles.*

magnetic pole *noun* one of the two poles of the Earth, near to but not identical with the geographical poles, which are the centres of the Earth's magnetic field and to which a compass points. Also called **geomagnetic pole**

magnetosphere *noun* a region surrounding the Earth, extending from about 500 to several thousand kilometres above the surface, in which charged particles are controlled by the Earth's magnetic field

magnification *noun* a measure of increase in size, especially in the apparent size of an image seen through a microscope

magnox power station *noun* a nuclear power station with a magnox reactor

COMMENT: The first magnox power station was built in the UK in 1956. The safety record has been very good, but magnox power stations are at the end of their commercial life and decommissioning began in 1990.

mahogany *noun* a tropical hardwood tree producing a dark timber, now becoming rare. Genus: especially: *Swietenia*.

main *adjective* the most important or principal

mains *noun* a system of pipes or cables which bring gas, water or electricity to a house ○ *mains gas* ○ *mains electricity*

maintain *verb* to keep something at the same level or standard

maintenance *noun* the action of keeping something at the same level or standard

maize *noun* a tall cereal crop grown in warm climates, that carries its grains on a large solid core (**cob**) of which there are only one or two per plant. Latin name: *Zea mays*. (NOTE: The US term is **corn**.)

make up water *noun* the water introduced into an irrigation or sewage system to replace water lost by leaking or evaporation

malaria *noun* a tropical disease caused by the parasite *Plasmodium* which enters the body after a bite from a mosquito

malarial *adjective* referring to malaria

malarious *adjective* referring to a region where malaria occurs frequently

malathion *noun* an organophosphorus insecticide used to kill aphids, mainly on flowers grown in glasshouses

male *adjective* **1.** referring to an animal that produces sperm **2.** referring to a flower that produces pollen, or a plant that produces such flowers ■ *noun* a male animal or plant

malignant melanoma *noun* a dark cancerous tumour that develops on the skin from a mole, caused by exposure to strong sunlight ○ *Cases of malignant melanoma could rise by between 5 and 7 per cent for each percentage decrease in ozone in the atmosphere.*

malnutrition *noun* **1.** the effect of an inadequate or unhealthy diet **2.** the state of not having enough to eat

mammal *noun* an animal that gives birth to live young, secretes milk to feed them, keeps a constant body temperature and is covered with hair. Class: Mammalia.

man *noun* **1.** an adult male human being **2.** all human beings considered in contrast to other animals ○ *Man is the only species to have made a global impact on the environment.* ◊ **humankind** (NOTE: This use of 'man' is now regarded as inappropriate in many non-technical contexts.)

manage *verb* **1.** to organise something or control the way in which something happens ○ *The department is in charge of managing land resources.* **2.** to succeed in doing something ○ *We managed to prevent further damage occurring.*

managed forest, **managed woodland** *noun* a wood or a forest producing commercial timber that is controlled by cutting down, coppicing or planting trees

management *noun* **1.** the organised use of resources or materials **2.** the people who control an organisation or business

manager *noun* a person who is in charge of an organisation or part of one

Man and the Biosphere Programme *noun* a programme of research and training organised by UNESCO to encourage the sensible use and conservation of the biosphere's resources and to improve relationships between people and their environment. Abbr **MAB**

mandible *noun* a biting mouthpart in insects and other invertebrates

manganese *noun* a metallic trace element. It is essential for biological life and is also used in making steel. (NOTE: The chemical symbol is **Mn**; the atomic number is **25** and the atomic weight is **54.94**.)

mangrove *noun* a salt-tolerant tropical shrub or tree that grows in areas such as river estuaries or tidal marshes that are covered by the sea at high tide

mangrove forest *noun* a group of salt-tolerant tropical trees and shrubs growing in an area that is covered by the sea at high tide

mangrove swamp *noun* an area that is covered by the sea at high tide where mangroves grow

manhole *noun* a hole in a roadway or pavement leading to a shaft down which an inspector can go to look at the sewers

man-made *adjective* referring to an object made or an event caused by human beings

mantle *noun* a layer of the interior of the Earth, between the solid crust and the core, formed of magma

manual *noun* a document or book containing instructions for doing something, especially carrying out a procedure or operating a machine ■ *adjective* carried out by someone without the help of a machine

manufacture *verb* **1.** to make a product using machines **2.** to produce a chemical naturally ○ *Ozone is constantly being manufactured and destroyed by natural processes in the atmosphere.*

manufacturer *noun* a person or company that produces machine-made products ○ *The company is a large manufacturer of farm machinery.*

manufacturing *noun* the production of machine-made products for sale

manure *noun* animal dung used as fertiliser (NOTE: In liquid form it is called 'slurry'.) ■ *verb* to spread animal dung on land as fertiliser

map *noun* **1.** a drawing that shows the location of geographical and urban features **2.** a diagram showing the position of something such as stars in the sky or genes on

MAP 132

chromosomes ■ *verb* to make a map of a place or area

MAP *abbr* Mediterranean Action Plan

maple *noun* a hardwood tree of northern temperate regions, some varieties of which produce sweet sap which is used for making sugar and syrup. Genus: *Acer.*

MAPPS model *noun* a global biological and geographical model that simulates the potential natural vegetation that will grow at any site in the world. Full form **mapped atmosphere–plant–soil model**

maquis *noun* in the Mediterranean area, shrubby vegetation, taller than garrigue, of evergreen shrubs and small trees with thick or spiny leaves

marble *noun* a form of limestone that has been metamorphosed, used especially in building and sculpture as it can be polished to give a flat shiny surface

margin *noun* **1.** the edge of a place or thing ○ *the eastern margin of the continent* ○ *unploughed strips at the margins of the fields* ○ *a leaf margin* **2.** an amount by which an amount or estimate may be different from the one expected without it causing a problem. Also called **margin of error** **3.** a blank space around a section of printed text

marginal *adjective* **1.** referring to areas of land such as field edges or banks beside roads which are at the edge of cultivated land **2.** referring to a plant which grows at the edge of two types of habitat ○ *marginal pond plants such as irises* **3.** referring to land of poor quality which results from bad physical conditions such as poor soil, high rainfall or steep slopes, and where farming is often difficult ○ *Cultivating marginal areas can lead to erosion.* **4.** situated in the spaces around a section of printed text ○ *marginal notes*

mariculture *noun* the breeding and keeping of sea fish or shellfish for food in seawater enclosures

marine *adjective* **1.** referring to the sea ○ *seals and other marine mammals* **2.** an animal or plant which lives in the sea

marine biocoenosis *noun* a varied community of organisms living in the sea

marine biology *noun* the scientific study of sea life

marine disposal *noun* the depositing of waste at sea

marine ecology *noun* the study of the relationship between organisms that live in the sea and their environment

marine environment *noun* the areas of the world usually covered by or containing sea water, including seas and oceans, river estuaries, and coasts and beaches

marine fauna *noun* the animals that live in the sea

marine flora *noun* the plants that live in the sea

marine habitat *noun* an area of sea coast, including features such as beaches, cliffs, salt marshes, dunes or mangrove swamps

marine park *noun* a natural park created on the bottom of the sea where visitors can go into observation chambers to look at the fish and plant life. Compare **oceanarium**

marine pollution *noun* the harmful effects of human activities such as disposal of waste into the sea on marine organisms and their environment, with resulting hazards to human food and health

maritime climate *noun* a climate that is modified by the influence of the sea, giving mild winters and warm summers, but with high rainfall

marked *adjective* clear and definite ○ *marked changes in climatic conditions*

marker *noun* same as **genetic marker**

market garden *noun* a place for the commercial cultivation of plants, usually vegetables, soft fruit, salad crops and flowers, found near a large urban centre which provides a steady outlet for the sale of its produce

marl *noun* a fine soil formed of a mixture of clay and lime, used for making bricks

MARPOL Convention *noun* the main international agreement for the prevention of pollution of the sea by ships, either accidentally or deliberately. Full form **Convention for the Prevention of Pollution from Ships**

marram grass *noun* a type of grass planted on sand dunes to prevent them being spread by the wind. Latin name: *Ammophila arenaria.*

MARS *noun* a computer network used by member countries of the EU and OECD for reporting and exchanging information on serious industrial accidents in a standard format. Full form **Major Accident Reporting System**

marsh *noun* an area of permanently wet land and the plants that grow on it (NOTE: Marshes may be fresh water or salt water and tidal or non-tidal. A marsh usually has a soil base, as opposed to a bog or fen, which is composed of peat.)

marsh gas *noun* same as **methane**

marshland *noun* land that is covered with marsh

marshy *adjective* referring to land that is permanently wet

marsupial *noun* a mammal with a pouch in which its young are carried, e.g. Australian kangaroos and wallabies or South American opossums (NOTE: Marsupials give birth to young at a much earlier stage of development than other mammals so that the young need to be protected in the mother's pouch for some months until they become able to look after themselves.)

mass *noun* **1.** a body of matter **2.** a large quantity or large number

mass extinction *noun* the disappearance of numerous species in a short period by a force of nature such as climate change or a volcanic eruption ○ *It has been suggested that the mass extinction of the dinosaurs 65 million years ago may have been caused by the impact of a comet or meteorite.*

mast *noun* **1.** a vertical pole for a flag or antenna ○ *Ice accretes on the leading edge of the detector mast.* **2.** the small hard fruits that have fallen from a beech tree

mate *noun* an animal that reproduces sexually with another ■ *verb* to reproduce sexually with another of same species

material *noun* **1.** a substance with a particular quality or used for a specific purpose ○ *waste material* ○ *construction materials* **2.** cloth

matter *noun* a physical substance ○ *organic matter*

maturation *noun* the process of becoming mature or fully developed

maturation lagoon, maturation pond *noun* a pond used in the final stages of sewage treatment

mature *adjective* referring to something that is fully developed ■ *verb* to become fully developed

maturing *adjective* referring to something that is in the process of becoming mature

maturity *noun* the state of being fully developed

Mauna Loa *noun* a volcano on the island of Hawaii where scientists have maintained the longest continuous collection of reliable daily atmospheric records

maximise, maximize *verb* to make something as large as possible. Opposite **minimise**

maximum *adjective* referring to the greatest possible ○ *maximum effect* ○ *The maximum capacity of the vehicle is 12.* Opposite **minimum**

maximum allowable concentration *noun* the largest amount of a pollutant with which workers are allowed to be in contact in their work environment. Abbr **MAC**

maximum–minimum thermometer *noun* a thermometer that shows the highest and lowest temperatures reached since it was last checked, as well as the current temperature

maximum permissible dose *noun* the highest amount of radiation to which a person may safely be exposed

maximum permissible level *noun* the highest amount of radiation that is allowed to be present in an environment

maximum residue level *noun* the maximum amount of a pesticide that can remain in crops or foodstuffs under European Union regulations. Abbr **MRL**

MCPA *noun* a herbicide that kills the most persistent broad-leaved weeds: nettle, buttercups, charlock, dock seedlings, plantains and thistles. Full form **2-methyl-4chlorophenoxy-acetic acid**

MCPP *abbr* mecoprop

meadow *noun* a field of grass and wild plants, sometimes grown for fodder. ◊ **water meadow**

mean *adjective* referring to an arithmetic mean ○ *mean daytime temperatures* ■ *noun* same as **arithmetic mean**

meander *noun* a large bend in the course of a river as it nears the sea ■ *verb* (*of a river*) to follow a winding course

mean lethal dose *noun* the dose of a substance that will kill half the organisms which absorb it

means *noun* a way of doing something that brings a result ○ *Turning down the central heating temperature by one or two degrees is a means of saving energy.*

mean sea level *noun* the level of the sea, measured relative to points on land, with wave movements and tide changes averaged out over a period of time ○ *Altitude is the vertical distance between a specific point and mean sea level.* Abbr **MSL**

mean temperature *noun* an average temperature ○ *The mean temperature for July in this area is 25 °C.*

meat *noun* animal flesh that is eaten as food

mechanical treatment *noun* the processing of sewage by mechanical means such as agitating or stirring

mechanism *noun* **1.** a machine or part of a machine **2.** a method of achieving something ○ *a mechanism for receiving feedback from consumers*

mecoprop *noun* a commonly used herbicide, mostly used to control weeds in cereal and grass crops, that is found as a contaminant of water. Abbr **MCPP**

media plural of **medium**

medicinal *adjective* referring to a substance or plant that has healing properties

medicinally *adverb* in the treatment of disease ○ *The herb can be used medicinally.*

medicine *noun* **1.** a drug or preparation taken to treat a disease or condition **2.** the study of diseases and how to cure or prevent them

Mediterranean Action Plan *noun* an agreement to protect the environment and encourage sustainable development in the Mediterranean area established by the European Union and the countries bordering the Mediterranean Sea. Abbr **MAP**

medium *adjective* middle or average ■ *noun* **1.** a substance through which something else is transmitted or carried ○ *Tubes convey the cooling medium.* (NOTE: The plural is **mediums** or **media**.) **2.** a substance in which an organism lives or is grown

medulla *noun* **1.** the soft inner part of an organ surrounded by the cortex **2.** same as **pith**

medullary ray *noun* a band or sheet of connective tissue between the pith and the bark in the stems of some woody plants

mega- *prefix* large. Opposite **micro-**

megadose *noun* a large dose ○ *received a megadose of radiation*

megalo- *prefix* unusually large. Opposite **micro-**

megalopolis *noun* a group of several small towns that grow to become one huge urban area

megaplankton *plural noun* large plankton more than 20 cm in length

megawatt *noun* one million watts ○ *power plants with a capacity larger than 50 megawatts*

megawatt-hour *noun* a measurement of power with respect to time (NOTE: One megawatt-hour is equal to one megawatt being used for a period of one hour.)

melanic *adjective* being unusually dark in appearance ○ *melanic moths*

melanin *noun* a dark pigment which gives colour to skin and hair

melanism *noun* a condition in which there are abnormal deposits of dark pigment on the skin of an animal

melanoma *noun* ♦ **malignant melanoma**

melt *verb* **1.** to heat a solid so that it becomes liquid ○ *The gradual rise in air temperature melted the glaciers.* **2.** (*of solid*) to become liquid after being heated ○ *The gradual rise in air temperature made the glaciers melt.* ◊ **molten**

meltdown *noun* a point in an accident in a nuclear reactor at which the fuel overheats and the core melts while the nuclear reaction is still in progress

meltwater *noun* water from melting ice, especially from a glacier or from winter snow

member *noun* an individual that belongs to a group ○ *Wheat is a member of the grass family.*

membrane *noun* **1.** a thin layer of tissue that lines or covers an organ ○ *mucous membranes in the nasal cavity* **2.** a thin layer of artificial material ○ *a waterproof membrane*

meniscus *noun* the curved surface of a narrow column of water

Mercalli ♦ **Modified Mercalli scale**

mercury *noun* a metal element that is liquid at room temperature. It is used in thermometers, barometers and electric batteries and is poisonous. Also called **quicksilver** (NOTE: The chemical symbol is **Hg**; the atomic number is **80** and the atomic weight is **200.59**.)

meridian *noun* an imaginary circle on the Earth's surface passing through the north and south geographic poles

meridional *adjective* referring to a meridian

meridionality *noun* a phenomenon of air blowing from north to south or from south to north

meristem *noun* a plant tissue at the tips of stems and roots in which cells are actively dividing

mes- *prefix* same as **meso-** (NOTE: used before vowels)

mesa *noun* a high plateau in the southwest of the USA, with steep sides and a flat top

mesarch *adjective* relating to the sequence of plant or animal communities (**sere**) that originates in a moist habitat

mesh size *noun* the diameter of the holes in a net (NOTE: The mesh size of fishing nets is used as a means of limiting catches.)

mesic *adjective* referring to an organism growing in or an environment characterised by moderate moisture

meso- *prefix* middle

mesobenthos *noun* the animals or plants living on the seabed, 250–1000m below the surface

mesoclimate *noun* the climate over a specific locality such as a hillside or valley, extending no more than a few kilometres in radius. ◊ **macroclimate, microclimate**

mesohaline *adjective* referring to water that contains a limited amount of salt

mesopause *noun* a thin cold layer of the Earth's atmosphere between the mesosphere and the thermosphere

mesophyll *noun* the tissue inside a leaf where photosynthesis takes place

mesophyte *noun* a plant that needs a standard amount of water to survive

mesoplankton *plural noun* organisms that take the form of plankton for part of their life cycle

mesosaprobic *adjective* referring to an organism that can survive in moderately polluted water

mesosphere *noun* the zone of the Earth's atmosphere between the stratosphere and the thermosphere (NOTE: It lies 50–80km above the surface, with the stratopause at the bottom and the mesopause at the top. The air temperature falls steadily with increasing ascent through the mesosphere.)

mesotherm *noun* a plant that grows in warm conditions

mesotrophic *adjective* referring to water that contains a moderate amount of nutrients. Compare **eutrophic, oligotrophic**

meta- *prefix* 1. changing 2. following

metabolic *adjective* referring to metabolism

metabolise *verb* to break down or build up organic compounds by metabolism ○ *The liver metabolises proteins and carbohydrates.*

metabolism *noun* the chemical processes of breaking down or building up organic compounds in organisms

metabolite *noun* a chemical produced as a result of metabolism

metal *noun* an element or a compound that can conduct heat and electricity

metaldehyde *noun* a substance used in the form of pellets to kill slugs and snails

metalimnion *noun* the middle layer of water in a lake. Also called **thermocline**. Compare **epilimnion, hypolimnion**

metallic *adjective* 1. referring to metal ○ *metallic materials* 2. referring to something that is like metal, especially in appearance

metamorphic *adjective* referring to rock that has changed because of external influences such as pressure from other rocks or temperature changes. ◊ **igneous, sedimentary**

metamorphism *noun* the process of forming metamorphic rock

metamorphose *verb* 1. (*of an animal*) to change into another form 2. (*of rock*) to undergo metamorphism

metamorphosis *noun* a process of change into a different form, especially the change of a larva into an adult insect

metapopulation *noun* a population belonging to a group of populations of the same species that exchange individuals through migration and recolonise sites in which other metapopulations have become extinct

meteor *noun* a solid body that enters the Earth's atmosphere from outer space, usually burning up as it does so

meteoric *adjective* referring to meteors

meteorite *noun* a solid body that falls from outer space onto the Earth's surface

meteorological *adjective* referring to meteorology or to climate

meteorologist *noun* a person who studies, reports and forecasts the weather

meteorology *noun* the scientific study of weather and weather conditions ○ *Terrestrial radiation plays an important part in meteorology.*

meter *noun* 1. a device to measure a physical property such as current, rate of flow or air speed 2. US spelling of **metre** ■ *verb* to count or measure with a meter

methanation *noun* the process of converting a mixture into methane. Also called **methanisation**

methane *noun* a colourless flammable gas produced naturally from rotting organic waste, as in landfill sites or animal excreta. Formula: CH_4. (NOTE: It is also found in marshes (**marsh gas**) and coal mines (**firedamp**).)

methane converter *noun* a process that turns into a usable form the gas produced by rotting waste in a landfill site

methanol *noun* an alcohol manufactured from coal, natural gas or waste wood, which is used as a fuel or solvent. Formula:

CH_3OH. Also called **methyl alcohol, wood alcohol**

methylated spirits *noun* almost pure alcohol, with wood alcohol and colouring added

methyl isothiocyanate *noun* a chemical compound used in the production of soil sterilants. Abbr **MIC**

metre *noun* an SI unit of length ○ *The area is four metres by three.* Symbol **m** (NOTE: The US spelling is **meter**.)

metres per second *noun* a system of measuring speed ○ *One metre per second is equal to 2.2 miles per hour.* Abbr **m/s** (NOTE: It is often used to measure wind speed.)

metric system *noun* a decimal measuring system, calculated in units of ten, e.g. the SI system

metric ton *noun* same as **tonne**

metropolis *noun* a very large town, usually the capital of a country

metropolitan *adjective* referring to a large town ○ *Smog covered the whole metropolitan area.*

mg *abbr* milligram

Mg *symbol* magnesium

MIC *abbr* methyl isothiocyanate

mica *noun* a silicate mineral that splits into thin transparent flakes. It is used as an insulator in electrical appliances.

micro- *prefix* very small. Opposite **macro-, mega-, megalo-**

microbe *noun* a microorganism (NOTE: Viruses, bacteria, protozoa and microscopic fungi are informally referred to as microbes.)

microbenthos *noun* plants or animals living at the bottom of a lake or the sea whose shortest dimension is equal to or more than 0.1 mm

microbial *adjective* referring to microbes

microbial insecticide *noun* an insecticide based on fungal, bacterial or other microorganisms that are pathogens of insects, or their toxins, as a form of biological control, e.g. the fungus *Verticillium lecanii* controlling whitefly in glasshouses

microbiological *adjective* referring to microbiology

microbiologist *noun* a scientist who specialises in the study of microorganisms

microbiology *noun* the scientific study of microorganisms

microclimate *noun* the climate over a very small area such as a pond, tree, field,

or even a leaf. ◊ **macroclimate, mesoclimate**

microenvironment *noun* same as **microhabitat**

microfauna *noun* **1.** very small animals which can only be seen with a microscope **2.** the animals living in a microhabitat

microgram *noun* a unit of measurement of weight, equal to one millionth of a gram. Symbol **µg**

microhabitat *noun* a single small area such as the bark of a tree, where fauna and/or flora live. Also called **microenvironment**

micro-hydro system *noun* a small system that uses water to produce electricity

micrometer *noun* an instrument for taking very small measurements such as of the width or thickness of very thin pieces of tissue

micrometre *noun* one thousandth of a millimetre. Symbol **µm**

micronutrient *noun* a nutrient which an organism uses in very small quantities, e.g. iron, zinc or copper

microorganism *noun* an organism that can only be seen with a microscope. Compare **microbe** (NOTE: Viruses, bacteria, protozoa and fungi are all forms of microorganism.)

microparasite *noun* a parasite which multiplies inside the body of its host, e.g. a virus

microplankton *plural noun* plankton in the size range 20–200 µm

micropollutant *noun* a pollutant which occurs in very small quantities

microscope *noun* a scientific instrument which makes very small objects appear larger ○ *The tissue was examined under the microscope.* ○ *Under the microscope it was possible to see the chloroplasts.*

COMMENT: In a light microscope the image is magnified by lenses. In an electron microscope the lenses are electromagnets and a beam of electrons is used instead of light, thereby achieving much greater magnifications.

microscopic *adjective* referring to something so small that it can only be seen through a microscope

microscopy *noun* the science of the use of microscopes

microtherm *noun* a plant which grows in cool regions

mid- *prefix* middle

mid-latitude desert *noun* a desert situated between the tropics, e.g. the Gobi

Desert or the Turkestan Desert. Also called **warm desert**

midrib *noun* the thick structure that runs along the middle of a leaf, providing for support and the movement of dissolved substances

migrant *noun* an animal or bird that moves from one place to another according to the season. Compare **nomad**

migrate *verb* **1.** (*of a bird or other animal*) to move from one place to another according to the season ○ *As winter approaches, the herds of deer migrate south.* **2.** to move to another place ○ *Waste materials may be allowed to migrate from landfill sites into the surrounding soil.*

migration *noun* **1.** the process of a bird or other animal moving from one place to another according to the season ○ *The islands lie along one of the main migration routes from Siberia to Australia.* (NOTE: Birds such as swallows breed in Northern Europe but fly south for the winter; fish such as salmon and eels spawn in one place, often a river, and then migrate to the sea.) **2.** the process of moving from one place to another

migratory *adjective* moving from one place to another according to the season ○ *Estuaries are important feeding grounds for migratory birds, and are also important for the passage of migratory fish such as salmon.*

mildew *noun* a disease caused by a fungus which produces a fine powdery film on the surface of an organism

mile *noun* an imperial measurement of distance, equal to 1.609 km. Also called **statute mile** (technical)

mileage *noun* a distance measured in miles

mill *noun* a factory where a substance is crushed to make a powder, especially one for making flour from the dried grains of cereals ■ *verb* to crush a substance to make a powder

millet *noun* a cereal crop grown in many of the hot, dry regions of Africa and Asia, where it is a staple food. Genera: especially: *Panicum* or *Eleusine*.

milli- *prefix* one thousandth or 10^{-3}. Symbol **m**

millibar *noun* a unit of pressure equal to one thousandth of a bar or 100 Pa. Symbol **mbar** (NOTE: This unit is often used in meteorology to express atmospheric pressure, standard atmospheric pressure at sea level being 1013.25 millibars.)

milligauss *noun* a unit of magnetic flux density ○ *A person living under a low-voltage power line is exposed to 20 milligauss of radiation.*

milligram *noun* a unit of measurement of weight, equal to one thousandth of a gram. Abbr **mg**

millilitre *noun* a unit of measurement of liquid equal to one thousandth of a litre. Abbr **ml** (NOTE: The US spelling is **milliliter**.)

millimetre *noun* a unit of measurement of length, equal to one thousandth of a metre. Abbr **mm** (NOTE: The US spelling is **millimeter**.)

milling *noun* **1.** the process of crushing and grinding mineral ores to separate out the useful materials **2.** the process of grinding cereal grains into flour

million tonnes of coal equivalent *noun* a measure of energy from a source that is not coal. Abbr **MTCE**

millisievert *noun* a unit of measurement of radiation. Abbr **mSv**

millisievert/year *noun* a number of millisieverts per year

millwheel *noun* a large wheel with wooden bars that is turned by the force of water

mimic *noun* an animal which imitates another ○ *Starlings are excellent mimics.* ■ *verb* to imitate another animal ○ *The starling mimicked the call of the thrush.*

mimicry *noun* a situation where one animal imitates another, often to prevent itself from being attacked

Minamata disease *noun* a form of mercury poisoning from eating polluted fish, first identified in Japan

mine *noun* a hole dug in the ground to extract a mineral ■ *verb* to dig into the ground to extract a mineral

mineral *noun* an inorganic solid substance with a characteristic chemical composition that occurs naturally (NOTE: The names of many minerals end with the suffix **-ite**.)

mineral deposit *noun* a deposit of rocks containing useful minerals

mineralisation *noun* the breaking down of organic waste into its inorganic chemical components

mineral nutrient *noun* an inorganic element other than carbon, hydrogen and oxygen that is absorbed by plants from the soil

mineral oil *noun* US oil which derives from petroleum and is made up of hydrocarbons (NOTE: The UK term is **liquid paraffin**.)

minimal *adjective* small in amount or importance ○ *the minimal area for sampling in which specimens of all species can be found*

minimisation *noun* the measures or techniques that reduce something such as the amount of waste generated during industrial production processes

minimise, minimize *verb* to make something as small as possible ○ *We minimised costs by cutting down the number of components.* Opposite **maximise**

minimum *adjective* referring to the smallest possible ○ *the minimum amount required* ○ *minimum requirements*

minimum lethal dose *noun* the smallest amount of a substance needed to kill an organism

minimum tillage *noun* a method of ploughing in which disturbance of the soil does not affect the deeper layers. The benefits are conservation of organic matter, leading to a better soil structure and less soil erosion, better soil biodiversity, and the use of less energy; disadvantages include the easier germination of grass seeds. Also called **min-till.** ◊ **no-till agriculture**

minimum viable population *noun* the smallest population which will allow a species to continue to exist and to avoid inbreeding, usually taken to be about 300 individuals. Abbr **MVP**

mining subsidence area *noun* a region in which the ground has subsided because of mines being dug

minute *adjective* extremely small ○ *minute hairs on leaves* ○ *minute traces*

mire *noun* an area of land saturated with water

miscanthus *noun* a plant related to sugar cane that is grown as an ornamental plant or for use as a fuel. Also called **elephant grass**

miscarry *verb* same as **abort 2** (*technical*)

mist *noun* **1.** the visible water vapour, in the form of very fine droplets, in the atmosphere ○ *an early morning mist on the fields* ○ *Mist is thinner than fog.* **2.** water vapour that has condensed on a cool surface **3.** liquid in the form of a spray ○ *an air/oil mist* ■ *verb* **1.** *also* **mist up** to form a mist on a cool surface ○ *The windows had misted up.* **2.** to spray plants with small drops of water to keep them wet

mister *noun* a device for spraying plants with small drops of water to keep them wet

mistral *noun* a strong, cold wind from the north which blows down the Rhone valley into the Mediterranean

misty *adjective* referring to mist ○ *a misty autumn morning* ○ *a misty window*

misuse *verb* to use something wrongly or inappropriately

mite *noun* a tiny animal of the spider family which may be free-living in the soil or on stored products, or parasitic on animals or plants

miticide *noun* a substance that kills mites

mixed *adjective* referring to something made up of different parts or categories

mixed cropping *noun* the practice of growing more than one type of plant on the same piece of land at the same time. Opposite **monocropping**

mixed farming *noun* the practice of combining arable and dairy farming

mixed fertiliser *noun* same as **compound fertiliser**

mixed woodland *noun* a wooded area where neither conifers nor broadleaved trees account for more than 75% of the total

mixture *noun* something which is the result of mixing a number of things together

ml *abbr* millilitre

mm *abbr* millimetre

MMHD *abbr* Mountain, Moor, Heath, Down

Mn *symbol* manganese

Mo *symbol* molybdenum

moder *noun* humus which is partly acid mor and partly neutral mull

Modified Mercalli scale *noun* a scale rising from 1 to 12 used for measuring the damage caused by an earthquake

module *noun* a part that together with other parts makes up another structure or system

Mohorovicic discontinuity, Moho *noun* a boundary layer in the interior of the Earth between the crust and the mantle, below which seismic shocks move more rapidly

moist *adjective* damp or humid

moist tropical forest *noun* a tropical forest which receives less rain than other types of tropical forest such as cloud forest

moisture *noun* water or other liquid

molar *adjective* referring to a solution containing one mole of solute per litre ■ *noun* a large back tooth

mold *noun, verb* US spelling of **mould**

mole *noun* **1.** a small dark-grey mammal which makes tunnels under the ground and eats worms and insects **2.** a dark raised spot on the skin ○ *She has a large mole on her chin.* **3.** an SI unit of measurement of the amount of a substance. Symbol **mol**

molecular *adjective* referring to molecules

molecular ecology *noun* the study of ecological problems using the techniques of molecular biology

molecule *noun* the smallest particle into which a substance can be divided without changing its chemical and physical properties ○ *The molecules of a gas move more quickly than the molecules of a liquid.*

mole drain *noun* an underground drain formed under the surface of the soil by a special plough (**mole plough**) as it is pulled across a field (NOTE: Mole drains are usually made 3 to 4 metres apart, and are used in fields with a clay subsoil.)

molehill *noun* a small heap of earth pushed up to the surface by a mole as it makes its tunnel

mollusc *noun* an invertebrate animal with a soft body, a muscular foot on the underside used for movement and, in many species, a protective shell (NOTE: Molluscs are found on land as well as in fresh and salt water; slugs, snails and shellfish are molluscs. The US spelling is **mollusk**.)

molluscicide *noun* a substance used to kill molluscs such as snails

molten *adjective* having become liquid when heated. ◊ **melt**

molybdenum *noun* a metallic trace element. It is essential to biological life and is also used in electric wiring. (NOTE: The chemical symbol is **Mo**; the atomic number is **42** and the atomic weight is **95.94**.)

monitor *noun* **1.** a screen for a computer display **2.** a piece of equipment for showing information or recording a process ■ *verb* to check or examine how something is working

monitoring *noun* a process of regular checking on the progress of something ○ *health monitoring* ○ *Scientists have set up a monitoring programme to record the changes in the Sun's radiation.*

monitoring well *noun* a well used to take water quality samples or to measure ground water levels

mono- *prefix* single or one. Opposite **multi-**

monoclimax *noun* a situation where one single community exists in a geographical region

monocline *noun* a rock formation where sedimentary rock slopes sharply on one side of a fold

monocot *noun* same as **monocotyledon** (*informal*)

monocotyledenous *adjective* referring to monocotyledons

monocotyledon *noun* a plant with seeds that have a single cotyledon, e.g. a grass or lily. Compare **dicotyledon**. ◊ **cotyledon**

monocropping, monocrop system, monoculture *noun* a system of cultivation in which a single crop plant such as wheat is grown over a large area of land often for several years. Opposite **mixed cropping**

monoecious *adjective* with male and female flowers on separate plants. Compare **dioecious**

monogamy *noun* a breeding arrangement where a male and female mate for life. Compare **polygamy**

monophagous *adjective* referring to an organism that feeds on only one kind of food. Compare **polyphagous**

monophagy *noun* the practice of feeding on only one kind of food. Compare **polyphagy**

monosodium glutamate *noun* a substance, labelled E621, added to processed food to enhance the flavour. Abbr **MSG** (NOTE: It can cause a bad reaction in some people.)

monotreme *noun* a type of mammal that lays eggs but feeds its young on milk in a pouch. The only monotremes are the duck-billed platypus and the spiny anteater.

monsoon *noun* **1.** a season of wind and heavy rain in tropical countries **2.** a wind which blows in opposite directions according to the season, especially the wind blowing north from the Indian Ocean in the summer

monsoon forest *noun* a tropical rainforest in an area where rain falls during the monsoon season

montane *adjective* referring to a plant or animal found in mountainous regions

Montreal Protocol *noun* an international agreement to control the production and use of chemicals containing bromine and chlorine, such as CFCs, that damage the ozone layer in the atmosphere. It was signed in 1987 and later updated. Full form **Montreal Protocol on Substances that Deplete the Ozone Layer**

Moon *noun* a natural satellite that orbits the Earth every 27 days

moor *noun* an area of often high land that is not cultivated, and is formed of acid soil covered with grass and low shrubs such as heather

moorland *noun* a large area of moor

mor *noun* a type of humus found in coniferous forests, which is acid and contains few nutrients. Compare **mull**

moraine *noun* a deposit of gravel and sand left by a glacier (NOTE: There are various types of moraine: ground moraine, which is a deposit left under a glacier; terminal moraine, which is the heap of soil and sand pushed by a glacier and left behind when it melts; and lateral moraines, which are deposits left at the sides of a glacier as it moves forward.)

moratorium *noun* a period when everyone agrees to stop a specific activity ○ *They voted to impose a ten-year moratorium on whaling.* ○ *The conference rejected a motion calling for a moratorium on nuclear reprocessing.*

morbidity *noun* a state of being diseased or sick

morbidity rate *noun* the number of cases of a disease per 100000 of population

morph *noun* an organism with a characteristic shape

morphology *noun* the study of the structure and form of living organisms. ◊ **geomorphology**

mortality *noun* the occurrence of death ○ *The population count in spring is always lower than that in the autumn because of winter mortality.*

mortality rate *noun* same as **death rate**

mosaic *noun* a disease of plants that makes yellow patterns on the leaves and can seriously affect some crops. It is often caused by viruses.

mosquito *noun* an insect which sucks blood and passes viruses or parasites into the bloodstream (NOTE: The plural is **mosquitoes** or **mosquitos**.)

mosquitocide *noun* a substance which kills mosquitoes

moss *noun* a very small plant without roots, which grows in damp places and forms mats of vegetation ○ *Sphagnum is a type of moss.*

moth *noun* an insect similar to a butterfly that is generally active at night. Order: Lepidoptera.

mother-of-pearl *noun* a hard shiny substance, mostly made up of calcium carbonate, which forms the inner layer of some shells such as oyster shells

mother rock *noun* a main layer of rock. Also called **parent rock**

motion *noun* the act of moving or changing position or place

mould *noun* **1.** a fungus, especially one that produces a fine powdery layer on the surface of an organism (NOTE: The US spelling is **mold**.) **2.** soft earth

moult *noun* an occasion of shedding feathers or hair at a specific period of the year ■ *verb* to shed feathers or hair at a specific period of the year ○ *Most animals moult at the beginning of summer.* (NOTE: The US spelling is **molt**.)

mount *verb* to fix something to a support ○ *to mount a specimen* ■ *noun* something such as a support or frame to which something else can be fixed

Mount *noun* a mountain. Abbr **Mt** (NOTE: used in the names of specific mountains: *Mount Everest*.)

mountain *noun* **1.** a natural structure of rock rising very high above the surrounding land surface **2.** a surplus or large amount of something, especially something that is being stored ○ *butter mountain* ○ *fridge mountain* ◊ **lake 2**

mountainous *adjective* referring to an area of land where there are high mountains

mountainside *noun* the sloping side of a mountain

mouth *noun* **1.** the part of an animal's body where food is taken in **2.** a place where a river widens and joins the sea

mouthpart *noun* a structure close to the mouth of an insect or other arthropod used to gather or chew food

MRL *abbr* maximum residue level

m/s *abbr* metres per second

MSG *abbr* monosodium glutamate

MSL *abbr* mean sea level

mSv *symbol* millisievert

Mt *abbr* Mount

MTCE *abbr* million tonnes of coal equivalent

mucilage *noun* slime secreted by some organisms such as seaweeds

mucin *noun* a glycoprotein that is a constituent of mucus

muck *noun* same as **manure**

mucus *noun* **1.** a slimy solution of mucin secreted by vertebrates onto a mucous membrane to provide lubrication **2.** a slimy substance secreted by invertebrates

mud *noun* a thick mixture of soil and water

muddy *adjective* containing mud, or covered with mud ○ *a muddy field* ○ *muddy boots*

mud flat *noun* a wide flat area of mud, usually in a river estuary

mudslide *noun* a large amount of mud that slips down a slope

mulch *noun* an organic material used to spread over the surface of the soil to prevent evaporation or erosion, e.g. dead leaves or straw ■ *verb* to spread organic material over the surface of the soil to prevent evaporation or erosion

mull *noun* a type of humus found in deciduous forests. Compare **mor** (NOTE: It is formed of rotted leaves, is PH neutral and contains many nutrients.)

Mullerian mimicry *noun* a form of mimicry where an animal mimics another animal which has an unpleasant taste

multi- *prefix* many or more than one. Opposite **mono-**

multicellular *adjective* referring to an organism composed of several or many cells. Compare **unicellular**

multicropping *noun* the cultivation of more than one crop on the same piece of land in one year

municipal *adjective* referring to a town or city

municipal dump *noun* a place where a town's rubbish is disposed of after it has been collected

municipality *noun* a town, city or region that has its own local government

municipal refuse, municipal waste *noun* the rubbish collected from homes and businesses in a town

municipal wastewater *noun* effluent from wastewater treatment plants that deal with sewage from homes and businesses and excess water after storms

mushroom *noun* a common edible fungus, often grown commercially

muskeg *noun* a bog in high cold plateau regions, especially in Canada

mutagen *noun* an agent that causes mutation, e.g. a chemical or radiation

mutagenic *adjective* referring to an agent that causes mutation

mutagenicity *noun* the ability of an agent to make genes mutate

mutant *adjective* referring to a gene in which a mutation has occurred, or to an organism carrying such a gene ○ *mutant mice* ■ *noun* an organism carrying a gene in which mutation has occurred ○ *New mutants have appeared.* Also called **mutation**

mutate *verb* (*of a gene or organism*) to undergo a genetic change that can be inherited ○ *Bacteria can mutate suddenly and become increasingly able to infect.*

mutation *noun* **1.** a heritable change occurring in a gene **2.** same as **mutant**

mutualism *noun* same as **symbiosis**

mutualist *noun* a species which benefits from symbiosis with another

MVP *abbr* minimum viable population

myc- *prefix* same as **myco-** (NOTE: used before vowels)

mycelium *noun* a mass of hyphae which forms the main part of a fungus

myco- *prefix* fungus or fungal

mycology *noun* the study of fungi

mycorrhiza *noun* a mutual association of a fungus with the roots of a plant in which the fungus supplies the plant with water and minerals and feeds on the plant's sugars (NOTE: Many different fungi form mycorrhizas, especially with trees, and many plants such as orchids cannot grow without them.)

mycotoxin *noun* a toxic substance produced by a fungus growing on crops in the field or in storage. There are regulations controlling the amount of some mycotoxins such as aflatoxin and ochratoxin permitted in food.

myiasis *noun* an infestation of animals by the larvae of flies

myxomatosis *noun* a usually fatal virus disease affecting rabbits, transmitted by fleas

N

N *symbol* **1.** nitrogen **2.** newton

Na *symbol* sodium

nacelle *noun* a part of a wind generator that contains the generator and gearbox at the top of the tower

nacreous clouds *plural noun* thin clouds, possibly made of ice crystals, which form a layer about 25 km above the Earth and look like mother-of-pearl

nanogram *noun* one billionth of a gram

nanoplankton *plural noun* plankton in the size range 10 –50 μm

NAO *abbr* North Atlantic Oscillation

nastic response *noun* a response of plants and flowers to a stimulus which is not connected with the direction from which the stimulus comes, e.g. the closing of flowers at night

-nasty *suffix* nastic response

natality *noun* birth

national *adjective* referring to a specific country ■ *noun* belonging to the people of a specific country

national grid *noun* same as **electricity grid**

National Nature Reserve *noun* a nationally important example of a type of habitat, established as reserve to protect the most important areas of wildlife habitat and geological formations. Abbr **NNR** (NOTE: There are over 200 National Nature Reserves in England, owned or controlled by English Nature or held by approved bodies such as Wildlife Trusts.)

national park *noun* a large area of land selected because of its scenic, recreational, scientific, or historical importance for special protection from development, and managed by a local government body for recreational use by the public and the benefit of the local community

National Radiological Protection Board *noun* an agency that monitors radiation risks to the UK population. Abbr **NRPB**

National Resources Institute *noun* a specialised research institute of the University of Greenwich, UK, working in the area of the sustainable management of natural and human resources in the developing world and elsewhere. Abbr **NRI**

National Rivers Authority *noun* a former UK statutory body responsible for water management, flood defence and the regulation of water quality. Abbr **NRA** (NOTE: Now part of the Environment Agency.)

National Scenic Area *noun* a national park in Scotland

National Trust *noun* **1.** in England, Wales and Northern Ireland, a charitable organisation that preserves historic buildings, gardens, parks, coastline and areas of natural beauty for the benefit of the public **2.** in Australia, an organisation that preserves historic monuments and areas of natural beauty for the benefit of the public

National Trust for Scotland *noun* in Scotland, a charitable organisation that preserves historic buildings, gardens, parks, coastline and areas of natural beauty for the benefit of the public

National Vegetation Classification *noun* a systemic scheme for classifying types of vegetation in the United Kingdom, covering all natural, semi-natural and major artificial habitats, including derelict urban sites. Abbr **NVC**

native *adjective* always having lived, grown or existed in a place ○ *Tigers are native to Asia.*

native species *noun* a species which exists naturally in an area

Natura 2000 *noun* in the European Union, a network of environmental sites designated by member states as of special interest for protection for their habitats or bird life

natural *adjective* **1.** not made by people ○ *natural materials* ○ *areas of natural beauty* **2.** usual or expected ○ *It's natural to be concerned about what's in the food you eat.*

natural amenities *plural noun* features of the landscape that are not made by humans and are regarded as contributing to a pleasant environment, e.g. rivers, lakes or moorland

Natural Area *noun* an area of the United Kingdom that is a biogeographical zone with a characteristic association of wildlife and natural features (NOTE: There are both terrestrial and marine Natural Areas, managed by English Nature.)

natural background *noun* the surrounding level of radiation or substances such as arsenic in a specific location

natural capital *noun* natural resources seen in economic terms as stock, goods and services

natural disaster *noun* a phenomenon such as a storm, earthquake or flood that destroys property and kills people and livestock

natural ecosystem *noun* an ecosystem where humans have had no more local influence than native species

natural environment *noun* **1.** same as **natural habitat 2.** the part of the Earth that has not been built or formed by humans. Compare **built environment**

natural forest *noun* a forest that has not been planted, maintained or exploited on a large scale by humans

natural gas *noun* a gas often found near petroleum deposits, although it can occur without petroleum, used as a domestic fuel (NOTE: It is mainly formed of methane but also contains small amounts of butane and propane. It contains no sulfur, unlike coal gas, and since it mixes with air it burns completely, creating very little carbon monoxide.)

natural habitat *noun* **1.** the usual surroundings in which an organism lives in the wild. Also called **natural environment 2.** an area of land or water where the majority of species are native and there has been very little human activity

natural historian *noun* same as **naturalist**

natural history *noun* the study of living organisms in their natural environments and of the features of the Earth not formed by humans

naturalise *verb* to introduce a species into an area where it has not lived or grown before so that it becomes established as part of the ecosystem ○ Rhododendron ponticum *has become naturalised in parts of Britain.*

naturalist *noun* a person who is interested in and studies the natural environment and its organisms. Also called **natural historian**

natural pollutant *noun* a polluting substance that occurs naturally, e.g. ash from a volcano

natural resource *noun* a naturally occurring material that can be put to use by humans, e.g. wood or oil (*often plural*)

natural science *noun* a science that deals with aspects of the physical world, e.g. biology, chemistry, geology or physics (*often plural*)

natural scientist *noun* a person who specialises in natural science

natural selection *noun* the process of evolutionary change, by which offspring of organisms with certain characteristics are more able to survive and reproduce than offspring of other organisms, thus gradually changing the composition of a population

natural vegetation *noun* the range of plant communities that exist in the natural environment without being planted or managed by people

nature *noun* all living organisms and the environments in which they live □ **to go back to nature** to return to a state similar to the one that existed before cultivation ○ *They've let the hillside go back to nature.* ◊ **back-to-nature**

Nature Conservancy Council *noun* a former UK organisation (1973–91) that took official responsibility for the conservation of fauna and flora. Abbr **NCC** (NOTE: Now replaced by English Nature, the Countryside Council for Wales and Scottish Natural Heritage.)

nature conservation *noun* the active management of the Earth's natural resources, plants, animals and environment, to ensure that they survive or are appropriately used

nature management *noun* the activity of managing a natural environment to encourage plant and animal life. Also called **habitat management**

nature reserve *noun* an area where plants, animals and their environment are protected

nature trail *noun* a path through the countryside with signs to draw attention to important and interesting features about plants, animals and the environment

NAWARAD *abbr* National Assembly for Wales Agriculture and Rural Affairs Department

NCC *abbr* Nature Conservancy Council

NDPB *abbr* non-departmental public body

Ne *symbol* neon

neap tide *noun* a tide which occurs at the first and last quarters of the Moon, when the difference between high and low water is less than usual. Compare **spring tide**

Nearctic Region *noun* a biogeographical region, part of Arctogea, comprising North America and Greenland

necrotroph *noun* a parasite which only feeds on dead organisms. Compare **biotroph**

nectar *noun* a sweet sugary liquid produced by flowers, which attracts birds or insects which pollinate the flowers

nectary *noun* a plant part that produces nectar, often found at the base of a flower (NOTE: Nectaries are usually in the flowers but may also develop on other plant parts such as the traps of pitcher plants.)

need *noun* something that is necessary or required ○ *the need for clean water* ■ *plural noun* **needs** something that a person must have for their health or well-being ○ *nutritional needs*

needle *noun* **1.** a thin hard leaf of a conifer **2.** a thin metal pointer in an instrument ○ *The needle on the dial indicated zero.*

-needled *suffix* with needles ○ *two needled or five-needled pines*

NEF *abbr* noise exposure forecast

negative *adjective* having a value of less than 0 ○ *The mechanism enables the propeller to be set to a negative pitch.* Symbol -. Opposite **positive**

negative feedback *noun* a situation in which the result of a process inhibits the action which caused the process

negative ion generator *noun* same as **ioniser**

neighbourhood noise *noun* the general noise from a local source such as a factory which is disturbing to people living in the area

nekton *plural noun* swimming sea animals such as fish, as opposed to floating or drifting animals such as plankton

nematicide *noun* a substance which kills nematodes

nematode *noun* a type of roundworm, some of which, such as hookworms, are parasites of animals while others, such as root knot and cyst nematodes, live in the roots or stems of plants

neo- *prefix* new

neo-Darwinism *noun* a revised form of Darwin's theory of evolution which accounts for modern genetics and other recent discoveries

Neogea *noun* one of the main biogeographical regions of the Earth, comprising Central and South America together with the islands in the Caribbean. Also called **Neotropical Region**. ◊ **Arctogea, Notogea**

neon *noun* an inert gas found in very small quantities in the atmosphere. It is used in illuminated signs. (NOTE: The chemical symbol is **Ne**; the atomic number is **10** and the atomic weight is **20.18**.)

Neotropical Region *noun* same as **Neogea**

neptunium *noun* a naturally radioactive element (NOTE: The chemical symbol is **Np**; the atomic number is **93** and the atomic weight is **237.05**.)

NERC *abbr* Natural Environment Research Council

neritic *adjective* referring to an animal or plant which lives in the shallow sea over the continental shelf

nervous system *noun* the network of specialised cells that transmit nerve impulses in most animals

nest *noun* **1.** a construction built by birds and some fish for their eggs **2.** a construction made by some social insects such as ants and bees for the colony to live in ■ *verb* to build a nest

nestling *noun* a very young bird that has not yet left its nest

net primary productivity *noun* the rate at which organic matter is incorporated into plants to produce growth. ◊ **gross primary productivity**

network *noun* a complex interconnected group or system of people or things ○ *A network of meteorological stations around the world exchange information.* ■ *verb* to link people or things together in a network

neurotoxicity *noun* the capacity to prevent nerve impulses from working

neurotoxin *noun* a substance which prevents nerve impulses from working, e.g. the poison of a snake or insect

neuston *plural noun* organisms such as plankton which float or swim in the surface film of a body of water

neutral *adjective* **1.** referring to the state of being neither acid nor alkali ○ *pH 7 is neutral.* **2.** referring to an electrical charge that is neither positive nor negative

neutralisation, neutralization *noun* a chemical process in which an acid reacts with a base to form a salt and water

neutralise, neutralize *verb* **1.** to make an acid neutral ○ *Acid in drainage water can be neutralised by limestone.* **2.** to make a bacterial toxin harmless by combining it with the correct amount of antitoxin **3.** to counteract the effect of something

neutralising, neutralizing *adjective* referring to a substance which acts against the effect of something

névé *noun* the spring snow on high mountains which becomes harder and more like ice during the summer

new chemicals *plural noun* the chemicals that were not listed in the European Inventory of Existing Commercial Chemical Substances between January 1971 and September 1981. Compare **existing chemicals**

newton *noun* an SI unit of measurement of force. Abbr **N** (NOTE: 1 newton is the force required to move 1 kilogram at the speed of 1 metre per second.)

NGO *abbr* non-governmental organisation

Ni *symbol* nickel

niche *noun* a place in an ecosystem which a species has adapted to occupy

nickel *noun* a metallic element (NOTE: The chemical symbol is **Ni**; the atomic number is **28** and the atomic weight is **58.71**.)

nicotine *noun* a harmful substance in tobacco. It is used as an insecticide.

nid- *prefix* nest

nidicolous *adjective* referring to a very young bird that is not well developed when it leaves the egg and remains in the nest for some time

nidifugous *adjective* referring to a very young bird that is well developed when it leaves the egg and can leave the nest immediately

night soil *noun* human excreta, collected and used for fertiliser in some parts of the world

nimbostratus *noun* a grey mass of cloud with precipitation in the form of rain or snow about 1000 m above the ground

NIMBY *noun* used to describe people who are willing· to accept development and building for various purposes, provided it is not near where they themselves are living. Full form **not in my backyard**

nitrate *noun* **1.** an ion with the formula NO_3 **2.** a chemical compound containing the nitrate ion, e.g. sodium nitrate

nitrate-sensitive area, nitrate-vulnerable zone *noun* a region of the country where nitrate pollution is likely and where the use of nitrate fertilisers is strictly controlled. Abbr **NSA, NVZ**

nitric *adjective* referring to a compound containing nitrogen

nitric acid *noun* a corrosive acid. It is a very reactive oxidising agent, used in making fertilisers. Formula: HNO_3.

nitric oxide *noun* a gas that is produced by burning at high temperatures, as in forest fires and internal combustion engines. Formula: NO. Also called **nitrogen monoxide** (NOTE: It converts to nitrogen dioxide in the atmosphere, is a major contributor to photochemical smog and is soluble in water. It contributes to acid rain (nitric acid) deposition, and is important in the catalytic destruction of ozone in the stratosphere.)

nitrification *noun* the process by which bacteria in the soil break down nitrogen compounds and form nitrates which plants can absorb (NOTE: It is part of the nitrogen cycle.)

nitrifier *noun* a microorganism that is involved in the process of nitrification

nitrify *verb* to convert nitrogen or nitrogen compounds into nitrates

nitrite *noun* **1.** an ion with the formula NO_2 **2.** a chemical compound containing the nitrite ion, e.g. sodium nitrite

nitrogen *noun* a chemical element that is the main component of air and an essential part of protein. It is essential to biological life. (NOTE: The chemical symbol is **N**; the atomic number is **7** and the atomic weight is **14.01**.)

nitrogen cycle *noun* the set of processes by which nitrogen is converted from a gas in the atmosphere to nitrogen-containing substances in soil and living organisms, then converted back to a gas (NOTE: Nitrogen is absorbed into green plants in the form of nitrates, the plants are then eaten by animals and the nitrates are returned to the ecosystem through animals' excreta or when an animal or a plant dies.)

nitrogen deficiency *noun* a lack of nitrogen in the soil, found where organic matter is low and resulting in thin, weak growth of plants

nitrogen dioxide *noun* a brown toxic irritant gas. Formula: NO_2. (NOTE: It is one of the pollutants produced by vehicle exhausts.)

nitrogen fertiliser *noun* a fertiliser containing mainly nitrogen, e.g. ammonium nitrate

nitrogen fixation *noun* the process by which nitrogen in the air is converted by bacteria in some plant roots into nitrogen compounds (NOTE: When the plants die the nitrogen is released into the soil and acts as a fertiliser.)

nitrogen-fixing bacteria *plural noun* bacteria such as *Rhizobium* in the soil which convert nitrogen in the air into nitrogen compounds by means of the process of nitrogen fixation in plants

nitrogen-fixing plant *noun* a leguminous plant which forms an association with bacteria that convert nitrogen from the air into nitrogen compounds in the soil, e.g. a pea plant

nitrogen monoxide *noun* same as **nitric oxide**

nitrogenous *adjective* referring to a compound containing nitrogen

nitrogen oxide *noun* an oxide formed when nitrogen is oxidised, e.g. nitric oxide or nitrogen dioxide. Formula: NO_x.

'The largest source of nitrogen oxides (NOx) emissions in the UK is the transport sector. (Delivering the evidence. Defra's Science and Innovation Strategy 2003–06)'

nitrous oxide *noun* a gas with a sweet smell that is one of the major greenhouse gases. Formula: HNO_2. (NOTE: It is produced by soil cultivation and fertilisation and by burning fossil fuels and biomass.)

nival *adjective* growing in or under the snow

NNI *abbr* noise and number index

NNR *abbr* National Nature Reserve

NOAEL *noun* the highest concentration of a substance that causes no harm which can be detected by existing testing methods. Full form **no-observed-adverse-effect-level**

noble gas *noun* a gas that does not react chemically with other substances. Also called **rare gas, inert gas** (NOTE: The noble gases include helium, neon, argon, krypton, xenon and radon.)

noble metal *noun* a metal such as gold or silver that resists corrosion and does not form compounds with non-metals. Compare **base metal**

nocturnal *adjective* **1.** referring to an organism that is active at night ○ *Owls and badgers are nocturnal.* Compare **diurnal 2.** happening at night

nocturnal animal *plural noun* an animal that is active at night and sleeps during the day

node *noun* a point on the stem of a plant where a leaf is attached

nodule *noun* a small lump found on the roots of leguminous plants such as peas which contains bacteria that can convert nitrogen from the air into nitrogen compounds

no dumping *noun* a sign telling people that they are not allowed to throw away waste in that particular place

NOEL *noun* the highest concentration of a substance that has no detectable effect on humans. Full form **no-observed-effect-level**

noise *noun* unwanted sound, especially an sound that is unpleasant or too loud

noise abatement *noun* measures taken to reduce unacceptable noise or vibrations, or to protect people from exposure to it

Noise Abatement Society *noun* an association of people who work to influence others to reduce loud or irritating noises

noise and number index *noun* a way of measuring noise from aircraft. Abbr **NNI**

noise charge *noun* a fee paid by a company to be allowed to make some amount of noise in the course of its business

noise criteria *plural noun* the levels of noise which are acceptable to people who hear them

noise exposure forecast *noun* a forecast of the effect that industrial or aircraft noise will have on people. Abbr **NEF**

noise level *noun* the degree of loudness of a noise, taken as a measurement ○ *The factory has announced plans to keep noise levels down to a minimum.*

noise nuisance *noun* a noise which is annoying, disturbing or unpleasant to someone

noise pollution *noun* annoying or physically dangerous noise to which people are exposed in their work or home environment and over which they often have no control

noise pollution level *noun* the degree of loudness of annoying or physically dangerous noise in a person's environment, taken as a measurement. Abbr **NPL**

noise zone *noun* an area which is classified according to the amount of noise that exists in it

noisy *adjective* **1.** making a loud noise **2.** referring to a place where there is a lot of noise

nomad *noun* an animal that moves from place to place without having a fixed range. Compare **migrant**

nomadic *adjective* referring to nomads

nomadism *noun* a habit of some animals that move from place to place without having a fixed range

nomenclature *noun* a system for giving names to organisms ○ *taxonomic nomenclature*

non- *prefix* not or no

non-biodegradable, **non-degradable** *adjective* referring to an object or substance that cannot be decomposed into environmentally safe waste materials by the action of soil bacteria

non-degradation *noun* the prevention of the pollution of clean air

non-departmental public body *noun* an organisation set up to carry out a specific role within government responsibilities, but which is not a government department or part of one. Abbr **NDPB**

non-disposable *adjective* referring to a product that is not thrown away after use, but can be recycled

non-ferrous *adjective* not containing iron

non-flammable *adjective* referring to a material that is difficult to set on fire

non-genetically modified *adjective* referring to an organism with a genetic composition that has not been altered by genetic modification. Abbr **non-GM**

non-governmental organisation *noun* an organisation which is not funded by a government and which works on a local, national or international level, e.g. a pressure group, charity or voluntary agency. Abbr **NGO**

non-indigenous *adjective* referring to a plant, animal or person that is not native to a place

non-metal *noun* a chemical element that lacks the physical and chemical properties of a metal, e.g. carbon or oxygen

non-native *adjective* relating to a species that did not originate where it is now found. Also called **alien**, **exotic**

non-organic *adjective* **1.** referring to a compound that does not contain carbon **2.** referring to crops that are not produced according to guidelines restricting the use of fertilisers and other practices

non-persistent *adjective* referring to a chemical, especially a pesticide, that decomposes quickly after it has been applied so that it does not enter the food chain

non-point source *noun* a source of pollution not associated with a specific discharge point. Compare **point source** (NOTE: Non-point sources include rainwater and runoff from agricultural land and industrial sites, as well as escaping gases from pipes and fittings.)

non-renewable *adjective* **1.** not able to be replaced when used up because a supply is limited ○ *non-renewable fuels* **2.** not able to be extended for a longer period ○ *non-renewable contract*

non-renewable energy *noun* power generated from a resource such as coil or oil that cannot be replaced once it has been used

non-renewable resource *noun* a natural resource which cannot be replaced once it has been used, e.g. coal or oil

non-resistant *adjective* referring to an organism that is not resistant to a disease, antibiotic, pesticide, herbicide or other agent

non-selective weedkiller *noun* a weedkiller that kills all plants

non-till *adjective* ▶ **no-till agriculture**

non-toxic *adjective* referring to a substance that is not poisonous or harmful to humans or other organisms or the environment

non-woody *adjective* referring to plants that do not form woody stems

normal environmental lapse rate *noun* the rate at which the temperature of the air falls with height above the Earth (NOTE: This is about 6.4°C per thousand metres, under conditions where there are no upward air currents or wind.)

normal room temperature *noun* the temperature regarded as comfortable for usual daily human activity

North Atlantic Conveyor *noun* an ocean current system carrying warm surface waters to the North Atlantic, where they cool and drop to a deeper level before flowing south again. Also called **Atlantic Conveyor Belt** (NOTE: Because it transfers heat to the atmosphere, it gives northwestern Europe a more temperate climate than other countries on a similar latitude such as Canada.)

North Atlantic Drift *noun* a current of warm water flowing north along the east coast of the USA from the Gulf of Mexico, then crossing the Atlantic to northern Europe (NOTE: It is part of the North Atlantic Conveyor.)

North Atlantic Oscillation *noun* an atmospheric mass that alternates between the North and South Poles and affects the strength and route of storms crossing the Atlantic from America to Europe as it changes in mass and pressure. Its effects are most obvious in November to April. Abbr **NAO**

northern hemisphere *noun* the upper half of the Earth

Northern Lights *plural noun* a spectacular illumination of the sky in the northern hemisphere caused by ionised particles striking the atmosphere. Also called **Aurora Borealis**

North Sea *noun* the sea to the north of the Netherlands and Germany, east of the UK and west of Scandinavia

North Sea oil *noun* oil extracted from the rocks under the North Sea

no smoking area *noun* a part of a public place such as a restaurant or airport where smoking is not allowed

notifiable disease *noun* a serious infectious disease of plants, animals or people that has to be officially reported so that steps can be taken to stop it spreading

notify *verb* to inform someone about something officially

no-till agriculture, no-till farming *noun* a system of cultivation in which mechanical disturbance of the soil by ploughing is kept to a minimum to reduce soil erosion. Also called **non-till.** ◊ **minimum tillage**

Notogea *noun* one of the main biogeographical regions of the Earth, comprising Australia, New Zealand and the Pacific Islands. ◊ **Arctogea, Neogea**

noxious *adjective* harmful to people or animals

noy *noun* a unit of measurement of perceived noise

Np *symbol* neptunium

NPK *noun* nitrogen, phosphorus and potassium, used in different proportions as a fertiliser

NPL *abbr* noise pollution level

NRA *abbr* National Rivers Authority

NRI *abbr* National Resources Institute

NRPB *abbr* National Radiological Protection Board

NSA *abbr* nitrate-sensitive area

nuclear *adjective* **1.** referring to an atomic nucleus, especially to the production of energy by fission or fusion of nuclei **2.** referring to a cell nucleus

nuclear accident *noun* an unexpected event in a nuclear power station which results in release of radiation into the environment above permitted safety levels

nuclear contamination *noun* the damage done to an object, person or substance because of contact with nuclear radiation

nuclear energy *noun* the energy released during a nuclear reaction

nuclear fallout *noun* the radioactive material which falls from the atmosphere after a nuclear explosion

nuclear-free *adjective* without nuclear reactors or nuclear weapons ○ *While some countries remain nuclear-free, nuclear reactors supply about 15% of all electricity generated in the world.*

nuclear-free zone *noun* an area in which the use of nuclear reactors or the use of nuclear weapons is not allowed

nuclear power *noun* the power generated by a nuclear reactor

nuclear power plant, nuclear power station *noun* a power station in which nuclear reactions are used to provide energy to run turbines which generate electricity

nuclear waste *noun* the radioactive waste from a nuclear reactor, including spent fuel rods and coolant

nuclear winter *noun* a period expected to follow a nuclear explosion, when there would be no warmth and light because dust particles would obscure the Sun and most life would be affected by radiation

nucleating agent *noun* a substance such as solid carbon dioxide that is scattered on clouds to make them release rain

nucleic acid *noun* a complex organic acid, either DNA or RNA, that exists in the nucleus and protoplasm of all cells

nucleus *noun* **1.** the central core of an atom, formed of neutrons and protons **2.** the central body in a cell, containing DNA and RNA, and controlling the function and characteristics of the cell **3.** a central part or focus round which something gathers

nué ardente *noun* a cloud of burning gas that flows downhill during a volcanic eruption

nuisance *noun* something annoying, disturbing or unpleasant

nuisance threshold *noun* the point at which something such as a noise or smell becomes annoying or unpleasant

nursery *noun* a place where plants are grown until they are large enough to be planted in their final positions

nut *noun* a hard indehiscent fruit with one seed

nutraceutical, nutriceutical *noun* same as **functional food**

nutrient *noun* a substance that an organism needs to allow it to grow, thrive and reproduce, e.g. carbon, hydrogen, oxygen, nitrogen, phosphorus, potassium, calcium, magnesium or sulfur. Plants obtain their nutrients from the soil, while humans and other animals obtain them from their food, including plants.

nutrient budget *noun* the calculation of the amount of a nutrient taken up by an individual and the amount lost by an individual to the environment

nutrient leaching *noun* the loss of nutrients from the soil caused by water flowing through it, which deprives the soil of nutrients and may pollute water courses

nutrient requirement *noun* the type and amount of nutrients needed by an organism

nutrient source *noun* the source of a nutrient for an individual or community

nutrition *noun* the process of taking in the necessary food components to grow and remain healthy. ◊ **soil nutrition**

nutritional *adjective* referring to nutrition ○ *the nutritional quality of meat*

nutritional requirement *noun* the type and amount of food needed by an organism

nutritious *adjective* referring to food that provides the nutrients that are needed for growth and health

nutritive *adjective* **1.** referring to a substance that provides the necessary components for growth and health ○ *plants grown in a nutritive solution* **2.** referring to nutrition

nutritive value *noun* the degree to which a food is valuable in promoting health ○ *The nutritive value of white flour is lower than that of wholemeal flour.*

NVC *abbr* National Vegetation Classification

NVZ *abbr* nitrate-vulnerable zone

nyct- *prefix* night

nyctinasty *noun* the opening or closing of flowers and leaves at night in response to darkness and falling temperature

nymph *noun* an insect at the stage in its development between the larval stage and adulthood

nymphal *adjective* referring to the stage in the development of some insects between the larval stage and adulthood

O

O *symbol* oxygen

oak *noun* a deciduous or evergreen hardwood tree of which there are many species. Latin name: *Quercus.*

oak apple, oak gall *noun* a small hard round growth found on oak trees, caused by a parasitic wasp

oakwood *noun* a number of oak trees growing together

oasis *noun* a place in an arid desert where the water table is near the surface and where vegetation can grow. In the oases of the hot desert regions, date palms form an important food supply. (NOTE: The plural is **oases.**)

oat *noun* a hardy cereal crop grown in most types of soil in cool wet northern temperate regions. Latin name: *Avena sativa.* (NOTE: Oats are regarded as environmentally friendly because they require fewer inputs than other cereals.)

objective *noun* a goal or target to be achieved ■ *adjective* referring to thoughts based on facts rather than personal feelings ○ *an objective assessment*

obligate *adjective* referring to an organism that exists or develops only in a particular set of circumstances ○ *an obligate parasite* ○ *an obligate anaerobe* Compare **facultative**

obliterative shading, obliterative countershading *noun* the grading of the colour of an animal, such as a dark back dark shading towards a light belly, which minimises shapes and gives a flat appearance

obscure *verb* **1.** to make something difficult to see or prevent something from being seen ○ *The ice forming on the window obscured vision.* **2.** to make something difficult to realise or understand ○ *The low temperatures in the years after the volcanic eruption obscured the general trend of gradual global warming.* ■ *adjective* not clearly expressed and therefore difficult to understand ○ *an obscure explanation*

observation *noun* the process of watching or studying someone or something carefully to find out information ○ *The type of cloud is established by observation and comparison with cloud photographs.* □ **under observation** being watched carefully

observations *plural noun* the pieces of scientific information gathered by using any of the five human senses, but especially sight ○ *observations of feeding patterns*

observe *verb* **1.** to watch or study something carefully to find out information ○ *They observed the birds' behaviour for several weeks.* **2.** to obey something such as an agreement or a guideline ○ *We expect everyone to observe the safety guidelines.*

OC *abbr* organic carbon

occidental *adjective* referring to the west

occluded front *noun* a weather front where warm and cold air masses meet and mix together, the warm air rising away from the surface of the ground

occlusion *noun* the forcing of air upwards from the Earth's surface, as when a cold front overtakes and flows under a warm front

occupational asthma *noun* asthma caused by materials with which people comes into contact at work, e.g. asthma in farm workers (**farmer's lung**), caused by hay

occupational exposure *noun* the situation of experiencing a health hazard while at work

ocean *noun* the body of salt water which covers the Earth (NOTE: American English prefers to use **ocean**, British English prefers to use **sea**.)

oceanarium *noun* a large saltwater aquarium where marine animals are kept for display

ocean dumping *noun* the discharging of waste, solid, liquid or radioactive, into the ocean, now banned

oceanic *adjective* **1.** referring to an ocean, especially to deep water beyond the continental shelf **2.** living in the ocean

ocean incineration *noun* the burning of toxic waste in special ships at sea, now banned

oceanography *noun* the study of all the physical aspects of the ocean, including the fauna and flora living there

oceanology *noun* the study of the geographical distribution of the ocean's economic resources

Ocean Thermal Energy Conversion *noun* the process whereby the difference in temperature between the upper and lower layers of water in tropical seas is used to generate electricity and fresh water. Abbr **OTEC** (NOTE: Warmer water from the upper layer is converted to steam to drive turbines and then condensed to provide fresh water.)

octa *noun* another spelling of **okta**

octane *noun* a liquid hydrocarbon that exists in 18 structurally different forms. Formula: C_8H_{18}.

COMMENT: Petrol without the addition of hydrocarbons will make the engine knock. Hydrocarbons, such as octane or aromatic hydrocarbons, or lead tetraethyl can be added to the petrol to give better performance, while increasing the octane rating. Unleaded petrol has a relatively low octane rating and leaded petrol, which contains an antiknock additive, has a high rating. Leaded petrol produces more atmospheric pollution than unleaded.

odour *noun* a smell, especially an unpleasant smell (NOTE: The US spelling is **odor**.)

odour nuisance *noun* a smell which is annoying or unpleasant

ODP *abbr* ozone-depleting potential *or* ozone-depletion potential

ODS *abbr* ozone-depleting substance

oestrogen *noun* a steroid hormone belonging to a group of hormones that controls the reproductive cycle and the development of secondary sexual characteristics in female primates (NOTE: The US spelling is **estrogen**.)

offpeak *adjective* referring to a period during which the consumption of something is low ○ *Offpeak electricity costs less.* ○ *By using thermal storage we can move 50% of electricity demand into offpeak hours.*

offshore *adjective, adverb* **1.** in sea water near a coast **2.** at a distance from a coast

offshore island *noun* an island situated up to 12.5 km or 20 miles from a coast

offshore windfarm *noun* a collection of wind turbines for the production of electricity situated in the sea at some distance from a coast (NOTE: Britain's first offshore windfarm is situated 1 km off the coast of Blyth, Northumberland.)

offspring *noun* a child, the young of an animal, or a descendant of a plant (NOTE: The plural is **offspring**: *The birds usually produce three or four offspring each year.*)

ohm *noun* the SI unit of measurement of electrical resistance. Symbol Ω

oil *noun* **1.** a liquid compound which does not mix with water, occurring as vegetable or animal oils, essential volatile oils and mineral oils **2.** mineral oil extracted from underground deposits, used to make petrol and other petroleum products

COMMENT: Oil is made up of different types of hydrocarbon together with sulfur compounds, and usually occurs in combination with natural gas or water. When these are removed it is called crude oil or crude petroleum. Refined crude oil gives products such as petrol, LPG, diesel oil, paraffin wax and tar. Crude oil is found in geological deposits, mainly in the Middle East, in the North Sea, Central America and Asia.

oil-bearing *adjective* referring to rock, sand or shale that contains oil

oil crop *noun* a crop grown for extraction of the oil in its seeds, e.g. sunflower or oilseed rape

oil-exporting country *noun* a country which produces enough oil from underground deposits for its own use and to sell to other countries

oilfield *noun* an area of rock under which lie one or more pools of oil that can be extracted ○ *The search is on for new oilfields to replace fields which have been exhausted.*

oil-fired *adjective* using oil as fuel ○ *oil-fired central heating*

oil-importing country *noun* a country which buys the fuel and industrial oil it uses from other countries

oil pollution *noun* damage to an area caused by oil, e.g. pollution of the sea by oil from a damaged oil tanker

oil sand *noun* a geological formation of sand or sandstone containing bitumen, which can be extracted and processed to give oil. Also called **tar sand, bituminous sand**

oilseed rape *noun* a plant of the cabbage family with bright yellow flowers, grown to provide an edible oil and animal feed from the processed seeds. Latin name: *Brassica napus*. Also called **rape** (NOTE: Oil produced from oilseed rape is often called 'vegetable oil'.)

oilseeds *plural noun* crops grown for the oil extracted from their seeds, e.g. oilseed rape or linseed

oil slick *noun* oil which has escaped into water and floats on the surface

oil spill *noun* an escape of oil into the environment, especially from a damaged ship, vehicle or pipeline

oily *adjective* containing oil

okta, octa *noun* a unit of visible sky equal to one eighth of total area visible to the horizon

old growth *noun* a long-established forest or woodland with some large old trees which supports a relatively stable and diverse community of plants and animals

old-growth forest *noun* a forest that has never been affected to any great extent by human activity

olefin, olefine *noun* an aliphatic hydrocarbon

olfactory *adjective* referring to the sense of smell

oligo- *prefix* few or little

oligohaline *adjective* (*of water*) having traces of salt. ◊ **mesohaline, polyhaline**

oligophagous *adjective* referring to animals that feed on only some types of prey

oligophagy *noun* the practice of feeding on only some types of prey

oligosaprobic *adjective* referring to an organism that is unable to survive in polluted water

oligotrophic *adjective* (*of water*) referring to water that contains few nutrients. ◊ **dystrophic, eutrophic, mesotrophic**

oligotrophy *noun* the state of being oligotrophic

olive *noun* a Mediterranean tree with small yellowish-green edible fruit from which an edible oil can be produced. Latin name: *Olea europaea*.

ombrogenous *adjective* referring to an area of land, such as a bog, or a plant that receives water only from rain and is therefore low in nutrients

ombudsman *noun* an official who investigates complaints by the public against government departments or other large organisations

omnivore *noun* an animal that eats both plant and animal foods. ◊ **carnivore, detritivore, frugivore, herbivore** (NOTE: Humans and pigs are examples of omnivores.)

omnivorous *adjective* referring to an animal that eats both plant and animal foods

onshore *adjective, adverb* **1.** situated on land ○ *onshore oil and gas exploration* **2.** towards the coast ○ *an onshore breeze*

ontogeny *noun* the development of a living organism from its earliest stage to maturity

ooze, ooze mud *noun* soft mud, especially at the bottom of a lake or the sea. Also called **ooze mud** ■ *verb (of liquid)* to flow slowly

opacity *noun* the characteristic of not allowing light or other rays to pass through ○ *Sometimes it is possible to estimate the depth and opacity of the layer of mist or fog from ground observations.*

opaque *adjective* referring to something that does not allow light or other rays to pass through it

OPEC *abbr* Organization of Petroleum Exporting Countries

open-air *adjective* referring to the environment outside buildings

open burner *noun* an outdoor site where waste such as automobile tyres or rags is destroyed by fire, thereby causing atmospheric pollution

open burning *noun* the burning of waste matter in the open air, creating pollution with smoke

open-cast mining *noun* a form of mining in which the mineral is dug from the surface instead of from under the ground. Also called **open-cut mining, strip mining**

open country, open land *noun* 1. an area of land that is not built on 2. an area of land that does not have many trees or high mountains 3. any area of land that is mountain, moor, heath or down or is registered as common land

open-cut mining *noun* same as **open-cast mining**

open dump *noun* a place where waste is left on the ground and not buried in a hole

open land *noun* land with no trees or bushes and no buildings

open ocean, open sea *noun* the ocean or sea well away from the coast

operation *noun* an organised activity designed to achieve something ○ *The clean-up operation after the oil spill lasted for months.*

opportunist, opportunistic *adjective* referring to an organism that quickly colonises an available habitat

opportunistic weed *noun* a weed that grows in a wide range of conditions

optic *adjective* referring to the eye or to sight

optimal *adjective* best or most effective

optimal foraging theory *noun* the theory that through evolution predators have adapted to maximise energy gain and minimise energy loss when foraging

optimise, optimize *verb* to make something as efficient as possible

optimum *adjective* referring to the point at which the condition or amount of something is the best ○ *optimum height* ■ *noun* the point at which the condition or amount of something is best

optimum sustainable population *noun* the number of individuals that are needed to maintain the existence of the species

oral *adjective* referring to the mouth, or to speech

orbit *noun* the curved path of a planet or satellite around another astronomical object

orbital *adjective* referring to the movement of an object around something

orbital road *noun* a road which goes right round a town, at some distance from the built-up areas. Compare **ring road**

order *noun* 1. a command or instruction 2. a classification of animals or plants, formed of several families (NOTE: Orders of animals have names ending in **-a**; orders of plants have names ending in **-ales**.) 3. the way in which things are arranged so that one comes before another □ **in order** in the correct order □ **in order of** according to ○ *in order of importance / priority / frequency* □ **in ascending order** with the lowest number or letter of the alphabet first □ **in descending order** with the highest number or letter of the alphabet first □ **in reverse order** in the opposite order from what is usual □ **out of order** in the wrong order

ore *noun* a mineral found in the ground containing a metal which can be extracted from it ○ *Iron ore deposits were found in the mountains.* ○ *The ore is heated to a high temperature to extract the metal.*

ore-bearing *adjective* referring to rock that contains ore

organ *noun* a part of an organism that is distinct from other parts and has a particular function, e.g. an eye or a flower

organic *adjective* 1. referring to a compound containing carbon 2. referring to food produced using only a restricted number of permitted pesticides and fertilisers, or to the production of such food 3. referring to organs in the body

COMMENT: Organic is a term that is used loosely in the media and elsewhere to mean 'natural' or 'wholesome' with reference to food. In fact, in the UK organic food can only be labelled as such if it meets various official criteria controlling the way in which it has been produced.

organic agriculture *noun* same as **organic farming**

organically *adverb* using only a restricted number of permitted pesticides and fertilisers in growing a crop

organic carbon *noun* carbon that comes from an animal or plant. Abbr **OC**

organic conversion *noun* the process of converting from conventional agriculture to organic production

organic farming *noun* a method of farming which does not involve the use of artificial fertilisers or pesticides ○ *Organic farming may become more economic than conventional farming.*

organic fertiliser *noun* a fertiliser made from dead or decaying plant matter or animal wastes, e.g. leaf mould, farmyard manure or bone meal

organic material, organic matter *noun* carbon-based material derived from organisms, e.g. decomposed plant material or animal dung

organic matter *noun* **1.** a combination found in soil of plant material that is decomposing, microorganisms such as fungi, and humus. Also called **soil organic matter 2.** same as **organic material**

organics *noun* **1.** the practice of managing the land and growing food according to organic principles **2.** organic material of all types including waste

organic waste *noun* substances consisting of material containing carbon compounds and disposed of as waste, e.g. plant or animal remains. Compare **inorganic waste**

organism *noun* any individual life form that is able to reproduce and grow, e.g. a plant, animal or microorganism

Organization of Petroleum Exporting Countries *noun* an association set up in 1960 to represent the interests of the major oil-exporting nations, to fix the price of oil and the amounts which can be produced. Abbr **OPEC**

organochlorine *noun* **1.** a chlorinated hydrocarbon **2.** a chemical compound containing chlorine, used as an insecticide

organophosphate *noun* a synthetic insecticide that attacks the nervous system, e.g. chlorpyrifos

organophosphorus compound *noun* an organic compound containing phosphorus

organo-tin paint *noun* a toxic paint based on tin that is used on ships' hulls to prevent the growth of marine organisms

origin *noun* **1.** a point where something starts or comes from ○ *the origin of life* ○ *An air mass takes on the characteristics of its place of origin.* **2.** a base from which a map projection is drawn ○ *The value of convergence used is correct at the parallel of origin.* ◊ **centre of origin**

ornamental *adjective* **1.** for use as decoration **2.** referring to a plant that is grown for its appearance rather than for food or other use ■ *noun* an ornamental plant, e.g. a rose or orchid

ornithological *adjective* referring to ornithology

ornithologist *noun* a scientist who studies birds

ornithology *noun* the study of birds

orographic effect *noun* an atmospheric disturbance that is caused by, or relating to, the existence of mountains or other high land

orphan site *noun* an area of contaminated land for which both polluter and owner reject responsibility

orthotropism *noun* growth directly towards or away from a stimulus

oscillation *noun* a regular movement from side to side

osmoregulation *noun* also called **osmotic regulation**

osmosis *noun* the movement of molecules from a solution of one concentration to a solution of a higher concentration through a semi-permeable membrane until the two solutions balance in concentration

osmotic pressure *noun* the pressure required to prevent the flow of a solvent into a solution through a semi-permeable membrane

osmotic regulation *noun* the control of osmotic pressure within cells and simple organisms, by which they maintain a balance between the fluid inside them and that outside in their environment. Also called **osmoregulation**

OSPAR *noun* an international agreement to prevent pollution of the northeast Atlantic and its coasts by continuously reducing discharges, emissions and losses of hazardous substances, with the aim of eventually achieving very low or zero concentrations. Full form **Oil Spill Preparedness and Response**

OTEC *abbr* Ocean Thermal Energy Conversion

outback *noun* a large area of wild or semi-wild land in the centre of the continent of Australia ○ *Many wild animals which used to live in the outback are be-*

coming rare as the land is reclaimed for farming.

outbreak noun the sudden start of something ○ an outbreak of disease ○ Showers are local outbreaks of precipitation from detached cumulus or cumulonimbus.

outbreeding noun 1. breeding between individuals that are not related 2. fertilisation between two or more separate plants, rather than within a flower or between flowers of the same plant ○ Outbreeding occurs in broad beans. ▶ compare **inbreeding**

outcompete verb to be more successful than other organisms of the same or different species in obtaining access to the same limited resources such as food, light or a mate

outcrop noun an area of rock that stands out above the surface of the soil ■ verb (of rock) to stand out above the surface of the soil

outer adjective furthest away from the centre ○ The outer coating of the seed is very hard.

outer suburbs noun a residential part of a town, a long way from the centre, but still within the built-up area

outfall noun a pipe from which sewage, either raw or treated, flows into a river, lake or the sea. Also called **outfall sewer**

outflow noun a flow in an outward direction ○ The outflow valve is controlled by the cabin pressure controller.

outgrowth noun something that is growing from a main part

outlet noun a passage or pipe through which something can leave ○ a water outlet

outlier noun 1. an organism that occurs naturally some distance away from the principal area in which its species is found 2. an area in which younger rocks are completely surrounded by older rocks

outline noun 1. a summary ○ an outline of the latest research results 2. a line that shows the external shape of something ○ The drawing shows the outline of the coast. ■ verb to form or draw round the shape of something ○ The additional material is outlined in red.

outline planning permission noun permission in principle to build a property on a piece of land, but not the final approval because further details must be submitted

output noun the product of a process ○ Air density will affect the output of the engine.

outwash noun the water which flows from a melting glacier and creates deposits of silt

outwash deposit, outwash fan noun a silt deposit formed by a melting glacier

ova plural of **ovum**

ovary noun 1. one of two organs in a woman or female animal that produce ova or egg cells and secrete the female hormone oestrogen 2. the part of a flower that contains the ovules, at the base of a carpel

over- prefix 1. above 2. excessively

overburden noun 1. in strip mining, the soil and rock lying on top of a layer of coal 2. a mineral which is dug away from the surface of the land to expose the coal or mineral below

overcropping noun the practice of growing too many crops on poor soil, which has the effect of greatly reducing soil fertility

overcultivated adjective referring to land that has been too intensively cultivated and has reduced fertility

overexploit verb 1. to work mineral deposits or use other resources in an uncontrolled way until there is very little left 2. to cultivate soil too intensely

overexploitation noun the uncontrolled use of natural resources until there is very little left ○ Overexploitation has reduced herring stocks by half.

overfertilisation noun the application of too much fertiliser to land (NOTE: Excess fertiliser draining from fields can cause pollution of the water in rivers and lakes.)

overfish verb to catch so many fish that the fish do not reproduce quickly enough and become rare

overfishing noun the practice of catching so many fish that the fish do not reproduce quickly enough and become rare ○ Herring stocks have been reduced by overfishing.

overflow noun excess liquid that flows over the edge of a container ■ verb to flow over the edge of a container ○ The floods made the reservoir overflow. ○ The river overflowed its banks and flooded hundred of hectares of farmland.

overgraze verb to graze a pasture so much that it loses nutrients and is no longer able enough to provide food for livestock

overgrazing noun the practice of grazing a pasture so much that it loses nutrients and is no longer able to provide food for livestock ○ Overgrazing has led to soil erosion and desertification.

overland flow *noun* a movement of rainwater or water melting from snow or ice over the surface of the ground in a broad thin layer

overnutrition *noun* **1.** the eating of too much food, or food containing too many calories **2.** same as **eutrophication**

overpopulate *verb* to increase the population of a place so much that available space, food, water or other resources are not adequate to support it

overpopulated *adjective* referring to a place containing too large a population to be adequately supported by the available resources

overproduction *noun* the production of more of something than is wanted or needed

overshot wheel *noun* a type of waterwheel where the water falls on the wheel from above. It is more efficient than an undershot wheel, where the water flows underneath the wheel.

overstorey *noun* the topmost vegetation layer in a forest, formed by the tallest trees. Also called **overwood**

overuse *noun* the excessive use of something ○ *The overuse of pesticides is contaminating the rivers.* ■ *verb* to use something too much ○ *Farmers are warned against overusing synthetic fertilisers.*

overwinter *verb* **1.** to spend winter in a particular place ○ *The herds overwinter on the southern plains.* **2.** to remain alive though the winter ○ *Many plants will not overwinter in areas that have frost.*

overwood *noun* same as **overstorey**

ovicide *noun* a substance, especially an insecticide, that kills eggs

oviparous *adjective* referring to an animal that carries and lays eggs. Compare **viviparous**

ovule *noun* an immature egg or an unfertilised seed

ovum *noun* a female egg cell which, when fertilised by a spermatozoon, begins to develop into an embryo (NOTE: The plural is **ova**.)

ox-bow lake *noun* a curved lake formed when a large curve of a river becomes cut off from the main body of the river by silt

oxidant *noun* same as **oxidising agent**

oxidation *noun* a chemical reaction in which a substance combines with oxygen with loss of electrons

oxidation ditch, oxidation pond *noun* a ditch or pond where sewage is purified by allowing biochemical reactions to take place in it over a period of time

oxidation–reduction *noun* a reversible chemical reaction between two substances where one is oxidised and the other is reduced

oxide *noun* a chemical compound of oxygen

oxidise, oxidize *verb* to form an oxide by the reaction of oxygen with another chemical substance ○ *Over a period of time, the metal is oxidised by contact with air.*

oxidising agent *noun* a substance that forms an oxide with another substance. Also called **oxidant**

oxidising atmosphere *noun* a mixture of gases that contains oxygen and converts elements into oxides through chemical reactions

oxychlorination *noun* the process of neutralising bacteria in water intended for drinking

oxygen *noun* a colourless, odourless gas, essential to human life, constituting 21% by volume of the Earth's atmosphere ○ *Our bodies obtain oxygen through the lungs in respiration.* (NOTE: The chemical symbol is O; the atomic number is **8** and the atomic weight is **16.00**.)

oxygenate *verb* to become filled with oxygen

oxygenation *noun* the process of becoming filled with oxygen

ozone *noun* poisonous form of oxygen found naturally in the atmosphere, which is toxic to humans at concentrations above 0.1 parts per million. Formula: O_3.

ozone-depleting substance *noun* a substance that is known to have unfavourable effects on the ozone layer in the atmosphere. Abbr **ODS**

ozone depletion *noun* the loss of ozone from the atmosphere

ozone-depletion potential, ozone-depleting potential *noun* a measurement of the effect of a substance on reducing the amount of ozone in the atmosphere. Abbr **ODP**

ozone-friendly *adjective* not harmful to the ozone layer in the atmosphere

ozone hole *noun* a thin part in the ozone layer in the atmosphere, which forms over Antarctica each year at the end of winter

ozone layer *noun* the layer of ozone in the atmosphere between 20 and 50 km above the surface of the Earth. Also called **ozonosphere**

COMMENT: The ozone layer in the stratosphere acts as a protection against the harmful effects of the Sun's radiation, and the destruction or reduction of the layer has the effect of allowing more radiation to pass through the atmosphere with harmful results such as skin cancer in humans. The first ozone hole was detected over Antarctica.

ozone monitoring device *noun* a device which measures the levels of ozone in the atmosphere

ozone precursor *noun* a chemical which contributes to the formation of ozone, e.g. nitrogen oxide

ozonosphere *noun* same as **ozone layer**

P

P *symbol* phosphorus

pack *noun* a group of predatory animals which live and hunt together (NOTE: **Pack** is especially used of animals of the dog family such as wolves, but also of other animals such as killer whales.)

package *noun* **1.** an object or set of objects wrapped in a covering **2.** a group of different items brought together ○ *a package of measures designed to reduce consumption*

packaged *adjective* referring to items wrapped in a covering

packaging *noun* the set of coverings used to wrap an object, especially a product that is going to be transported, displayed and sold (NOTE: Packaging may be paper, cardboard, plastic, polystyrene or some other material.)

packaging material *noun* a type of covering such as paper or plastic used to wrap an object, especially a product that is going to be transported, displayed and sold ○ *Many of the packaging materials we used to throw away may now be re-used or recycled to save energy and raw materials.*

packaging waste *noun* material such as paper or plastic used as packaging that is thrown away

COMMENT: In the European Union, member states must have systems for the return and/or collection of used packaging to attain the following targets: recovery 50% to 60% and recycling 25% to 45%, with a minimum of 15% by weight for each packaging material. There are also requirements covering the composition and the re-use, recovery and recycling of packaging.

paddy, padi *noun* a rice crop growing in shallow water ○ *Paddies can be breeding grounds for mosquitoes.*

paddy field *noun* a field filled with shallow water, in which rice is grown ○ *It is thought that paddy fields may contribute to the methane in the atmosphere.*

PAH *abbr* polycyclic aromatic hydrocarbon

paint *noun* a liquid substance put on a surface to give it colour or to protect it ○ *Antifouling paint used on ships' hulls kills marine organisms.*

Palaearctic Region *noun* a biogeographical region, part of Arctogea covering Europe, North Asia and North Africa

palaeo- *prefix* ancient or prehistoric (NOTE: The US spelling is **paleo-**.)

palaeoecology *noun* the study of the ecology of fossils

palaeomagnetism *noun* the study of the magnetism of ancient rocks

palm *noun* a large tropical plant like a tree with branching divided leaves, that produces fruits which give oil and other foodstuffs

palmate *adjective* referring to leaves that split from a central part like the fingers on a hand. Also called **digitate**

palm oil *noun* an edible oil produced from the seed or fruit of an oil palm

paludal *adjective* relating to or living in swamps or marshes

palynology *noun* the scientific study of pollen, especially of pollen found in peat and coal deposits. Also called **pollen analysis**

pampas *noun* a wide area of grassy plains found in South America

PAN *abbr* peroxyacetyl nitrate

pan- *prefix* affecting everything or everywhere

pandemic *adjective, noun* referring to an epidemic disease which affects many parts of the world. ◊ **endemic, epidemic**

panemone *noun* a type of windmill in which flat surfaces spin round a vertical axis

panicle *noun* a flower head (**inflorescence**) with many branches that carry small flowers, e.g. the flower head of a rice plant

paper *noun* a substance made from the pulp of wood, rags or fibre rolled flat into sheets, used for writing on, printing, wrapping objects and other purposes

para- *prefix* **1.** similar to **2.** changed or beyond

paraben *noun* a chemical used in toiletries and as a food preservative (NOTE: It is reported as a possible cause of reproductive or developmental problems because its action is similar to that of the hormone oestrogen.)

paraffin *noun* **1.** a saturated aliphatic hydrocarbon **2.** same as **paraffin oil**

paraffin oil *noun* oil produced from petroleum, used as a fuel in aircraft engines, for domestic heating and lighting, and as a solvent. Also called **paraffin**

parallel *noun* **1.** same as **parallel of latitude 2.** a line representing a parallel on a map or chart

parallel of latitude *noun* an angular distance north or south of the Earth's equator, measured in degrees, minutes and seconds, along a meridian. Also called **parallel**

parameter *noun* **1.** a factor that defines the limits or actions of something ○ *The X parameter defines the number of characters displayed across a screen.* ○ *The size of the array is set with this parameter.* **2.** a variable quantity or value for which a measurement is attempted, e.g. mean height

parapatric speciation *noun* the development of new species in areas which are next to each other and so not completely isolated

paraquat *noun* a herbicide that destroys a wide range of plants by killing their foliage and becomes inert on contact with the soil

parasite *noun* a plant or animal which lives on or inside another organism, the host, and derives its nourishment and other needs from it ○ *a water-borne parasite*

parasitic *adjective* referring to animal or plant parasites ○ *a parasitic worm* ○ *Dodder is a parasitic plant.*

parasiticide *noun* a substance that kills parasites

parasitise, **parasitize** *verb* to live as a parasite on another organism ○ *Sheep are parasitised by flukes.*

parasitism *noun* a state in which one organism, the parasite, lives on or inside another organism, the host, and derives its nourishment and other needs from it

parasitoid *noun* an organism that is a parasite only at one stage in its development

parasitoidism *noun* the state of being a parasite only at one stage of development, as when an insect lays eggs inside the body of a host

parasitology *noun* the scientific study of parasites

parcel *noun* **1.** a package **2.** a plot of land **3.** a quantity of wood, either growing in a forest or cut down, which is sold

parent *noun* a male or female that has produced offspring

parent rock *noun* same as **mother rock**

park *noun* an area of open land used as a place of recreation

parkland *noun* grazed grassland or heathland with large individual trees or small groups of large trees, usually part of a designed and managed landscape

parthenocarpy *noun* the production of seedless fruits without fertilisation having taken place

parthenogenesis *noun* a form of reproduction in which an unfertilised ovum develops into an individual

particle *noun* **1.** a very small piece of a substance ○ *soil particles* ○ *Particles of volcanic ash were carried into the upper atmosphere.* **2.** ♦ **elementary particle**

particulate *adjective* made up of separate particles ■ *noun* a tiny solid piece of a substance

COMMENT: The finest particulates in the air are the most dangerous pollutants as they are easily inhaled into the bronchioles in the lungs. Fine particulates from volcanic eruptions can enter the stratosphere and have a cooling effect by preventing the heat from the Sun reaching the Earth's surface, i.e. the opposite of the greenhouse effect.

particulate matter *noun* any matter in the atmosphere except water, including dust particles, pollen or particles produced by internal combustion engines. Abbr **PM**

parts per billion *noun* a measure of the concentration of a substance in a gas, liquid or solid. Abbr **ppb**

parts per million *noun* a measure of the concentration of a substance in a gas, liquid or solid. Abbr **ppm**

passage *noun* 1. a long narrow channel or corridor 2. a movement from one place to another

passerine *noun* a bird belonging to an order of birds which typically come to rest on branches. Order: Passeriformes. ■ *adjective* referring to a passerine

passive *adjective* not actively participating. Opposite **active**

passive smoking *noun* a situation in which someone breathes in tobacco smoke from the atmosphere around them. This process may cause lung cancer.

pastoral *adjective* 1. referring to agriculture based on grazing animals 2. referring to land available for pasture

pastoralist *noun* a farmer who keeps grazing animals on pasture ○ *The people most affected by the drought in the Sahara are nomadic pastoralists.*

pasture *noun* land covered with grass or other small plants, used by farmers as a feeding place for animals ○ *a mixture of pasture and woodland* ○ *Their cows are on summer pastures high in the mountains.* □ **to put cattle out to pasture** to put cattle onto land covered with grass or other small plants ■ *verb* to put animals onto land covered with grass or other small plants ○ *Their cows are pastured in fields high in the mountains.*

pasture agronomist *noun* a person who specialises in the study of types of plants grown in pastures

pastureland *noun* land covered with grass or other small plants, used by farmers as a feeding place for animals

patch dynamics *noun* a process in which the disturbance of a community creates gaps which are then colonised by the same or another species

path *noun* 1. a way from one place to another, especially one travelled on foot. ◊ **bridle path, cycle path, footpath** 2. a way to achieve something

patho- *prefix* disease

pathogen *noun* an agent, usually a microorganism, that causes a disease

pathogenesis *noun* the origin, production or development of a disease

pathogenetic *adjective* referring to pathogenesis

pathogenic *adjective* able to cause or produce a disease

pathogenicity *noun* the ability of a pathogen to cause a disease

pathogenic organism *noun* an organism responsible for causing a disease

pathological *adjective* 1. referring to a disease 2. caused by a disease 3. indicating a disease

pathologist *noun* 1. a scientist who specialises in the study of diseases 2. a person who checks tissue and other samples for evidence of disease 3. a doctor who examines dead bodies to find out the cause of death

pathology *noun* the study of diseases and the changes in structure and function which diseases can cause

pathway *noun* 1. a path, especially a footpath, or a route 2. the route by which a contaminant can reach a receptor and cause harm

Pb *symbol* lead

PBB *abbr* polybrominated biphenyl

PCB *abbr* polychlorinated biphenyl

PCF *abbr* process(ed) chlorine-free

PCW *abbr* post-consumer waste

PE *abbr* production efficiency

peak *noun* 1. the top of a mountain 2. the highest point of something ○ *The intensity of solar radiation reaches a peak around noon.*

peak average *noun* the average of all the highest points on a graph or in a series of figures

peak traffic *noun* the largest number of vehicles that travel in an area within a specific period ○ *The hours of peak traffic at the junction are 8–9 a.m. and 5–7 p.m.*

peasouper *noun* a type of thick dark yellow fog caused by sulfur particles from burning coal, formerly common in the winter time in London before the 1960s (*informal*)

peat *noun* the accumulated partly decayed mosses and other plants which form the soil of a bog, often forming a deep layer (NOTE: Peat was used as a fuel in some areas and was widely used in gardens to improve the texture of the soil or mixed with soil or other materials to grow plants in pots. These practices are now discouraged in order to prevent the overuse of peat bogs.)

peat bog *noun* an area of wet acidic land, low in nutrients, in which peat has formed

peat-free *adjective* referring to material that does not contain peat

peat-free compost *noun* material in which plants can be grown in pots that does not contain peat ○ *Coir fibre from coconut shells can be used as a peat-free compost.*

peatland *noun* an area of land covered with peat bog

peaty *adjective* containing peat ○ *peaty soil* ○ *peaty water*

pebble *noun* a small, often rounded piece of rock, less than 64 mm in diameter

pedestrian *noun* a person who travels by walking

pedestrian area, pedestrian zone *noun* a part of a town where only people who are walking are allowed

pedestrianisation, pedestrianization *noun* the process of making part of a town into an area where only people who are walking are allowed

pedestrianise, pedestrianize *verb* to make part of a town into an area where only people who are walking are allowed

pedicel *noun* a stalk that carries a single flower within a flower head (**inflorescence**)

peduncle *noun* 1. a stalk-like structure such as that attaching a polyp to the rock on which it lives 2. the main flower stalk of a plant

pelagic *adjective* referring to the top and middle layers of sea water. Compare **demersal**

pelagic deposits *plural noun* material that has fallen to the sea floor. Also called **pelagic sediment**

pelagic species *noun* fish that live at or near the surface of the sea, e.g. swordfish, tuna, anchovies and sardines

pelagic zone *noun* the part of the sea that is not near the shore and not immediately above the seabed

Pelton wheel *noun* a type of water turbine that has specially shaped buckets attached to the edge of a wheel which are struck by a jet of water

penalty *noun* a fine or other action taken to punish someone for doing something ○ *The government has imposed penalties on industrial concerns which emit too much pollution.*

peneplain *noun* a plain formed after mountains have been completely eroded

peninsula *noun* a long narrow piece of land, surrounded on three sides by sea

peninsular *adjective* referring to a peninsula

pentad *noun* a five-day period (NOTE: This term is used especially in meteorological forecasting and recording.)

per *preposition* for each or every ○ *the recommended daily dose per person*

perceived noise level *noun* a measurement of the loudness of a sound as heard by the human ear. Abbr **PNL**

perceived noise level in decibels *noun* a measurement of sound pressure in decibels. Abbr **PNdB**

percentage *noun* 1. the proportion or rate equivalent to a total divided by a hundred ○ *Some 20% of infected plants died, a much higher percentage than expected.* 2. an inexact proportion or amount ○ *Developing countries possess the largest percentage of the world's rainforest.*

percentile *noun* one of a series of 99 figures below which a particular percentage of the total falls

percolate *verb* to move slowly through a quantity of solid particles ○ *Water percolates through the soil.*

perennial *adjective* lasting for many years ■ *noun* a plant that lives for a long time, flowering each year without dying. ♦ **annual, biennial** (NOTE: In herbaceous perennials the parts above ground die back in winter, but the plant persists under the ground and produces new shoots in the spring. In woody perennials, permanent stems remain above the ground in the winter.)

perfluorocarbons *plural noun* a group of synthetic chemical compounds that are potent greenhouse gases. Abbr **PFCs**

perform *verb* to carry out an action or role ○ *to perform a biological experiment* ○ *The kidneys perform the function of eliminating nitrogenous waste.*

perianth *noun* the outer parts of a flower, made up of a calyx, corolla or both

pericarp *noun* the part of a fruit that encloses the seed or seeds

period *noun* 1. a length of time ○ *a 24 hour period* ○ *a period of 3 minutes* 2. an interval of geological time, the subdivision of an era and itself divided into epochs ○ *the Cretaceous period*

periodic *adjective* happening from time to time ○ *a periodic review of the company's performance*

periphyton *noun* a dense mass of strands of algal growth that covers the water surface between emerging aquatic plants

peri-urban *adjective* on the edge of a built-up area

permaculture *noun* a system of permanent agriculture, which involves carefully designing human habitats and food production systems

permafrost *noun* ground that is permanently frozen, as in the Arctic regions (NOTE: Although the top layer of soil melts and softens in the summer the soil beneath remains frozen.)

permanent *adjective* lasting or remaining without change

permanent grassland, permanent pasture *noun* land that remains as grassland for a long time and is not ploughed

permeability *noun* 1. the ability of a rock to allow water to pass through it 2. the ability of a membrane to allow fluid or chemical substances to pass through it

permeable *adjective* with a degree of permeability (NOTE: The US term is **pervious**.)

peroxyacetyl nitrate *noun* a substance contained in photochemical smog, which is extremely harmful to plants. Abbr **PAN**

persist *verb* 1. to continue to exist ○ *Snow cover tends to persist on north-facing slopes of mountains.* 2. (*of a chemical compound*) to remain active without breaking down in the environment for a period of time ○ *The chemical persists in the soil.* 3. (*of a plant*) to grow for several seasons

persistence *noun* 1. the ability to persist ○ *The persistence and movement of cols is governed by the movement of the adjacent pressure systems.* 2. the ability of a chemical to remain active without breaking down in the environment for a period of time 3. (*of a plant*) the ability to grow for several seasons

persistent *adjective* 1. continuing for some time ○ *persistent flickering of the screen* 2. remaining active without breaking down for some time ○ *persistent chemicals* 3. growing for several seasons ○ *persistent species*

persistent insecticide, persistent pesticide *noun* a chemical compound used to kill insect or other pests that remains without breaking down in the soil or in the body of an animal and is passed from animal to animal through the food chain

personal *adjective* referring to direct relationships between people ○ *The information came through a personal contact.*

personal communication *noun* information given by one person directly to another

pervious *adjective* US same as **permeable**

pest *noun* an organism that carries disease or harms plants or animals ○ *a spray to remove insect pests*

pesticide *noun* a chemical compound used to kill pests such as insects, other animals, fungi or weeds

pesticide residue *noun* the amount of a pesticide that remains in the environment after application

Pesticides Trust *noun* a group that works to minimise and eventually eliminate the hazards of pesticides

pesticide tax *noun* a proposed tax to restrict the use of pesticides

PET *abbr* polyethylene terephthalate

petal *noun* a single part of the corolla of a flower ○ *A buttercup flower has yellow petals.*

petiole *noun* the stalk of a leaf

petrifaction *noun* the process of turning a substance into stone

petrify *verb* to turn a substance into stone

petrochemical *noun* a chemical derived from petroleum or natural gas

petrochemistry *noun* 1. the scientific study of the chemical composition of petroleum and substances derived from it 2. the scientific study of the chemical composition of rocks

petrol *noun* a liquid made from petroleum, used as a fuel in internal combustion engines ○ *We are looking for a car with a low petrol consumption.* (NOTE: The US term is **gasoline**.)

petroleum *noun* oil that is extracted from the ground

petrology *noun* the study of rocks and minerals (NOTE: Petrology has no direct connection with **petrol**.)

PFA *abbr* pulverised fuel ash

PFBC *abbr* pressurised fluidised-bed combustion

PFCs *abbr* perfluorocarbons

pH *noun* a measure of the acidity of a solution, determined as the negative logarithm of the hydrogen ion concentration, on a scale from 0 to 14 ○ *soil pH* (NOTE: A pH less than 7 is acid, and a pH more than 7 is alkaline.)

phalanx *noun* a plant species that invades a community as a dense mass. Compare **guerrilla**

phase *noun* a stage or part of a larger process ○ *the vegetative phase* ○ *A result may occur during any phase of the experiment.*

phenology *noun* the effect of climate on annually recurring phenomena such as animal migration or plant flowering

phenomenon *noun* an event that exists and is experienced ○ *Chemical reactions in the atmosphere generate phenomena such as acid rain and photochemical smog.* (NOTE: The plural is **phenomena**.)

phenotype *noun* the physical characteristics of an organism, produced by its genes. Compare **genotype**

phenotypic *adjective* relating to a phenotype

phenotypic plasticity *noun* the ability of a phenotype to vary as a result of environmental influences on its genetic makeup

pheromone *noun* a chemical substance produced and released into the environment by an animal, influencing the behaviour of another individual of the same species ○ *Some insects produce pheromones to attract mates.*

pH factor *noun* ▸ **pH**

-philia *suffix* attraction towards or liking for something

philoprogenitive *adjective* referring to an organism that produces many offspring

phloem *noun* the vascular tissue in a plant that is formed of living cells and conducts organic substances from the leaves to the rest of the plant. ◊ **xylem**

phosphate *noun* a salt of phosphoric acid which is formed naturally by weathering of rocks (NOTE: It is an essential plant nutrient.)

COMMENT: Natural organic phosphates are provided by guano and fishmeal, otherwise phosphates are mined. Artificially produced phosphates are used in agriculture and are known as superphosphates because they are highly concentrated. Phosphates escape into water from sewage, especially waste water containing detergents, and encourage the growth of algae by eutrophication.

phosphorous *adjective* containing phosphorus

phosphorus *noun* a chemical element that is essential to biological life (NOTE: The chemical symbol is **P**; the atomic number is **15** and the atomic weight is **30.97**.)

phosphorus cycle *noun* a cycle by which phosphorus atoms are circulated through living organisms

phot- *prefix* same as **photo-** (NOTE: used before vowels)

photic zone *noun* same as **euphotic zone**. Compare **aphotic zone**

photo- *prefix* light

photoautotrophic *adjective* using light energy to create a source of food. Compare **chemoautotrophic**

photocell *noun* same as **photoelectric cell**

photochemical *adjective* referring to a chemical reaction that is caused by light ○ *Gases rise into the upper atmosphere and undergo photochemical change.*

photochemical oxidant *noun* a substance which is produced by a chemical reaction with light, e.g. ozone

photochemical pollution *noun* pollution caused by the action of light on chemicals in the lower atmosphere

COMMENT: When the atmosphere near ground level is polluted with nitrogen oxides from burning fossil fuels together with hydrocarbons, ultraviolet light from the Sun sets off a series of reactions that result in photochemical pollution, containing, among other substances, ozone.

photochemical reaction *noun* a chemical reaction started by the absorption of light (NOTE: Photosynthesis and photochemical smog are examples of such a reaction.)

photochemical smog *noun* air pollution caused by the effect of strong sunlight on nitrogen dioxide and hydrocarbons emitted by motor vehicles, creating a harmful haze of minute droplets in the air

photochemistry *noun* the study of chemical changes brought about by light and other forms of radiation

photoconverter *noun* a device that converts energy from light into electric energy

photodecomposition *noun* the breaking down of a substance by the action of light

photoelectric cell *noun* a cell in which light falling on the cell is converted to electricity. Also called **photocell**

photogenic *adjective* **1.** produced by the action of light **2.** referring to an organism producing light

photolysis *noun* the breakdown of a chemical by light or other electromagnetic radiation

photonastic *adjective* referring to photonasty

photonasty *noun* a response of plants to light without movement towards the light source. ◊ **phototaxis**

photo-oxidant *noun* a chemical compound produced by the action of sunlight on nitrogen oxides and hydrocarbons

photo-oxidation *noun* a change in the chemical constitution of a compound by the action of sunlight ○ *Photo-oxidation breaks down polluted air and converts the gases to sulfur dioxide.*

photoperiod *noun* the period in every 24 hours when an organism is exposed to daylight ○ *Short-day plants require a photoperiod of less than 12 hours for flowering.* (NOTE: Photoperiod has an effect on activities such as flowering and mating.)

photoperiodicity *noun* the degree to which plants and animals react to changes in the length of the period of daylight from summer to winter

photoperiodism *noun* the response of an organism in its growth and behaviour to the amount of daylight it receives in every 24 hours

photophilic, photophilous *adjective* referring to an organism that grows best in strong light

photorespiration *noun* a reaction that occurs in plants, alongside photosynthesis, in which the plant fixes oxygen from the air and loses carbon dioxide (NOTE: Photorespiration reduces the production of sugars by photosynthesis. Some crop plants have been bred to reduce their photorespiration rate.)

photosensitive *adjective* **1.** sensitive to light **2.** stimulated by light

photosensitivity *noun* the state of being sensitive to or stimulated by light

photosynthesis *noun* the process by which green plants convert carbon dioxide and water into sugar and oxygen using sunlight as energy

photosynthesise, photosynthesize *verb* to carry out photosynthesis ○ *Acid rain falling on trees reduces their ability to photosynthesise.*

photosynthetic *adjective* referring to photosynthesis

photosynthetic capacity *noun* the calculation of the efficiency of conversion of solar energy by photosynthesis

phototaxis *noun* a movement of all or part of an organism in response to light either towards or away from it

phototroph *noun* an organism that obtains its energy from sunlight. Compare **chemotroph**

phototrophic *adjective* obtaining energy from sunlight. Compare **chemotrophic** (NOTE: Plants are phototrophic.)

phototropic *adjective* referring to a plant or a cell that turns or grows towards or away from light

phototropism *noun* the response of plants or cells to light by turning or growing towards or away from it (NOTE: Most plant shoots show positive phototropism, i.e. they grow towards the light.)

photovoltaic *adjective* converting the energy from electromagnetic radiation such as light into electricity

photovoltaic cell, photovoltaic panel *noun* a device that converts the energy from light into electricity. Also called **photovoltaic, photovoltaic panel** (NOTE: As light strikes the cell the electrons in it become mobile and create electricity.)

phreatic *adjective* referring to the water table

phreatophyte *noun* a plant whose roots go down into the water table

phthalate *noun* a chemical compound used to soften plastics and in many toiletries (NOTE: It is reported as a possible cause of reproductive or developmental problems because its action is similar to that of the hormone oestrogen.)

pH value *noun* ♦ pH

phycology *noun* the scientific study of algae

phylogenesis, phylogeny *noun* the evolutionary history of an organism or group of organisms

phylum *noun* a major subdivision in the classification of organisms, below kingdom (NOTE: The plural is **phyla**.)

physical *adjective* **1.** referring to matter and energy or the sciences dealing with them, especially physics **2.** referring to the body rather than the mind ○ *physical discomfort* ○ *describe its physical appearance* **3.** being touched or able to be touched or felt ○ *physical contact*

physics *noun* the scientific study of matter, including electricity, radiation, magnetism and other phenomena that do not change the chemical composition of matter

physio- *prefix* physiology

physiological *adjective* referring to physiology

physiological ecology *noun* the study of the physiology of an individual and the effects on function and behaviour in its habitat

physiological specialisation *noun* a phenomenon whereby some members of a population look identical but differ biochemically

physiologist *noun* a scientist who specialises in the study of the functions of living organisms

physiology *noun* the scientific study of the functions of living organisms

phyto- *prefix* plant

phytoaccumulation *noun* same as **phytoextraction**

phytobenthos *noun* the plants that live on the bottom of the sea, lake or river

phytochemical *noun* a substance occurring naturally in a plant ■ *adjective* referring to phytochemistry

phytochemistry *noun* the study of the chemistry of substances found in plants

phytochrome *noun* a pigment molecule in plants which is sensitive to slight changes in day length and controls the plant's growth timetable

phytoextraction *noun* the absorption by plants of metal contaminants through their roots and subsequent storage in their upper parts, allowing the decontamination of land. Also called **phytoaccumulation**

phytogeography *noun* the study of plants and their geographical distribution

phytome *noun* a plant community

phytonutrient *noun* a substance in plants that is beneficial to human health, e.g. a vitamin or antioxidant

phytophagous *adjective* referring to an animal that eats plants

phytoplankter *noun* a single microscopic plant that floats in the sea or in a lake

phytoplankton *plural noun* microscopic plants that float in the sea or in a lake (NOTE: Phytoplankton, formed mainly of diatoms and using the sunlight in the surface layers of the water to photosynthesise, are the basis of the food chain of almost all aquatic animals.)

phytoplankton bloom *noun* a large mass of plankton that develops regularly at different periods of the year and floats on the surface of the sea or of a lake

phytoplanktonic *adjective* referring to phytoplankton

phytoremediation *noun* the decontamination of land by growing plants to absorb heavy metals or other soil contaminants

phytosociology *noun* the branch of ecology concerned with the identification, analysis, and classification of the species composition of plant communities or plant associations

phytostabilisation, **phytostabilization** *noun* the use of plants to trap soil contaminants in their roots and prevent them from polluting ground water

phytotoxic *adjective* poisonous to plants

phytotoxicant *noun* a substance that is phytotoxic

phytotoxin *noun* a poisonous substance produced by a plant

PIC *abbr* product of incomplete combustion

picogram *noun* one trillionth of a gram

piezometer *noun* an instrument for measuring the pressure of a liquid

piezometric, piezometrical *adjective* referring to the level reached by water under its own pressure in a borehole or in a piezometer

pigment *noun* a substance that gives colour to a part of an organism, e.g. melanin in animals or chlorophyll in plants

pigmentary *adjective* referring to or producing pigment

pigmentation *noun* the colouring of an animal's body, especially that produced by deposits of pigment

pileus *noun* **1.** the domed or bell-shaped part of the body of a jellyfish **2.** the cap of a mushroom or toadstool

pilot project *noun* a small-scale project carried out to see whether a large-scale project will work ○ *They are running a pilot project in the area for three months before deciding on the next stage.*

pine *noun* an evergreen coniferous tree. Genus: *Pinus.* ○ *The north of the country is covered with forests of pine.*

pine cone *noun* a hard scaly structure bearing the seeds of a pine tree

pine forest *noun* a large wooded area containing mainly pines

pine tree *noun* same as **pine**

pinetum *noun* an area where different types of pine have been planted

pinewood *noun* a wooded area containing mainly pines

pinna *noun* **1.** a thin, flat, tapering body part such as a feather or fin **2.** one of the small leaves on a pinnate leaf

pinnate *adjective* with small leaves arranged on each side of a central stalk

pioneer, pioneer species *noun* a species that is one of the first to begin to grow in a previously unoccupied site, e.g. a moss growing on a scree slope

pipeline *noun* a long tube through which a fluid or gas flows from one place to another

pisciculture *noun* the breeding of edible fish in special pools for sale as food

pit *noun* **1.** a large hole in the ground, e.g. for burying or planting something **2.** an

area of land from which minerals, especially coal, are removed, and the buildings associated with the activity. Also called **mine**
3. a small indentation in a surface

pitch *noun* **1.** the frequency of a sound (NOTE: A low-pitched sound has a low frequency and a high-pitched sound has a high frequency.) **2.** a dark sticky substance obtained from tar, used to make objects watertight **3.** the angle of the blades of a wind or water turbine in relation to the flow of wind or water

pith *noun* the tissue found in the centre of plant stems. Also called **medulla**

pitted *adjective* with small indentations ○ *a pitted surface*

placental mammal *noun* same as **eutherian** (NOTE: All mammals are placental except for monotremes and marsupials.)

plagioclimax *noun* a stage in the development of a plant ecosystem where the system is kept stable by human intervention, as in managed woodlands

plagiosere *noun* a succession of plants that takes a new course because of the effect of a biotic factor

plague *noun* **1.** an infectious disease that occurs in epidemics which kill many organisms **2.** a widespread infestation by a pest ○ *A plague of locusts has invaded the region and is destroying crops.*

plain *noun* a level area of land with few trees ■ *plural noun* **plains** a large area of flat country with few trees, especially in the middle of North America

plan *noun* **1.** an organised way of doing something **2.** a drawing that shows how something is arranged or how something will be built ■ *verb* to organise carefully how something should be done

plane *noun* a deciduous hardwood tree, frequently grown in towns because of its resistance to air pollution. Genus: *Platanus*.

planet *noun* a large body in the solar system, e.g. Earth, Mars or Mercury

planetary *adjective* referring to a planet

plankter *noun* a single microscopic animal or plant that lives and drifts in water (NOTE: The plural is **plankton**.)

planktivorous *adjective* referring to an animal that eats plankton

plankton *plural noun* the microscopic animals and plants that drift near the surface of the water, belonging to two groups: zooplankton, which are microscopic animals, and phytoplankton, which are microscopic plants capable of photosynthesis (NOTE: A single organism is a **plankter**.)

planktonic *adjective* referring to plankton ○ *Blooms are population explosions of planktonic plants.*

planner *noun* a person responsible for planning an activity or development

planning *noun* **1.** the careful organisation of how something should be done **2.** the organisation of how land and buildings are to be used

planning authority *noun* a local authority which gives permission for development such as changes to existing buildings or new use of land

planning controls *plural noun* legislation used by a local authority to control building

planning department *noun* a section of a local authority which deals with requests for planning permission

planning inquiry *noun* a hearing before a government inspector relating to a decision of a local authority in planning matters

planning permission *noun* an official agreement allowing a person or company to plan new buildings on empty land or to alter existing buildings

plant *noun* **1.** an organism containing chlorophyll with which it carries out photosynthesis **2.** a very large factory or industrial site ○ *A nuclear power plant is to be built near the town.* **3.** large heavy equipment and vehicles ■ *verb* to put plants in the ground ○ *to plant a crop of rice*

plantation *noun* **1.** an estate, especially in the tropics, on which large-scale production of cash crops takes place (NOTE: Plantations specialise in the production of a single crop such as cocoa, coffee, cotton, tea or rubber.) **2.** an area of land planted with trees for commercial purposes. Also called **plantation forest**

plant breeding *noun* the practice of producing new forms of ornamental and crop plants by artificial selection

plant community *noun* a group of plants growing together in an area

plant cover *noun* the percentage of an area occupied by plants ○ *Plant cover at these altitudes is sparse.*

plant ecology *noun* the study of the relationship between plants and their environment

plant genetic resources *plural noun* the gene pool of plants, especially of plants regarded as of value to humans for food or pharmaceuticals

plant health *noun* the areas related to the prevention of pests and diseases affecting plants and plant produce, including the control of imports and exports

plant hormone *noun* a hormone that affects plant growth

plant kingdom *noun* the category of all organisms classified as plants

plantlet *noun* BOT a young plant

PlantNet *noun* a national network of botanic gardens, arboreta and other documented plant collections in Britain and Ireland

plant nutrient *noun* a mineral whose presence is essential for the healthy growth of plants

plant plankton *plural noun* same as **phytoplankton**

plant population *noun* the number of plants found in a particular area

plant protection *noun* the activity of protecting plants from disease by biocontrol, cultivation practices and especially by the application of pesticides

plant science *noun* the scientific study of plants

plant scientist *noun* a scientist who studies plants

plant sociology *noun* the study of communities of plants

plastic *noun* an artificial, usually organic, material made from petroleum and used to make many objects

COMMENT: Plastics are moulded by heating a substance under pressure and they retain their shape after being formed. Thermoplastics are heated while being shaped and can be heated and shaped again for re-use. Thermosetting plastics are heated while being shaped but cannot be reheated for recycling. Waste plastics containing chlorine can produce hydrogen chloride when incinerated. Plastics formed from ethylene or propylene (i.e. polyethylene and polypropylene) are not degradable and must be recycled or destroyed by incineration.

plastic foam *noun* same as **foam plastic**

plasticiser, plasticizer *noun* a substance, usually a synthetic organic chemical, that is added to a material to make it more flexible

plasticity *noun* variability in the growth of a plant in response to differences in the supply of resources

plate *noun* same as **tectonic plate**

plateau *noun* an area of high flat land (NOTE: The plural is **plateaux**.)

platinum *noun* a rare metallic element that does not corrode (NOTE: The chemical

symbol is **Pt**; atomic number is **78** and the atomic weight is **195.09**.)

Pleistocene, Pleistocene epoch *noun* the period in the Earth's evolution that lasted until about ten thousand years ago, including the main Ice Ages

plough *noun* an agricultural implement used to turn over the surface of the soil in order to cultivate crops ■ *verb* to turn over the soil with a plough (NOTE: [all senses] The US spelling is **plow**.)

plug *noun* a round block of igneous rock forming the central vent of an old volcanic opening

plumbism *noun* lead poisoning caused by taking in lead salts

plume *noun* **1.** a tall cloud of smoke or gas escaping from a factory chimney ○ *a gas plume* **2.** a tall cloud of smoke or gas escaping from a volcano **3.** a long expanse of pollution in ground water or an aquifer **4.** a cloud of powdered snow blowing from a mountain crest **5.** a large feather

plumule *noun* the tiny structure in a plant embryo from which a shoot will develop

plutonium *noun* a toxic and carcinogenic radioactive element extracted from uranium ore (NOTE: The chemical symbol is **Pu**; the atomic number is **94** and the atomic weight is **244**.)

PM *abbr* particulate matter

PNdB *abbr* perceived noise level in decibels

pneum- *prefix* same as **pneumo-** (NOTE: used before vowels)

pneumatophore *noun* a root growing down from a branch in plants such as mangrove growing in wet ground

pneumo- *prefix* air, the lungs or breathing

pneumoconiosis *noun* a lung disease in which fibrous tissue forms in the lungs because the patient has inhaled particles of stone or dust over a long period

PNL *abbr* perceived noise level

Po *symbol* polonium

Poaceae *noun* a very large family of plants, the grasses, including bamboo and cereals such as wheat and maize. Former name **Gramineae**

poach *verb* to catch animals, birds or fish illegally on someone else's land

poacher *noun* a person who catches animals, birds or fish illegally on someone else's land

poaching *noun* the illegal activity catching animals, birds or fish on someone else's land

pod *noun* **1.** a container for several seeds, e.g. a pea pod or bean pod **2.** a small group of whales, dolphins, or seals

podsol, podzol *noun* a type of acid soil where oxides have been leached from the light-coloured top layer into a darker lower layer through which water does not flow and which contains little organic matter

podsolic, podzolic *adjective* referring to podsol

podsolic soil *noun* a soil that has formed a podsol. Also called **podsolised soil**

podsolisation, podsolization *noun* the process by which a podsol forms

podsolised soil, podsolized soil *noun* same as **podsolic soil**

poikilo- *prefix* irregular or varied

poikilosmotic *adjective* referring to an aquatic animal whose body fluids change by osmosis depending on the composition of the surrounding water

poikilotherm *noun* same as **ectotherm**

pointer *noun* an indication of how something will develop ○ *a pointer to future research priorities*

point out *verb* to make someone aware of a piece of information

point source *noun* a discharge of a pollutant or radiant energy from a single place, e.g. a pipe, ship or installation. Compare **non-point source**

poison *noun* a substance which can kill or harm a person or animal when eaten, drunk, breathed in or touched ■ *verb* to expose an organism to a poison ○ *They were poisoned by toxic fumes.*

poisoning *noun* the act of killing or harming an organism with a poison

poisonous *adjective* containing poison ○ *a poisonous gas* ○ *Some fungi are good to eat and some are poisonous.*

polar *adjective* referring to the North Pole or South Pole ○ *polar air* ○ *a polar region*

polar ice cap *noun* a large area of thick ice covering the regions around the North or South Pole, which is slowly disappearing as the Earth warms

polar vortex *noun* same as **circumpolar vortex**

polder *noun* a piece of low-lying land which has been reclaimed from the sea and is surrounded by earth banks, especially in the Netherlands

pole *noun* **1.** one of two opposite points on an axis **2.** the extreme north or south point of the Earth's axis ○ *A meridian is a line joining pole to pole.*

policy *noun* a plan for dealing with a situation ○ *transport policy*

political *adjective* concerning politics

politician *noun* a person actively involved in politics, especially a member of a parliament or assembly

politics *noun* the practice or study of how to govern a country

pollard *noun* a tree of which the branches have been cut back to a height of about 2 m above the ground ■ *verb* to cut back the branches on a tree every year or every few years to a height of about 2 m above the ground. Compare **coppice**

pollen *noun* the mass of small grains in the anthers of flowers which contain the male gametes

pollen analysis *noun* same as **palynology**

pollen count *noun* a measurement of the amount of pollen in a sample of air (NOTE: A high pollen count is bad for people who have hay fever.)

pollinate *verb* to transfer pollen from anther to stigma in a flower

pollination *noun* the action of pollinating a flower (NOTE: There is no English noun 'pollinisation'.)

pollinator *noun* **1.** an organism which helps pollinate a plant, e.g. a bee or bird ○ *Some apple trees need to be planted with pollinators as they are not self-fertile.* ○ *Birds are pollinators for many types of tropical plant.* **2.** a plant from which pollen is transferred by bees to pollinate another plant, especially a fruit tree, that is not self-fertile ○ *Some apple and pear trees need to be planted with pollinators.*

pollinosis *noun* inflammation of the nose and eyes caused by an allergic reaction to pollen, fungal spores or dust in the atmosphere. Also called **hay fever**

pollutant *noun* **1.** a substance that causes pollution **2.** noise, smell or another unwanted occurrence that affects a person's surroundings unfavourably

pollute *verb* to discharge harmful substances in unusually high concentrations into the environment ○ *Polluting gases react with the sun's rays.* ○ *Polluted soil must be removed and buried.*

polluter *noun* a person or company that causes pollution

polluter-pays principle *noun* the principle that, if pollution occurs, the person or company responsible should be required to pay for the consequences of the pollution and for avoiding it in future. Abbr **PPP**. ◊ **user-pays principle**

polluting agent *noun* a substance that causes pollution

pollution *noun* the presence of unusually high concentrations of harmful substances or radioactivity in the environment, as a result of human activity or a natural process such as a volcanic eruption, or the unwanted presence of noise or artificial light ○ *In terms of pollution, gas is by far the cleanest fuel.* ○ *Pollution of the atmosphere has increased over the last 50 years.* ○ *Soil pollution round mines poses a problem for land reclamation.*

pollution abatement *noun* a reduction of pollution

pollution alert *noun* a warning that pollution levels are or will be high

pollution charges *plural noun* the costs of repairing or stopping environmental pollution

pollution control, pollution prevention *noun* the activity of taking measures to limit the human activities that produce pollution

polonium *noun* a natural radioactive element (NOTE: The chemical symbol is **Po**; the atomic number is **84** and the atomic weight is **209**.)

poly- *prefix* many

polyandry *noun* a breeding arrangement in which a female has several mates

polybrominated biphenyl *noun* a highly toxic aromatic compound containing benzene and bromine. It is used in plastics, electrical equipment and fire-retardant materials and is either banned or very restricted in use in many countries. Abbr **PBB**

polychlorinated biphenyl, polychlorobiphenyl *noun* one of a group of compounds produced by chlorination of biphenyl. Abbr **PCB**

COMMENT: PCBs are stable compounds and formerly were extensively used in electrical fittings and paints. Although they are no longer manufactured they are extremely persistent and remain in large quantities in landfill sites. They are not water-soluble and float on the surface of water where they are eaten by aquatic animals and so enter the food chain. PCBs are fat-soluble, and are therefore easy to take into the system, but difficult to excrete.

polycondensed plastic *noun* a type of plastic which can be recycled, e.g. nylon

polycrystalline silicon *noun* silicon used to manufacture photovoltaic panels

polyculture *noun* the rearing or growing of more than one species of plant or animal on the same area of land at the same time

polycyclic aromatic hydrocarbon *noun* one of a group of chemical compounds which are carcinogenic. Abbr **PAH**

polyethylene *noun* same as **polythene**

polyethylene terephthalate *noun* a type of plastic that can be recycled, used to make artificial fibres and plastic bottles. Abbr **PET**

polygamy *noun* a breeding arrangement in which a male has several mates. Compare **monogamy**

polyhaline *adjective* (*of water*) containing almost as much salt as sea water. Compare **mesohaline, oligohaline**

polymorphic *adjective* existing in different forms

polymorphism *noun* **1.** the existence of different forms during the life cycle of an organism, as in the example of a butterfly, which exists as a caterpillar, then a pupa, before becoming a butterfly **2.** the existence of different forms of an organism in a social system, as in the example of bees, which exist as workers, queens and drones

polymorphous *adjective* same as **polymorphic**

polynyas *noun* in a frozen sea, an area of water that is not frozen, created by local water currents in northern oceans

polyp *noun* a water animal that does not swim about, e.g. a sea anemone

polyphagous *adjective* referring to an organism that eats more than one type of food ○ *a polyphagous animal* Compare **monophagous**

polyphagy *noun* the practice of eating more than one type of food. Compare **monophagy**

polypropylene *noun* a type of plastic used to make artificial fibres, bottles, pipes, and other articles, which is not degradable and must be recycled or destroyed by incineration

polysaprobe *noun* an organism which can survive in heavily polluted water

polysaprobic *adjective* referring to organisms that can survive in heavily polluted water

polystyrene *noun* a type of plastic which can be made into hard lightweight foam by blowing air or gas into it, used as an insulating and packaging material

polythene *noun* a type of plastic used to make artificial fibres, packaging, boxes and other articles. Also called **polyethylene**

polyvinyl chloride *noun* full form of **PVC**

pome *noun* a fruit with a core containing the seeds enclosed in a fleshy part that develops from the receptacle of a flower and not from the ovary (NOTE: The fruit of apples and pears are pomes.)

pomology *noun* the study of fruit cultivation

pond *noun* **1.** a small area of still water formed artificially or naturally. ◊ **dew pond** **2.** an open storage area for liquids used in industrial processes

pond life *noun* the community of organisms that live in a pond

pond scum *noun* a layer of green freshwater algae on the surface of stagnant water

pondweed *noun* a small plant that grows in a pond

pool *noun* **1.** a small area of still water, especially one formed naturally **2.** an area of oil or gas which collects in porous sedimentary rock **3.** a group or combination of things or people. ◊ **gene pool**

POP *abbr* persistent organic pollutant

populate *verb* to fill an area with organisms ○ *Starlings soon populated the whole eastern seaboard of the USA.*

population *noun* **1.** a number of people living in a country or town ○ *The government has decided to screen the whole population of the area.* ○ *Population growth is a major threat to conservation efforts.* **2.** a number of individuals of the same species living and breeding in a specific area ○ *The fish population has been severely reduced.*

population age structure *noun* the numbers of individuals of each age in a population

population change *noun* the change in a population caused by births and deaths

population concentration *noun* the number of individuals found in one place

population control *noun* the process of limiting the number of individuals living in a specific area

population cycle *noun* a series of regular changes in the population of a species, usually a cycle in which the population gradually increases and then falls away again

population decrease *noun* a reduction in the number of individuals living in a specific area

population density *noun* the number of individuals living in a specific area

population dispersion *noun* the spreading out of the members of a population over an area

population distribution *noun* the pattern of the spread of a population across an area

population dynamics *noun* the study of changes in the number of individuals living in a specific area

population ecology *noun* the study of the factors determining abundance and fluctuations in the population of a species

population equilibrium *noun* a situation in which the population stays at the same level, because the number of deaths is the same as the number of births

population explosion *noun* a rapid increase in the number of individuals in a population

population growth *noun* an increase in the size of a population

population momentum *noun* a continuation of population growth for several generations after the population has achieved the ability to replace itself

population pyramid *noun* a graphical representation showing the distribution of a population according to age, sex or other characteristics

population transfer *noun* a movement of individuals from one place to another

pore *noun* **1.** a tiny space in a rock formation or in the soil **2.** same as **stoma**

porosity *noun* the degree to which a substance is porous ○ *Clay has a lower porosity than lighter soils.*

porous *adjective* **1.** referring to a substance with many holes or spaces **2.** referring to rock which has many small pores in it and can absorb water (NOTE: Porous rock is not necessarily permeable.) **3.** referring to tissue which allows fluid to pass through it ○ *a porous membrane*

positive *adjective* having a value of more than 0. Symbol **+**. Opposite **negative**

post- *prefix* after or later

postclimax *noun* a climax community that still exists in a place where the environmental conditions are no longer suitable for it

post-consumer waste *noun* any material that has been used by someone and then thrown away. Abbr **PCW**. Compare **industrial waste**

potable *adjective* referring to water that is suitable for drinking

potamology *noun* the scientific study of rivers

potamoplankton *plural noun* plankton that live in rivers

potamous *adjective* referring to animals that live in rivers

potash *noun* any potassium salt (NOTE: Potash salts are crude minerals and contain much sodium chloride.)

potash fertiliser *noun* a fertiliser based on potassium, e.g. potassium sulfate

potassium *noun* a soft metallic element, essential to biological life (NOTE: The chemical symbol is **K**; the atomic number is **19** and the atomic weight is **39.10**.)

potent *adjective* having a strong effect ○ *a potent drug*

potential evapotranspiration rate *noun* the amount of water transpired from a site assuming that there is no soil water limitation and complete vegetation cover

potentially renewable resources *plural noun* resources that could be replaced by natural environmental processes if they are depleted

potentiate *verb* (*of two substances*) to increase each other's toxic effects

potentiation *noun* the degree of probable increased damage caused by the combined action of toxic substances compared with their individual effects

potting compost *noun* a mixture usually of soil and fibrous matter used to fill containers in which plants are grown (NOTE: Peat has often been used in such composts, but alternatives such as coir fibre from coconut husks are being introduced in an attempt to conserve peat bogs.)

powder *noun* a substance made of ground or otherwise finely dispersed solid particles ○ *Dry chemical fire-extinguishers contain a non-toxic powder.*

powdered *adjective* crushed to a fine dry dust

powdery *adjective* having the texture or appearance of powder ○ *The fungus forms as a powdery layer on leaves.*

power *noun* the energy, especially electricity, which makes a machine or device operate

power cable *noun* a wire carried across the countryside on pylons along which electric current travels from the power station where it was generated. Also called **power line**

-powered *suffix* operated by a particular type of energy ○ *a wind-powered pump*

power failure *noun* a loss of electrical power supply

power generation *noun* the production of electricity from various energy sources

power line *noun* same as **power cable**

power station, power plant *noun* a building with machines that make electricity

power surge *noun* a sudden increase in the flow of electricity

ppb *abbr* parts per billion

ppm *abbr* parts per million

PPP *abbr* polluter-pays principle

prairie *noun* a large area of grass-covered plains in North America, mainly without trees (NOTE: The prairies of the United States and Canada are responsible for most of North America's wheat production. In Europe and Asia, the equivalent term is **steppe**.)

pre- *prefix* before or in front of

precautionary approach, precautionary principle *noun* a decision-making policy to take action to prevent possible environmental damage even before there is scientific evidence that damage will certainly occur

precession *noun* the tendency of the Earth's axis to wobble in space over a period of 23000 years (NOTE: The Earth's precession is one of the factors that results in the planet receiving different amounts of solar energy over long periods.)

precipitant *noun* a substance added to a solution to make solid dissolved particles separate from it

precipitate *noun* the mass of solid particles that separate from a solution during a chemical reaction ■ *verb* to make solid dissolved particles separate from a solution

precipitation *noun* **1.** water which falls from clouds as rain, snow or hail ○ *Annual precipitation is high in the mountain areas.* **2.** the action of forming solid particles in a solution

precipitation scavenging *noun* the removal of particles of polluting substances from the air in the form of acid rain

precise *adjective* exact or accurate

precision *noun* **1.** exactness or accuracy **2.** the accuracy to which a calculation is performed, indicated as a specific number of significant figures

precursor *noun* a substance or cell from which another substance or cell is developed ○ *The biggest share of ozone precursors comes from emissions from vehicles.*

predation *noun* the killing and eating of other animals

predator *noun* an animal that kills and eats other animals ○ *The larvae are predators of aphids.* Opposite **prey**

predatory *adjective* referring to a predator ○ *predatory animals such as lions and tigers*

predictive agriculture *noun* same as **intensive agriculture**

predominance *noun* the condition of being more powerful than others

predominant *adjective* **1.** more powerful than others ○ *The predominant airstream is from the west.* **2.** most common ○ *The predominant hair colour in this population is black.*

predominate *verb* **1.** to be more powerful than others **2.** to be more common than others ○ *A cold northerly airstream predominates during the winter.*

preferendum *noun* the area where a species flourishes best

preservation *noun* the process of protecting something from damage or decay ○ *the preservation of herbarium specimens* ○ *Food preservation allows some types of perishable food to be eaten during the winter when fresh food is not available.*

preservationist *noun* a person who is concerned to preserve things of natural or historical interest for future generations

preservation order *noun* an order from a local government department that stops a building from being demolished or a tree from being cut down

preservative *noun* a substance added to food to preserve it by slowing natural decay caused by microorganisms (NOTE: In the EU, preservatives are given E numbers E200 – E297.)

preserve *noun* US same as **reserve 2** ■ *verb* to protect something from damage or decay

pressure *noun* **1.** the physical action of squeezing or forcing **2.** the force of something on its surroundings ○ *population pressure* □ **pressure of numbers** too many of something ○ *The park is suffering from pressure of numbers – it's too popular with visitors.* **3.** strong influence to make someone take or change an action

pressure group *noun* a group that tries to influence governments and public opinion on a specific issue ○ *The environmental association set up a pressure group to lobby parliament.*

pressurise, pressurize *verb* to increase the atmospheric pressure in a container

pressurised fluidised-bed combustion *noun* an economic method of burning low-grade coal in a furnace in which air is blown upwards through the burning fuel. Abbr **PFBC**

pressurised water reactor *noun* a type of nuclear reactor in which water is heated to steam under high pressure to turn turbines to generate electricity. Abbr **PWR**

prevailing wind *noun* the wind direction that is most frequent in a specific place ○ *The prevailing wind is from the south.*

prevalence *noun* frequency of occurrence ○ *the prevalence of malaria in some tropical countries* ○ *the prevalence of cases of malnutrition in large towns*

prevalent *adjective* occurring frequently ○ *a fungus which is more prevalent in deciduous forests* ○ *The disease is prevalent in some African countries.*

prevent *verb* to stop something happening

prevention *noun* an act or process of stopping something from happening

prey *noun* an animal which is killed and eaten by another ○ *Small mammals are the prey of owls.* Opposite **predator** ■ *verb* **prey on** to kill and eat another animal ○ *Water snakes prey on frogs and small fish.*

primary *adjective* **1.** first, basic or most important **2.** being first or before something else. ◊ **secondary, tertiary**

primary commodity *noun* a basic raw material or food

primary consumer *noun* an animal that eats plants, which are producers in the food chain. ◊ **secondary consumer**

primary forest *noun* a forest which originally covered a region before changes in the environment brought about by human activity

primary host *noun* a host which a parasite settles on finally

primary particulates *plural noun* particles of matter sent into the air from fires, industrial processes, vehicle emissions, especially diesel, volcanic eruptions, sandstorms and similar phenomena

primary producer *noun* an organism which takes energy from outside an ecosystem and channels it into the system, e.g. a green plant (NOTE: Primary producers are the first level in the food chain and are eaten by herbivores, which are secondary producers.)

primary product *noun* a product which is a basic raw material, e.g. wood, milk or fish

primary production *noun* the amount of organic matter formed by photosynthesis

primary productivity *noun* **1.** the rate at which plants produce organic matter through photosynthesis **2.** the amount of organic matter produced in a specific area over a specific period, e.g. the yield of a crop during a growing season

primary sere *noun* the first plant community that develops on ground such as cooled lava from a volcano where no plants have grown before

primary succession *noun* an ecological community that develops in a place where nothing has lived before

primary treatment *noun* the first stage in a treatment. In primary treatment of sewage, suspended solids are removed.

primate *noun* a mammal such as a monkey, ape or human being

prime meridian *noun* a line of longitude situated at 0° and passing through Greenwich, England

primitive *adjective* **1.** referring to very early or prehistoric times **2.** referring to an early stage in an organism's development

primitive area *noun* an area of undeveloped land such as a forest that is protected as a national park or reserve

primordial *adjective* in a very early stage of development

principal *adjective* most important

priority effect *noun* a situation where the individual that arrives at a site first has the best chance of establishing itself

priority habitat *noun* a habitat that urgently needs to be protected because of its rarity or functional importance

priority species *noun* a species that is reducing in numbers and urgently needs to be protected

prisere *noun* the succession of plants from bare earth to climax vegetation

probability *noun* a statistical assessment of how likely something is ○ *It is important to identify the most significant threats to the population and what actions might be taken to reduce the probability of extinction.*

probability refuge *noun* a situation where the number of competing species in an environment is limited by the bad state of the environment

probe *noun* a device inserted into something to investigate the inside or to obtain information ■ *verb* to investigate the inside of something

process *noun* a series of actions or changes that achieve a particular result ○ *the cooling process* ■ *verb* **1.** to deal with something in a particular way ○ *The core samples are being processed by the laboratory.* **2.** to produce something by treating a raw material in a factory **3.** to make a substance undergo a chemical reaction **4.** to examine or to test samples

process chemical *noun* a chemical that is manufactured by an industrial process

process chlorine-free, processed chlorine-free *adjective* referring to paper that has been made or recycled without the use of chlorine to bleach it. Abbr **PCF**

processing *noun* the activity of treating a raw material in a factory to make it into something different

produce *verb* to make something ○ *a factory producing agricultural machinery* ○ *a drug which increases the amount of milk produced by cows* ■ *noun* what is produced ○ *a stall selling fruit and other farm produce*

producer *noun* **1.** a person or company that produces something **2.** an organism that takes energy from outside an ecosystem and channels it into the system, e.g. a green plants (**primary producers**) and herbivores (secondary producers). Compare **consumer** (NOTE: Producers are the first level in the food chain.)

producer gas *noun* same as **air gas**

producer responsibility *noun* the duty of manufacturers or producers to be responsible for their products when these eventually become waste, e.g. by taking them back from consumers

product *noun* **1.** something that is produced by manufacture or in a chemical reaction **2.** the result or effect of a process

production *noun* **1.** the act of manufacturing or producing something **2.** the amount of heat or energy produced by the biomass in an area

production ecology *noun* the study of groups of organisms from the point of view of the food which they produce

production efficiency *noun* the amount of energy which is taken into the biomass after consumption. Abbr **PE**

production residue *noun* the waste left after a production process

productive *adjective* **1.** producing a lot of something that can be used or sold ○ *highly efficient and productive forms* ○ *making productive use of waste ground* **2.** giving a good outcome ○ *a productive collaboration*

productive agriculture *noun* same as **intensive agriculture**

productivity *noun* the rate at which something is produced ○ *With new strains of rice, productivity per hectare can be increased.*

product of incomplete combustion *noun* a compound formed when combustion does not destroy all the material being incinerated. Abbr **PIC**

profession *noun* all the chemical, physical and biological characters that determine the position of an organism or species in an ecosystem (NOTE: Examples are 'aquatic predator' or 'terrestrial herbivore'.)

profundal zone *noun* an area of water in a lake below the limnetic zone

programme *noun* a planned course of action ○ *a research programme* ■ *verb* **1.** to analyse or plan something ○ *The review is programmed to take place next month.* **2.** to make an organism behave in a particular way ○ *Some plants are naturally programmed to respond to day length.*

prohibit *verb* **1.** to say that something should not be done ○ *prohibit the gathering of bulbs from the wild for sale* ○ *Smoking is prohibited in this area.* **2.** to prevent something from happening ○ *The persistence of DDT prohibits its general use for malaria control.*

project *noun* a plan or scheme of work ○ *a land reclamation project* ■ *verb* **1.** to stick out ○ *The groynes project into the sea.* **2.** to estimate something in the future from current information ○ *Research costs are projected to rise sharply.*

projectile *adjective* **1.** moving forwards with force **2.** able to push suddenly forward, as are the jaws of some fish or the mouthparts of a dragonfly larva

projection *noun* **1.** a part that sticks out **2.** an estimate or assessment of something that will happen in the future **3.** a technique for making a map

prokaryote *noun* a simple organism such as a bacterium whose DNA is not contained within a nucleus. Compare **eukaryote**

prokaryotic *adjective* referring to prokaryotes. Compare **eukaryotic**

prolonged *adjective* lasting for a long time ○ *prolonged drought*

promontory *noun* an area of high land which projects into the sea

promote *verb* to encourage or enable something to take place ○ *Growth-promoting hormones are used to increase the weight of beef cattle.*

promoter *noun* a substance that increases the activity of a catalyst

promotion *noun* the activity of encouraging or enabling something to take place ○ *the promotion of recycling schemes*

propagate *verb* **1.** to reproduce **2.** to produce new plants by a technique such as taking cuttings, grafting, budding or layering ○ *fuschias propagated from cuttings*

propagation *noun* the production of new plants ○ *propagation by runners* ◊ **vegetative propagation**

propagator *noun* a closed but transparent container in which seed can be sown or cuttings grown in a moist, warm atmosphere

propellant *noun* **1.** a gas used in an aerosol can to make the spray come out **2.** a substance used to make something move forwards, e.g. rocket fuel

propene *noun* same as **propylene**

property *noun* **1.** something which belongs to someone ○ *The institute is the property of a large corporation.* ○ *Inventions are regarded as intellectual property.* **2.** land and buildings

prophylactic *adjective* referring to an activity that helps to prevent the development of disease or infection

prophylaxis *noun* the practice of taking of measures to prevent disease or infection

proportionality principle *noun* the concept that control measures or response to a situation should generally be proportional to the risk identified

propylene *noun* a substance obtained from petroleum, used in the manufacture of plastics and chemicals. Formula: C_3H_6. Also called **propene**

protect *verb* to stop something being damaged or harmed

protected *adjective* referring to a species that has been legally identified as in danger of extinction, or an area of sea or land that has special value for the maintenance of biological diversity and natural resources

protection *noun* the act or an instance of keeping something from harm, injury or damage

protective *adjective* intended or able to keep something else from harm, injury or damage

protein *noun* a nitrogen compound formed by the condensation of amino acids that is present in and is an essential part of living cells

protest *noun* an act of showing disagreement ○ *There was a protest against cutting* *down the trees.* ■ *verb* □ **to protest against something** to show you disagree with something ○ *Crowds protested against the killing of seals.*

proto- *prefix* first

protocol *noun* an addition to an international legal measure ○ *the Montreal protocol on CFCs*

protozoan *adjective* referring to organisms in the Protozoa ■ *noun* a single-celled organism that is able to move and feeds on organic nitrogen and carbon compounds, e.g. an amoeba (NOTE: Protozoans are now regarded as part of the kingdom *Protoctista*.)

province *noun* a biogeographical area within a region that is defined by the plants and animals that inhabit it

proximal *adjective* nearer to the centre or point of attachment. Compare **distal**

pseudo- *prefix* similar to something, but not the same

pseudokarst *noun* a terrain like karst, but not in limestone country and not due to weathering

Pt *symbol* platinum

pteridophyte *noun* a plant that does not produce flowers or seeds and reproduces by means of spores, e.g. ferns or some mosses. Division: *Pteridophyta.*

Pu *symbol* plutonium

public *adjective* concerning or available to all people in general

public amenities *plural noun* facilities that make the surroundings more pleasant and are open to the general public

public amenity point *noun* a place where people can take their household waste for recycling or safe disposal

public domain *noun* the condition of not being protected by copyright and available to all people in general ○ *The information is now in the public domain.*

public enquiry *noun* 1. a set of official meetings that members of the public may attend to investigate why something happened or whether something should happen in future ○ *They called for a public enquiry on the road plans.* 2. a request for information to an organisation made by a member of the public

Public Health Inspector *noun* an official of a local authority who examines the environment and tests for air pollution, bad sanitation or noise pollution

public transport *noun* a system of buses, trains, aircraft, trams or boats which everyone may use for travel

public utility *noun* an essential service which is available to all people in general, e.g. electricity, gas, water, telephone, railway

puddingstone *noun* a type of stone which is formed from other stones fused together

pulp *noun* 1. the soft inside of a fruit or vegetable 2. a thick soft substance made by crushing ○ *wood pulp*

pulse *noun* 1. a short burst of current or voltage 2. a pressure wave that can be felt in an artery each time the heart beats to pump blood 3. any regular recurring variation in quantity 4. a leguminous plant that produces seeds eaten as food, e.g. a bean or pea ○ *Pulses provide a large amount of protein.*

pulverise, pulverize *verb* to reduce something to small particles

pulverised fuel ash *noun* fine ash from furnaces used to make construction blocks. Abbr **PFA**

pumice, pumice stone *noun* a light glass-like substance formed from foam at the edge of a lava flow

pump *noun* a machine which forces liquid or air into or out of something ○ *a water pump* ○ *a bicycle pump* ■ *verb* to force liquid or air into or out of something

pupa *noun* a stage in the development of some insects such as butterflies when the larva becomes encased in a hard shell (NOTE: The plural is **pupae**.)

pupal *adjective* referring to a pupa

pupate *verb* (*of an insect*) to move from the larval to the pupal stage

pure *adjective* uncontaminated or unmixed ○ *Magnesium does not possess sufficient strength in its pure state for structural uses.*

purebred *adjective* referring to an animal which is the offspring of parents which are themselves the offspring of parents of the same breed

pure strain *noun* a group of plants bred by self-fertilisation whose characteristics remain always the same

purification *noun* the action of making something pure or of removing impurities ○ *Activated sludge speeds up the process of purification.*

purify *verb* to make something pure or remove impurities from something

purity *noun* the state of being pure

putrefaction *noun* the decomposition of dead organic substances by bacteria

putrefy *verb* to decompose or rot

putrescibility *noun* the ability of waste matter to decompose or rot

putrescible *adjective* referring to waste matter that can decompose or rot

PVC *noun* a type of plastic that is not bio-degradable, used for floor coverings, clothes, shoes, pipes, etc. Full form **polyvinylchloride**

PWR *abbr* pressurised water reactor

pylon *noun* a tall metal construction for carrying high-tension electric cables from a power station

pyr- *prefix* same as **pyro-** (NOTE: used before vowels)

pyramid of biomass *noun* a graphical representation of the different amounts of biomass at each trophic level, with the highest biomass at producer level and the lowest at secondary consumer level. Also called **pyramid** (NOTE: The biomass at each level is about 10% of that of the level beneath.)

pyramid of energy *noun* a graphical representation of the amounts of energy consumed at each trophic level

pyramid of numbers *noun* a graphical representation of the structure of an ecosystem in terms of what eats what (NOTE: The base is composed of producer organisms, usually plants, then herbivores, then carnivores.)

pyrethrum *noun* an organic pesticide, developed from a form of chrysanthemum, which is not very toxic and is not persistent

pyrite, pyrites *noun* a gold-coloured form of iron sulfide. Formula: Fe_2S.

pyro- *prefix* burning

pyroclastic flow *noun* the flow of lava from a volcano

pyrolysis *noun* the decomposition or conversion of one substance into another by heat

Q

quadrant *noun* a device for measuring the height of stars, formerly used in calculating direction at sea

quadrantal *adjective* referring to a quarter of a circle

quadrat *noun* an area of land measuring one square metre, chosen as a sample for research on plant populations ○ *The vegetation of the area was sampled using quadrats.*

quake *noun* same as **earthquake** (*informal*)

qualitative *adjective* referring to quality

quality *noun* how good or bad something is □ **quality of life** the set of characteristics that determine the type of life that people live or hope to live ○ *The aim of the ban on emitting polluting gases is to improve the quality of life in the surrounding regions.* ○ *Trees in urban areas improve the quality of life for people living there.* ■ *adjective* of a high standard ○ *a quality product* □ **quality farm produce** farm produce of the best quality

quality assurance *noun* the system of procedures used in checking that the quality of a product is good

quango *noun* a group set up by a government to investigate or deal with a specific problem. Full form **quasi-autonomous non-governmental organisation.** ◊ **non-departmental public body**

quantifiable *adjective* able to be shown in figures ○ *The effect of the change in the waste disposal systems is not easily quantifiable.*

quantify *verb* to state something as a quantity or in figures ○ *to quantify the effect of the new legislation on pollution levels* ○ *The environmental benefits are difficult to quantify.*

quantitative *adjective* referring to quantity

quantity *noun* an amount or number of items ○ *He bought a large quantity of spare parts.* □ **to carry out a quantity survey** to estimate the amount of materials and the cost of the labour required for a construction project

quarantine *noun* the period when an animal, person, plant or ship just arrived in a country is kept separate in case it carries a serious disease, to allow the disease time to develop and so be detected

quarry *noun* a place where rock is removed from the ground for commercial purposes ∎ *verb* to remove rock from the ground for commercial purposes

quartile *noun* one of three figures below which 25%, 50% and 75% of a total falls

quartz *noun* a mineral form of silica, often found as crystals in igneous rocks (NOTE: Pure quartz is known as rock crystal.)

quasi- *prefix* almost ○ *a quasi-official body*

quaternary *adjective* consisting of four parts

Quaternary period *noun* the geological period which is still currently in existence

quicklime *noun* a calcium compound made from burnt limestone (NOTE: It is used in the composition of cement and in many industrial processes.)

quicksilver *noun* same as **mercury**

quiescent *adjective* **1.** referring to a volcano that is not active **2.** referring to a seed that is not germinating because the conditions for germination are unsatisfactory

quota *noun* a fixed amount of something which is allowed ○ *A quota has been imposed on the fishing of herring.*

R

Ra *symbol* radium

race *noun* a group of individuals within a species that are distinct, especially physiologically or ecologically, from other members of the species □ **the human race** all people

raceme *noun* an inflorescence in which flowers are borne on individual stalks on a main flower stem with the youngest flowers at the top of the main stalk

rachis *noun* the main stem that supports an inflorescence or a compound leaf

rad *noun* a former unit of measurement of absorbed radiation dose. ◊ **gray, becquerel** (NOTE: The gray is now used for 100 rad.)

radar *noun* a method of detecting distant objects and establishing their position, velocity or other characteristics by analysis of radio waves reflected from their surfaces. Full form **radio detection and ranging**

radiant *adjective* sent out in the form of rays

radiate *verb* **1.** to spread out in all directions from a central point **2.** to send out rays ○ *Heat radiates from the body.* ○ *Beta rays are radiated from a radioactive isotope.*

radiation *noun* **1.** the process or state of spreading out in all directions from a central point **2.** the waves of energy which are given off when heat is transferred **3.** the waves of energy which are given off by a radioactive substance

radiation ionisation *noun* same as **ionising radiation**

radiation pollution *noun* the contamination of the environment by radiation from a radioactive agent

radiation sickness *noun* an illness caused by exposure to a radioactive agent

radiation zone *noun* an area that is contaminated by radiation and which people are not allowed to enter

radiative forcing *noun* a change in balance between incoming solar radiation and outgoing infrared radiation

radicle *noun* the tiny structure in a plant embryo from which the root will develop

radio- *prefix* **1.** radiation **2.** radioactive substances

radioactive *adjective* referring to a substance whose nucleus disintegrates and gives off energy in the form of radiation that can pass through other substances

COMMENT: The most common naturally radioactive substances are radium and uranium. Other substances can be made radioactive for industrial or medical purposes by making their nuclei unstable, so forming radioactive isotopes. Radioactive wastes are classified as low-level, i.e. not considered to be very dangerous, intermediate and high-level, i.e. emitting dangerous levels of radiation.

radioactive isotope *noun* a natural or artificial isotope which gives off radiation

radioactive waste *noun* used radioactive materials produced by nuclear power stations, industrial plants, hospitals and other installations

radioactive waste conditioning *noun* the processing of radioactive waste to use it again or to make it safe for disposal

radioactive waste isolation *noun* keeping radioactive waste separate so that it does not contaminate other things

radioactivity *noun* the energy in the form of radiation emitted by a radioactive substance

radiobiologist *noun* a scientist who specialises in radiobiology

radiobiology *noun* the scientific study of radiation and its effects on living things

radiocarbon *noun* a radioactive isotope of carbon with an atomic number of 14

radiodermatitis *noun* an inflammation of the skin caused by exposure to a radioactive agent

radio detection and ranging *noun* full form of **radar**

radiogenic heat *noun* the heat generated by the decay of a radioactive substance

radium *noun* a naturally radioactive metallic element (NOTE: The chemical symbol is **Ra**; atomic number is **88** and the atomic weight is **226**.)

radon *noun* an inert naturally radioactive gas formed by the radioactive decay of radium that occurs naturally in soil, in construction materials and ground water. It can seep into houses and cause radiation sickness. (NOTE: The chemical symbol is **Rn**; the atomic number is **86** and the atomic weight is **222**.)

rain *noun* 1. water that falls from clouds as small drops (NOTE: Rain is normally slightly acid, about pH 5.6, but becomes more acid when pollutants from burning fossil fuels are released into the atmosphere.) 2. a period of wet weather ■ *plural noun* **rains** in some countries, repeated heavy falls of rain during a season of the year

rainbow *noun* a natural phenomenon that occurs when light strikes water droplets, especially when sunlight hits rain or spray from a waterfall, creating a semicircle of rings of each of the colours of the spectrum

raincloud *noun* a cloud that carries moisture in droplet form which can fall as rain

raindrop *noun* a drop of water that falls from a cloud

rainfall *noun* the amount of water that falls as rain on an area over a period of time ○ *an area of high/low rainfall*

rainforest *noun* a thick tropical forest which grows in regions where the rainfall is very high

rainmaking *noun* the attempt to create rain by releasing crystals of salt, carbon dioxide and other substances into clouds

rainout *noun* a process whereby particles in the atmosphere act as centres round which water can form drops which then fall as rain. Compare **washout**

rainstorm *noun* a period of heavy rain accompanied by wind

rainwash *noun* the erosion of soil by rain

rainwater *noun* the water which falls as rain from clouds

rainy season *noun* the period in some countries when a lot of rain falls. Also called **wet season**. Compare **dry season**

raise *verb* 1. to make something higher 2. to make plants germinate and nurture them as seedlings ○ *The plants are raised from seed.* 3. to breed and keep livestock

ramet *noun* a single cloned organism such as one produced by tissue culture

ram pump *noun* a water pumping device that is powered by falling water

Ramsar site *noun* a site designated by the Ramsar convention on the conservation of wetland habitats and species

ranching *noun* the raising of cattle on large grassland farms

range *noun* 1. a series of different but similar things ○ *a range of books on biology* 2. the difference between the lowest and highest values in a series of data ○ *The temperature range is over 50°C.* 3. an area within two or more points ○ *The geographical range of the plant is from the Arctic Circle to southern Europe.* 4. a large area of grass-covered farmland used for raising cattle or sheep 5. a group of mountains ■ *verb* 1. to vary between limits ○ *The temperature ranges from 13°C to 18°C in that month.* 2. to include many things ○ *The lecture ranged over the whole area of medical and agricultural genetic modification.* 3. to move over a wide area

ranger *noun* a person in charge of the management and protection of a forest, park or reserve

rape, rapeseed *noun* same as **oilseed rape**

rapid *adjective* acting, moving or changing quickly

raptor *noun* a bird of prey

raptorial *adjective* referring to raptors

rare *adjective* 1. not common 2. (*of a species*) existing only in small local populations 3. (*of air*) not containing much oxygen, especially at high altitudes

rare gas *noun* same as **noble gas**

rarity *noun* the state of being rare

rate *noun* **1.** an amount or proportion of something compared to something else **2.** the number of times something happens

rate of natural increase *noun* the difference between the crude birth rate and the death rate

rate of population growth *noun* the increase in population in a specific area divided by the initial population

rating *noun* a classification according to a scale

ratio *noun* a relationship between two quantities expressed as the quotient of one divided by the other ○ *The air/fuel ratio is 15:1.* ○ *Chart scale is the ratio of the chart distance to Earth distance.* (NOTE: The ratio of 7 to 4 is written 7:4 or 7/4.)

ration *noun* an amount of food given to an animal or person

raw *adjective* **1.** (*of food*) uncooked **2.** (*of a substance*) unprocessed or unrefined **3.** (*of sewage, water or waste*) untreated **4.** (*of data*) not yet subjected to analysis

raw material *noun* a substance which is used to manufacture something, e.g. ore for making metals or wood for making furniture

ray *noun* **1.** a line of light, radiation or heat **2.** an arm of a starfish **3.** a distinct radial band of tissue in the stem of a plant **4.** same as **ray floret**

ray floret *noun* a long thin part among those around a flower head of a plant belonging to the Compositae such as a daisy or sunflower. Compare **disc floret**

RBE *abbr* relative biological effectiveness

RDA *noun* Recommended Daily Amount

RDF *abbr* refuse-derived fuel

RDZ *abbr* resource depletion zone

REACH *abbr* Registration, Evaluation, Authorisation and Restrictions of Chemicals

react *verb* **1.** to act in response to an action **2.** to change chemical composition on contact with a substance ○ *Ozone is produced as a result of oxides reacting with sunlight.* □ **to react with something** to change because of the presence of another substance ○ *ozone is produced as a result of oxides reacting with sunlight*

reaction *noun* **1.** an action that takes place because of something that happened earlier **2.** an effect produced by a stimulus **3.** a chemical change that occurs when two substances come into contact and cause each other to change

reactive *adjective* referring to a chemical that reacts easily with other substances

reactivity *noun* the degree to which a substance reacts

reading *noun* a piece of information indicated by an instrument or gauge

reafforest *verb* to plant trees again in an area which was formerly covered by forest

reafforestation *noun* the planting of trees in an area which was formerly covered by forest

reagent *noun* a chemical substance which reacts with another substance, especially one used in an experiment, test or process

realised niche *noun* the portion of a fundamental niche that is actually occupied by a species, resulting from the sharing of resources in an ecosystem

real time *noun* □ **in real time** happening at the same time as something else, without a time delay ○ *The scan allowed us to watch the baby moving in real time.*

real-time *adjective* referring to something that happens at the same time as something else, such as the processing of data as soon as they are received

rear *verb* to look after young animals until they are old enough to look after themselves

receiving waters *plural noun* rivers, lakes, oceans, streams or other bodies of water into which waste water or treated effluent is discharged

receptacle *noun* **1.** the top part of a flower stalk that supports the flower (NOTE: In some plants such as strawberry it develops into the fruit.) **2.** the plant part that carries the reproductive organs in lower plants such as mosses and liverworts

receptor *noun* **1.** a nerve ending which senses a change such as cold or heat in the surrounding environment or in the body and reacts to it by sending an impulse to the central nervous system **2.** a site on a cell surface to which a specific molecule such as an antigen binds **3.** someone or something adversely affected by a pollutant ○ *The ground water is the receptor in this case of land contamination.*

recessive *adjective* (*of a gene or genetically controlled characteristic*) suppressed by the presence of a corresponding dominant gene. Compare **dominant**

recessiveness *noun* the characteristic of a gene that leads to its not being expressed in the individual carrying it when a corresponding dominant gene is present. Compare **dominance**

recharge verb 1. to restore the electric charge of a battery 2. to replace or renew something

rechargeable battery noun a type of battery that uses a reversible chemical reaction to produce electricity, allowing it to be recharged and used again ○ *A rechargeable battery is used for backup when the system is switched off.*

recharge area noun an area of land where there is a net transfer of water each year from the surface to ground water

recharge well noun a well through which surface water is introduced to an underground aquifer

reclaim verb 1. to make available for agricultural or commercial purposes marshy land, a waste site, land which has previously been built on or used for industry, or land which has never been cultivated ○ *to reclaim land from the sea* 2. to recover useful materials from waste

reclamation noun 1. the act of reclaiming land ○ *land reclamation schemes in urban centres* 2. land which has been reclaimed 3. the recovery of useful materials from waste

recognition noun 1. the ability to recognise someone or something 2. respect or official acceptance □ **in recognition of** *or* **for** as a mark of respect for ○ *He was awarded the Nobel prize in recognition of his work on the human genome.*

recombination noun any process that results in offspring that have combinations of genes different from those of either parent, e.g. the crossing-over and independent assortment of chromosomes during gamete formation

recommend verb to suggest that something should be done ○ *The report recommended excluding deer from the woodland in order to protect the young growth of plants.*

recommendation noun a strong suggestion that something should be done ○ *The council accepted the committee's recommendations about disposal of waste.*

reconstitute verb to put something back into its original state ○ *The mining company should reconstitute the site after the open-cast mining operation has closed down.*

record noun a written account of facts and information for future reference ■ verb to write down information or data ○ *Record the results in this column.* ○ *Measure the*

angles *and distances and record them in a log.*

recover verb 1. to return to a more usual condition ○ *The fish populations may never recover from overfishing.* 2. to obtain metals or other useful materials from waste by separating and purifying it

recovery noun 1. a return to a more usual condition ○ *The area has been overfished to such an extent that the recovery of the fish population is impossible.* 2. the process of obtaining metals or other useful materials from waste

recrystallisation noun the purification of a substance by repeatedly forming crystals from a solution

rectification noun the purification of a liquid by distillation

rectify verb to purify a liquid by a repeated process

recyclable adjective referring to waste that can be processed so that it can be used again

recycle verb to process waste so that it can be used again ○ *The glass industry recycles tonnes of waste glass each year.*

recycled adjective made from waste ○ *recycled aluminium*

recycled paper noun paper made from waste paper

recycling noun the activity of processing waste so that it can be used again

'Waste production in the UK continues to rise at 3% per year – faster than GDP growth. Defra's target is to enable 25% of household waste to be recycled or composted by 2005/6. (Delivering the evidence. Defra's Science and Innovation Strategy 2003–06).'

red adjective referring to a colour like the colour of blood

Red Data Book noun a catalogue formerly published by the IUCN, listing species which are rare or in danger of becoming extinct. The information is now available in a searchable database. ◊ **Red list**

redevelop verb to demolish the buildings on an area of land and build new ones ○ *The company has put forward a plan to redevelop the area around the railway station.*

redevelopment noun the act of redeveloping an area of land ○ *The council's planning committee has approved the redevelopment plan for the town centre.*

redistribution of land noun the practice of taking land from large landowners and splitting it into smaller plots for many people to own

red lead *noun* a poisonous red oxide of lead, used as a colouring in paints. Formula: Pb_3O_4.

Red list *noun* **1.** a searchable database maintained by IUCN that records the conservation status of different organisms in throughout the world. Full form **IUCN Red List of Threatened Species.** ◊ **IUCN 2.** a list recording the conservation status of a particular type of organism in a specific geographical area ○ *the Red list of the epiphytic lichens of Switzerland*

redox *noun* same as **oxidation–reduction**

redox potential *noun* **1.** a measure of the ability of the natural environment to bring about an oxidation or a reduction process **2.** the cell potential required relative to a standard hydrogen electrode to cause oxidation at an anode and reduction at a cathode ▶ abbr **rH**

reduce *verb* **1.** to make something less, smaller or lower, or to become less, smaller or lower. Opposite **increase 2.** to add electrons or hydrogen to a substance

reducer *noun* an organism that breaks down dead organic matter, e.g. an earthworm, fungus or bacterium

reducing atmosphere *noun* an atmosphere that does not contain free oxygen gas and in which compounds combine chemically with hydrogen

reduction *noun* **1.** the process of making something less, smaller or lower, or of becoming less, smaller or lower ○ *The key to controlling acid rain must be the reduction of emissions from fossil-fuelled power stations.* Opposite **increase 2.** the addition of electrons or hydrogen to a substance

redundancy *noun* the situation of not being needed because other similar things exist

redundant *adjective* no longer useful ○ *recycling redundant containers*

redwood *noun* a tall North American conifer. Latin name: *Sequoia sempervirens*.

reed *noun* a grass that grows in water near the shores of lakes (NOTE: The common reed *Phragmites communis* is used for thatching roofs. The Spanish reed *Arundo donax* has been used in musical instruments for more than 5000 years.)

reedbed *noun* a mass of reeds growing together

reedbed filter *noun* a reedbed used as part of a system of cleaning sewage or dirty water

reef *noun* a series of low rocks or coral near the surface of the sea

re-emerging *adjective* starting to reappear

refine *verb* **1.** to process something to remove impurities ○ *a by-product of refining oil* **2.** to make changes in order to improve something ○ *We've refined the procedures.*

refined *adjective* having had impurities removed ○ *refined oil*

refinement *noun* the process of removing impurities in something

refinery *noun* a processing facility where impurities are removed from raw materials such as ore, oil or sugar

reflection *noun* the process of light, sound or heat being transmitted back towards its source

reflex *noun* a rapid automatic reaction to a stimulus

reflux *noun* a backward flow of a liquid from a boiler in the opposite direction to normal flow, collecting vapour and condensing it so that it can return to the boiler again

reforest *verb* same as **reafforest**

reforestation *noun* same as **reafforestation**

refract *verb* to cause a wave such as light or sound to change direction or turn as it passes from one medium into another of different density ○ *On reaching the ionosphere, a direct wave is refracted and returns to the Earth's surface.*

refrigerant *noun* a substance used to provide cooling or freezing either as the working substance of a refrigerator or by direct absorption of heat

refrigerate *verb* to keep something cold to prevent deterioration

refrigeration *noun* the process of keeping something cold to prevent deterioration

refrigerator *noun* a machine which keeps things cold

refuge *noun* a safe place where a species can escape environmental change and continue to exist as before

refugium *noun* same as **refuge** (NOTE: The plural is **refugia**.)

refuse *noun* rubbish or other forms of waste

refuse collection and disposal *noun* the action of gathering waste together and getting rid of it

refuse-derived fuel *noun* a fuel that is made or processed from refuse. Abbr **RDF**

refuse disposal *noun* same as **waste disposal**

refuse dump *noun* a place where waste is thrown away

regenerate *verb* to grow again, or grow something again ○ *A forest takes about ten years to regenerate after a fire.* ○ *Salamanders can regenerate limbs.*

regeneration *noun* the process of vegetation growing back on land which has been cleared or burnt ○ *Grazing by herbivores prevents forest regeneration.*

regenerative *adjective* 1. restoring or renewing ○ *regenerative capacity* 2. allowing new growth to replace damaged tissue

regime *noun* a general pattern or system ○ *a strict dietary regime* ○ *The two rivers have very different flow regimes: one has rapid flow down from high mountains, while the other is slower and mainly crosses fertile plains.*

region *noun* 1. a large area of land with distinct geographic, political, or biological characteristics ○ *the polar regions* ○ *The troposphere is deepest over equatorial regions and shallowest near the Poles.* 2. an area of a surface ○ *the outer region of the stained area* □ **in the region of** approximately ○ *The burning temperature of the fuel is in the region of 2000° C.*

register *verb* 1. to show or display information or data ○ *Several lakes have registered a steady increase in acidity levels until their natural fish populations have started to decline.* ○ *The earthquake registered 6.2 on the Richter scale.* 2. to make something known formally or officially ○ *We registered our concern about the procedure.* ■ *noun* an official record, or a list of items ○ *a register of authorized users*

regolith *noun* a layer of weathered rock fragments which covers most of the Earth's land area

regress *verb* to return to a more primitive earlier state

regression *noun* the process of returning to a more primitive earlier state, e.g. when cultivated land returns to a wild state

regressive *adjective* (*of a water level*) getting lower

regrowth *noun* the growth that occurs after a cut or harvest, or after accidental damage or fire

regulate *verb* 1. to control a process or activity 2. to change or maintain something by law ○ *Development is regulated by local authorities.*

regulation *noun* 1. the control of a process or activity 2. a rule ○ *The pamphlet lists the regulations concerning visits to nature reserves.*

regulator *noun* 1. something or someone controlling a process or activity 2. a device used to limit the current and voltage in a circuit ○ *Regulators allow the correct charging of batteries from solar panels and wind generators.*

regulatory *adjective* controlling a process or activity according to specific rules ○ *a regulatory body*

rehabilitation *noun* reclaiming and redeveloping land and buildings which have been abandoned

reheater *noun* a section of a power station where steam which has been used to turn the first turbine is heated again to create enough pressure to turn the second turbine

reintroduce *verb* to help a species to live successfully again in an area it had formerly inhabited

reintroduction *noun* the process of helping a species to live successfully again in an area it had formerly inhabited

relate *verb* to make a connection or link between two things ○ *Orientating the chart relates the direction of land features to their representation on the chart and aids recognition.*

-related *suffix* connected to ○ *a heat-related change*

relationship *noun* the way in which someone or something is related to another

relative *noun* something such as a species that has developed from the same origin as another similar thing ○ *onions and their wild relatives* ■ *adjective* describing how one thing is compared with another

relative abundance *noun* the number of individual specimens of an animal or plant seen over a period in a specific place

relative biological effectiveness *noun* a measure of the different degrees of effectiveness of different types of radiation in producing effects in biological systems, used in radiation protection contexts. Abbr **RBE**

relative humidity *noun* a ratio between the amount of water vapour in air and the amount that would be present if the air was saturated, shown as a percentage

release *verb* 1. to let something go that has been contained ○ *Acid rain leaches out nutrients from the soil and releases harmful substances such as lead into the soil.* ○ *Us-*

ing an aerosol spray releases CFCs into the atmosphere. **2.** to allow a bird or other animal that has been reared or kept in captivity to live freely in the environment ○ *They released 93 birds and there are now 177 breeding pairs.* **3.** to make something available, especially for the first time ■ *noun* **1.** the act of letting something out from where it is contained ○ *The report points out the danger of radiation releases from nuclear power stations.* **2.** the act of making something available for the first time

releaser *noun* a stimulus that provokes a reaction in an animal, e.g. the sight of a hawk or the sound of a gun

relevé *noun* a small plot into which a larger area is divided, used as a sample for analysing vegetation

reliable *adjective* referring to someone or something that can be trusted ○ *It is not a very reliable method of measuring the depth.*

relict *noun* a species that still exists, even though the environment in which it originally developed does not

relief *noun* a difference in height between points on the Earth's surface

rely on *verb* to trust someone or something ○ *He relies on his skill and experience to identify poisonous fungi.* (NOTE: **relies – relying – relied**)

rem *abbr* roentgen equivalent man

remedial investigation *noun* investigation of a polluted site, including taking samples of soil or water, to determine what sort of action needs to be taken to improve it. Abbr **RI**

remediation *noun* a course of action intended to reverse environmental damage. ◊ **bioremediation**

remote sensing *noun* the collection of information via satellite observation and aerial photography about physical aspects of the Earth such as the location of mineral deposits, or the movement of water or pests

renew *verb* to replace something

renewable *adjective* referring to something that can be replaced or can renew itself by regrowing, reforming or breeding ○ *Herring stocks are a renewable resource if the numbers being caught are controlled.* □ **renewable sources of energy** energy from the sun, wind, waves, tides or from geothermal deposits or from burning waste, none of which uses up fossil fuel reserves

renewable resource *noun* a natural resource that replaces itself unless overused,

e.g. animal or plant life, fresh water or wind energy

renewables obligation *noun* the requirement for power generators to reduce their use of fossil fuels and replace them over time with sources of energy that can be renewed

repel *verb* to push something away by force, or to resist something (NOTE: **repelling – repelled**)

repellent *adjective* referring to a substance that causes something to which it is applied to resist something ○ *a repellent insecticide* ■ *noun* a substance that causes something to which it is applied to resist something ○ *The coating of wax on the leaves acts as a repellent to pollutants.*

-repellent *suffix* resisting something ○ *a water-repellent coating*

replacement fertility *noun* the fertility rate needed to ensure that a population remains constant as each set of parents is replaced by its offspring

replant *verb* to grow plants in an area again ○ *After the trees were felled the land was cleared and replanted with mixed conifers and broadleaved species.*

replicate *verb* **1.** to do something again in the same way ○ *The routine will replicate your results with very little effort.* **2.** (*of a cell or microorganism*) to reproduce

replication *noun* **1.** the process in the division of a cell during which DNA makes copies of itself **2.** the process of reproduction of a cell or microorganism ○ *virus replication* **3.** the repetition of an experiment several times in order to achieve a reliably consistent result

report *noun* a document giving an account of something, stating what action has been taken, what the current state is or what the results of a test or experiment are ○ *a report on global warming* ■ *verb* to give an account of something

repository *noun* *US* a place where something can be stored ○ *a nuclear waste repository*

repower *verb* to rebuild an old power station, converting it to a more modern combustion system

reprocess *verb* to process something into another form

reprocessing *noun* the processing of something such as spent nuclear fuel and subjecting it to chemical processes which produce further useful materials such as plutonium

reproduce *verb* **1.** to produce offspring **2.** (*of bacteria*) to produce new cells **3.** to do a test again in exactly the same way

reproduction *noun* the production of offspring

reproductive *adjective* referring to the production of offspring ○ *Pollination is a reproductive process.*

reproductive cloning *noun* the use of cloning techniques to produce new individuals

reproductive value *noun* the number of offspring an individual can be expected to produce during a lifetime

reptile *noun* a cold-blooded animal that lays eggs and has a scaly skin, e.g. a crocodile, tortoise or snake. Class: Reptilia.

requirement *noun* something that is needed ○ *a change in water requirements* ○ *The regulations contain a requirement for regular monitoring.*

research *noun* a scientific study that investigates something new ○ *recent research into the relationship between skin cancer and exposure to sunlight* ○ *environmental research* ○ *a research programme*

reservation *noun* an area of land set aside for a special purpose

reserve *noun* **1.** an amount stored or kept back for future use **2.** an area of land maintained for the benefit of plant or animal life where no commercial exploitation is allowed. ◊ **game reserve, nature reserve, wildlife reserve**

reservoir *noun* **1.** an artificial or natural area of water, used for storing water for domestic or industrial use ○ *The town's water supply comes from reservoirs in the mountains.* ○ *After two months of drought the reservoirs were beginning to run dry.* **2.** a natural hole in rock that contains water, oil or gas

reservoir rock *noun* rock that is porous and permeable, from which oil or natural gas may be extracted

residence time *noun* the amount of time during which something remains in the same place or in the same state until it is lost or transformed into something else

resident *adjective* referring to an organism or a person living in a place, especially for a long time ○ *The introduced species wiped out the resident population of flightless birds.* ■ *noun* a bird, insect or other animal that does not migrate ○ *The birds are year-round residents in this particular area.*

residential environment *noun* an area characterised principally by the presence of houses and apartment blocks

residual *adjective* referring to the amount of something that is left behind

residual risk *noun* a risk which still remains after pollution-prevention measures have been applied

residue *noun* the material left after a process has taken place or after a material has been used

resilience *noun* **1.** the ability of an organism to resist or recover from adverse conditions **2.** the ability of an ecosystem to return to its usual state after being disturbed

resin *noun* **1.** a sticky oil secreted by some conifers or other trees, especially when they are cut **2.** a solid or liquid organic compound used in the making of plastic

resinous *adjective* referring to resin

resistance *noun* the ability of an organism not to be affected by something such as a disease, stress factor, process or treatment ○ *Increasing insect resistance to chemical pesticides is a major problem.* ○ *Crop plants have been bred for resistance to disease.*

resistant *adjective* referring to something which is unaffected by a disease, stress factor, process or treatment ○ *Some alloys are less resistant to corrosion than others.* ○ *The plants were not resistant to mildew.*

-resistant *suffix* not adversely affected by something ○ *heat-resistant* ○ *a DDT-resistant strain of insects* ○ *disease-resistant genetic material* ○ *a new strain of virus-resistant rice*

resorption *noun* **1.** the absorption of a substance already produced back into the organism that produced it **2.** the melting of solid rock which falls into magma

resource *noun* **1.** a useful source of something ○ *reference resources such as encyclopaedias* **2.** anything in the environment which can be used ○ *Fossil fuel resources are being depleted.* ○ *Woodland is a valuable resource.* ◊ **natural resource**

resource depletion zone *noun* an area where a resource is depleted, e.g. where water is removed from the soil around a plant. Abbr **RDZ**

resource economics *noun* the study of the economics of an ecosystem, showing the value of the services provided by that system in financial terms

resource partitioning *noun* the way in which resources in an ecosystem are divided up by the species who need them, each using them in a different way

respiratory heat *noun* the energy lost to a community in plant respiration

respond *verb* to react to something

response *noun* a reaction to a stimulus

responsibility *noun* the state of being answerable for something, or in charge of something ○ *the responsibility of using limited resources wisely* ○ *take responsibility for stewardship of the countryside*

responsible *adjective* answerable for something or in charge of something ○ *responsible for safety checks*

responsible care *noun* an initiative of the chemical industry which requires member firms to follow codes of conduct on such matters as toxic materials, waste reduction, chemical-accident minimisation, worker safety and community consultation

restock *verb* to provide another supply of something that has been used up, or provide somewhere with a new supply ○ *We'll restock next year.* ○ *So many animals died that they had to restock the farm in the spring.*

restoration *noun* the act or process of giving something back, or putting something back to a previous state or position

restore *verb* to give something back, or put something back to a previous state or position

result *noun* a consequence or outcome ○ *The abundance and diversity of flowers in the meadow was the result of careful management.*

returnable *adjective* referring to something such as a bottle which can be taken back to the place where it was bought and then be reused or recycled

reuse *noun* the use of a product or a material for an additional time or a different purpose, usually as an alternative to throwing it away ■ *verb* to use a product or a material for an additional time or a different purpose, usually as an alternative to throwing it away

reverse *adjective* referring to an object or a process going backwards or in the opposite direction ■ *verb* to change a decision and do the opposite of what was done before ○ *The decision of the planning committee was reversed and the planning application went ahead.*

reversed fault *noun* same as **thrust fault**

reverse osmosis *noun* a process in which water is forced through a membrane which removes impurities

rH *abbr* redox potential

rhino *noun* same as **rhinoceros** (NOTE: The plural is **rhinos.**)

rhinoceros *noun* a very large herbivorous animal with thick skin and either one horn or two horns, one behind the other, on a projecting part of its head above the nose and mouth (NOTE: The plural is **rhinoceroses** or **rhinoceros.**)

COMMENT: There are five species of rhinoceros, three found Asia (two of which have only one horn) and two in Africa, and all are in danger of extinction. Although they have few natural predators, 97% of rhinos have been lost in the last 30 years and is believed there are only about 11 000 wild rhinos in existence. Rhinos have been hunted especially for their horn which is used in traditional Chinese medicine and for carving.

rhizobium *noun* a bacterium that lives in soil and forms nodules on plant roots, taking up nitrogen from the atmosphere and fixing it in the soil

rhizofiltration *noun* the use of plants to absorb or precipitate ground-water contaminants in their roots

rhizoid *noun* a thin structure in lower plants such as mosses and liverworts that resembles a root

rhizome *noun* a plant stem that lies on or under the ground and has leaf buds and adventitious roots

rhizosphere *noun* the soil surrounding the roots of a plant

Rhodophyta *plural noun* a phylum of red algae, mainly found on the seabed

RI *abbr* remedial investigation

ria *noun* a valley that has been filled by the sea

ribbon development *noun* the building of houses in an uninterrupted row along a main road, usually with fields remaining behind them

ribonucleic acid *noun* full form of **RNA**

rice *noun* a plant that is the most important cereal crop and the staple food of half the population of the world. Latin name: *Oryza sativa.*

rich *adjective* **1.** (*of soil*) having many useful nutrients for plant growth **2.** (*of food*) having a high calorific value **3.** (*of a mixture of fuel and air*) having a high ratio of fuel to air **4.** □ **rich in** having a lot of something ○ *Green vegetables are rich in miner-*

als. ○ *The forests are rich in mosses and other forms of moisture-loving plants.*

-rich *suffix* having a lot of something ○ *a nutrient-rich detergent* ○ *a protein-rich diet* ○ *a species-rich habitat* ○ *oil-rich seeds*

richness *noun* the quality of having a lot of something. ◊ **species richness**

Richter scale *noun* a scale of measurement of the force of an earthquake from 0 to 10, earthquakes of 5 or more causing damage ○ *There were no reports of injuries after the quake which reached 5.2 on the Richter scale.* (NOTE: The Richter scale measures the force of an earthquake: the damage caused is measured on the Modified Mercalli scale. The strongest earthquake ever recorded was 8.9.)

ridge *noun* **1.** a long raised section of ground, occurring as part of a mountain range, in a field, on a beach or on the ocean floor **2.** a long narrow band of high pressure leading away from the centre of an anticyclone ○ *A ridge of high pressure is lying across the country.*

rift valley *noun* a long valley with steep walls, formed when land between two fault lines sinks or possibly when a fault widens as plates forming the Earth's crust move apart

right of common *noun* the right to walk on land, graze animals on it, or gather wood

rigid *adjective* hard or stiff and not easy to bend ○ *rigid pipes* ○ *a rigid structure*

rigidity *noun* **1.** hardness or stiffness and an inability to bend ○ *Extra strength and rigidity must be provided in the tail section for aircraft with a tail wheel unit.* **2.** strictness of control or adherence to a way of doing something ○ *the rigidity of the guidelines*

rill *noun* a very narrow stream

rime *noun* the feathery ice formed when freezing fog settles on surfaces

ring *verb* to attach a numbered ring to the leg of a bird so that its movements can be recorded

Ringelmann chart *noun* a chart which uses numbers from 0 to 5 to identify the blackness of smoke

ring road *noun* a road which goes round a town centre, usually quite close to built-up areas, allowing traffic to bypass the town and not go through the middle. Compare **orbital road**

Rio Declaration *noun* a statement laying down the broad principles of environ-

mentally sound development adopted at the Earth Summit in Rio de Janeiro in 1992

riparian *adjective* referring to the bank of a river ○ *riparian fauna*

rip current *noun* same as **riptide**

ripple *noun* a little wave on the surface of water ○ *Ripple marks can be seen in some sedimentary rocks showing where the sand was marked by the movement of water.*

riptide *noun* **1.** an area of rough water in the sea where currents meet **2.** a current that flows against the flow of the incoming waves ▶ also called **rip current**

risk *noun* **1.** a combination of the likelihood of injury, damage or loss being caused by a potentially dangerous substance, technology or activity, or by a failure to do something, and the seriousness of the possible consequences **2.** something that is regarded as likely to cause injury, damage or loss ○ *a fire risk* ○ *a health risk* Compare **hazard**

COMMENT: A substance or practice may have the potential to cause harm, i.e. may be a hazard, but risk only arises if there is a likelihood that something will be harmed by it in a specific set of circumstances. A highly dangerous thing may in fact present only a small risk. Risk assessment is used to decide what the degree and nature of the risk, if any, may be so that measures to reduce or avoid it can be taken.

risk assessment *noun* a process used to determine the risk from a substance, technology or activity

risk management *noun* the activity of controlling the factors affecting risk

river *noun* a large flow of water, running from a natural source in mountains or hills down to the sea □ **river in flood** a river that contains an unusually large amount of water

river authority *noun* an official body which manages the rivers in an area

riverine *adjective* referring to a river ○ *The dam has destroyed the riverine fauna and flora for hundreds of kilometres.*

river terrace *noun* same as **alluvial terrace**

Rn *symbol* radon

RNA *noun* a nucleic acid chain that takes coded information from DNA and translates it into specific proteins. Full form **ribonucleic acid**. ◊ **DNA**

RO *abbr* renewables obligation

roadside verge *noun* ▶ **verge**

road user *noun* a person who drives on public roads

rock *noun* a solid mineral substance which forms the outside crust of the Earth

rock pool *noun* a pool of salt water left in rocks by the sea

rodent *noun* a mammal that has sharp teeth for gnawing, e.g. a rat or mouse

roentgen, röntgen *noun* a unit of measurement of the amount of exposure to X-rays or gamma rays. Symbol **R**

roentgen equivalent man *noun* a unit of measurement of ionising radiation equivalent to the effect of absorbing one roentgen. Abbr **rem** (NOTE: It has been replaced by the sievert.)

role *noun* the set of characters, chemical, physical and biological, that determine the position of an organism or species in an ecosystem, e.g. aquatic predator or terrestrial herbivore

root *noun* a part of a plant which is usually under the ground and absorbs water and nutrients from the surrounding soil ■ *verb* (*of a plant*) to produce roots ○ *The cuttings root easily in moist sand.*

root crop *noun* a plant that stores edible material in a root, corm or tuber and is grown as food (NOTE: Root crops include carrots, parsnips, swedes and turnips. Starchy root crops include potatoes, cassavas and yams.)

root cutting *noun* a piece of root cut from a living plant and put in soil, where it will sprout and grow into a new plant

rootstock *noun* a plant with roots onto which a piece of another plant is grafted. ◊ **scion**

root system *noun* all the roots of a plant

rot *verb* (*of organic tissue*) to decay or become putrefied because of bacterial or fungal action

rotate *verb* **1.** to turn around on an axis or fixed point ○ *The Earth rotates on its axis approximately every 24 hours.* **2.** to grow different crops from year to year in a field (NOTE: The advantages of rotating crops include: different crops utilising soil nutrients differently, pests specific to one crop being discouraged from spreading, and some crops such as legumes increasing the nitrogen content of the soil if their roots are left in the soil after harvesting.)

rotation *noun* the process of turning around an axis or fixed point ○ *the rotation of the Earth* ○ *The speed of rotation determines the frequency of the generator output.*

rotation of crops *noun* same as **crop rotation**

rotenone *noun* the active ingredient of the insecticide derris

rotor *noun* **1.** a rapidly turning mass of air, surrounded by clouds **2.** the central shaft of a generator, which turns inside the stator

rough *adjective* having an irregular surface or action

roughage *noun* fibrous matter in food, which cannot be digested. Also called **dietary fibre**

rough fish *noun* fish which are not used for sport or food

roundworm *noun* a type of worm with a round body, some of which are parasites of animals, others of roots of plants

ROW *abbr* rest of the world

Royal Society for Nature Conservation *noun* a UK charity that supports environmental projects and coordinates the activities of Wildlife Trusts. Abbr **RSNC**

Royal Society for the Protection of Birds *noun* a UK charity that works to ensure a good environment for birds and wildlife. Abbr **RSPB**

RSNC *abbr* Royal Society for Nature Conservation

R strategy *noun* a form of reproduction where the mother produces large numbers of offspring which need little attention. Compare **K strategy**

rubber *noun* a material which can be stretched and compressed, made from a thick white fluid (**latex**) from a tropical tree

rubbish *noun* things that are of no longer of any use and are thrown away

ruderal *adjective* growing in rubbish or on wasteland

ruminant *noun* an animal that has a stomach with several chambers, e.g. a cow

rumination *noun* the process by which food taken to the stomach of a ruminant is returned to the mouth, chewed again and then swallowed

runoff *noun* **1.** the removal of water from a system by opening sluices **2.** the flow of rainwater or melted snow from the surface of land into streams and rivers **3.** the flow of excess fertiliser or pesticide from farmland into rivers ○ *Nitrate runoff causes pollution of lakes and rivers.* ○ *Fish are extremely susceptible to runoff of organophosphates.*

runoff rate *noun* the amount of excess fertiliser or pesticide from farmland that flows into rivers in a specific period

rural *adjective* referring to the country, as opposed to the town ○ *Many rural areas have been cut off by floods.*

rural affairs *noun* the activities and concerns of rural communities

rural area *noun* an area in the countryside where the main activities are farming or forestry and where relatively few people live

rural development *noun* a programme of activities undertaken to ensure that rural areas remain economically and socially sustainable

rural economy *noun* farming and other businesses in rural areas

Rural Enterprise Scheme *noun* a system of government support for the adaptation and development of the rural economy, community, heritage and environment. It is part of the England Rural Development Programme.

rural environment *noun* the countryside

rural migration *noun* a movement of people away from the country and into towns in order to find work

rural planning *noun* same as **country planning**

rural recreation *noun* same as **countryside recreation**

Rural Stewardship Scheme *noun* in Scotland, a scheme of payments to encourage farmers to be involved in the protection and enhancement of the environment, to support sustainable rural development and to maintain the prosperity of rural communities

rural tourism *noun* holiday and leisure activities carried out in the countryside

rurban *adjective* referring to areas that combine the characteristics of agricultural activities found in rural zones with those of suburban living areas and industrialised zones

COMMENT: Rapid extension of urbanisation the world over has created areas that have both urban and rural characteristics. Land planning specialists talk about 'rurban areas' and the 'rurbanisation' process.

rurbanisation *noun* the process of rural areas becoming more like urban areas in the type of housing and activities that develop

rust *noun* **1.** a reddish powder that forms on the surface of iron and iron compounds on contact with damp air **2.** a fungal disease that gives plants a reddish powdery covering ■ *verb* to become covered with reddish powder through contact with damp air

R-value *noun* a unit of measurement of resistance to the flow of heat (NOTE: An insulated outside wall has an R-value of R-11, while an internal ceiling has a value of R-19.)

rye *noun* a hardy cereal crop grown in temperate areas. Latin name: *Secale cereale*.

S

S *symbol* sulfur

SAC *abbr* Special Area of Conservation

safe *adjective* not likely to hurt or cause damage ○ *It is not safe to drink the water here.*

safety *noun* the condition of being safe or without danger □ **to take safety precautions** to take measures which make your actions or condition safe

safety guidelines *plural noun* a series of recommendations indicating appropriate practices and procedures to ensure safe conditions

safety zone *noun* an area in which people are not at risk

Sahara *noun* a large desert region in North Africa

Saharan *adjective* referring to the Sahara

Sahel *noun* a semi-desert region south of the Sahara where desert conditions are spreading

Sahelian *adjective* referring to the Sahel

salination *noun* a process by which the salt concentration of soil or water increases, especially as a result of irrigation in hot climates. Also called **salinisation**

saline *adjective* referring to salt

saline lagoon *noun* an area of water partially or completely separated from the sea by sandbanks, shingle, rocks or sea defences and containing a mixture of sea water and freshwater. It may be tidal or non-tidal, but always contains water even at very low tide.

saline lake *noun* a low-lying inland lake with water that contains a lot of salt because of evaporation and a lack of fresh water flowing into it. Also called **salt lake**

salinisation, salinization *noun* same as **salination**

salinised, salinized *adjective* referring to soil where evaporation leaves salts as a crust on the dry surface

salinity *noun* the concentration of salt in an amount of water or soil

salinometer *noun* an instrument for measuring the amount of salt in a saline solution or in sea water

salmon *noun* a large sea fish that returns to a freshwater river to lay its eggs

salmonid *noun* a fish belonging to a family that is sensitive to pollution in water and whose presence indicates that the water is pure, e.g. a trout

salt *noun* **1.** a chemical compound formed from an acid and a metal **2.** sodium chloride as part of the diet ○ *a salt-restricted diet* ○ *He should reduce his intake of salt.* ■ *adjective* same as **salty**

salt dome *noun* an area where salt from beneath the surface of the soil has risen to form a small hill

salting *noun* an area of land that is regularly flooded with salt water

salt lake *noun* same as **saline lake**

salt lick *noun* **1.** a naturally occurring deposit of salt which animals lick **2.** a block of salt given to animals to lick

salt marsh *noun* an area of land over which the sea flows at high tide

saltpan *noun* an area where salt from beneath the soil surface rises to form crystals on the surface

salt water *noun* water which contains salt, e.g. sea water. Compare **fresh water**

saltwater *adjective* **1.** containing salt water **2.** living in salt water

salty *adjective* **1.** containing salt ○ *Excess minerals in fertilisers combined with naturally saline ground to make the land so salty that it can no longer produce crops.* **2.** tasting of salt

sample *noun* a small amount which is representative of the whole ○ *A sample of water was taken from the lake for analysis.* ○ *A seed sample was tested for germination.* ○ *Factories were asked to provide samples from outflow pipes.* ■ *verb* to take a small quantity of something to test

sanctuary *noun* an area where the wildlife it contains is protected ○ *A bird sanctuary has been created on the island.*

sand *noun* fine grains of weathered rock, usually round grains of quartz, found especially on beaches and in the desert

sand bar *noun* a long bank of sand in shallow water either in a river or the sea

sand beach *noun* same as **sandy beach**

sand dune *noun* an area of sand blown by the wind into a small hill or ridge, often crescent-shaped in the desert and sometimes covered with sparse grass when near the sea

sandpit *noun* a place where sand is extracted from the ground

sandstone *noun* a sedimentary rock formed of round particles of quartz

sandstorm *noun* a high wind in the desert, which carries large amounts of sand with it

sandy beach *noun* a beach covered with sand rather than pebbles or shingle. Also called **sand beach**

sandy soil *noun* soil containing a high proportion of sand particles

sanitary *adjective* referring to hygiene or to health

sanitary landfill, sanitary landfilling *noun* a method of disposing of solid waste on land in lined pits to avoid contaminating surface or ground water and other public health and environmental risks

sanitation *noun* the systems of waste disposal and water provision that are the basis of public hygiene ○ *Poor sanitation in crowded conditions can result in the spread of disease.*

sap *noun* a liquid carrying nutrients which flows inside a plant

SAP *abbr* Species Action Plan

sapele *noun* a fine African hardwood, formerly widely exploited but now becoming rarer. Genus: *Entandrophragma.*

sapling *noun* a young tree

sappy *adjective* referring to tree trunks or branches, or wood, that are full of sap

sapro- *prefix* decay or rotting

saprobe *noun* a bacterium that lives in rotting matter

saprobic *adjective* referring to a classification of organisms according to the way in which they tolerate pollution. ◊ **mesosaprobic, oligosaprobic, polysaprobic**

saprogenic, saprogenous *adjective* referring to organisms that grow on decaying organic matter

sapropel *noun* a layer of decaying organic matter at the bottom of a body of water

saprophagous *adjective* referring to organisms that feed on decaying organic matter

saprophyte *noun* an organism that lives and feeds on dead or decaying organic matter, e.g. a fungus

saprophytic *adjective* referring to organisms that live and feed on dead or decaying organic matter

saproplankton *plural noun* plankton that live and feed on dead or decaying organic matter

saproxylic *adjective* referring to invertebrate animals, fungi and other organisms that live in the rotting wood of dead trees

sapwood *noun* an outer layer of wood on the trunk of a tree, which is younger than the heartwood inside and carries the sap. ◊ **heartwood**

sarcoma *noun* a cancer of connective tissue such as bone, muscle or cartilage

Sargasso Sea *noun* an area of still water in the North Atlantic Ocean, which is surrounded by currents and contains drifting weed

satellite *noun* **1.** an astronomical object that orbits a larger body in space ○ *The Moon is the Earth's only satellite.* **2.** a manmade device that orbits the Earth, receiving, processing and transmitting signals and generating images such as weather pictures

saturate *verb* to fill something with the maximum amount of a liquid that can be absorbed ○ *Nitrates leached from forest soils, showing that the soils are saturated with nitrogen.*

saturation *noun* the state of being filled with the maximum amount of something which can be absorbed ○ *The various types of fog are classified by the manner in which saturation is reached.*

saturation zone *noun* the ground below the water table

saturnism *noun* same as **plumbism**

savanna, savannah *noun* a dry grass-covered plain with few trees, especially in South America or Africa, where growth is abundant during the rainy season but vegetation dies back during the dry season

save-all *noun* a container for keeping waste products so that they can be reused or recycled

scale *noun* **1.** a series of marks at fixed intervals used as a reference standard in measurement ○ *This rule has scales in inches and centimetres.* **2.** a small overlapping plate of tissue on the skin of reptiles and fish **3.** a hard white calcium layer that forms in containers and pipes carrying hot water in areas where the water supply contains a lot of calcium

scaly *adjective* covered in flakes of tissue, like a reptile or fish

scarce *adjective* **1.** not available in sufficient amounts **2.** uncommon or rare

scarcity noun **1.** a shortage in the supply of something **2.** the infrequency with which something occurs

scavenge verb **1.** (of organisms) to feed on dead and decaying matter **2.** to remove impurities or pollutants from a substance

scavenger noun **1.** a mammal or bird that feeds on animals which have been killed by lions or other predators **2.** same as **detritivore 3.** generally, any organism which feeds on dead animals, dead plants or refuse left unconsumed by other organisms **4.** a substance added to a chemical reaction or mixture to remove impurities or neutralise something

scavenging noun **1.** the activity of eating organic matter or dead animals ○ Vultures and hyenas sometimes feed by scavenging. **2.** the removal of impurities from a gas

scenery noun the landscape or surroundings, especially when regarded as attractive ○ beautiful mountain scenery

scent noun **1.** a smell given off by a substance that stimulates the sense of smell **2.** a pleasant smell ○ the scent of flowers

schist noun a type of metamorphic rock that splits easily into flakes

schistosomiasis noun a tropical disease caused by flukes taken in from water affecting the intestine or bladder. Also called **bilharziasis**

school noun a group of water animals which all move together and keep an equal distance apart, e.g. fish or whales

SCI abbr Site of Community Importance

scientific method noun the systematic method used in investigations of the natural world, which include designing controlled experiments, collecting data and developing and testing hypotheses

scion noun a piece of a plant which is grafted onto a rootstock

sclerophyll noun a woody plant that grows in hot dry regions, with thick leathery evergreen leaves that lose very little moisture

-scope suffix an instrument for examining by sight

Scots pine noun a common commercially grown European conifer. Latin name: Pinus sylvestris.

Scottish Natural Heritage noun an official body responsible for the conservation of fauna and flora in Scotland

scrap noun **1.** waste material ○ scrap paper ○ scrap metal ○ Some 50% of steel is made from recycled scrap. (NOTE: no plural)

2. a small piece of something ○ Scraps of paper had blown all over the grass.

scrapie noun a brain disease of sheep and goats

scree noun an area of loose rocks and stones at the base of the side of a mountain

screen noun **1.** something which protects **2.** a display device capable of showing a quantity of information, e.g. a computer monitor **3.** a hedge or row of trees grown to shelter other plants, to protect something from the wind or to prevent something from being seen ■ verb **1.** to examine people, animals or plants to test for the presence of something ○ All air passengers, parcels and freight will be screened for the presence of radioactivity. **2.** to select somebody or something as suitable for a particular purpose

screening noun **1.** the process of testing for the presence of something **2.** the process of selecting somebody or something as suitable for a particular purpose

scree slope noun a part of a mountain side covered with loose rock and stones

scrub noun **1.** small trees and bushes **2.** an area of land covered with small trees and bushes ■ verb to remove sulfur and other pollutants from waste gases produced by power stations

scrubber noun a device for removing sulfur and other pollutants from waste gases

scrubland noun land covered with small trees and bushes

Se symbol selenium

seabed noun the bottom of the sea ○ These fish feed on minute debris on the seabed.

seabird noun a bird which lives near the sea and eats fish, e.g. a seagull

seaboard noun an area of land along a stretch of sea ○ the eastern seaboard of the USA

sea defences plural noun same as **coastal defences**

sea fog noun fog that forms when cold air is above much warmer water

seagull noun a bird, of several species, that lives near the sea and has a heavy build, a rather hooked beak and webbed feet

sea level noun the average level of the surface of the sea. ◊ **mean sea level**

COMMENT: Sea level is taken as the base for references to altitude: a mountain 300 m high is three hundred metres above sea level. The Dead Sea is 395 m below sea level. Sea levels in general have risen over the past 100 years and much more rapid rises are forecast if the greenhouse effect results in the melting of the polar ice caps. Sea level is also used as a basis for measuring barometric pressure.

sea loch *noun* a long inlet of the sea in Scotland

seam *noun* a layer of mineral in rock beneath the Earth's surface ○ *The coal seams are 2 m thick.* ○ *The gold seam was worked out some years ago.*

sea mist *noun* mist that forms over the sea when the air is colder than the water

season *noun* one of the four parts into which a year is divided, i.e. spring, summer, autumn and winter ■ *verb* to allow the sap in timber to dry so that the wood can be used for making things

seasonal *adjective* referring to or occurring at a season ○ *seasonal changes in temperature* ○ *Plants grow according to a seasonal pattern.*

seasonal boundary layer *noun* the layer of water immediately above the thermocline

seasonality *noun* the characteristic of being seasonal

sea wall *noun* a wall built along a stretch of coast to protect it against erosion by the action of the waves

seawater *noun* the salty water in the sea

seaweed *noun* any of the large algae that grow in the sea and are usually attached to a surface

second *noun* **1.** a base SI unit of measurement of time, equal to one sixtieth of a minute **2.** a unit of measurement of the circumference of a circle, equal to one sixtieth of a degree ■ *adjective* coming after the first

secondary *adjective* **1.** less important than something else ○ *a secondary reason* **2.** coming after something else ○ *secondary thickening of stems in plants* ◊ **primary, tertiary**

secondary consumer *noun* an animal such as a carnivore that eats other consumers in the food chain. ◊ **primary consumer**

secondary forest *noun* natural growth occurring in a forest after a major disruption such as fire damage or logging activities

secondary host *noun* a host which a parasite settles on before moving to its primary host

secondary particulates *plural noun* particles of matter formed in the air by chemical reactions such as smog

secondary productivity *noun* the rate at which primary material is converted into animal tissue by a herbivore

secondary substance *noun* a chemical substance found in plant leaves, believed to be a form of defence against herbivores

secondary succession *noun* an ecological community which develops in a place where a previous community has been removed as a result of fire, flooding, cutting down of trees or some other event

second home *noun* same as **holiday home**

secrete *verb* (*of a gland*) to produce a substance such as a hormone, oil or enzyme

secretion *noun* a substance produced by a gland

sedentary *adjective* **1.** referring to marine invertebrates that do not swim about and remain attached to a rock for most of their lives **2.** referring to animals that do not migrate **3.** referring to a person who remains seated for long periods or takes little exercise in a way that can be bad for health ○ *a sedentary lifestyle*

sediment *noun* a mass of solid particles, usually insoluble, that fall to the bottom of a liquid

sedimentary *adjective* referring to rock formed from material deposited by water, wind or ice and then subjected to pressure. ◊ **igneous, metamorphic**

sedimentation *noun* **1.** the process of formation of sedimentary rock **2.** the process of solid particles falling to the bottom of a liquid, e.g. in the treatment of sewage

sedimentation tank *noun* a tank in which sewage is allowed to stand so that solid particles can sink to the bottom

seed *noun* a fertilised ovule that forms a new plant on germination □ **to set seed** to produce seed ○ *plants left after flowering to set seed* ■ *verb* **1.** (*of a plant*) to produce offspring by dropping seed which germinates and grows into plants in following seasons ○ *The poppies seeded all over the garden.* ○ *The tree was left standing to allow it to seed the cleared area around it.* **2.** to sow seeds in an area ○ *The area of woodland was cut and then seeded with pines.* **3.** to drop crystals of salt, carbon dioxide and other substances onto clouds from an aeroplane in order to encourage rain to fall

seed bank *noun* **1.** all the seeds existing in the soil **2.** a collection of seeds from plants, kept for conservation or research purposes

seedcase *noun* a hard outside cover that protects the seeds of some plants

seedling *noun* a young plant that has recently grown from a seed

seed tree *noun* a tree left standing when others are cut down, to allow it to drop seeds on the cleared land around it

seep *verb* (*of a liquid*) to flow slowly through a substance ○ *Water seeped through the rock.* ○ *Chemicals seeped out of the container.*

seepage *noun* the action of flowing slowly

seepage tank, seepage pit *noun* in some septic tank systems, a deep hole into which partly decomposed sewage drains before dispersing slowly into the surrounding soil

SEERAD *abbr* Scottish Executive Environment and Rural Affairs Department

seiche *noun* a tide in a lake, usually caused by the wind or by movements in water level

seism *noun* an earthquake

seismic *adjective* referring to earthquakes

seismograph *noun* an instrument for measuring earthquakes. ◊ **Richter scale**

seismological *adjective* referring to the study of earthquakes

seismologist *noun* a scientist who studies earthquakes

seismology *noun* the scientific study of earthquakes

seismonasty *noun* a response of plants to a physical stimulus such as touch

select *verb* to identify plants or animals with desirable characteristics such as high yield or disease resistance as part of the activity of breeding new varieties

selection *noun* **1.** the process of identifying plants or animals with desirable characteristics such as high yield or disease resistance as part of the activity of breeding new varieties **2.** an individual chosen from a group in a breeding programme on the basis of distinctive characteristics

selective herbicide, selective weedkiller *noun* a weedkiller which is designed to kill only plants with specific characteristics and not others

selenium *noun* a non-metallic trace element, used in photoelectric cells. Symbol Se (NOTE: The chemical symbol is **Se**; the atomic number is **34** and the atomic weight is **78.96**.)

self- *prefix* **1.** of itself **2.** automatic

self-fertilisation, **self-fertilization** *noun* the fertilisation of a plant or invertebrate animal with its own pollen or sperm

self-pollination *noun* the pollination of a plant by pollen from its own flowers. Compare **cross-pollination**

self-purification *noun* the ability of water to clean itself of polluting substances

self-regulating *adjective* controlling itself without outside intervention ○ *Most tropical rainforests are self-regulating environments.*

self-seeded *adjective* referring to a plant that grows from seed that has fallen to the ground naturally rather than being sown intentionally ○ *Several self-seeded poppies have come up in the vegetable garden.*

self-sterile *adjective* referring to a plant that cannot fertilise itself from its own flowers

self-sterility *noun* the inability of a plant to fertilise itself

self-sufficiency *noun* a simple traditional way of farming with little use of modern technology that provides only enough food and other necessary materials for a family

self-sufficient *adjective* **1.** able to provide enough food and other necessary materials for a family, often by means of a simple traditional way of farming with little use of modern technology ○ *We're self-sufficient in salad crops from the garden in the summer time.* **2.** referring to provision of the required quantity of a product locally or for yourself, without needing to purchase or import it ○ *The country is self-sufficient in barley.*

self-thinning *noun* a process by which only a few individuals survive in a group of plants of the same age, since plants cannot escape competition by moving away to a different place

sell-by date *noun* a date on the label of a food product which is the last date on which the product should be sold and be guaranteed as of good quality

selva *noun* tropical rainforest in the Amazon basin

semeloparity *noun* a form of reproduction where the animal or plant reproduces once only, as in the case of salmon

semi- *prefix* half

semi-arid *noun* receiving very little rain

semiconductor *noun* a material with conductive properties between those of a conductor such as a metal and an insulator

semi-desert *noun* an area of land which has very little rain

semi-natural forest *noun* a wooded area that contains mainly native trees and shrubs which have not been planted

semiochemical *adjective* a chemical released by animals, especially insects, as a means of communication, e.g. a pheromone

semi-parasitic *adjective* referring to an organism living as a parasite but also undergoing photosynthesis

semi-permeable *adjective* referring to something such as a membrane that allows a liquid to pass through but not substances dissolved in the liquid

senescence *noun* the process of growing older

sensitise, sensitize *verb* to make someone sensitive to a substance such as an allergen or drug

sensitive *adjective* **1.** referring to the ability to respond to stimuli ○ *The leaves of the plant are sensitive to frost.* **2.** referring to devices that are able to record very small changes ○ *The earthquake was a small one and only registered on the most sensitive equipment.*

sensitivity *noun* **1.** the ability or tendency to respond to stimuli. Also called **irritability 2.** the ability to record very small changes ○ *the scanner's sensitivity to small objects*

sensory *adjective* referring to the senses

SEPA *abbr* Scottish Environment Protection Agency

sepal *noun* a part of the calyx of a flower, usually green and sometimes hairy

separate *adjective* **1.** distinct and not related **2.** not joined or together ■ *verb* **1.** to move or keep something apart **2.** to distinguish one thing from another **3.** to divide or split something into its parts

separate collection, separated collection *noun* the collection of different types of solid waste separately, often in containers of different colours, so that they can be recycled, reused or disposed of in different ways

separate system *noun* a drainage system where sewage and rainwater are not collected together but drain through different channels

separator *noun* a device which removes a component from a mixture or combination ○ *The water separator will extract a percentage of free moisture from the air.*

septic *adjective* referring to the process of decomposition of organic matter

septic tank *noun* **1.** an underground tank for household sewage that is not connected to the main drainage system and in which human waste is decomposed by the action of anaerobic bacteria **2.** a tank at a sewage treatment works in which sewage is collected to begin its treatment by anaerobic bacteria

sere *noun* a series of plant communities which succeed one another in an area

sessile *adjective* **1.** attached directly to a branch or stem without a stalk ○ *The acorns of a sessile oak tree have no stalks or very short stalks.* **2.** permanently attached to a surface

set aside *verb* to use a piece of formerly arable land for something other than growing food crops. It may be allowed to lie fallow, be planted as woodland or with industrial crops, or be used for recreation.

set-aside *noun* a piece of formerly arable land used for something other than growing food crops

settle *verb* **1.** to stop moving and stay in one place **2.** (*of sediment*) to fall to the bottom of a liquid

settlement *noun* **1.** a place where people have established a community **2.** (*of sediment*) the process of falling to the bottom of a liquid

settling basin, settling pond *noun* a tank in which a liquid is allowed to stand so that solid particles can sink to the bottom

Seveso *noun* a town in Italy, scene of a disaster in 1976 when tetrachlorodibenzoparadioxin gas escaped from a chemical factory during the manufacture of 2,4,5-T

sewage *noun* waste water and other material such as faeces, carried away in sewers. Also called **sewage waste**

sewage disposal *noun* the removal of sewage from houses and other buildings for processing

sewage effluent *noun* liquid or solid waste carried away in sewers

sewage lagoon *noun* a pond used to purify sewage by allowing sunlight, oxygen and bacteria to act on the mixture of sewage and water

sewage sludge *noun* the solid or semi-solid part of sewage

sewage treatment plant *noun* a place where sewage from houses and other buildings is brought for processing. Also called **sewage farm, sewage works**

COMMENT: A modern sewage treatment plant works by passing the sewage through a series of processes. It is first screened to remove large particles, then passed into sedimentation tanks where part of the solids remaining in the sewage settle. The sewage then continues into an aerator which adds air to activate the bacteria. The sewage then settles in a second sedimentation tank before being discharged into a river or the sea and the resulting sludge is digested anaerobically by bacteria in digestion tanks before being put on the land as biosolids, burnt, or otherwise disposed of.

sewage waste *noun* same as **sewage**

sewage works *noun* same as **sewage treatment plant**

sewer *noun* a large pipe or tunnel which takes waste water and material such as faeces away from buildings

sewerage *noun* a system of pipes and treatment plants which collect and dispose of sewage in a town

shade plant *noun* a plant which tolerates and grows in shade

shading *noun* the action of cutting off the light of the sun ○ *Parts of the field near tall trees suffer from shading.*

shale *noun* sedimentary rock formed from clay, which cracks along horizontal straight lines

shear wave *noun* a type of slow seismic wave that alters direction as it passes through different types of rock

shed *verb* to let something fall off as part of a natural process ○ *Deciduous trees shed their leaves in autumn.* ○ *Deer shed their antlers after the mating season.*

sheep *noun* an animal farmed for its wool, meat and milk

sheet lightning *noun* lightning which lights up the sky rather than producing a single visible flash

shelf *noun* a layer of rock or ice which juts out

shelf-life *noun* the number of days or weeks for which a product can stay on the shelf of a shop and still be good to use

shell *noun* a hard outer covering of an animal, egg or seed

shellfish *noun* a sea animal that has a hard shell and is used as food

shelter *noun* a structure or feature providing protection from wind, sun, rain or other weather conditions ■ *verb* to protect something from weather conditions

shelter belt *noun* a row of trees planted to give protection from wind

shelterwood *noun* a large area of trees left standing when others are cut, to act as shelter for seedling trees

shield *noun* a large area of very old rocks ○ *the Canadian shield*

shifting cultivation *noun* **1.** an agricultural practice using the rotation of fields rather than crops, short cropping periods followed by long fallows and the maintenance of fertility by the regeneration of vegetation. ◊ **fallow 2.** a form of cultivation practised in some tropical countries, where land is cultivated until it is exhausted and then left as the farmers move on to another area

shingle *noun* the small pebbles found on beaches, 1–7 cm in diameter

shock *noun* a sudden violent impact

shore *noun* land at the edge of the sea or a lake

COMMENT: The shore is divided into different zones. The upper shore is the area which is only occasionally covered by sea water at the very highest tides. The middle shore is the main area of shore which is covered and uncovered by the sea at each tide. The lower shore is the area which is very rarely uncovered and only at the lowest tides.

shorebird *noun* a bird which lives and nests on the shore

shoreline *noun* an area of land at the edge of the sea or a lake

shoreline management plan *noun* a official plan for flood and coastal defence for a specific area of coast, taking into account local social and economic issues as well as environmental concerns

short-day plant *noun* a plant that flowers as the days get shorter in the autumn, e.g. a chrysanthemum. Compare **long-day plant**

short ton *noun* US same as **ton**

shower *noun* a brief fall of rain or snow

shrivel *verb* to become dry and wrinkled ○ *The leaves shrivelled in the prolonged drought.*

shrub *noun* a perennial plant with several woody stems

shrubby *adjective* growing like a shrub

Si *symbol* silicon

SI *noun* the international system of metric measurements. Full form **Système International**

sib, sibling *noun* one of the offspring of the same parents ○ *Brothers and sisters are all siblings.*

SIC *abbr* Site of Community Importance

sick building syndrome *noun* a set of symptoms that affect people when they are in a building and not when they leave the building, but that cannot be traced to specific pollutants or sources within the building. Compare **building-related illness**

COMMENT: Symptoms of sick building syndrome include headaches, sore throats, dry skin, general tired feeling and depression. Some features that seem to be common to the buildings causing these symptoms are artificial ventilation systems with windows that do not open and energy-efficient heating, bright lighting and carpeting on floors.

-side *suffix* side or edge ○ *eroded hillsides* ○ *waterside plants*

side effect *noun* a secondary often undesirable effect ○ *Draining the marsh has had several unexpected side effects.*

sievert *noun* a unit of measurement of the absorbed dose of radiation, calculated as the amount of radiation from one milligram of radium at a distance of one centimetre for one hour. Symbol **Sv**

significant *adjective* **1.** important, considerable or notable ○ *There has been a significant reduction in the amount of raw sewage being released into the sea.* **2.** too closely linked statistically to be the result of chance ○ *The difference is not statistically significant.*

significant figures *plural noun* the figures in a decimal number that express accuracy, beginning with the first non-zero figure on the left and ending with the figure on the right ○ *shown to three significant figures*

significantly *adverb* **1.** to any considerable or notable degree ○ *The amount has not been significantly reduced.* **2.** in a way that is linked statistically

silage *noun* food for cattle formed of grass and other green plants, cut and stored in silos

silencer *noun* a device to reduce noise, fitted to a machine

silica *noun* a mineral which forms quartz and sand, and is used to make glass. Also called **silicon dioxide**

silicate *noun* **1.** a chemical compound of silicon and oxygen, the most widespread form of mineral found in most rocks and soils **2.** particles of silica found in clay

silicon *noun* an element with semiconductor properties, used in crystal form as a base for the manufacture of integrated circuits (NOTE: The chemical symbol is **Si**; the atomic number is **14** and the atomic weight is **28.09**.)

silicon dioxide *noun* same as **silica**

silicosis *noun* a type of pneumoconiosis caused by inhaling silica dust from mining or stone-crushing operations, which makes breathing difficult and can lead to emphysema and bronchitis

silo *noun* a large container for storing grain or silage

silt *noun* **1.** soft mud which settles at the bottom of water **2.** particles of fine quartz with a diameter of 0.002–0.06 mm ■ *verb* □ **to silt up** (*of a harbour or river*) to become full of silt, so that boats can no longer sail

siltation, silting *noun* the action of depositing silt at the bottom of water, or the state of having a silt deposit ○ *increased sedimentation and siltation in backwaters*

silver *noun* a white metallic element which is not corroded by exposure to air (NOTE: The chemical symbol is **Ag**; the atomic number is **47** and the atomic weight is **107.87**.)

silvi- *prefix* trees or woods

silvicide *noun* a substance which kills trees

silvicolous *adjective* living or growing in woodland

silvicultural *adjective* referring to the cultivation of trees

silviculture *noun* the cultivation of trees as part of forestry

simazine a herbicide that kills germinating seedling, used as a ground spray (NOTE: It is under review for withdrawal from use in the European Union.)

similarity coefficient *noun* the degree to which two things such as areas of vegetation are alike

sink *verb* to fall to the bottom of water ○ *sank to the river bed* (NOTE: **sinks – sank – sunk**) ■ *noun* **1.** a place into which a substance passes to be stored or to be absorbed. ◊ **carbon sink 2.** a low-lying piece of land where water collects to form a pond

sinkhole *noun* same as **sink** *noun* 2

sirenian *noun* a large marine animal living in warm estuaries, e.g. a manatee. Order: Sirenia.

sirocco *noun* a dry wind blowing from the desert northwards in North Africa

site *noun* **1.** a place or position of something ○ *The rare orchid grows on only two sites.* ○ *Hazardous chemicals found on the site include arsenic, lead mercury and cyanide.* ◊ **honeypot site, landfill site 2.** a geographically defined area whose extent is clearly marked

Site of Community Importance *noun* a place recognised by the European Commission as important in maintaining or restoring the conservation status of the region in which it occurs. Abbr **SCI**

Site of Special Scientific Interest *noun* in England, Wales and Scotland, an area of land which is officially protected to maintain its fauna, flora or geology. Abbr **SSSI**

siting *noun* the act of putting something or being in a particular place ○ *Siting the windfarm offshore has attracted criticism from bird conservation groups.*

Sitka spruce *noun* a temperate softwood coniferous tree, that is fast-growing. It is used for making paper. Latin name: *Picea sitchensis.*

skyline *noun* a line of hills or buildings seen against the sky ○ *They want to protect mountain skylines from the planting of conifers.*

slack *noun* a valley with a high water table between sand dunes

slack water *noun* the part of the tidal cycle occurring between the ebb and flood tides at the point when the flows are reversing direction

slag *noun* waste matter which floats on top of the molten metal during smelting, used to lighten heavy soils, e.g. clay, and also for making cement

slag heap *noun* a large pile of waste material from an industrial process such as smelting or from coal mining

slash and burn agriculture *noun* a form of agriculture in which forest is cut down and burnt to create open space for growing crops. Also called **swidden farming** (NOTE: The space is abandoned after several crops have been grown and then more forest is cut down.)

slate *noun* a hard metamorphic rock which splits easily along cleavage lines, used especially for making roofs

slaughter *noun* the killing of a large number of animals ■ *verb* **1.** to kill animals for food **2.** to kill large numbers of animals ○ *Thousands of seals were slaughtered annually.*

sleet *noun* icy rain ■ *verb* to fall as icy rain

slick *noun* a patch of something thin or slippery on a surface, especially of oil floating on water

slime *noun* **1.** a mucous substance secreted by an organism such as a snail **2.** a coating of green algae on rocks or other surfaces **3.** an unpleasant slippery substance

slip-off slope *noun* a gently sloping bank on the inside of a river with large bends (**meanders**)

slough *noun* dead tissue, especially dead skin, which has separated from healthy tissue ■ *verb* (*of a snake*) to let dead skin fall off as part of a natural process

sludge *noun* **1.** a thick wet substance, especially wet mud or snow **2.** the solid or semi-solid part of sewage

sludge composting *noun* the decomposition of sewage for use as a fertiliser or mulch

sludge digestion *noun* a final treatment of sewage when it is digested anaerobically by bacteria

sludge gas *noun* methane mixed with carbon dioxide which is given off by sewage

sludge gulper *noun* a large truck which removes sludge from cesspits and septic tanks

sludge processing *noun* treatment of the solid or semi-solid part of sewage so that it can safely be dumped or used as a fertiliser

slug *noun* an invertebrate animal without a shell. It causes damage to plants by eating leaves or underground parts, especially in wet conditions.

slug pellet *noun* a small hard piece of a mixture containing a substance such as metaldehyde which kills slugs. Slug pellets are usually coloured blue-green.

sluice *noun* a channel for water, especially through a dam or other barrier

sluice gate *noun* a mechanism for controlling the amount of water that passes through a channel

slum *noun* an area of a city where the buildings are in bad condition and often where a lot of people live very closely together ■ *adjective* referring to a slum ○ *slum housing* ○ *slum conditions*

slurry *noun* liquid or semi-liquid waste from animals, stored in tanks or lagoons and treated to be used as fertiliser

small-scale *adjective* small in size or limited in scope. Compare **large-scale**

smelt *verb* to extract metal from ore by heating it

smelter *noun* a processing facility where ore is heated and metal extracted from it

smelting *noun* the process of extracting metal from ore by heating

smog *noun* a form of air pollution in towns, caused by warm damp air combined with exhaust fumes from cars. ◊ **photochemical smog**

smoke *noun* a white, grey or black mass of small particles in the air, produced by something which is burning ■ *verb* to emit smoke ○ *The volcano is still smoking.*

smoke control area *noun* an area of a town where it is not permitted to produce smoke from chimneys or fires

smokeless *adjective* **1.** referring to a place where there is no smoke or where smoking is not allowed **2.** referring to a fuel which does not produce smoke when it is burned

smokeless zone *noun* an area of a town where it is not permitted to produce smoke from chimneys or fires

smokestack *noun* a very tall industrial chimney, usually containing several flues

smoky *adjective* **1.** full of smoke ○ *a smoky room* **2.** producing a lot of smoke ○ *a smoky fire*

smut *noun* **1.** a small black piece of carbon emitted from a fire ○ *Smuts from the oil depot fire covered the town.* **2.** a disease of cereal plants, caused by a fungus, that affects the development of the grain and makes it look black

Sn *symbol* tin

SNF *abbr* spent nuclear fuel

snow *noun* water which falls as light pieces of white ice in cold weather ■ *verb* to fall as snow ○ *It snowed heavily during the night.*

snowfall *noun* a quantity of snow that comes down at any one time ○ *A heavy snowfall blocked the main roads.*

snowflake *noun* a small piece of snow formed from a number of ice crystals

snow-melt *noun* the melting of snow in spring, often the cause of floods

snowstorm *noun* a heavy fall of snow accompanied by wind

snowy *adjective* referring to weather or a period when a lot of snow falls ○ *a period of snowy weather* ○ *a snowy night*

soakaway *noun* a channel in the ground filled with gravel, which takes rainwater from a downpipe or liquid sewage from a septic tank and allows it to be absorbed into the surrounding soil

soar *verb* (*of a bird*) to fly high up or stay airborne without any movement of the

wings by floating on the upward movement of warm air

SoCC *abbr* Species of Conservation Concern

social *adjective* referring to a group of animals or people

social carnivore *noun* a meat-eating animal that lives and hunts in a group, e.g. a lion or wolf. Compare **herbivore, omnivore**

social cost *noun* the full cost to society of an activity, including hidden costs as well as direct costs

social insect *noun* an insect such as an ant or termite that lives in a large group

social responsibility *noun* concern for the effects upon society of activities that are undertaken, such as a concern for the effects on people's health of environmental pollution and industrial processes

society *noun* **1.** a group of people or animals that live together in an organised way **2.** a group of plants within a larger community

sociology *noun* the study of human or other societies

soda *noun* same as **sodium hydroxide**

soda lake *noun* a salt lake with a high concentration of sodium in the water

sodium *noun* a chemical element which is a constituent of common salt and essential to animal life (NOTE: The chemical symbol is **Na**; the atomic number of **11** and the atomic weight is **22.99**.)

sodium chloride *noun* common salt. Formula: NaCl.

sodium hydroxide *noun* a compound of sodium and water which is used to make soap and to clear blocked drains. Formula: NaOH. Also called **caustic soda, soda**

softwood *noun* **1.** the open-grained wood produced by pine trees and other conifers **2.** a pine tree or other conifer that produces such wood. Compare **hardwood**

soil *noun* the earth in which plants grow. ◊ **chernozem, loess, podsol, subsoil, topsoil**

COMMENT: Soil is a mixture of mineral particles, decayed organic matter and water. Topsoil contains chemical substances which are leached through into the subsoil where they are retained. Soils are classified according to the areas of the world in which they are found, according to the types of minerals they contain or according to the stage of development they have reached.

Soil Association *noun* a UK organisation that certifies organically grown food

soil compaction *noun* the process of developing a close, densely packed soil structure, as a result of pressure or heavy loads, or the state of being densely packed

soil conservation *noun* the use of a range of methods to prevent soil from being eroded or overcultivated

soil creep *noun* a slow movement of soil downhill

soil erosion *noun* the removal of soil by the effects of rain, wind, sea or cultivation practices

soil fauna *plural noun* invertebrate animals that live in soil, e.g. earthworms

soil fertility *noun* the potential capacity of soil to support plant growth based on its content of nitrogen and other nutrients

soil flora *plural noun* microorganisms such as fungi and algae that live in soil

soil horizon *noun* a layer of soil that is of a different colour or texture from other layers (NOTE: There are four soil horizons: the A horizon or topsoil containing humus; the B horizon or subsoil containing minerals leached from the topsoil and little organic matter; the C horizon or weathered rock; and the D horizon or bedrock.)

soilless gardening *noun* same as **hydroponics**

soil map *noun* a map showing the different types of soil found in an area

soil nutrition *noun* **1.** the condition of soil in terms of the plant nutrients it contains **2.** the application of fertilisers to soil ○ *use muck and some seaweed for soil nutrition*

soil organic matter *noun* decayed or decaying vegetation that forms part of soil. Abbr **SOM**

soil profile *noun* a vertical section through the soil showing the different layers. ◊ **soil horizon**

soil salinity *noun* the quantity of mineral salts found in a soil (NOTE: High soil salinity is detrimental to most agricultural crops, although some plants are adapted to such conditions.)

soil sample *noun* a small quantity of soil used for testing

soil science *noun* the scientific study of all aspects of soil, including its formation, distribution and structure

soil sterilant *noun* something used to remove microorganisms from soil, e.g. a chemical or steam

soil structure *noun* the arrangement of soil particles in groups or individually, giving a loose or firm texture

soil texture *noun* the structure of soil based on the relative proportions of particles of different sizes it is composed of (NOTE: There are four main classes of soil texture: clay, silt, sand and loam. Loam, which contains a mixture of soil particles, is the most suitable for growing crops.)

solar *adjective* **1.** referring to the Sun **2.** using the energy of the Sun or driven by power from the Sun

solar cell *noun* a photoelectric device that converts solar energy into electricity

solar collector *noun* same as **solar panel**

solar eclipse *noun* a situation when the Moon passes between the Sun and the Earth during the daytime and the shadow of the Moon falls across the Earth, so cutting off the Sun's light. Compare **lunar eclipse**

solar energy *noun* electricity produced from the Sun's radiation. Also called **solar power, solar-generated energy, solar-generated power**

COMMENT: The Sun emits radiation in the form of ultraviolet rays, visible light and infrared heating rays. Solar energy can be collected by various methods, most often by heating water, which is then passed into storage tanks. Although solar energy is easy to collect, the problem is in storing it in order to make sure that power is available for use during the night or when it is cloudy.

solar gain *noun* the amount of heat in a building derived from solar radiation through windows or transparent walls

solar-generated energy, solar-generated power *noun* same as **solar energy**

solar heating *noun* the use of the Sun's energy to heat water as it passes through heat-absorbing panels

solarisation, solarization *noun* exposure to the rays of the Sun, especially for the purpose of killing pests in the soil, by covering the soil with plastic sheets and letting it warm up in the sunshine

solar panel *noun* a device with a dark surface which absorbs the sun's radiation and uses it to heat water. Also called **solar collector, collector panel**

solar power *noun* same as **solar energy**

solar-powered *adjective* powered by energy derived from the Sun's rays ○ *a solar-powered steam pump*

solid *adjective* not liquid or gaseous ○ *a lump of solid matter* ○ *a solid object* ○ *Visibility is reduced by the presence of solid particles such as dust or sand in the atmosphere.*

solidification *noun* the process of becoming solid

solidify *verb* to become solid ○ *Carbon dioxide solidifies at low temperatures.*

solid waste *noun* a type of waste matter that is hard and not liquid

solifluction *noun* a gradual downhill movement of wet soil

solstice *noun* one of the two times of year when the Sun is at its furthest point, either north or south, from the equator

solubility *noun* the ability of a substance to dissolve in another substance or solvent at a given temperature and pressure

soluble *adjective* referring to a substance that can be dissolved ○ *fat-soluble* ○ *water-soluble*

solum *noun* soil, including both topsoil and subsoil

solute *noun* a solid substance which is dissolved in a solvent to make a solution

solution *noun* **1.** the act or means of solving a problem or difficulty ○ *The solution was to protect the plants from trampling.* **2.** the answer to or a way of removing a problem or difficulty ○ *found a solution* **3.** a change of a solid or gas into a liquid by dissolving in water or some other liquid **4.** a mixture of a solid substance dissolved in a liquid ○ *a dilute solution of sodium bicarbonate*

solvent *noun* a liquid in which a solid substance can be dissolved

SOM *abbr* soil organic matter

sonar *noun* a method of finding objects under water by sending out sound waves and detecting returning sound waves reflected by the object

sonde *noun* a device attached to a balloon or rocket, for measuring and taking samples of the atmosphere

sonic *adjective* referring to sound waves

soot *noun* a black deposit of fine particles of carbon which rise in the smoke produced by the burning of material such as coal, wood or oil

sorghum *noun* a drought-resistant cereal plant grown in semi-arid tropical regions such as Mexico, Nigeria and Sudan. Latin name: *Sorghum vulgare.*

sound *noun* something that can be heard and is caused by vibration of the surrounding air

sound insulation *noun* preventing sound escaping or entering

source *noun* **1.** a substance or object which produces something ○ *Hot rocks are* a potential energy source. ○ *Plants tend to turn towards a light source.* **2.** the place where a river starts to flow ○ *The source of the Nile is in the mountains of Ethiopia.*

southern hemisphere *noun* the lower half of the Earth

Southern Lights *plural noun* a spectacular illumination of the sky in the southern hemisphere caused by ionised particles striking the atmosphere. Also called **Aurora Australis**

sow *verb* to put seeds into soil so that they will germinate and grow

soya *noun* a plant that produces edible beans which have a high protein and fat content and very little starch. Latin name: *Glycine max.* Also called **soya bean, soybean**

soya bean, soybean *noun* **1.** a bean from a soya plant **2.** same as **soya**

sp. *abbr* species (NOTE: The plural, for several species, is **spp.**)

sparse *adjective* having only a small number of items or individuals in a specific area ○ *a few sparse bushes in the desert* ○ *a sparse population*

spate *noun* □ **in (full) spate** very full of water and overflowing its banks ○ *The river was in full spate.*

spathe *noun* a large funnel-shaped bract, often coloured, around a flower head

spawn *noun* a mass of eggs produced by a fish or reptile ○ *Frog spawn develops into tadpoles.* ■ *verb* (*of a fish or reptile*) to produce a mass of eggs

SPEC *abbr* Species of European Conservation Concern

Special Area of Conservation *noun* a site designated to meet the requirements of the Habitats and Species Directive of the European Union. Abbr **SAC**

specialisation, specialization *noun* **1.** the activity of being concerned with one particular area of knowledge in detail **2.** a particular area of knowledge

specialise, specialize *verb* to be concerned with one particular area of knowledge in detail ○ *She specialises in the study of conifers.*

specialist *noun* **1.** a person who specialises in a particular area of knowledge ○ *They have called in a contamination specialist.* **2.** an organism which only lives on one type of food or in a very restricted habitat

specialist species *noun* a species which only lives on one type of food or in a very restricted habitat

speciality *noun* a particular area of knowledge that a person is concerned with in detail

special protection area *noun* an area designated under the Birds directive for the conservation of wild birds

specialty *noun US* same as **speciality**

speciation *noun* the process of developing new species

species *noun* a group of organisms that can interbreed. A species is a division of a genus. Abbr **sp.** (NOTE: The plural is **species.**)

Species Action Plan *noun* a scheme aimed at protecting species that are at risk by collecting all the available ecological data and listing appropriate conservation actions

species barrier *noun* the inability of members of different species to produce healthy offspring if they mate or cross

species diversity *noun* the range of species found in an area

species of conservation concern *noun* a species that is in decline, rare or scarce in the wild. Abbr **SoCC**

species of European concern *noun* a species that is in decline, rare or scarce in Europe. Abbr **SPEC**

species pool *noun* the group of all members of a species

species richness *noun* the number of species found in an area

species richness map *noun* a map showing the distribution of species in an area

specific *adjective* **1.** clearly defined and definite ○ *The plants have specific requirements for growth.* **2.** characteristic of something **3.** referring to species. ♭ **interspecific, intraspecific**

specificity *noun* the characteristic of having a specific range or use ○ *Parasites show specificity in that they live on only a limited number of hosts.*

specific name *noun* the scientific name by which a species is differentiated from other members of the genus (NOTE: It is the second name in the binomial classification system, the first being the name which identifies the genus. It is written with a small letter.)

specimen *noun* **1.** a representative of a group, especially an animal or plant ○ *a rare double-flowered specimen* **2.** a small quantity of something given for testing ○

Scientists have taken away soil specimens for analysis.

spectrography *noun* the recording of a spectrum on photographic film

spectroscope *noun* an instrument used to analyse a spectrum

spent fuel *noun* fuel which has been used in a nuclear reactor but which is still fissile and can be reprocessed ○ *Tonnes of spent fuel are sent for reprocessing.*

spent nuclear fuel *noun* radioactive material that has undergone one year of decay since being taken from a nuclear reactor but has not been separated into its components by reprocessing. Abbr **SNF**

sperm *noun* same as **spermatozoon** (NOTE: The plural is **sperm.**)

spermatogenesis *noun* the formation and development of spermatozoa

spermatophyte *noun* a seed-producing plant such as an angiosperm or a gymnosperm

spermatozoon *noun* a mature male sex cell, which is capable of fertilising an ovum (NOTE: The plural is **spermatozoa.**)

sperm whale *noun* a large toothed whale with a massive head inside which is a cavity containing sperm oil for which it was formerly hunted

sphagnum *noun* a type of moss which grows in bogs

spider *noun* one of a large group of animals, with two parts to their bodies and eight legs. Class: Arachnida.

spike *noun* a tall pointed flower head (**inflorescence**) in which small flowers without stalks grow from a central flower stem

spill *noun* a quantity of liquid which has escaped from a container or confined area

spillage *noun* **1.** the process of escaping from a container or confined area ○ *spillage of the river onto the adjacent land* **2.** a quantity of liquid which has escaped from a container or confined area

spillway *noun* a channel down which water can overflow from the reservoir behind a dam

spirochaete *noun* a bacterium with a spiral shape

spit *noun* a long, narrow accumulation of sand or gravel that projects from the shore into the sea

spoil *noun* waste left after minerals have been dug out of the ground

spoilage *noun* the process of food becoming inedible, especially because of poor storage conditions

spoil heap *noun* a large pile of waste left after minerals have been dug out of the ground

sporangium *noun* the organ that produces spores in some fungi, ferns and some other non-flowering plants (NOTE: The plural is **sporangia**.)

spore *noun* the microscopic reproductive body of fungi, bacteria and some non-flowering plants such as ferns

sporicidal *adjective* able to kill spores

sporicide *noun* a substance that kills spores

sporophyll *noun* a leaf with spore-producing organs, e.g. the fertile frond of a fern

sporophyte *noun* the spore-producing non-sexual phase in the life cycle of some plants such as ferns

sporozoon *plural noun* a parasitic protozoan, e.g. *Plasmodium*, the cause of malaria (NOTE: The plural is **sporozoa**.)

sports utility vehicle, sport utility vehicle *noun* a large strongly built car designed to carry people and equipment in rough countryside but usually used for everyday driving. Abbr **SUV** (NOTE: There are environmental concerns about the poor fuel economy of such cars.)

SPOT *abbr* Système Probatoire d'Observation de la Terre

sprawl *noun* an area that has been built up in a disorderly way ○ *urban sprawl* ■ *verb* to spread out in a disorderly way

spray *noun* 1. a mass of tiny drops of liquid 2. special liquid for spraying onto a plant to prevent insect infestation or disease ■ *verb* 1. to send out a liquid in a mass of tiny drops ○ *They sprayed the plants with water at regular intervals.* 2. to send out a special liquid onto a plant to prevent insect infestation or disease ○ *Apple trees are sprayed twice a year to kill aphids.*

sprayer *noun* a machine which forces a liquid through a nozzle under pressure, used to distribute liquids such as herbicides, fungicides, insecticides and fertilisers

spread *verb* 1. to move out over a large area ○ *The locusts spread right across the country.* ○ *Invasive plants spread rapidly.* 2. to put something such as manure, fertiliser or mulch on an area of ground

spring *noun* 1. a place where water comes naturally out of the ground 2. the season of the year following winter and before summer, when days become longer and the weather progressively warmer

spring tide *noun* a tide which occurs at the new and full moon when the influence of the Sun and Moon act together and the difference between high and low water is more than normal. Compare **neap tide**

springwood *noun* wood that develops just below the bark of trees in spring. Compare **summerwood**

sprout *noun* a little shoot growing out from a plant, with a stem and small leaves ■ *verb* (*of a plant*) to send out new growth

spruce *noun* a temperate softwood coniferous tree. Genus: *Picea.*

spur *noun* 1. a ridge of land that descends towards a valley floor from higher land above 2. a tubular projection from a flower sepal or petal often containing nectar 3. a short leafy branch of a tree with a cluster of flowers or fruits

squall *noun* a sharp gust of wind

squally *adjective* (*of weather*) with sharp gusts of wind

Sr *symbol* strontium

SSSI *abbr* Site of Special Scientific Interest

stabilisation lagoon *noun* 1. a pond used for storing liquid waste 2. a pond used for purifying sewage by allowing sunlight to fall on a mixture of sewage and water

stabilisation pond *noun* same as **sewage lagoon**

stabilise, stabilize *verb* 1. to become steady and not change, or to make something remain without change 2. to take measures to prevent soil being eroded, especially from a hillside

stabiliser, stabilizer *noun* 1. an artificial substance added to processed food such as sauces containing water and fat to stop the mixture from changing (NOTE: In the EU, emulsifiers and stabilisers have E numbers E322 to E495.) 2. an artificial substance added to plastics to prevent degradation

stabilising agent *noun* same as **stabiliser**

stability *noun* the state of being stable and not changing

stable *adjective* 1. steady and not easily moved ○ *a stable surface* 2. not changing ○ *In parts of Southeast Asia, temperatures remain stable for most of the year.* 3. referring to a chemical compound that does not react readily with other chemicals

stable climax *noun* a community of plants and animals in equilibrium with its environment, the final stage of an ecological succession

stable population *noun* a population which remains at a constant level because births and deaths are equal

stack *noun* **1.** a very tall industrial chimney, usually containing several flues ○ *The use of high stacks in power stations means that pollution is now more widely spread.* **2.** a steep-sided pillar of rock which stands in the sea near a cliff **3.** a large neat pile of things ○ *a stack of boxes* ■ *verb* to place things in a neat pile one on top of the other

stain *noun* **1.** a coloured mark on a surface **2.** a substance used to increase contrast in the colour of something such as a piece of tissue or a bacterial sample before examining it under a microscope ■ *verb* to treat something such as a piece of tissue or a bacterial sample with a dye so as to increase contrast in the colour before examining it under a microscope

stakeholder *noun* a person who has an interest in seeing that something does or does not happen, e.g. a shareholder in a business, an employee or a supplier

stalactite *noun* a long pointed growth of mineral from the ceiling of a cave, formed by the constant dripping of water which is rich in minerals

stalagmite *noun* a long pointed growth of mineral upwards from the floor of a cave, formed by the constant dripping of water which is rich in minerals from the tip of a stalactite

stalk *noun* **1.** the main stem of a plant which holds the plant upright **2.** a subsidiary stem of a plant, branching out from the main stem or attaching a leaf, flower or fruit

stamen *noun* a male part of a flower consisting of a stalk (**filament**) bearing a container (**anther**) in which pollen is produced

stand *noun* a group of plants or trees growing together ○ *a stand of conifers*

standard *noun* **1.** something which has been agreed on and is used to measure other things by ○ *set higher standards for water purity* **2.** a plant grown on a single long stem that is kept from forming branches except at the top **3.** a large tree in a woodland ○ *a coppice with standards*

standing crop *noun* **1.** a crop such as wheat which is still growing in a field **2.** the numbers and weight of the living vegetation of an area, calculated by weighing the vegetation growing in a sample section

staphylococcal *adjective* caused by staphylococci

staphylococcus *noun* a bacterium that causes boils and food poisoning. Genus: *Staphylococcus*. (NOTE: The plural is **staphylococci**.)

staple commodity *noun* a basic food or raw material

starch *noun* a substance composed of chains of glucose units, found in green plants (NOTE: It is the usual form in which carbohydrates exist in food, especially in bread, rice and potatoes, and is broken down by the digestive process into forms of sugar.)

starchy *adjective* containing a lot of starch ○ *Potatoes are a starchy food.*

starfish *noun* one of a group of flat sea animals that have five arms branching from a central body

starvation *noun* the state of having very little or no food

starve *verb* to have little or no food or nourishment

stasis *noun* a state when there is no change, growth or movement

static *adjective* not changing, moving or growing

station *noun* a building used for a particular purpose, e.g. a research station or railway station

statistics *plural noun* figures relating to measurements taken from samples ○ *Population statistics show that the birth rate is slowing down.*

stator *noun* a fixed part of a rotary machine ○ *The low pressure compressor has large rotor blades and stator blades.*

steady state *noun* a situation where the input, output and properties of a system remain constant over time

steam *noun* vapour that comes off boiling water and condenses in the atmosphere

stearic acid *noun* a colourless insoluble fatty acid found in animal and vegetable fats. It is used for making candles and soap. Formula: $C_{18}H_{36}O_3$.

steel *noun* an alloy mainly of iron and carbon

steelworks *noun* a factory where steel is produced from iron ore

stele *noun* the core of roots and stems, consisting of vascular tissue arranged in different patterns in different types of plant

stem *noun* **1.** the main stalk of a plant that holds it upright **2.** a subsidiary plant stalk, branching out from the main stalk or attaching a leaf, flower or fruit

steno- *prefix* narrow or constricted

stenohaline *adjective* **1.** referring to an organism that cannot tolerate variations in salt concentration in its environment **2.** referring to an organism that cannot survive variations in osmotic pressure of soil water ▶ compare **euryhaline**

stenothermous *adjective* referring to an organism that cannot tolerate changes of temperature. Compare **eurythermous**

steppe *noun* a wide grassy plain with no trees, especially in Europe and Asia (NOTE: The North American equivalent of a steppe is a **prairie**.)

sterile *adjective* **1.** free from microorganisms **2.** infertile or not able to produce offspring

sterilisation, sterilization *noun* **1.** the action of making something free from microorganisms **2.** the action of making an organism unable to produce offspring

sterilise, sterilize *verb* **1.** to make something sterile by killing the microorganisms in it or on it ○ *The soil needs to be sterilised before being used for intensive greenhouse cultivation.* **2.** to make an organism unable to have offspring (NOTE: This may be done by various means including drugs, surgery or irradiation.)

sterility *noun* **1.** the state of being free from microorganisms **2.** the inability to produce offspring

Stevenson screen *noun* a shelter that contains meteorological instruments, arranged to give standard readings

stewardship *noun* the protection of the environment for the future benefit of generations of human beings by developing appropriate institutions and strategies

stigma *noun* the part of a flower's female reproductive organ that receives the pollen grains (NOTE: It is generally located at the tip of the **style**.)

stimulate *verb* to make an organism or organ react or respond

stimulus *noun* something that makes an organism or organ react or respond, e.g. light, heat or noise (NOTE: The plural is **stimuli**.)

sting *noun* **1.** an organ with a sharp point, used by an insect or scorpion to pierce the skin of its victim and inject a toxic substance into the victim's bloodstream **2.** the action of using a sting **3.** a raised area on the skin produced by a sting **4.** a small itchy lump that is the result of touching a plant such a nettle that irritates the skin ■ *verb* **1.** (*of an insect or scorpion*) to use a sting to pierce a victim ○ *Do not touch the scorpion or it will sting you.* **2.** (*of a plant*) to produce a small itchy lump on somebody's skin

stinger *noun* a plant such as a nettle that irritates the skin

stock *noun* **1.** animals or plants that are derived from a common ancestor **2.** a plant with roots onto which a piece of another plant, the **scion**, is grafted. ◊ **rootstock 3.** a supply of something available for future use ○ *Stocks of herring are being decimated by overfishing.* ■ *verb* to provide a supply of something for future use ○ *a well-stocked garden* ○ *We stocked the ponds with a rare breed of fish.*

stockpile *noun* a large supply of something held for future use

stolon *noun* **1.** a stem that grows along the ground and gives rise to a new plant when it roots **2.** a structure found in some simple animals, sometimes used to anchor an organism to a surface

stoma *noun* a pore in a plant, especially in the leaves, through which carbon dioxide is taken in and oxygen is sent out. Each stoma in a leaf is surrounded by a pair of guard cells, which close the stomata if the plant needs to conserve water. (NOTE: The plural is **stomata**.)

stone *noun* **1.** a single small piece of rock **2.** a mineral formation **3.** a hard endocarp that surrounds a seed in a fruit such as a cherry

stoneground *adjective* referring to flour which has been made by grinding between flat heavy stones

stony *adjective* with many stones

storage *noun* the act of keeping something until it is needed

storage organ *noun* a plant part that stores food from the previous growing season and allows the plant to survive without leaves over winter, e.g. a potato tuber or a daffodil bulb

storage tank *noun* a large tank for storing a liquid

store *verb* to keep something until it is needed ○ *Whales store energy as blubber under the skin.*

storm *noun* a period of violent weather, with wind and rain or snow ○ *There was a storm during the night.* ○ *Storms swept the northern region.* ◊ **Beaufort scale**

storm cloud *noun* a dark-coloured cloud in which vigorous activity produces heavy rain or snow and sometimes other pronounced meteorological effects such as squalls of wind

storm drain *noun* a specially wide channel for taking away large amounts of rainwater which fall during heavy storms

storm sewage *noun* sewage mixed with storm water after a heavy rainfall

storm sewer *noun* a specially large pipe for taking away large amounts of rainwater

storm surge *noun* a rise in sea level as a hurricane or other severe storm moves over water, causing flooding when the storm comes ashore

storm swell *noun* a long, often massive and wave or succession of waves without crests caused by a hurricane

storm water *noun* water that falls as rain during a storm

straight fertiliser *noun* a fertiliser that supplies only one nutrient such as nitrogen. Compare **compound fertiliser**

strain *noun* a group within a species with distinct characteristics ○ *They have developed a new strain of virus-resistant rice.*

strait *noun* a narrow passage of sea between two larger areas of sea

strata plural of **stratum**

strategic environmental assessment *noun* an official assessment of the environmental effect of policies, plans and projects. ◊ **environmental impact assessment**

stratification *noun* the formation of several layers in substances such as sedimentary rocks, or water in a lake or air in the atmosphere

stratified *adjective* formed of several layers

stratigraphy *noun* the science of studying rock strata

stratocumulus *noun* a layer of small cumulus clouds below 3000 m

stratopause *noun* a thin layer of the Earth's atmosphere between the stratosphere and the mesosphere

stratosphere *noun* a layer of the Earth's atmosphere, above the troposphere and the tropopause and separated from the mesosphere by the stratopause

COMMENT: The stratosphere rises from about 18 km to 50 km above the surface of the Earth. It is formed of nitrogen (80%), oxygen (18%), ozone, argon and trace gases. The ozone in it forms the ozone layer.

stratospheric *adjective* referring to the stratosphere ○ *CFCs are responsible for damage to the ozone in the Earth's stratospheric zone.*

stratum *noun* a layer of rock (NOTE: The plural is **strata**.)

stratus *noun* a type of grey cloud, often producing light rain

straw *noun* **1.** the dry stems and leaves of crops such as wheat and oilseed rape left after the grains have been removed **2.** grass which is mowed after flowering. Compare **hay**

stream *noun* a narrow and shallow river

stream erosion *noun* the wearing away of soil or rock by the effect of a stream of water

streamflow *noun* the amount and speed of water flowing in a stream

stress *noun* a condition where an outside influence changes the composition or functioning of something ○ *Plants in dry environments experience stress due to lack of water.* ■ *verb* to subject something to stress

stress-tolerant *adjective* referring to a plant which can survive some degree of stress

striation *noun* **1.** a pattern of parallel lines or grooves **2.** a narrow groove or scratch on rock, caused by the action of a glacier

strip *noun* a long narrow piece, usually of the same width from end to end ○ *a strip of paper* ○ *a strip of land* ■ *verb* to remove a covering from something ○ *Spraying with defoliant strips the leaves off all plants.*

strip cropping *noun* a method of farming in which long thin pieces of land across the contours are planted with different crops in order to reduce soil erosion

strip cultivation *noun* a method of communal farming in which each family has a long thin piece or several long thin pieces of land to cultivate

strip mining *noun* a form of mining where the mineral is dug from the surface instead of digging underground. ◊ **opencast mining**

strontium *noun* a radioactive metallic element (NOTE: The chemical symbol is **Sr**; the atomic number is **38** and the atomic weight is **87.62**.)

structural *adjective* referring to the structure of something ○ *The structural limitations must never be exceeded.*

structure *noun* **1.** something that has been constructed ○ *a glass and steel structure* **2.** the different parts that make up a whole, or the arrangement of parts ○ *the structure of DNA*

stubble *noun* the short stems left in the ground after a crop such as wheat or oilseed rape has been cut

stunt *verb* to reduce the growth of something ○ *The poor soil stunts the growth of the trees.*

style *noun* the elongated structure that carries the stigma at its tip in many flowers

sub- *prefix* less important than

subatomic particle *noun* same as **elementary particle**

subclass *noun* a division of a class in the scientific classification of organisms

subclimax *noun* a stage in the development of a plant community where development stops before reaching its final stable state or **climax**

subcontinent *noun* a very large land mass, that is a distinct part of a continent ○ *the Indian subcontinent*

subculture *noun* a culture of microorganisms or cells that is grown from another culture ■ *verb* to grow a culture of microorganisms or cells from another culture

subdivision *noun* a group within a division in the scientific classification of organisms

subdominant *adjective* referring to a species that is not as important as the dominant species

subduct *verb* to pull something underneath ○ *The oceanic crust is being subducted under the continents which surround it.*

subduction *noun* the process by which a tectonic plate such as the oceanic crust is slowly being pulled under another plate

subgroup *noun* a small group distinguished in some way from the larger group to which it belongs

sublimate *verb* to transform directly from the solid to the gaseous state or from the gaseous to the solid state without becoming a liquid ○ *At low temperatures water vapour is directly sublimated into ice crystals.*

sublime *verb* same as **sublimate**

sublittoral *adjective* further inland from a shore than the littoral zone

submarine *adjective* situated or existing beneath the sea ○ *Shellfish collect round warm submarine vents.*

submerge *verb* to cover something with water or to become covered with water ○ *The coast is dangerous, with rocks submerged at intervals along it.*

submicroscopic *adjective* too small to be seen with a light microscope

sub-Saharan *noun* referring to the area south of the Sahara ○ *Rural supplies of wood for fuel are falling in many countries of sub-Saharan Africa.*

subsere *noun* the development of a plant and animal community after destruction of an existing community by fire, flood or human action

subside *verb* **1.** to go down or to become less violent ○ *After the rainstorms passed, the flood waters gradually subsided.* **2.** to sink or fall to a lower level ○ *The office block is subsiding owing to the shrinkage of the clay it is built on.*

subsidence *noun* **1.** (*of a piece of ground or a building*) the process of sinking or falling to a lower level ○ *Subsidence caused by the old mine shaft closed the main road.* **2.** a gradual downward movement of a mass of air

subsidy *noun* money given by a government or organisation to help an industry, charity or other organisation ○ *The reform will result in subsidies for farming being replaced by payments for caring for the environment.*

subsistence *noun* the condition of managing to live on the smallest amount of resources including food needed to stay alive

subsistence farming *noun* the activity of growing just enough crops to feed the farmer's family and having none left to sell

subsoil *noun* a layer of soil under the topsoil (NOTE: The subsoil contains little organic matter but chemical substances from the topsoil leach into it.)

subspecies *noun* a group of organisms that is part of a species but which shows slight differences from the main group, with which it can still interbreed

substance *noun* material of a particular type ○ *a sticky substance* ○ *a harmful substance* ○ *toxic substances*

substitute *noun* a thing used in place of another ■ *verb* to replace one thing with another ○ *Farmers have been told to plough up pastureland and substitute woodlots.*

substitution *noun* the replacement of one thing by another ○ *the substitution of natural fibres by synthetic materials*

substitution effect *noun* the effect on the environment of substituting one form of action for another

substrate *noun* **1.** a substance that is acted on by a catalyst such as an enzyme **2.** the matter or surface on which an organism lives

substratum *noun* a layer of rock beneath the topsoil and subsoil (NOTE: The plural is **substrata**.)

subterranean *adjective* below the ground

subtropical *adjective* referring to the subtropics ○ *The islands enjoy a subtropical climate.* ○ *Subtropical plants grow on the sheltered parts of the coast.*

subtropics *plural noun* an area between the tropics and the temperate zone

suburb *noun* a residential part of a town, away from the centre, but still within the built-up area

suburban *adjective* referring to the suburbs

succession *noun* a series of stages, one after the other, by which a group of organisms living in a community reaches its final stable state or **climax**

successive *adjective* referring to events or things following on one after another

succulent *noun* a plant that has fleshy leaves or stems in which it stores water, e.g. a cactus

sudden oak death *noun* a serious disease caused by the fungus *Phytophthora ramorum* that affects many tree species (NOTE: It has killed various species of oak in the US states of California and Oregon, but European species of oak appear to be less at risk.)

sufficiency *noun* a large enough amount of something

suffrutescent, suffruticose *adjective* referring to a perennial plant that is woody at the base of the stem and does not die down to ground level in winter

sugar *noun* any chemical of the saccharide group

sulfate *noun* a salt of sulfuric acid and a metal

sulfide, sulphide *noun* an ion of sulfur present in chemical compounds and mineral ores

sulfite, sulphite *noun* a salt of sulfuric acid that forms part of several chemical compounds and is used in processing paper

sulfonation, sulphonation *noun* the incorporation of sulfonic acid into an organic substance

sulfonator, sulphonator *noun* an apparatus for adding sulfur dioxide to water to remove excess chlorine

sulfur, sulphur *noun* a yellow non-metallic chemical element that is essential to biological life. It is used in the manufacture of sulfuric acid and in the vulcanisation of rubber. (NOTE: The chemical symbol is **S**; the atomic number is **16** and the atomic weight is **32.06**. The usual and recommended scientific spelling of sulphur and derivatives such as sulphate, sulphide and sulphonate is with an -f-, though the spelling with -ph- is still common in general usage.)

COMMENT: In the United Kingdom, the removal of sulfur from the atmosphere means that some crops such as oilseed rape are deficient and sulfur needs to be added to fertilisers.

sulfur cycle, sulphur cycle *noun* the process by which sulfur flows from the environment, through organisms and back to the environment again

sullage *noun* **1.** mud brought down by mountain streams **2.** the liquid waste from a building

summer *noun* the season following spring and before autumn, when the weather is warmest, the Sun is highest in the sky and most plants flower and set seed ■ *verb* to spend the summer in a place ○ *The birds summer on the shores of the lake.*

summerwood *noun* dense wood formed by trees during the later part of the growing season. Compare **springwood**

summit *noun* **1.** the highest point of a hill or mountain ○ *The climber reached the summit of the mountain.* **2.** a meeting between heads of government. ◊ **Earth Summit**

sun *noun* sunlight or the rays of the Sun ○ *sitting in the sun*

Sun *noun* a very hot star round which the Earth and other planets orbit and which gives energy in the form of light and heat

sunburn *noun* damage to the skin by excessive exposure to sunlight

sunlight *noun* the light from the Sun

sunrise *noun* the time when the Sun appears above the eastern horizon

sunset *noun* the time when the Sun disappears below the western horizon

sunshine *noun* bright light from the Sun

sunspot *noun* a darker patch on the surface of the Sun, caused by a stream of gas shooting outwards

super- *prefix* more than

superbug *noun* a bacterium that is resistant to most antibiotics that could be used to treat it

supercell *noun* the centre of a very large tornado or thunderstorm

supercool *verb* to reduce the temperature of a substance below its usual freezing point without freezing actually occurring

superficial *adjective* referring to features on or near the surface ○ *superficial scratches*

superheated *adjective* referring to steam that is heated to a high temperature in a power station

superinsulate *verb* to equip a building with completely effective insulation

superorder *noun* one of the groups in the scientific classification of organisms, ranking next above order

superorganism *noun* a group or community of individual organisms that functions as a single unit (NOTE: A forest, a termite colony and even human society can all be viewed as superorganisms.)

superphosphate *noun* a chemical compound formed from calcium phosphate and sulfuric acid, used as a fertiliser

supersaturated *adjective* referring to air which contains more moisture than the amount required to saturate it

superweed *noun* a weed resistant to herbicides that might develop in future as hybrid of a weed and a genetically modified plant

supply *noun* 1. the provision of something that is needed ○ *safeguard the generation and supply of power* 2. a stock of something that is needed ○ *a year's supply of food*

support *verb* to provide what is necessary for an activity or way of life ○ *These wetlands support a natural community of plants, animals and birds.*

supra- *prefix* above or over

surface *noun* 1. the outer covering or top layer of something 2. the land, water or sea of Earth's surface

surface-active agent *noun* same as **surfactant**

surface air temperature *noun* the temperature recorded in the shade at a height just above ground level

surface area *noun* the total of all the outer surfaces of an object ○ *a surface area of 10 square metres*

surface drainage *noun* the removal of surplus water from an area of land by means of ditches and channels

surface evaporation *noun* the evaporation of water from the surface of a body of water

surface heating *noun* the heating of the ground by the Sun

surface runoff *noun* a flow of rainwater, melted snow or excess fertiliser from the surface of land into streams and rivers

surface soil *noun* same as **topsoil**

surface water *noun* water that flows across the surface of the soil as a stream after rain and drains into rivers rather than seeping into the soil itself. Compare **ground water**

surfactant *noun* a substance that reduces surface tension. Also called **surface-active agent**

surge *noun* a sudden increase in the flow of something such as water or electrical power

surplus *adjective* excess ○ *Surplus water will flow away in storm drains.* ■ *noun* something that is more than is needed ○ *produced a surplus of wheat*

surplus yield *noun* a yield which is more than necessary for a population

survey *noun* 1. an investigation or inspection of something ○ *a survey of garden birds* ○ *a survey of people's views on smoking in public places* 2. the taking of measurements of the height of buildings or mountains and the length of roads, rivers and other features in order to make a detailed plan or map 3. a document, plan or map showing the results of an investigation or of the measurements taken ■ *verb* 1. to investigate or inspect something 2. to ask people for their opinion of something

survival *noun* the situation of continuing to live, especially if conditions are difficult

survive *verb* 1. to continue to live in a difficult situation ○ *After the fire, only a few trees survived.* 2. to overcome a difficult situation ○ *The plants can survive even the hottest desert temperatures.*

survivor *noun* an individual that continues to live when others have died

survivorship *noun* the number of individuals of a population surviving at a specific time

suspend *verb* 1. to hang something from above ○ *The bird-feeder was suspended from a tree.* 2. to hold particles in a liquid or in air ○ *an aerosol of suspended particles*

suspension *noun* 1. the state of being suspended 2. a liquid with solid particles in it, not settling to the bottom nor floating on the surface □ **in suspension** held in a liquid, not floating or settling

sustain *verb* to provide the necessary conditions for something ○ *The land is fertile enough to sustain a wide variety of fauna and flora.*

sustainability *noun* the ability of a process or human activity to meet present needs but maintain natural resources and leave the environment in good order for future generations

sustainable *adjective* referring to an activity that does not deplete or damage natural resources ○ *hardwood from a sustainable source*

sustainable agriculture *noun* environmentally friendly methods of farming that allow the production of crops or livestock without damage to the ecosystem

sustainable development *noun* development that balances the satisfaction of people's immediate interests and the protection of future generations' interests

sustainable energy *noun* energy produced from renewable resources that does not deplete natural resources

sustainable existence *noun* a way of life that ensures that the resources of the ecosystem are not depleted

Sustainable Farming and Food Strategy *noun* a strategy produced by Defra to support farming and food industries in working towards practices that will lead to a better environment and healthy and prosperous communities

sustainable society *noun* a society which exists without depleting the natural resources of its habitat

sustainable tourism *noun* the management of tourist activities to ensure minimum disruption of local infrastructure and environment

sustainable yield *noun* the greatest productivity that can be derived from a renewable resource without depleting the supply in a specific area

SUV *abbr* sport(s) utility vehicle

Sv *symbol* sievert

swallow hole *noun* a hole that forms in limestone rock as rainwater drains through it, dissolving minerals in the rock and sometimes forming underground caverns

swamp *noun* an area of permanently wet land and the plants that grow on it

swampland *noun* an area of land covered with swamp

swampy *adjective* referring to land that is permanently wet

swarm *noun* a large number of insects such as bees or locusts flying as a group ■ *verb* (*of insects*) to fly in a large group

swash *noun* a rush of water up a beach from a breaking wave. Compare **backwash**

swidden farming *noun* same as **slash and burn agriculture**

swollen *adjective* **1.** increased in size ○ *A tuber is a swollen underground stem.* **2.** containing more water than usual ○ *swollen rivers or streams*

sycamore *noun* a large hardwood tree of the maple family. Latin name: *Acer pseudoplatanus*.

symbiont *noun* one of the set of organisms living in symbiosis with each other. Compare **commensal**

symbiosis *noun* a condition where two or more unrelated organisms exist together enabling both to survive. Also called **mutualism**

symbiotic *adjective* referring to symbiosis ○ *The rainforest has evolved symbiotic mechanisms to recycle minerals.*

symbiotically *adverb* in symbiosis ○ *Colonies of shellfish have parasites that live symbiotically with them.*

symbiotic relationship *noun* a relationship of cooperation between two or more unrelated organisms

sympatric speciation *noun* the development of new species in the same areas as other new species

symphile *noun* an insect or other organism that lives in the nests of social insects such as ants or termites and is fed by them

symptom *noun* a change in the functioning or appearance of an organism, which shows that a disease or disorder is present

symptomatic *adjective* referring to a symptom

syn- *prefix* joint or fused

syncline *noun* a concave downward fold of rock, with the youngest rock on the inside. Compare **anticline**

syndrome *noun* a group of symptoms and other changes in an organism's functions which, when taken together, show that a particular disease or disorder is present

synecology *noun* the study of communities of organisms in their environments. Compare **autecology**

synergism *noun* a phenomenon where two substances act more strongly together than they would independently

synergist *noun* a substance that increases the effect of another

synfuel *noun* a fuel similar to those produced from crude oil but produced from more plentiful resources, e.g. coal, shale or tar

synroc *noun* an artificial mineral compound formed of nuclear waste fused into minerals and so will never deteriorate

synthesis *noun* 1. the process of combining things to form a whole 2. the process of producing a compound by a chemical reaction

synthesise, synthesize *verb* 1. to combine things to form a whole 2. to produce a compound by a chemical reaction ○ *The body cannot synthesise essential fatty acids and has to absorb them from food.*

synthetic *adjective* made in an industrial process and not occurring naturally ○ *synthetic rubber*

synthetically *adverb* by an industrial process ○ *synthetically produced hormones*

synusia *noun* a group of plants living in the same habitat

system *noun* 1. an arrangement of things or phenomena that act together ○ *a weather system* 2. an arrangement of parts of the body that work together ○ *the nervous system* 3. a way of classifying something scientifically ○ *the Linnaean system*

systematic *adjective* organised in a planned way

systematics *noun* the scientific study of systems, especially of the system of classifying organisms

Système International *noun* full form of **SI**

Système Probatoire d'Observation de la Terre *noun* a French observation satellite transmitting data which gives images of the Earth. Abbr **SPOT**

systemic *adjective* affecting a whole organism

systemic fungicide *noun* a fungicide that is absorbed into a plant's sap system through its leaves or roots and protects the plant from infection by fungi without killing the plant itself. ◊ **systemic pesticide**

systemic herbicide *noun* a herbicide that is absorbed into a plant's sap system through its leaves or roots and is transported through the plant to kill the roots. Also called **systemic weedkiller**

systemic pesticide *noun* a pesticide that is absorbed into a plant's sap system through its leaves or roots and protects the plant from pests without killing the plant itself

systemic weedkiller *noun* same as **systemic herbicide**

T

T *symbol* tera-

Ta *symbol* tantalum

tableland *noun* an area of high flat land

TAC *abbr* total allowable catch

taiga *noun* a forested region between the Arctic tundra and the steppe

tailings *plural noun* refuse or waste ore from mining operations

tailpipe *noun* US a tube at the back of a motor vehicle from which gases produced by burning petrol are sent out into the atmosphere (NOTE: British English is **exhaust pipe**.)

tall-grass prairie *noun* same as **long-grass prairie**

tank *noun* a large container for storing fluid ○ *water tank* ○ *fuel tank*

tanker *noun* 1. a large ship used to carry petrol or oil 2. a truck used to carry liquids such as petrol or milk

tantalum *noun* a rare metal that does not corrode (NOTE: The chemical symbol is **Ta**; the atomic number is **73** and the atomic weight is **180.95**.)

tap *noun* a pipe with a handle that can be turned to make a liquid or gas come out of a container ■ *verb* to remove or drain liquid from something □ **to tap oil resources** to bring up oil from the ground. ◊ **untapped**

taproot *noun* the thick main root of a plant which grows straight down into the soil (NOTE: A taproot system has a main root with smaller roots branching off it, as opposed to a fibrous root system which has no main root.)

tap water *noun* the water that has been supplied by pipes to a building and is sometimes stored in tanks before being used

tar *noun* a thick black sticky substance derived from coal

tardigrade *noun* a tiny animal that lives in moss

tarn *noun* a small lake in a depression on a mountainside

tar sand *noun* same as **oil sand**

tartrazine *noun* a yellow substance added to food to give it an attractive colour (NOTE: It is coded E102. Although widely used, tartrazine provokes bad reactions in some people and is banned in some countries.)

taungya, taungya system *noun* a system used in the tropics in which food crops and crops such as coffee that need shade are grown below useful trees until the trees become large

taxa plural of **taxon**

-taxis *suffix* the response of an organism moving towards or away from a stimulus

taxon *noun* a grouping in a scientific classification of organisms, e.g. a family, genus or species (NOTE: The plural is **taxa**.)

taxonomic *adjective* referring to taxonomy

taxonomy *noun* the techniques and system of classifying organisms according to their characteristics

TBT *abbr* tributyltin

TCDD *noun* a highly toxic persistent by-product of the herbicide 2,4,5-T. Full form **tetrachlorodibenzoparadioxin**

TDI *abbr* Tolerable Daily Intake

teak *noun* a tropical tree that produces a hardwood which is resistant to water. Latin name: *Tectona grandis*.

technical *adjective* referring to practical or scientific work

technician *noun* a person who does practical work in a laboratory or scientific institution ○ *a laboratory technician*

technique *noun* a way of doing something such as scientific or medical work using a special method or skill ○ *a new technique for dating fossils*

technological *adjective* referring to technology

technology *noun* the application of scientific knowledge to industrial processes ○ *The technology has to be related to user requirements.*

technosphere *noun* an environment built or modified by humans

tectonic *adjective* referring to faults or movements in the Earth's crust

tectonic plate *noun* a large area of solid rock in the Earth's crust, which floats on the mantle and moves very slowly

temperate *adjective* neither very hot nor very cold

temperate climate *noun* a climate that is neither very hot in summer nor very cold in winter

temperate region *noun* a region that is neither very hot in summer nor very cold in winter

temperature *noun* a measurement of heat

temperature chart *noun* a chart showing changes in temperature over a period of time

temperature lapse rate *noun* same as **lapse rate**

temporary *adjective* lasting for a short time and not permanent

tender *adjective* **1.** soft or susceptible to damage **2.** referring to a plant which cannot tolerate frost

tendril *noun* a stem, leaf or petiole of a plant modified into a thin touch-sensitive organ that coils around objects, providing support for climbing plants

tera- *prefix* one trillion, 10^{12}. Symbol **T**

teratogen *noun* a substance or agent that causes birth defects

teratogenesis *noun* the production of birth defects

teratogenic *adjective* causing birth defects

terawatt *noun* a unit of measurement of electric energy, equal to one billion watts. Abbr **TW**

terminal *adjective* coming at the end ○ *a terminal inflorescence* ○ *terminal moraine*

termitarium *noun* a nest made by termites formed in the shape of a hill of hard earth

termite *noun* an insect resembling a large ant, which lives in colonies and eats cellulose

tern *noun* a type of small gull

terrace *noun* a flat strip of land across a sloping hillside, lying level along the contours ■ *verb* to build terraces on a mountainside ○ *The hills are covered with terraced rice fields.*

terrain *noun* the ground or an area of land in terms of its physical surface features ○ *mountainous terrain*

terrestrial *adjective* **1.** referring to the Earth, as opposed to space ○ *terrestrial and satellite links* **2.** referring to dry land, as opposed to the sea or the air ○ *terrestrial ecology* ○ *terrestrial and marine sites*

terrestrial animal *noun* an animal that lives on dry land

terrestrial equator *noun* same as **equator**

terricolous *adjective* referring to an animal that lives in or on soil

territorial *adjective* referring to territory

territorialism, territoriality *noun* a pattern of behaviour involving the establishment and defence of a territory

territorial species *noun* a species that occupies and defends a territory

territorial waters *plural noun* the sea near the coast of a country that is under the control of that country

territory *noun* an area of land occupied and defended by an animal, which may be all or part of the animal's home range ○ *A robin defends its territory by attacking other robins that enter it.*

tertiary *adjective* coming after two other things. ◊ **primary, secondary**

tertiary consumer *noun* a carnivore that only eats other carnivores. ◊ **primary consumer, secondary consumer**

test *noun* a process designed to find out if a sample of something matches criteria, if a device is working well, or if a product is satisfactory ○ *Laboratory tests showed that the sample was positive.* ○ *Government officials have carried out tests on samples of drinking water.* ■ *verb* to examine a sample or device to see if it is working well ○ *They tested the water sample for microorganisms.*

tetrachlorodibenzoparadioxin *noun* full form of **TCDD**

tetraethyl lead *noun* a substance sometimes added to petrol to prevent knocking in an engine

texture *noun* the roughness or smoothness of a surface or substance

Th *symbol* thorium

thatch *verb* to cover a roof with reeds, straw, grass or other plant material ○ *Reeds provide the longest-lasting material for thatching.* ■ *noun* a covering for a roof made of reeds, straw, grass or other plant material ○ *birds nesting in the old thatch*

thaw *noun* a period when the weather becomes warmer after a heavy frost, and ice and snow melt ■ *verb* to melt or make something melt ○ *As the polar ice thaws, the sea level rises.* ○ *It is possible that rising atmospheric temperatures will thaw the polar ice caps and raise the level of the sea.*

thaw water *noun* water from melting snow and ice

theodolite *noun* an instrument formed of a telescope mounted in such a way that it can turn around, used for measuring angles

theoretical *adjective* **1.** about, involving or based on theory **2.** dealing with theory or speculation rather than with practical applications **3.** existing only as a theory

theoretically *adverb* possibly, on the basis of a theory

theorise, theorize *verb* to produce ideas to explain something

theory *noun* a possible explanation of how or why something happens which has not been confirmed by experimental evidence

thermal *adjective* referring to heat ○ *Intense surface heating causes thermal currents to develop and create convection.*

thermal accumulator *noun* same as **heat accumulator**

thermal discharge *noun* same as **heat discharge**

thermal pollution *noun* a change in the quality of an environment by increasing its temperature, e.g. the release of heat from the cooling towers of a power station or from the discharge of a coolant

thermal power plant *noun* an industrial site that produces energy from heat, especially by burning fossil fuels or using nuclear energy

thermal storage *noun* same as **heat storage**

thermo- *prefix* heat or temperature

thermocline *noun* same as **metalimnion**. ♦ epilimnion, hypolimnion

thermodynamic temperature *noun* temperature measured on a scale that is independent of the substance being used, expressed in kelvin

thermograph *noun* an instrument that records changes in temperature on a roll of paper

thermolysis *noun* a reduction in body temperature, e.g. by sweating

thermometer *noun* an instrument for measuring temperature

thermometry *noun* the science of measuring temperature

thermonasty *noun* a response of plants to heat

thermoneutral zone *noun* a range of environmental temperatures in which an endotherm can easily maintain a constant body temperature

thermonuclear energy *noun* energy produced by fusion of atomic nuclei

thermoperiodic *adjective* referring to an organism that reacts to regular changes in temperature

thermoperiodicity, **thermoperiodism** *noun* the effect on an organism of regular changes in temperature

thermophilic *adjective* referring to organisms such as algae living in the hot water of thermal springs that need a high temperature to grow

thermoplastic *adjective* able to be recycled by heating and cooling ○ *thermoplastic materials*

thermoregulation *noun* the control of body temperature by processes such as sweating and shivering

thermosphere *noun* the zone of the atmosphere above 80 km from the surface of the Earth, where the temperature increases with altitude

therophyte *noun* an annual plant that completes its life cycle rapidly in favourable conditions, growing from a seed and dying within one season and then surviving the unfavourable season in the form of seeds (NOTE: Many desert plants and plants growing on cultivated land are therophytes.)

Third World *noun* the developing countries of Africa, Asia and Latin America (NOTE: This term is now less-often used.)

thorium *noun* a natural radioactive element which decomposes to radioactive radon gas (NOTE: The chemical symbol is **Th**; the atomic number is **90** and the atomic weight is **232.04**.)

thorn *noun* a sharp woody point on plant stems or branches

thornbush *noun* a shrub or bush which has sharp woody points on its stems and branches

thorn scrub *noun* an area of land covered with bushes and small trees which have sharp woody points on their stems and branches

thorn woodland *noun* an area of land covered with trees which have sharp woody points on their stems and branches

threat *noun* something dangerous which may cause harm or damage ○ *Water pollution is a threat to public health.* □ **under threat (of)** likely to be harmed or damaged ○ *under threat of flooding*

threaten *verb* to be a danger or harmful to something ○ *Plant species growing in arid or semi-arid lands are threatened by the expansion in keeping livestock.*

threatened *adjective* in danger of being harmed, damaged, or reduced in numbers ○ *a threatened habitat*

threatened species *noun* a species which is in danger of becoming extinct and needs protection

COMMENT: IUCN defines three categories of threatened species, in order of danger of extinction: critically endangered, endangered and vulnerable.

Three Mile Island *noun* a nuclear power station in Pennsylvania, USA, where an accident in 1979 almost caused the release of large quantities of radioactive substances

threshold *noun* **1.** a point or limit at which something changes **2.** the limit below which a significant adverse effect is not expected

thrive *verb* (*of an animal or plant*) to develop and grow strongly ○ *These plants thrive in very cold environments.*

throw *noun* the amount of up or down movement of rocks at a fault line

thrust *noun* a force in the crust of the Earth that squeezes and so produces folds

thrust fault *noun* a fault in which the upper layers of rock have been pushed forward over the lower layers

thunder *noun* a loud sound generated by lightning in the atmosphere ○ *The storm was accompanied by thunder and lightning.*

thunderstorm *noun* a storm with rain, thunder and lightning

Ti *symbol* titanium

tick *noun* a tiny parasite that sucks blood from the skin. Order: Acarida.

tidal *adjective* referring to the tide

tidal energy, tidal power *noun* electricity produced by using the force of the tides to drive turbines. Also called **wave power**

tidal prism *noun* a model of water flow in an estuary or other tidal area, used to assess the way in which pollutants are flushed through the area and dispersed

till *noun* a boulder clay soil mixed with rocks of different sizes, found in glacial deposits ■ *verb* to prepare the soil, especially by digging or ploughing, to make it ready for the cultivation of crops

tillage *noun* the activity of preparing the soil for cultivation

tilth *noun* a good light crumbling soil prepared to be suitable for growing plants ○ *Work the soil into a fine tilth before sowing seeds.*

timber *noun* trees which have been or are to be cut down and made into logs

timberline *noun US* same as **treeline** ○ *The slopes above the timberline were covered with boulders, rocks and pebbles.*

tin *noun* **1.** a metallic element, used especially to form alloys (NOTE: The chemical symbol is **Sn**; the atomic number is **50** and the atomic weight is **118.69**.) **2.** a metal container for food or drink, made of iron with a lining of tin or of aluminium. Also called **tin can** (NOTE: The US term is **can**.)

tip *noun* **1.** the end part of a plant stem where growth takes place ○ *a shoot tip* **2.** a place where rubbish or waste is thrown away ○ *The siting of the council refuse tip has caused a lot of controversy.* ■ *verb* to throw away rubbish

tipping *noun* the process of disposing with rubbish ○ *a ban on tipping* ◊ **fly-tipping**

tissue *noun* a group of cells that carries out a specific function, of which the organs of an animal or plant are formed ○ *photosynthetic tissue in leaves* ○ *Most of an animal's body is made up of soft tissue, with the exception of the bones and cartilage.*

titanium *noun* a light metal used to make strong alloys (NOTE: The fatigue resistance of titanium is greater than that of aluminium or steel. The chemical symbol is **Ti**; the atomic number **22** and the atomic weight is **47.90**.)

titration *noun* a process for measuring the concentration of a solution

titre *noun* a measurement of the concentration of a solution, as determined by titration (NOTE: The US spelling is **titer**.)

toadstool *noun* a poisonous fungus that resembles an edible mushroom

TOE *abbr* tonnes of oil equivalent

TOID, toid *noun* the unique 16-digit number attached to buildings and each feature of the landscape on a digital map. Full form **topographical identifier**

tolerable daily intake *noun* the amount of a substance that it is estimated can be taken in without risk to health on a daily basis. Abbr **TDI**

tolerance *noun* **1.** the ability of an organism to accept something, or not to react to something ○ *plants with frost tolerance* **2.** an allowable variation in something which can be measured ○ *a tolerance of 2°* ○ *a tolerance of 1mm*

tolerant *adjective* not reacting adversely to something ○ *a salt-tolerant plant*

tolerate *verb* not to react adversely to something

toleration *noun* the ability to tolerate something, or the act of tolerating something ○ *poor toleration of high temperatures*

ton *noun* **1.** a unit of measurement of weight, equal to 1016 kg. Also called **long ton 2.** *US* a unit of measurement of weight, equal to 907 kg. Also called **short ton**

tonne *noun* a unit of measurement of weight, equal to 1000 kg. Also called **metric ton**

tonnes of oil equivalent *noun* a unit of measurement of the energy content of a fuel, calculated by comparing its heat energy with that of oil. Abbr **TOE**

toothed *adjective* **1.** having teeth **2.** having many small indentations around the edge ○ *toothed leaves*

toothed whale *noun* a whale that has teeth, e.g. a sperm whale, killer whale, porpoise or dolphin. Suborder: Odontoceti.

top-down control *noun* the system of regulation of trophic levels by which the abundance of herbivores in the lower trophic levels is determined by factors such as predators in the higher levels. Compare **bottom-up control**

topographic, topographical *adjective* referring to topography

topography *noun* the study of the physical features of a geographical area

topotype *noun* a population which has become different from other populations of a species because of adaptation to local geographical features

topset bed *noun* a layer of fine-grained sediment in a river delta

topsoil *noun* the top layer of soil, often containing organic material, from which chemical substances are washed by water into the subsoil below

tor *noun* a pile of blocks or rounded granite rocks found on summits and hillsides

tornado *noun* a violent storm with a column of rapidly turning air at the centre of an area of very low pressure, giving very high winds and causing damage to buildings

torrent *noun* a violent rapidly flowing stream of water or lava

torrential *adjective* referring to very heavy rain ○ *The storm brought a torrential downpour of rain.*

total *adjective* complete or entire ○ *The total world population of the animal is no more than four or five hundred pairs.*

total allowable catch *noun* the maximum amount of fish permitted to be caught. Abbr **TAC**

total fertility rate *noun* an average number of children expected to be born to a female during her lifetime

town *noun* a collection of buildings, an urban area smaller than a city and larger than a village

town hall *noun* a building in a town where the administrative offices of the town are situated and where the local council has its meetings

town planner *noun* a person who supervises the design of a town and the way the streets and buildings are laid out and developed

town planning *noun* the process of designing a town or city, including the way the streets and buildings are laid out and developed

townscape *noun* the appearance of a town, the way in which the streets and buildings are laid out

tox-, toxi- *prefix* poison

toxic *adjective* referring to a substance that is poisonous or harmful to humans, animals or the environment

toxic emissions *plural noun* poisonous chemicals discharged into the air, water or land

toxicity *noun* the degree to which a substance is poisonous or harmful ○ *They were concerned about the high level of toxicity of the fumes.*

toxico- *prefix* poison

toxicological *adjective* referring to toxicology ○ *Irradiated food presents no toxicological hazard to humans.*

toxicologist *noun* a scientist who specialises in the study of poisons

toxicology *noun* the scientific study of poisons and their effects on the human body

toxicosis *noun* poisoning

toxic site *noun* land contaminated with one or more toxic substances, usually not suitable for human habitation

toxic substance *noun* a substance that is poisonous or harmful to humans, animals or the environment

toxic waste *noun* industrial or chemical waste that is poisonous or harmful to humans, animals or the environment

toxin *noun* a poisonous substance produced by microorganisms. ◊ **mycotoxin**

TPO *abbr* tree preservation order

trace *noun* **1.** a very small amount of something ○ *There are traces of radioactivity in the sample.* **2.** a line or pattern made on a screen or piece of paper by a device recording an electrical signal

trace element *noun* a chemical element that is essential to organic growth but only in very small quantities

COMMENT: Plants require traces of copper, iron, manganese and zinc. Humans require the trace elements chromium, cobalt, copper, magnesium, manganese, molybdenum, selenium and zinc.

trace gas *noun* a gas that exists in the atmosphere in very small quantities, e.g. xenon or helium

tracer *noun* a substance inserted into an organism so that its movements may be tracked from its colour, radioactivity, fluorescence or other characteristic

tract *noun* a wide area of land ○ *Large tracts of forest have been destroyed by fire.*

trade wind *noun* a wind that blows towards the equator, from the north-east in the northern hemisphere and from the south-east in the southern hemisphere

traditional *adjective* referring to something that has always been done in the same way ○ *a traditional system of agriculture* ○ *Traditional technologies met basic subsistence needs.*

traffic *noun* **1.** the vehicles that are travelling in an area at the same time ○ *rush-hour traffic* **2.** aircraft, train and ships that travel from one place to another ○ *Lower fares have resulted in a large increase in air traffic.*

traffic-calming measure *noun* a means of reducing the number and speed of motor vehicles using a road, e.g. speed humps or a speed limit

traffic concentration *noun* a large number of vehicles in one place

traffic congestion, traffic jam *noun* a blockage caused by too many vehicles on a road. ◊ **congestion charging**

trail *noun* **1.** a path or track ○ *created a new nature trail in the forest* **2.** a mark or scent left by an animal ○ *on the trail of a badger*

trait *noun* a genetically controlled characteristic

trans- *prefix* through or across

transboundary pollution *noun* airborne or waterborne pollution produced in one country which crosses to another. Also called **transfrontier pollution**

transect *noun* a line used in ecological surveys to provide a way of measuring and showing the distribution of organisms

transform *verb* to change the structure or appearance of something

transformation *noun* a change in structure or appearance

transfrontier pollution *noun* same as **transboundary pollution**

transgenic *adjective* **1.** referring to an organism into which genetic material from a different species has been transferred using the techniques of genetic modification **2.** referring to the techniques of transferring genetic material from one organism to another ■ *noun* an organism produced by genetic modification

transhumance *noun* the practice of moving flocks and herds up to high summer pastures and bringing them down to a valley again in winter

transition *noun* a change from one state to another

transitional waters *noun* the area of surface water in a river mouth that is partly salty

translocate *verb* to move substances through the tissues of a plant

translocated herbicide *noun* a herbicide that kills a plant after being absorbed through its leaves

translocation *noun* a movement of substances through the tissues of a plant

transmissible disease *noun* a disease which can be transmitted to other individuals

transmit *verb* **1.** to send something somewhere else ○ *The charts are transmitted from one station to another by fax.* **2.** to pass on a disease to another animal or plant ○ *Some diseases are transmitted by insects.* (NOTE: **transmitting – transmitted**)

transpiration *noun* the loss of water from a plant through its stomata

transpire *verb* (*of a plant*) to lose water through stomata ○ *In tropical rainforests, up to 75% of rainfall will evaporate and transpire into the atmosphere.*

transplant *noun* a plant taken from one place and planted in the soil in another place ■ *verb* to take a growing plant from one place and plant it in the soil in another place

transport *noun* **1.** a system of moving things from one place to another ○ *road and rail transport* ○ *an integrated transport policy* Also called **transportation 2.**

the activity of moving something from one place to another

transportation *noun* same as **transport**

transuranic element *noun* an artificial radioactive element which is beyond uranium in the periodic table

trash *noun US* unwanted material or household waste

trawl, trawl net *noun* a very long net with a wide mouth tapering to a pointed end, towed behind a fishing boat at any depth in the sea

treat *verb* to apply a chemical or physical process to something in order to get a specific result ○ *The fabric has been treated to make it waterproof.*

treatment *noun* the application of a chemical or physical process ○ *anti-corrosion treatment* ○ *heat treatment* ○ *the treatment of sewage*

tree *noun* a plant typically with one main woody stem that may grow to a great height

tree cover *noun* the percentage of an area occupied by trees

treehugger *noun* somebody who is regarded as devoted to environmental protection in an extreme or foolish way (*informal*)

treeline *noun* **1.** a line at a specific altitude, above which trees will not grow ○ *The slopes above the treeline were covered with boulders, rocks and pebbles.* **2.** a line in the northern or southern hemisphere, north or south of which trees will not grow

tree preservation order *noun* an order from a local government department that prevents a tree from being cut down. Abbr **TPO**

tree ring *noun* same as **annual ring**

tree savanna *noun* a dry grass-covered plain with some trees

tree-sit *noun* a protest carried out by spending a period in shelter built in a tree in an effort to prevent tree-felling or construction activities

treeware *noun* paper and paper products such as books made from wood pulp

tremor *noun* **1.** a slight shaking movement **2.** a minor earthquake

trench *noun* a long narrow hole in the ground

trend *noun* a gradual development ○ *a trend towards organic farming*

tributary *noun* a stream or river flowing into a larger river

tributyltin *noun* a very toxic organic compound containing tin that is a component of the paint used on ships' hulls and structures that stand in seawater to prevent organisms growing on them. Abbr **TBT**. ◊ **antifouling paint**

trifuralin *noun* a commonly used herbicide incorporated into the soil before planting a wide range of crops (NOTE: It is under review for withdrawal from use in the European Union.)

trigger *verb* to cause something to operate or come into effect ○ *The indicator triggers an aural warning if specific limits are exceeded.* ○ *It is not known what triggered the avalanche.*

triple bottom line *noun* the three criteria of environmental sustainability, social responsibility and sound financial performance, used in making ethical investment decisions

tritium *noun* a rare isotope of hydrogen

trophic *adjective* referring to nutrition

trophic cascade *noun* the effect that a change in the size of one population in a food web has on the populations below it

trophic chain *noun* same as **food chain**

trophic level *noun* one of the levels in a food chain

COMMENT: There are three trophic levels. Producers, organisms such as plants, take energy from the Sun or the environment and convert it into matter. Primary consumers, organisms such as herbivores, eat producers. Secondary consumers are carnivores that eat herbivores; tertiary consumers eat only other carnivores.

trophic pyramid *noun* a chart showing the structure of an ecosystem in terms of trophic levels

trophic structure *noun* the structure of an ecosystem, shown by food chains and food webs. ◊ **dystrophic, eutrophic, mesotrophic, oligotrophic**

tropho-, troph- *prefix* referring to food or nutrition

-trophy *suffix* **1.** nourishment **2.** development of an organ

-tropic *suffix* turning towards

tropical *adjective* referring to the tropics ○ *The disease is carried by a tropical insect.*

tropical desert *noun* same as **hot desert**

tropics *plural noun* the region between the Tropic of Cancer and the Tropic of Capricorn, where the climate is hot and often humid ○ *a disease which is endemic in the tropics*

tropism *noun* the action of a plant organ turning towards a stimulus

tropopause *noun* a layer of the atmosphere between the troposphere and the stratosphere

troposphere *noun* the lowest region of the atmosphere, extending to about 12 km above sea level

tropospheric *adjective* referring to the troposphere

tropospheric ozone *noun* the ozone that is located in the troposphere and plays a significant role in the greenhouse gas effect and urban smog

trough *noun* **1.** a low point in a cycle ○ *The graph shows the peaks and troughs of pollution over the seasons.* **2.** a long narrow area of low pressure with cold air in it, leading away from the centre of a depression

trunk *noun* **1.** the main woody stem of a tree **2.** the long muscular tube at the front of the head of an elephant, used for grasping things and taking up water

tuber *noun* a swollen underground stem or root, which holds nutrients and which has buds from which shoots develop ○ *A potato is the tuber of a potato plant.*

tuberous *adjective* **1.** like a tuber **2.** referring to a plant that grows from a tuber

tufa *noun* a form of calcareous deposit found near hot springs

tundra *noun* a cold Arctic region without trees which may be covered with low shrubs, grasses, mosses and lichens

turbid *adjective* referring to a liquid which is cloudy because of particles suspended in it

turbidity *noun* cloudiness of a liquid, because of particles suspended in it

turbine *noun* a mechanical device which converts moving liquid, steam or air into energy by turning a generator

turbocline *noun* the lower layer of water at the base of the seasonal boundary layer

turgor *noun* the normal state of a plant cell when the vacuole is full of water

TW *abbr* terawatt

twin *noun* one of two babies or animals born at the same time from two ova fertilised at the same time or from one ovum that splits in two

twister *noun US* a tornado (*informal*)

2,4-D *noun* a herbicide that is absorbed into a plant through its leaves and is especially effective against broadleaved weeds growing in cereals

typhoon *noun* a tropical cyclone in East Asia

U

U *symbol* uranium

UKAEA *abbr* United Kingdom Atomic Energy Authority

ultra- *prefix* beyond

ultrabasic *adjective* referring to rock which has less silica and more magnesium than basic rock

ultramicroscopic *adjective* too small to be seen with a light microscope

ultrananoplankton *plural noun* plankton less than 2 μm in size

ultraplankton *plural noun* plankton in the size range 0.5–10 μm

ultrasonic *adjective* referring to the frequencies in the range of 20000Hz which cannot be heard by the human ear

ultrasonics *noun* the study of ultrasound

ultrasonic waves *plural noun* sound waves in the range of 20000Hz

ultrasound *noun* sound in the range of 20000Hz which cannot be heard by the human ear

ultraviolet *adjective* referring to the range of invisible radiation wavelengths just greater than those of the visible spectrum. Abbr **UV**

ultraviolet rays *plural noun* the short invisible rays, beyond the violet end of the colour spectrum, which form the tanning and burning element in sunlight

COMMENT: UV rays form part of the high-energy radiation which the Earth receives from the Sun. UV rays are classified as UVA and UVB rays. UVB rays form only a small part of radiation from the Sun but they are dangerous and can cause skin cancer if a person is exposed to them for long periods. The effect of UVB rays is reduced by the ozone layer in the stratosphere

UN *abbr* United Nations

un- *prefix* not

unblock *verb* to remove a blockage from something

unconfined *adjective* referring to ground water or an aquifer of which the upper surface is at ground level

uncontaminated *adjective* not having been contaminated

uncontrollable *adjective* unable to be controlled

uncontrolled dumping *noun* the throwing away of waste in places that are not officially approved

uncontrolled dumpsite *noun* a place where waste is left without permission or control

uncontrolled fire *noun* a fire which has ignited accidentally and burns out of control

uncoordinated *adjective* not joined together or working together

uncropped land *noun* land on which crops are not currently being grown or have never been grown

uncultivated *adjective* not cultivated ○ *uncultivated land and semi-natural areas* ○ *The field was left uncultivated over winter to allow ground-nesting birds such as skylarks to nest and rear young.*

under- *prefix* below or underneath

underbrush *noun* same as **undergrowth**

underdeveloped country *noun* a country which has not been industrialised (NOTE: The term that is now preferred is **developing country**.)

underground *adjective, adverb* beneath the surface of the ground ○ *underground power cables* ○ *swollen underground stems* ○ *Foxes live in underground holes.* ○ *Worms live underground.*

undergrowth *noun* shrubs and other plants growing under large trees

undershot wheel *noun* a type of waterwheel where the wheel rests in the flow of water which passes underneath it and makes it turn. Compare **overshot wheel** (NOTE: It is not as efficient as an overshot wheel where the water falls on the wheel from above.)

understorey *noun* the lowest layer of small trees and shrubs in a wood, below the canopy

underwood *noun* the small trees in a wood, below the canopy

UNFCCC *abbr* United Nations Framework Convention on Climate Change

ungulate *adjective* having hoofs (NOTE: Ungulates are divided into two groups, odd-toed such as horses or even-toed such as cows.) ■ *noun* a grazing animal that has hooves, e.g. a horse

uni- *prefix* one

unicellular *adjective* referring to an organism formed of one cell. Compare **multicellular**

unit *noun* **1.** a component of something larger **2.** a quantity or amount used as a standard, accepted measurement ○ *The internationally agreed unit of pressure is the millibar.* ○ *The higher the Sun is in the sky, the more intense is the radiation per unit area.*

United Kingdom Atomic Energy Authority *noun* the official organisation in the United Kingdom responsible for all aspects of atomic energy, both commercially and in research. Abbr **UKAEA**

United Nations Framework Convention on Climate Change *noun* an agreement by nearly all world governments to act on issues affecting climate. Abbr **UNFCCC**

unlawful *adjective* not permitted by law

unleaded petrol *noun* petrol with a low octane rating, which has no lead additives such as tetraethyl lead and therefore creates less lead pollution in the atmosphere

unlined *adjective* referring to something with no lining, such as a landfill site from which waste liquids can leak out into the surrounding soil

unnatural *adjective* not found in nature

unneutralised, unneutralized *adjective* not having been made neutral

unpolluted *adjective* not affected by pollution ○ *the relatively unpolluted atmosphere in mountain areas*

unsettled *adjective* referring to weather which changes frequently from rainy to fine and back again

unsightly *adjective* not pleasant to look at ○ *The company is proposing to run a line of unsightly pylons across the moors.*

unspoilt *adjective* referring to a landscape which has not been damaged by development ○ *an area of unspoilt woodland* ○ *The highland region is still unspoilt.*

unstable *adjective* not stable and liable to change easily

unsterilised, unsterilized *adjective* not free from microorganisms ○ *unsterilised bottles*

unsustainable *adjective* referring to a development or process which depletes or damages natural resources and which does not leave the environment in good order for future generations

untapped *adjective* not yet used ○ *untapped mineral resources*

untreated *adjective* not subjected to a treatment process ○ *Untreated sewage leaked into the river.*

updraught *noun* a rising air current, usually of warm air

upfreezing *noun US* a phenomenon in which loose rocks rise to the surface of the soil in spring, caused by the freezing of the soil in winter

upland *noun* an inland area of high land ○ *The uplands have different ecosystems from the lowlands.* ■ *adjective* referring to an upland ○ *upland farming*

upland farm *noun* same as **hill farm**

uplands *plural noun* an inland region of high land

upstream *adverb, adjective* towards the source of a river ○ *The river is contaminated for several miles upstream from the estuary.* ○ *Pollution has spread into the lake upstream of the waterfall.* ○ *Upstream communities have not yet been affected.* Compare **downstream**

upwelling *noun* the process by which warmer surface water in the sea is drawn away from the shore and replaced by colder water from beneath the surface

uranium *noun* a naturally radioactive metallic element which is an essential fuel for nuclear power (NOTE: The chemical symbol is U; the atomic number is 92 and the atomic weight is 283.04.)

urban *adjective* referring to towns

urban area *noun* a town or city, area which is completely built up

urban blight *noun* an unattractive, dirty and dilapidated area in a city or town

urban decay, urban erosion *noun* the condition where part of a city or town becomes old, dirty or ruined, because businesses and wealthy families have moved away from it

urban design *noun* the process of deciding how to lay out a town and what type and style of buildings to have

urban fringe *noun* land at the edge of a city or town

urban growth *noun* an increase in the size and number of towns

urbanisation, urbanization *noun* the spread of built-up areas into the surrounding countryside

urban landscape *noun* the visual appearance of a town

urban redevelopment, urban regeneration, urban renewal *noun* the process by which large areas of derelict and industrial land and rundown housing areas are re-

urine *noun* a liquid secreted as waste from an animal's body

user-pays principle *noun* the principle that a user of a service or resource pays directly for the amount they use, rather than the cost being shared by all the users or a community equally. ◊ **polluter-pays principle**

utilitarian justification *noun* a reasoning for conservation based on the idea that the environment should provide direct economic benefits to the population

utility *noun* a company that organises an essential public service such as electricity, gas or public transport

UV *abbr* ultraviolet

UVR *abbr* ultraviolet radiation

stored to become thriving communities once more

urban sprawl *noun* the uncontrolled spread of new houses and other buildings on the edges of towns and cities into the countryside ○ *There is a need to protect the remaining open spaces from urban sprawl.*

urban wastewater *noun* water from homes, or the total of water from homes, businesses and rainfall, that flows into the sewage system

urea *noun* a crystalline solid produced in the liver from excess amino acids and excreted by the kidneys into the urine (NOTE: It is made commercially from carbon dioxide and ammonia and is used as a fertiliser and in other products.)

V

vadose *adjective* referring to an area which lies between the surface of the ground and the water table

vagrant *noun* a bird which only visits a country or region occasionally

vale *noun* same as **valley** (*used especially in place names*)

valley *noun* a long low area, usually with a river at the bottom, between hills or mountains. Also called **vale**

value *noun* a quantity shown as a number

vaporise, vaporize *verb* to turn into vapour, or to turn something into a vapour ○ *Water vaporises when heated.*

vapour *noun* a gaseous form of a liquid (NOTE: The US spelling is **vapor**.)

variable *adjective* changing or changeable ○ *Winds are more variable in the northern hemisphere than in the southern hemisphere.*

variant *noun* a specimen of a plant or animal that is different from the usual type

variation *noun* **1.** the existence of a difference in amount, concentration, number or other feature **2.** a difference within a possible range or from a standard **3.** something that is slightly different from other similar things

variety *noun* **1.** a number of different things ○ *a wide variety of reasons why people like and dislike cities* **2.** a type of something ○ *Green vegetables are a source of dietary fi-*

thing **3.** a named cultivated plant ○ *a new variety of wheat* Also called **cultivar**

vascular bundle *noun* a strand of plant tissue containing the xylem and phloem tubes that transport water and food to and from different parts of the plant

vascular plant *noun* a plant that has specialised tubes within it for transporting sap (NOTE: All flowering plants, conifers, ferns, clubmosses and horsetails, but not mosses and liverworts, are vascular plants.)

vascular system *noun* **1.** (*in animals*) a system of tubes that carry liquid, e.g. blood **2.** (*in plants*) a system of conducting tissues that carry nutrients from the roots to the upper parts of the plant

vascular tissue *noun* a specialised plant tissue consisting of phloem and xylem, which transports dissolved sugar, water and dissolved minerals throughout the plant

vector *noun* an insect or animal which carries a disease or parasite and can pass it to other organisms ○ *The tsetse fly is a vector of sleeping sickness.*

veer *verb* (*of wind*) to change in a clockwise direction, in the northern hemisphere ○ *Winds veer and increase with height ahead of a warm front.* Opposite **back**

vegetable *noun* a plant grown for food, especially plants grown for leaves, roots or pods or seeds that are usually cooked ○ *bre.*

vegetable farming *noun* the activity of growing vegetables for sale

vegetable kingdom *noun* the category of all organisms classed as plants

vegetarian *noun*, *adjective* a person who does not eat meat

vegetation *noun* 1. plants that are growing ○ *The vegetation was destroyed by fire.* ○ *Very little vegetation is found in the Arctic regions.* 2. the set of plants that is found in a particular area ○ *He is studying the vegetation of the island.*

vegetation loss *noun* the loss of plants from an area by processes such as pollution or clearing

vegetation map *noun* a map showing the pattern of vegetation in an area

vegetative *adjective* 1. referring to plants ○ *The loss of vegetative cover increases the accumulation of carbon dioxide in the atmosphere.* 2. referring to the process of growth and development 3. referring to reproduction that does not involve sex cells

vegetative propagation *noun* the artificial reproduction of plants by taking cuttings or by grafting, not by seed

vegetative reproduction *noun* a form of reproduction in which a plant reproduces itself from parts such as bulbs or tubers rather than from seed

veil *noun* a thin layer of cloud or mist

vein *noun* a thin tube that forms part of the structure of a leaf or the circulation system of an animal, allowing the flow of liquids

vent *noun* 1. a hole through which air, smoke or gas can leave a building or other structure 2. a hole through which gases or lava escape from a volcano

ventilate *verb* to cause air to pass in and out of a place freely

ventilation *noun* the process of air passing in and out of a place freely

ventilation system *noun* a system that allows fresh air to move around a building

ventilator *noun* a device that causes fresh air to pass into a room or building

ventral *adjective* referring to the abdomen or the front of the human body

venturi effect *noun* the rapid flow of a liquid or a gas as it passes through a narrower channel

verge *noun* 1. the edge or boundary of something 2. an area of grass and other plants at the side of a road ○ *Roadside verges, especially motorway verges, offer security from human disturbance, and the wildlife quickly adapts to the noise and wind generated by passing vehicles.* □ **on the verge of** at the point where something starts to happen

vermicide *noun* a substance that kills worms

vermiculite *noun* a substance that is a form of silica processed into small pieces. It is used instead of soil in horticulture because it retains moisture.

vermin *noun* an organism that is regarded as a pest ○ *Vermin such as rats are often carriers of disease.* ◊ **pest** (NOTE: Usually treated as plural.)

vernacular *adjective* limited to a specific area

vernacular building *noun* a building built in the distinctive local style of the place where it is found

vernacular material *noun* a building material found in an area and not brought from elsewhere

vernal *adjective* referring to the spring

vernalisation, **vernalization** *noun* 1. a requirement by some plants for a period of cold in order to develop normally 2. the technique of making a seed germinate early by refrigerating it for a time

vertebra *noun* one of the ring-shaped bones which link together to form the backbone (NOTE: The plural is **vertebrae**.)

vertebrate *noun* an animal that has a backbone ■ *adjective* referring to animals that have a backbone ▶ compare (all senses) **invertebrate**

vertical-axis wind turbine *noun* a type of wind turbine with a vertical main shaft

vertical-looking radar *noun* radar equipment used for analysis of features such as insect populations and movement. Abbr **VLR**

vertical stratification *noun* an area in water or soil where layers are found on top of each other

vessel *noun* 1. a container for liquids 2. a tubular structure which carries liquid around the body of an animal or plant 3. a ship or boat

vestigial *adjective* existing in a simple and reduced form ○ *Some snakes have vestigial legs.*

veteran tree *noun* same as **ancient tree**

victim *noun* a person or animal that is injured, harmed or attacked

vigorous *adjective* growing strongly ○ *Plants put out vigorous shoots in a warm damp atmosphere.*

viral *adjective* referring to or caused by a virus ○ *a viral disease*

virgin *adjective* in its natural state, untouched by humans ○ *Virgin rainforest was being cleared at the rate of 1000 hectares per month.*

viscid *adjective* same as **viscous**

viscosity *noun* the internal resistance of a liquid to flowing

viscous *adjective* referring to a liquid which is thick, sticky and slow-moving. Also called **viscid**

visibility *noun* the degree to which unlit objects can be seen by day and lighted objects can be seen by night ○ *Measurement of visibility by day is made by direct observation of objects at known distances and is therefore an estimated value.*

visible *adjective* referring to something that can be seen ○ *The Sun will be clearly visible through cumulus cloud.*

visitor, visitant *noun* a bird that comes to a region regularly when migrating ○ *Flycatchers are summer visitors to Britain.*

vital *adjective* important, or essential for life ○ *Vital nutrients are leached from the topsoil.* ○ *Oxygen is vital to the human system.*

vitamin *noun* a substance not produced in the body, but found in most foods, and needed for good health

viviparous *adjective* **1.** referring to an animal such as a mammal or some fish that give birth to live young. Compare **oviparous** (NOTE: Birds, reptiles and some fish lay eggs and are oviparous.) **2.** reproducing by buds that form plantlets while still attached to the parent plant or by seeds that germinate within a fruit

vivisection *noun* the dissection of a living animal under experimental conditions

VLR *abbr* vertical-looking radar

VOC *abbr* volatile organic compound

volatile *adjective* referring to a liquid which easily changes into a gas or vapour

volatile oil *noun* same as **essential oil**

volatile organic compound *noun* an organic compound which evaporates at a relatively low temperature. Abbr **VOC** (NOTE: Volatile organic compounds such as ethylene, propylene, benzene and styrene contribute to air pollution.)

volcanic *adjective* referring to volcanoes

volcano *noun* a mountain surrounding a hole in the Earth's crust, formed of solidified molten rock sent up from the interior of the Earth

COMMENT: Volcanoes occur along faults in the Earth's surface and exist in well-known chains. Some are extinct, but others erupt relatively frequently. Some are always active, in that they emit sulfurous gases and smoke, without actually erupting. Volcanic eruptions are a major source of atmospheric pollution, in particular of sulfur dioxide. Very large eruptions cause a mass of dust to enter the atmosphere, which has a noticeable effect on the world's climate.

voltage *noun* an electrical force measured in volts

voltage drop *noun* the voltage lost along a wire or conductor due to the resistance of that conductor

volume *noun* **1.** the amount of space occupied by a solid, a liquid or a gas ○ *If the pressure of a given mass of gas is maintained constant, the volume of gas increases as its temperature is increased.* **2.** the loudness of a transmission

-vore *suffix* an organism that eats a particular diet

-vorous *suffix* eating a particular diet

vortex *noun* a flow of a liquid in a whirlpool or of a gas in a whirlwind ○ *The most destructive winds are in the vortex, where the rotation of the whirlwind produces very high wind speeds.*

VU *abbr* vulnerable

vulcanism *noun* a movement of magma or molten rock onto or towards the Earth's surface

vulnerability *noun* the degree to which a person, organism, environment or system is likely to be caused harm by an activity

vulnerable *adjective* **1.** liable to be easily harmed **2.** referring to a species that is likely to become endangered unless protective measures are taken. Abbr **VU**

vulture *noun* a large bird of prey that feeds on carrion

W

wader *noun* a bird that feeds on organisms or plants found in shallow water

wadi *noun* a gully with a stream at the bottom, found in the desert regions of North Africa. Compare **arroyo**

Waldsterben *noun* same as **forest dieback** (NOTE: From a German word meaning 'the dying of trees'.)

Wallace's line *noun* a line dividing the Australasian biogeographical region from the Southeast Asian region

wane *verb* (*of the Moon or a planet*) to appear to grow smaller as less of the illuminated face is visible. Compare **wax**

warfarin *noun* a substance used to poison rats, to which many rats in some areas are now resistant

warm *adjective* pleasantly hot ○ *These plants grow fast in the warm season.* ■ *verb* to make something hotter ○ *The greenhouse effect has the result of warming the general atmospheric temperature.*

warm-blooded *adjective* referring to an animal such as a mammal that can control its body temperature. ◊ **endotherm**

warm desert *noun* same as **mid-latitude desert**

washland *noun* an area of land that is regularly flooded

wash out *verb* to remove a mineral by the action of running water ○ *Minerals are washed out of the soil during heavy rains.*

washout *noun* a process in which drops of water form in the atmosphere and then collect pollutant particles as they fall. Compare **rainout**

wastage *noun* the act of wasting something ○ *There is an enormous wastage of mineral resources.*

waste *noun* material that is thrown away by people or is an unwanted by-product of a process ○ *household waste* ○ *industrial waste* ■ *adjective* without a specific use and unwanted ○ *Waste products are dumped in the sea.* ○ *Waste matter is excreted by the body in the faeces or urine.* ■ *verb* to use more of something than is needed

'There are estimated to be 300 000 tonnes of non-natural wastes produced on agricultural holdings in England and Wales each year. These include a wide range of materials such as waste packaging, silage plastics, metal, tyres, oils and animal health products. (Agricultural Waste: Opportunities for Change. Information from the Agricultural Waste Stakeholders' Forum 2003)'

waste disposal *noun* the process of getting rid of household or industrial waste

waste disposal site *noun* same as **waste dump**

waste disposal unit *noun* a device that fits into the hole in a kitchen sink and grinds household waste into very small pieces so that it can be flushed away

waste dump *noun* a place where household or industrial waste is left. Also called **waste disposal site**

waste ground *noun* an area of land that is not used for any purpose

wasteland *noun* an area of land that is no longer used for agriculture or for any other purpose ○ *Overgrazing has produced wastelands in Central Africa.*

waste management *noun* the action of controlling and processing household or industrial waste

waste neutral *adjective* relating to activities designed to reduce waste and lead to a balance between the production of waste to be recycled and the amount of recycled products used

wastepaper *noun* paper that has been thrown away after use

waste processing *noun* the activity of treating waste material to make it suitable for reuse or safe disposal. Also called **waste treatment**

waste processing plant *noun* a facility where waste material is treated to make it suitable for reuse or safe disposal

waste product *noun* a substance which is produced in a process but is not needed

waste site *noun* same as **waste dump**

waste sorting *noun* the process of separating waste into different categories of material such as glass, metal, paper or plastic

waste stream *noun* a quantity of separated waste that is all of the same type, e.g. paper or glass (NOTE: A major obstacle to recycling is the accidental contamination of waste streams – plastic wrapping thrown in a paper bin and so on.)

waste treatment *noun* same as **waste processing**

wastewater *noun* water that is part of effluent or sewage, especially from industrial processes ○ *There is considerable interest in the anaerobic treatment of industrial wastewaters.* ○ *Wastewater will add small but significant quantities of heavy metals to the aquatic environment.*

wastewater treatment *noun* the processing of wastewater to make it suitable for reuse or safe disposal

wastewater treatment plant *noun* a place where liquid waste is processed

water *noun* a liquid which forms rain, rivers, lakes and the sea and which makes up a large part of the bodies of organisms. Formula: H_2O. ■ *verb* to give water to a plant

water balance *noun* a state in which the water lost in an area by evaporation or by runoff is replaced by water received in the form of rain

waterborne *adjective* carried in water

waterborne disease, waterborne infection *noun* a disease or infection that is spread by water ○ *After the floods diarrhoea, dysentery and other waterborne diseases spread rapidly.*

water closet *noun* a toilet in which the excreta are flushed into the sewage system by running water. Abbr **WC**

water column *noun* the open water of the ocean between the surface and the sea bed

watercourse *noun* a stream, river, canal or other flow of water

water cycle *noun* the circulation of water between the atmosphere, land and sea (NOTE: The Sun causes water to evaporate from seas, other bodies of water and land; it condenses in clouds and then falls back to the Earth's surface as rain.)

water dispersal *noun* the spreading of plant seeds by water

waterfall *noun* a place where a river or stream falls over a steep vertical drop (NOTE: Some waterfalls only appear in very wet weather.)

waterfowl *plural noun* birds which live on water, e.g. ducks

Water Framework Directive *noun* a basis for future policy decisions in the European Union, setting objectives for water use and management and waste water disposal. Abbr **WFD**

waterhole *noun* **1.** a place where water rises naturally to the surface ○ *In the evening, the animals gather round the waterholes to drink.* **2.** a pool of water created by boring holes in the ground

waterlogged *adjective* referring to soil that is saturated with water and so cannot keep oxygen between its particles (NOTE: Most plants cannot grow in waterlogged soil.)

water management *noun* the careful and appropriate use of water

water meadow *noun* a grassy field near a river, which is often flooded

water mill *noun* a mill powered by water

water plant *noun* a plant that grows in water. Also called **aquatic plant**

water pollution *noun* the introduction of pollutants into watercourses or the sea, rivers, lakes or canals

water pollution abatement *noun* a reduction of pollution in watercourses or the sea

water power *noun* power derived from a descending water supply that is converted to electricity by hydraulic turbines

waterproof *adjective* not allowing water to pass through

water purification *noun* the removal of impurities from water

water quality *noun* the suitability of water for human consumption and bathing and for animals to live in ○ *Fish have returned to many rivers because of the improvement in water quality.*

water resources *plural noun* rivers, lakes and other surface waters that supply water for human use

water–salt balance *noun* a state where the water in the soil balances the amount of salts in the soil

watershed *noun* a natural dividing line between the sources of river systems, dividing one catchment area from another

waterside *adjective* referring to a plant which grows next to a river, lake or other area of water

water solubility *noun* the degree to which something is able to be dissolved in water

water-soluble *adjective* able to dissolve in water

waterspout *noun* a phenomenon caused when a rapidly turning column of air forms over an area of water, sucking water up into the column

water table *noun* the area below the soil surface at which the ground is saturated with water

watertight *adjective* not leaking water or other fluid

water turbine *noun* a device that converts the motion of the flow of water into the turning movement of a wheel ○ *Water turbines are often used to drive generators or pumps.*

water vapour *noun* air containing suspended particles of water

waterway *noun* a river or canal used as channel for moving from one place to another

waterwheel *noun* a wheel with wooden steps or buckets that is turned by the flow of water against it and itself turns machinery such as a mill wheel or an electric generator. ◊ **overshot wheel, undershot wheel**

waterworks *noun* a plant for treating and purifying water before it is pumped into pipes for distribution to houses, factories, schools and other places for use

watt *noun* an SI unit of measurement of electrical power. The work done by an electrical circuit or the power consumed is measured in watts. Symbol **W**

watt-hour *noun* a measurement of power with respect to time. One watt-hour is equal to one watt being used for a period of one hour.

wave *noun* **1.** a mass of water moving across the surface of a lake or the sea, rising higher than the surrounding water as it moves **2.** the form in which heat, light, sound or electric current is spread

wave power *noun* electricity produced by using the force of waves (NOTE: In harnessing wave power, the movement of waves on the surface of the sea is used to make large floats move up and down. These act as pumps which supply a continuous flow of water to turn a turbine.)

wave refraction *noun* the tendency of wave crests to turn from their original direction and become more parallel to the shore as they move into shallower water

wax *noun* a semi-solid or solid substance of animal, plant or mineral origin ■ *verb* (*of the Moon or a planet*) to appear to grow bigger as more of the illuminated face becomes visible. Compare **wane** (NOTE: The Moon waxes between its new and full phases.)

waxy *adjective* **1.** smooth and shiny **2.** covered with wax

waymarking *noun* the practice of indicating the direction of a public path by special signs

WC *abbr* water closet

weather *noun* daily atmospheric conditions such as sunshine, wind and precipitation in an area ■ *verb* to change the state of soil or rock through the action of natural agents such as rain, sun, frost or wind or by artificially produced pollutants

weather chart *noun* a chart showing the state of the weather at a specific moment or changes which are expected to happen in the weather in the near future. Also called **weather map**

weather front *noun* the edge of mass of air where it meets another of different temperature or density. Also called **front**

weathering *noun* the alteration of the state of soil or rock through the action of natural agents such as rain, sun, frost or wind or by artificially produced pollutants

weather map *noun* same as **weather chart**

web *noun* a structure of threads secreted by a spider in the form of a net

webbed *adjective* with skin between the toes ○ *Ducks and other aquatic birds have webbed feet.*

weed *noun* a plant that grows where it is not wanted, e.g. a poppy in a wheat field (NOTE: Some weeds are cultivated plants, for example oilseed rape growing in hedgerows.)

weedkiller *noun* same as **herbicide**

weedy *adjective* **1.** like a weed **2.** weak and not growing well

weedy habit *noun* the tendency of some species of plant to spread onto wasteland

well *noun* a hole dug in the ground to the level of the water table, from which water can be removed by a pump or bucket

wellhead *noun* the top structure of a well above the ground

Wentworth-Udden scale *noun* a scale for measuring and describing the size of grains of minerals

- COMMENT: The scale runs from the largest size, the boulder, down to the finest grain, clay. The approximate diameters of each grain are: boulder, up to 256 mm; cobble, above 64 mm; pebble, between 4 and 64 mm; gravel, between 2 and 4 mm; sand, between 0.06 and 2 mm; silt and clay are the finest sizes.

wet *adjective* with a lot of moisture

wetfall *noun* the fall of polluting substances in rain or snow. Compare **dryfall**

wetland *noun* an area of land where the soil surface is almost level with the water table and where specially adapted vegetation has developed (*often plural*)

wetland hydrology *noun* the study of periodic flooding or soil saturation which creates anaerobic conditions in the soil of wetlands

wet season *noun* same as **rainy season**

WFD *abbr* Water Framework Directive

whale *noun* a very large mammal living in the sea. Order: Cetacea.

COMMENT: Whales are the largest mammals still in existence. There are two groups of whales: the toothed whales and the baleen whales. Baleen whales have no teeth and feed by sucking in large quantities of water which they then force out again through their baleen, which is a series of fine plates like a comb hanging down from the upper jaw. The baleen acts like a sieve and traps any plankton and krill which are in the water. The toothed whales have teeth and eat fish. They include the sperm whale, the killer whale and porpoises and dolphins. Whales are caught mainly for their oils, though also in some cases for food. Some species of whale have become extinct because of overexploitation and the population of many of the existing species is dangerously low. Commercial whaling is severely restricted.

whaler *noun* a boat which is specially equipped for catching whales. Also called **whaling boat**

whaling *noun* the catching of whales to use as food or for their oil and other commodities

whaling boat *noun* same as **whaler**

whaling fleet *noun* a group of boats specially equipped for catching whales

wheat *noun* a cereal crop grown in temperate regions. Genus: *Triticum*. (NOTE: Wheat is one of the major arable crops.)

wheatgerm *noun* the central part of the wheat seed, which contains valuable nutrients

wheatmeal *noun* brown flour with a large amount of bran, but not as much as is in wholemeal

whirlpool *noun* a rapidly turning eddy of water

whirlwind *noun* a column of rapidly turning air at the centre of an area of very low pressure (NOTE: Over water a whirlwind becomes a **waterspout** and over desert a **dust devil**.)

wholefood *noun* food such as brown rice or wholemeal flour that has not been processed and so contains the vitamins, minerals and fibre that are removed by processing

wholegrain *noun* a cereal grain containing the whole of the original seed, including the bran

wholemeal *noun* flour that contains a large proportion of the original wheat seed, including the bran

wild *adjective* not domesticated

wilderness *noun* an area of wild uncultivated land, usually a long way from human habitation

wilderness area *noun* an area of undeveloped land that is protected, as a national park or other conservation area

Wildfowl and Wetlands Trust *noun* full form of **WWT**

wildland *noun* uncultivated land in its natural state, especially considered as a habitat for wildlife

wildlife *noun* wild animals of all types, including birds, reptiles and fish ○ *Plantations of conifers are poorer for wildlife than mixed or deciduous woodlands.* ○ *The effects of the open-cast mining scheme would be disastrous on wildlife, particularly on moorland birds.*

Wildlife and Countryside Act *noun* in the UK, the main legislation under which native wildlife is protected

wildlife refuge *noun* an area maintained for the preservation of the habitats of some types of wild animals such as migratory waterfowl or for animals in an urban setting, but which people are allowed to visit

wildlife reserve *noun* an area where animals and their environment are protected

Wildlife Trust *noun* any of a network of organisations working to protect wildlife

wildscape *noun* remote countryside in a natural state with a wild, rough character

willow *noun* a temperate hardwood tree that often grows near water. Genus: *Salix*. (NOTE: Willow is sometimes grown as a crop and is coppiced or pollarded to produce biomass for fuel.)

wind *noun* air which moves in the lower atmosphere, or a stream of air ○ *The weather station has instruments to measure the speed of the wind.*

wind chill factor *noun* a way of calculating the risk of exposure in cold weather by adding the speed of the wind to the number of degrees of temperature below zero

wind dispersal *noun* the spread of plant seeds as a result of being blown by the wind

wind-driven *adjective* powered by the wind

wind erosion *noun* erosion of soil or rock by wind

wind farm *noun* a group of large windmills or wind turbines, built to harness the wind to produce electricity ○ *Wind farms in estuaries may adversely affect bird populations.* Also called **wind park**

wind generator *noun* a machine used to produce electricity from the wind

windmill *noun* 1. a construction with sails which are turned by the wind, providing the power to drive a machine. ◊ **panemone 2.** same as **wind turbine**

wind park *noun* same as **wind farm**

wind pollination *noun* pollination of flowers by pollen which is blown by the wind

wind power *noun* the power generated by using wind to drive a machine or turbine which creates electricity

wind pump *noun* a pump driven by the wind, which raises water out of the ground

windrow *noun* a row of the cut stalks of a crop, gathered together and laid on the ground to be dried by the wind

wind turbine *noun* a turbine driven by wind

windward *adjective* referring to a position exposed to the wind ○ *The trees provide shelter on the windward side of the house.*

wing *noun* 1. one of the feather-covered limbs of a bird or membrane-covered limbs of a bat that are used for flying 2. an outgrowth on a seed case of seeds such as sycamore dispersed by wind

wing span *noun* the distance between the tip of one wing to the tip of the other wing

wing tip *noun* the outermost end of a wing

winter *noun* the season of the year, following autumn and before spring, when the weather is coldest, the days are short, most plants do not flower or produce new shoots and some animals hibernate ■ *verb* to spend the winter in a place

winterbourne *noun* a stream which flows only in the wetter part of the year, usually in winter

wintering ground *noun* an area where birds come each year to spend the winter

wither *verb* (*of plants, leaves, flowers*) to shrivel and die

wolds *plural noun* areas of low chalk or limestone hills

wood *noun* 1. a large number of trees growing together 2. a hard tissue which forms the main stem and branches of a tree 3. a construction material that comes from trees

-wood *suffix* referring to wood ○ *an elm-wood stool*

wood-burning pollution *noun* pollution caused by burning wood

wood-burning stove *noun* same as **woodstove**

woodfuel *noun* wood which is used as fuel

woodland *noun* an area in which the main vegetation is trees with some spaces between them

woodland burial *noun* an act of burial designed to have low environmental impact, typically placing a corpse that has not been embalmed in a biodegradable coffin or bag and burying it in a natural woodland setting without a headstone. ◊ **green burial**

woodland management *noun* the controlling of an area of woodland so that it is productive, e.g. by regular felling, coppicing and planting

woodlot *noun* a small area of land planted with trees

wood pasture *noun* a long-established area of parkland, in which trees are often very old

wood pulp *noun* softwood that has been pulverised into small fibres and mixed with water, used to make paper

woodstove *noun* a heating device that burns wood. Also called **wood-burning stove**

working environment *noun* the surroundings in which a person works

workings *plural noun* 1. the parts of something such as a machine that allow it to operate 2. underground tunnels in a mine

work out *verb* to use up something such as a mineral resource completely ○ *The coal mine was worked out years ago.*

world *noun* 1. the Earth ○ *a map of the world* ○ *to sail round the world* 2. a particular society, community or situation ○ *the bird world* ○ *the world of work*

worldwide *adjective, adverb* referring to or covering the whole world ○ *the worldwide energy crisis* ○ *We sell our products worldwide.*

worm *noun* 1. an invertebrate animal with a soft body and no limbs, e.g. a nematode or flatworm 2. an invertebrate animal with a long thin body and no legs that lives in large numbers in the soil. Also called **earthworm**

WWF *abbr* World Wide Fund for Nature

WWT *abbr* Wildfowl and Wetlands Trust

XYZ

Xe *symbol* xenon

xeno- *prefix* different

xenobiotics *plural noun* chemical compounds that are foreign to an organism

xenon *noun* an inert gas, traces of which are found in the atmosphere (NOTE: The chemical symbol is **Xe**; the atomic number is **54** and the atomic weight is **131.30**.)

xeric *adjective* referring to a dry environment. Compare **hydric**

xero- *prefix* dry

xeromorphic *adjective* referring to a plant which can prevent water loss from its stems during hot weather

xerophilous *adjective* referring to a plant which lives in very dry conditions

xerophyte *noun* a plant which is adapted to living in very dry conditions

xerosere *noun* a succession of communities growing in very dry conditions

xerothermic *adjective* referring to an organism which is adapted to living in very dry conditions

X-ray *noun* a ray with a very short wavelength, which is invisible, but can go through soft tissue and register as a photograph on a film

xylem *noun* the tissue in a plant which transports water and dissolved minerals from the roots to the rest of the plant. Compare **phloem**

xylophagous *adjective* wood-eating

xylophilous *adjective* preferring to grow on wood

yeast *noun* a single-celled fungus that is used in the fermentation of alcohol and in making bread

yellowing *noun* **1.** a condition where the leaves of plants turn yellow, caused by lack of light **2.** a sign of disease or of nutrient deficiency

yield *noun* the quantity of a crop or a product produced from a plant or from an area of land ○ *The usual yield is 8 tonnes per hectare.* ○ *The green revolution increased rice yields in parts of Asia.* ■ *verb* to produce a quantity of a crop or a product ○ *The rice can yield up to 2 tonnes per hectare.* ○

The oil deposits may yield 100 000 barrels a month.

zero emission vehicle *noun* an electric-powered vehicle with no direct emissions from its tailpipe or fuel evaporation. Abbr **ZEV**

zero population growth *noun* a state when the numbers of births and deaths in a population are equal and so the size of the population remains the same

ZEV *abbr* zero emission vehicle

zinc *noun* a white metallic trace element, essential to biological life. It is used in alloys and as a protective coating for steel. (NOTE: The chemical symbol is **Zn**; the atomic number is **30** and the atomic weight is **65.38**.)

zonal *adjective* referring to a zone

zonation *noun* a pattern of changes in the structure of a community depending on moisture levels, soil type and altitude ○ *zonation of seaweeds on the seashore*

zone *noun* an area of land, sea or of the atmosphere

zoning *noun* an order by a government or local council that an area of land shall be used only for a specific type of building or for a specific purpose, e.g. agricultural, industrial, recreational or residential

zoo- *prefix* animal

zoobenthos *noun* the invertebrate animals that live in or on the seabed, including the intertidal zone

zooecology *noun* the scientific study of the relationship between animals and their environment

zoogeographical *adjective* referring to animals and geography

zoogeographical region *noun* a large area of the world where the fauna is different from that in other areas. ◊ **biogeographical region**

zoological *adjective* referring to zoology

zoologist *noun* a scientist who specialises in zoology

zoology *noun* the scientific study of animals

zoonosis *noun* a disease that a human can catch from an animal

zoonotic *adjective* referring to a disease that a human can catch from an animal

zoophyte *noun* an animal that looks like a plant, e.g. a sea anemone

zooplankton *plural noun* microscopic animals that live and drift in water

zooxanthellae *plural noun* microscopic algae that live inside cells of sea animals, especially corals, each organism benefiting from the relationship

zygote *noun* a fertilised ovum, the first stage of development of an embryo

SUPPLEMENTS

Nitrogen Cycle, Carbon Cycle
Beaufort scale
Richter scale
Outline Criteria for Threatened Species
Critically Endangered Species
Natural Disasters
Manmade Disasters

Nitrogen Cycle

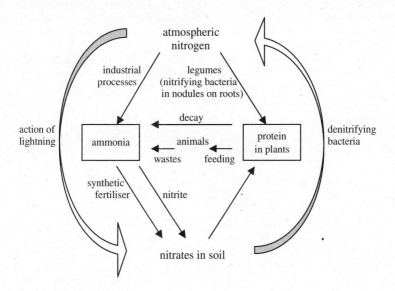

Carbon Cycle

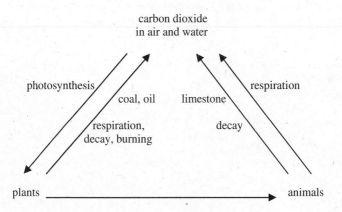

Beaufort scale

The Beaufort scale was devised in 1805 by Sir Francis Beaufort, a captain (later admiral) in the British Royal Navy, to measure the observable effects of wind force at sea. It was later adapted to include effects on land, and wind speed equivalents were officially incorporated in 1926.

Sailors and forecasters use the Beaufort scale as a standardised way to rate wind speed. Warnings of potentially dangerous conditions for people in small boats are usually issued at a rating of six on the scale. The Beaufort number is also referred to as a 'Force' number, for example 'Force 10 Gale'.

Beaufort number	Wind speed km/h	Wind speed mph	Description
0	below 1	below 1	Calm
1	1 - 6	1 - 3	Light air
2	7 - 12	4 - 7	Light breeze
3	13 - 19	8 - 12	Gentle breeze
4	20 - 30	13 - 18	Moderate breeze
5	31 - 39	19 - 24	Fresh breeze
6	40 - 50	25 - 31	Strong breeze
7	51 - 62	32 - 38	Moderate gale
8	63 - 74	39 - 46	Fresh gale
9	75 - 87	47 - 54	Strong gale
10	88 - 102	55 - 63	Whole gale
11	103 - 117	64 - 72	Storm
12	above 118	above 73	Hurricane

Richter scale

The Richter scale measures the magnitude of an earthquake based on how much the ground shakes at a distance of 100 km (60 miles) from the epicentre of an earthquake (the site on the earth's surface directly above its origin). Other systems used by seismologists to measure earthquakes include the Modified Mercalli scale, a 12-point scale that measures intensity at different locations.

Richter number	Increase in the motion of the ground	Results
1	1	Generally not felt, but recorded on seismometers
2	10	
3	100	
4	1 000	Felt by many people; trees sway
5	10 000	Poorly built structures damaged
6	100 000	Specially designed structures damaged; others collapse
7	1 000 000	Many structures destroyed; cracks in ground
8+	10 000 000	Severe destruction; very wide cracks in ground

Outline Criteria for Threatened Species

Based on the IUCN Red List of Threatened Species where full details of the full criteria for each category will be found. The list includes more than 12 000 species (2003).

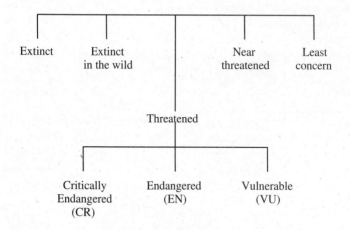

	CR	EN	VU
Population size reduction in 10 years or 3 generations	more than 80-90%	more than 50-70%	more than 30-50%
Geographic range: extent of occurrence	less than 100 km^2	less than 5 000 km^2	less than 20 000 km^2
Geographic range: area of occupancy	less than 10 km^2	less than 500 km^2	less than 2 000 km^2
Population	less than 50-250 mature individuals	less than 250-2 500 mature individuals	less than 1 000-10 000 mature individuals

Critically Endangered Species

The following species are among those categorised by IUCN - The World Conservation Union as 'Critically Endangered'. This category of threat means that the species faces a probability of extinction in the immediate future. A full list of threatened species in various categories can be found in the IUCN Red List of Threatened Species (2003).

Amsterdam Albatross *(Diomedea amsterdamensis)* Antarctic, Oceania

Bachman's Warbler *(Vermivora bachmanii)* Caribbean, North America

Bahia Tapaculo *(Scytalopus psychopompus)* South America

Beck's Petrel *(Pseudobulweria becki)* Oceania

Bogota Sunangel *(Heliangelus zusii)* South America

Bottle Palm *(Hyophorbe lagenicaulis)* Subsaharan Africa

Bulo Burti Boubou / Bush-shrike *(Laniarius liberatus)* Subsaharan Africa

California Condor *(Gymnogyps californianus)* North America, Central America

Campbell Island Teal *(Anas nesiotis)* Oceania

Chinese Crested Tern *(Sterna bernsteini)* East Asia, Southeast Asia

Clay's Hibiscus *(Hibiscus clayi)* North America

Cone-billed Tanager *(Conothraupis mesoleuca)* South America

Crested Shelduck *(Tadorna cristata)* North Asia, East Asia

Dwarf Olive Ibis *(Bostrychia bocagei)* Subsaharan Africa

Eskimo Curlew *(Numenius borealis)* North America, South America

Garrido's Hutia *(Mysateles garridoi)* Caribbean

Glaucous Macaw *(Anodorhynchus glaucus)* South America

Grey Wood-pigeon / Silvery Wood-pigeon *(Columba argentina)* SE Asia

Guadaloupe Storm-petrel *(Oceanodroma macrodactyla)* Central America

Hainan Sonneratia *Sonneratia hainanensis* East Asia

Hawaiian Thrush *(Myadestes lanaiensis or Myadestinus)* North America

Himalayan Quail *(Ophrysia superciliosa)* Southeast Asia

Hooded Seedeater *(Sporophila melanops)* South America

Imperial Woodpecker *(Campephilus imperialis)* Central America

Irrawaddy Dolphin *(Orcaella brevirostris)* Southeast Asia

Ivory-billed Woodpecker *(Campephilus principalis)* North America, Caribbean

Jamaica Petrel *(Pterodroma caribbaea)* Caribbean

Jamaican Paraque *(Siphonorhis americanus)* Caribbean

Javanese Lapwing / Sunda Plover *(Vanellus macropterus)* Southeast Asia

Kakapo / Owl Parrot *(Strigops habroptilus)* Oceania

Kalinowski's Tinamou *(Nothoprocta kalinowskii)* South America

Land Lobster *(Dryococelus australis)* Australia

Ley's Whitebeam *(Sorbus leyana)* Europe

Critically Endangered Species *continued*

Little Blue Macaw / Spix's Macaw *(Cyanopsitta spixii)* South America

Luquillo Mountain Manjack / Wagner's Cordia *(Cordia wagnerorum)* Caribbean

Madeira Petrel / Zino's Petrel *(Pterodroma madeira)* Europe

Magdalena Tinamou *(Crypturellus saltuarius)* South America

Makira Moorhen / San Cristobal Moorhen *(Gallinula silvestris)* Oceania

Mauritius Parakeet *(Psittacula eques)* Subsaharan Africa

Mongarlowe Mallee *(Eucalyptus recurva)* Oceania

Mount Glorius Torrent Frog *(Taudactylus diurnis)* Oceania

Negros Fruit Dove *(Ptilinopus arcanus)* Philippines

New Caledonian Rail *(Gallirallus lafresnayanus)* Oceania

New Caledonian Lorikeet *(Charmosyna diadema)* Oceania

New England Owlet-nightjar *(Aegotheles savesi)* Oceania

Newton's Fiscal / São Tomé Fiscal *(Lanius newtoni)* Subsaharan Africa

Night Parrot *(Geopsittacus occidentalis)* Oceania

Nukupuu *(Hemignathus lucidus)* North America

Oahu Creeper / Oahu Alauahio *(Paroreomyza maculata)* North America

Ou *(Psittirostra psittacea)* North America

Owl Parrot / Kakapo *(Strigops habroptilus)* Oceania

Pear Clermontia *(Clermontia pyrularia)* Hawaiian Islands

Peppered Tree Frog *(Litoria piperata)* Australia

Père David's Deer *(Elaphurus davidianus)* East Asia

Pink-headed Duck *(Rhodonessa caryophyllacea)* Southeast Asia

Pohnpei Mountain Starling / Pohnpei Starling *(Aplonis Pelzelni)* Oceania

Puerto Rican Amazon / Puerto Rican Parrot *(Amazona vittata)* Caribbean

Red Wolf *(Canis rufus)* North America

Rueck's Blue-flycatcher / Rueck's Niltava *(Cyornis ruckii)* Southeast Asia

Samoan Moorhen *(Gallinula pacifica)* Oceania

San Cristobal Moorhen / Makira Moorhen *(Gallinula silvestris)* Oceania

São Tomé / Canary / Goldfinch / Grosbeak *(Neospiza concolor)* Subsaharan Africa

Sebucan *(Leptocereus quadricostatus)* Caribbean

Semper's Warbler *(Leucopeza semperi)* Caribbean

Seychelles Magpie-robin *(Copsychus sechellarum)* Subsaharan Africa, Southeast Asia

Siau Scops-owl *(Otus siaoensis)* Southeast Asia

Sicilian Fir *(Abies nebrodensis)* Europe

Silvery Wood-pigeon / Grey Wood-pigeon *(Columba argentina)* SE Asia

Skulpin *(Physiculus helenaensis)* Subsaharan Africa

Spiny Logwood *(Xylosma pachyphyllum)* Caribbean

Critically Endangered Species *continued*

Spix's Macaw / Little Blue Macaw *(Cyanopsitta spixii)* South America

St Helena Dragonet *(Callionymus sanctaheclenae)* Subsaharan Africa

Stresemann's Bristlefront *(Merulaxis stresemannii)* South America

Sumatran Ground-cuckoo *(Carpococcyx viridis)* Southeast Asia

Sunda Plover / Javanese Lapwing *(Vanellus macropterus)* Southeast Asia

Tahiti Flycatcher / Tahiti Monarch *(Pomarea nigra)* Oceania

Thick-billed Ground-dove *(Gallicolumba salamonis)* Oceania

Three-nerved Alsunidendron *(Alsunidendron trinerve)* Hawaiian Islands

Turquoise-throated Puffleg *(Eriocnemis godini)* South America

Virginia Round-leaf Birch *(Betula uber)* North America

Wagner's Cordia / Luquillo Mountain Manjack *(Cordia wagnerorum)* Caribbean

Waikane Valley Cyrtandra *(Cyrtandra kaulantha)* Hawaiian Islands

White-breasted Silver-eye / White-breasted White-eye *(Zosterops albogularis)* Oceania

White-eyed River-martin *(Eurychelidon sirintarae)* Southeast Asia

Yellow-spotted Tree Frog *(Litoria castanea)* Australia

Zino's Petrel / Madeira Petrel *(Pterodroma madeira)* Europe

Natural Disasters

Jul 1979-May 1981 Drought. *China (Hebei).* Worst for sixty years. Much of area normally one of the most fertile in China, became a virtual desert. 14 000 000 peasants left dependent on government grain rations. It was estimated 2 000 000 children were suffering from malnutrition.

Aug-Sept 1980 Hurricane David. *Dominican Republic.* 20 killed. 60 000 homeless. Banana and grapefruit crops destroyed.

May 1980 Volcanic eruption. *USA (Washington State).* 2 000 people evacuated. Large quantities of volcanic ash blanketed communities to a depth of several feet in parts of Washington, Idaho and Montana.

Oct 1980 Earthquakes. *El Asnam, Algeria.* 7.5 and 6.5 on Richter scale. 3 600 dead. 8 252 injured. 300 000 homeless. The town had been destroyed in 1954 by another earthquake which killed 1 000. It was rebuilt by the French with supposedly 'quake-proof' structures. These were the worst affected by the 1980 earthquake.

Nov 1980 Earthquake. *Southern Italy.* 6.8 on Richter scale. Aftershocks continued for 10 days. 200 towns and villages affected: Naples, Salerno, Avellino worst affected. 4 500 dead. 8 000 injured. 350 000 homeless.

Jul 1981 Floods. *China (Sechuan).* 1 385 dead. 14 109 injured. Affected 10 million people in 135 of the province's 212 counties, threatened the Gezhouba dam and destroyed more than 1 000 000 acres of crops.

Late 1982-1983 Floods. *Eastern Bolivia.* 40 500 hectares (100 000 acres) of prime agricultural land destroyed. In the high valleys of Bolivia and in southern Peru drought conditions devastated the potato crop affecting about 2 million people.

Dec 1982 Earthquake. *Northern Yemen (Dhamar).* 6.0 on Richter scale. 1 588 killed. 1 604 injured. 200 000 homeless.

Feb 1983-Jul 1984 Drought. *Northeastern Brazil.* Fifth year of drought. 850 000 sq kms affected. 70% of population suffering from malnutrition.

May 1985 Cyclone and tsunami. *Southeastern Bangladesh.* 11 000 killed. 250 000 homeless.

Sept 1985 Earthquake. *Mexico City, Mexico.* 8.1 on Richter scale. More than 7 000 dead. 30 000 injured. 10 000 seriously. 100 000 homeless.

Nov 1985 Volcanic eruption. *Colombia.* The Nevado del Ruiz volcano erupted leaving 22 000 dead, 4 000 injured and 20 000 homeless. The village of Armero was totally engulfed by a torrent of mud when La Lagunilla river burst its banks. 11 000 hectares of agricultural land ruined.

Aug 1986 Toxic gases following volcanic eruption. *Cameroon.* Toxic gases (a mixture of carbon dioxide and hydrogen sulphide) were released from volcanic Lake Nyos, near the Nigerian border, killing 1 746 and injuring 3 000, though exact numbers of casualties will probably never be known. In Nyos village only 2 out of a population of 700 survived.

10 Oct 1986 Earthquake. *San Salvador, El Salvador.* 7.5 on Richter scale. 1 500 killed. 300 000 homeless. On the outskirts of the city a landslide buried 100 people.

Mar 1987 Earthquake. *Ecuador.* 7.3 on Richter scale. Followed by 1 300 aftershocks. 2-4 000 killed. 50 000 homeless. Mudslides entombed whole villages.

Aug-Sept 1987 Floods. *Bangladesh.* 70 killed (a very low estimate). 24 000 000 homeless and without food (from a total population of 100 000 000. 2 000 000 homes, 2 600 kms of road and 4 300 000 acres of land devastated.

Natural Disasters *continued*

Sept 1987 Heavy rains and mudslides. *Medellin, Columbia.* Shanty town of Villa Tina buried by mud. 355 people dead. 200 seriously injured. 2 100 homeless.

Feb 1988 Mudslides. *Rio de Janeiro, Brazil.* In a shanty town in Rio after weeks of torrential rain. 300 killed. 735 seriously injured. 11 000 homeless.

Mid 1988 Drought. *USA.* Farming lands were turned into disaster areas and world food production fell.

Aug-Sept 1988 Floods. *Bangladesh.* Widespread flooding on a similar scale to the floods of 1987.

Sept 1988 Hurricane Gilbert. *Jamaica.* Over 200 mph winds. Left a trail of destruction across Jamaica, Grand Cayman, the Yucatan Peninsula, Mexico, Texas. At least 240 killed, most of those in Yucatan.

Nov 1988 Earthquake. *China.* 7.6 on Richter scale. 900 people killed.

Dec 1988 Earthquake. *Armenia.* 6.7 on Richter scale. 55 000 dead. 250 000 left homeless. 80% were still living in makeshift huts and tents in April 1991.

Apr 1989 Tornado. *Bangladesh.* 1 000 people killed and many villages destroyed.

Sept 1989 Hurricane Hugo. *USA.* Widespread devastation in the northeastern Caribbean and southeastern USA. Winds reached up to 140 mph. Guadeloupe and Leeward Islands: 6 killed, 10 000 homeless and many crops destroyed. Montserrat: 10 killed, hospital and houses destroyed and airport runway blocked. Puerto Rico: 25 killed, 100 000 homeless. Dominica: much of banana crop destroyed. South Carolina: 5 killed, houses damaged, services disrupted.

Oct 1989 Earthquake. *San Francisco, USA.* 6.9 on Richter scale. About 100 people killed, mostly when the elevated section of Interstate 880 highway collapsed crushing people in their cars.

Feb 1990 Mudslide. *Peru.* The village of San Miguel de Rio Mayo, 800 km north of Lima, was buried. 200 people killed or missing.

May 1990 Earthquake. *Peru.* 5.8 on Richter scale. About 200 people killed, villages flattened by landslides.

Jan 1991 Epidemic. *Latin America.* Cholera broke out in Peru and spread to Brazil, Colombia, Chile and Ecuador. WHO estimates 42 000 people could die unless steps are taken to combat malnutrition and lack of basic sanitary and medical facilities. Famine. Still critical in Sudan, Ethiopia, Somalia, Mozambique and Angola, all countries in which armed conflict exacerbated food distribution problems.

2 Feb 1991 Earthquake. *Afghanistan.* 6.5-6.8 on Richter scale. 1 000 killed, many more injured. Resulting floods killed 200 and left 3.000 people homeless.

Mar 1991 Floods and mudslides. *Malawi.* 516 people dead or missing. 40-50 000 homeless.

Apr 1991 Earthquake. *Peru.* Three earthquakes, the worst of which was 6.9 on the Richter scale. 35 killed. 750 injured.

Apr 1991 Earthquake. *Costa Rica, Panama.* 7.5 on Richter scale. About 80 people killed, 800 injured, thousands of homes destroyed.

Apr 1991 Cyclone. *Bangladesh.* Winds up to 145 mph. 139 000 killed and thousands more threatened by epidemic. Up to 10 000 000 people homeless, 4 000 000 at risk from starvation. Toll would have been worse but for 300 cyclone shelters built under Cyclone Preparedness Programme set up by Red Crescent.

Apr 1991 Earthquake. *Georgia, Russia.* 7.2 on Richter scale. 100 people killed, several villages totally destroyed.

Natural Disasters *continued*

Jun 1991 Volcano. *Philippines*. After lying dormant for 600 years Mount Pinatubo suffered several eruptions, some shooting volcanic ash and rock 19 miles into the air. At least 343 people were killed and 100-200 000 made homeless. 600 000 Filipinos lost their means of livelihood.

Dec 1991 Earthquake. *Romania*. 5.7 on Richter scale. 1 700 people made homeless.

Dec 1991 Floods. *Texas, USA*. 13.3 inches of rain fell in six days. At least 14 people were killed.

Late Dec 1991 Cyclone. *Hanoi, Vietnam*. 220 people killed.

Feb 1992 Avalanche. *South Eastern Turkey*. Avalanches smothered remote villages killing at least 167 people, most of them soldiers.

Aug 1992 Hurricane Andrew. *USA (Bahamas, Florida and Louisiana)*. Winds up to 264 km/hr. Hurricane Andrew caused extensive damage to property, estimated at $20 000 million in Florida. 38 people killed. Up to 200 000 people homeless.

Sept 1992 Flooding. *Pakistan*. Floods engulfed thousands of villages and vast acres of cropland especially in Punjab, the worst affected province. More than 2 000 people killed. At least 3 000 000 homeless.

Sept 1992 Tidal wave. *Nicaragua*. Coastal settlements devastated by tidal wave up to 15 metres high, triggered by earthquake beneath Pacific Ocean. Over 200 people dead. 4 200 homeless.

Oct 1992 Earthquake. *Cairo, Egypt*. 5.9 on Richter scale. 552 people killed. About 3 000 injured. Hundreds made homeless.

Dec 1992 Mudslide. *Bolivia*. Town of Caranavi engulfed. Homes pushed into Tipuani River. Around 350 people killed. 135 injured.

Dec 1992 Earthquake. *Indonesia (Nusa Tenggara)*. 6.8 on Richter scale. As many as 2 000 people killed. Created a 24 metre-high tidal wave, devastating the coastal town of Maumere, killing over 1 000 and damaging a third of the buildings.

Feb 1993 Floods. *Yemen, Iran*. Widespread damage. At least 500 people killed. More than 1 500 people displaced.

Mar 1993 Severe storms. *USA*. Heavy snow and floods caused widespread destruction from the Florida Keys through the Deep South to northern New England. 50 tornadoes hit Florida. At least 163 people killed.

Mar 1993 Earthquake. *Erzincan, Turkey*. 6.8 on Richter scale. More than 500 people killed. Over 1 000 injured.

Apr 1993 Floods and landslides. *Colombia*. At least 59 people killed in north-west area. Thousands homeless.

May 1993 Floods and mudslides. *Tadjikistan*. At least 200 people killed.

May 1993 Landslide. *Ecuador*. Over 200 people killed in a village in south Ecuador as 15 000 tonnes buried the community.

Jun 1993 Floods. *Bangladesh*. About 100 people killed. More than 1 million displaced. Worst affected area was Sylhet district.

Jun 1993 Mudslide. *Kabul, Afghanistan*. 115 people reported killed.

Jul 1993 Torrential rains and mudslides. *India, Nepal, Bangladesh*. Worst hit areas of India in Assam and West Bengal. More than 3 700 people killed, and millions made homeless.

Jul 1993 Flooding. *USA*. Midwest affected as Mississippi-Missouri river system burst its banks. 40 000 sq km flooded. At least 45 dead. 30 000 homes ruined.

Natural Disasters *continued*

Jul 1993 Earthquake. *Japan*. 7.8 on Richter scale. Ensuing tidal waves struck parts of Hokkaido, Honshu and devastated coastal regions of Okushiri. Triggered landslides and fires. Over 150 people killed.

Aug 1993 Tropical storm. *Venezuela*. Torrential rain and high winds caused mudslides in shanty towns above Caracas. At least 150 killed. More than 400 injured.

Sept 1993 Earthquake. *India*. 6.5 on Richter scale. Devastation in states of Maharashtra, Karnataka and Andhra Pradesh. Over 9 000 people killed. Umarga and Khilari worst hit towns. More than 30 villages flattened.

Jan 1994 Earthquake. *Los Angeles, USA*. 57 people killed, thousands injured and about 25 000 homeless. Damage estimated at costing up to $20 000 million.

Feb 1994 Earthquake. *Indonesia*. Struck southern Sumatran province of Lampung, killing 200 people and injuring 2 700.

May 1994 Cyclone. *Bangladesh*. 165 people officially reported killed as cyclone hit southeastern coast.

Jun 1994 Earthquake. *Colombia*. 250 people killed as earthquake triggered mudslide in southwestern region. 11 000 homeless.

Aug 1994 Earthquake. *Western Algeria*. 5.6 on Richter scale. 149 people killed.

Jan 1995 Flooding. *North Western Europe*. More than 300 000 people fled their homes in Belgium, France, Germany and The Netherlands. 40 people killed. Immediate natural cause of flood was heavy rain and snow-melt.

Jan 1995 Earthquake. *Kobe, Japan*. 7.2 on Richter scale. About 5 000 people killed. 250 000 homeless. Widespread damage estimated at $50 000 million.

Jan 1995 Avalanches and snowstorms. *Kashmir, India*. More than 200 deaths.

Feb 1995 Earthquake. *Colombia*. 6.4 on Richter scale. 37 people killed and 200 injured in south-west region.

Mar 1995 Landslide. *Afghanistan*. 354 people killed in village of Qara Luk, in the northern province of Badakhshan.

May 1995 Earthquake. *Sakhalin Island, Russia*. 7.5 on Richter scale. Estimated 2 000 people killed. Many thousands homeless.

Jun 1995 Earthquake. *Greece*. 6.1 on Richter scale. 25 people killed and 60 injured in western Greece.

Jun-Jul 1995 Flooding. *China (Hunan)*. 1 200 people killed, 1 200 000 displaced.

Jul 1995 Flooding. *Pakistan*. Floods caused by heavy rains in provinces of Baluchistan, Punjab and Sind killed more than 120 people.

mid-Jul 1995 Flooding. *Bangladesh*. More than 200 people died amid spread of disease following devastating floods which engulfed 38 districts.

Jul 1995 Typhoon. *Southern Korea*. Southern coast hit by Typhoon Faye. Winds of 154 mph caused a 140 000-ton oil tanker to run aground off city of Yeosoo, spreading an oil slick over a 50-km area which caused considerable damage to marine life.

Jul-Aug 1995 Flooding. *North Korea*. More than 5 000 000 people affected in Pyongyang. Damage estimated at $15 billion.

Sept 1995 Hurricane Ismael. *Mexico*. Pacific states of Sinaloa and Sonoro hit by Hurricane Ismael. 107 people killed and 52 000 homeless. 20 000 hectares of agricultural land devastated.

Oct 1995 Earthquake. *Turkey*. 6.0 on Richter scale. Hit South Western town of Dinar. 84 people killed and at least 200 injured.

Natural Disasters *continued*

Oct 1995 Tropical storm. *Philippines*. Widespread destruction throughout country caused by Tropical Storm Sybil. More than 100 people killed. At end of Oct at least 100 more people killed by Tropical Storm Zack.

Oct 1995 Hurricane Opal. *USA*. 17 people killed by Hurricane Opal in Florida and neighbouring states.

Oct 1995 Earthquake. *Sumatra, Indonesia*. 7.0 on Richter scale. Triggered landslides and killed at least 70 people. About 10 000 buildings destroyed.

Oct 1995 Flooding. *Vietnam*. Severe floods followed torrential rains in central province of Quang Ngai. 85 people killed. 176 000 houses covered by flood waters.

Oct 1995 Earthquake. *Mexico*. 7.6 on Richter scale. 66 people killed, hundreds injured and thousands homeless in western coastal states of Jalisco and Colima.

Oct 1995 Earthquake. *China*. 6.5 on Richter scale. At least 29 people killed and 20 000 homeless in Southwestern Yunan. More than 12 000 buildings collapsed.

Dec 1995 Volcanic eruption. *Nicaragua*. Relief efforts focused on clearing town of Leon (94 999 inhabitants) from ash fall to prevent spread of respiratory diseases, notably among children.

Dec 1995-Jan 1996 Flooding. *South Africa*. At least 147 people killed in Kwazulu-Natal when Umsunduzi River and its main tributary burst their banks following heavy seasonal rains. 4 000-5 000 homeless.

Jan 1996 Flooding. *Indonesia*. Affected 50 600 households. 24 600 people evacuated. 480 seriously injured and 18 killed.

Jan 1996 Forest fire. *Argentina*. Thousands of hectares of ancient forests destroyed in national parks in southern Chebut and Rio Negro provinces.

Jan 1996 Snowstorm. *USA*. Major disruption caused to transport services in north-eastern region. At least 59 people killed.

Feb 1996 Flooding. *USA*. Melting snow and heavy rain produced severe flooding in the North Western region. Mudslides blocked roads and 16 000 people forced to flee their homes. At least 3 people killed in Oregon.

Feb 1996 Earthquake. *China (Yunnan)*. 7.0 on Richter scale. 322 people killed and about 4 000 seriously injured. 319 600 homeless. 358 000 housing units collapsed. Total economic loss estimated at $47.1 million.

Feb 1996 Earthquake. *Eastern Indonesia*. 7.5 on Richter scale. 108 people killed, over 400 injured and 1 018 houses destroyed. Generated tsunami that hit Irian Jaya.

Mar 1996 Cyclone. *Madagascar*. 100 000-150 000 people affected by Cyclone Bonita. 9 killed.

Mar 1996 Avalanche. *India (Kashmir)*. 36 people killed and 27 injured in remote village in Pakistan-ruled part of disputed Kashmir.

Mar 1996 Earthquake. *Ecuador*. 5.7 on Richter scale. 21 people killed, 66 injured and 3 000 homeless in central Ecuador.

Apr 1996 Forest fire. *Mongolia*. 30 000 sq km of forests and 50 000 sq km of pasture destroyed. 8 people killed, 20 injured.

May 1996 Earthquake. *China*. 6.4 on Richter scale. At least 18 people killed and 297 injured. 50 000 buildings damaged or destroyed around city of Baotou, 540km north-west of Beijing.

May 1996 Tornado. *Northern Bangladesh*. More than 600 people killed.

Jan 1997 Snowstorms. *China*. 34 deaths and 100 000 cut off in their homes.

Natural Disasters *continued*

Jan 1997 Storms. *Brazil*. 65 people killed and nearly 20 000 homeless in states of Minais Gerais and Rio de Janeiro.

Feb 1997 Earthquake. *Iran*. 965 people killed and more than 2 600 injured in north-west province of Ardabil.

Feb 1997 Earthquake. *Pakistan*. 7.3 on Richter scale. At least 100 people killed in Harnai, Balushistan province.

May 1997 Earthquake. *Iran*. 7.1 on Richter scale. More than 1 600 people killed, 2 200 injured and 50 000 homeless in northeastern province of Khorasan.

May 1997 Cyclone. *Bangladesh*. 112 people killed in coastal areas.

May 1997 Earthquake. *India*. 6.0 on Richter scale. At least 38 people killed and over 1 000 injured in Madhya Pradesh state in central India.

May 1997 Tornadoes. *Texas, USA*. Series of tornadoes killed 27 people, most of them in the town of Jarrell, 40km north of Austin.

Jun 1997 Volcanic eruption. *Montserrat*. Eruption of Soufriere Hills volcano devastated two-thirds of the island. At least 23 people killed. 5 000 evacuated from island. Disaster compounded by huge eruption of Chance's Peak volcano.

Jul 1997 Flooding. *Eastern Germany, Poland, Czech Republic*. Thousands affected by worst floods in central Europe in 20th century. Heavy rain destroyed vast areas in eastern Germany. Many people homeless after dyke holding back torrential Oder river burst. At least 48 people killed.

Jul 1997 Earthquake. *Cariaco, Venezuela*. 6.9 on Richter scale. At least 59 people killed and 320 injured.

Aug 1997 Flooding. *India*. Heavy rains in northern state of Pradesh led to rivers flooding. At least 135 people killed.

Sept 1997 Drought. *Papua New Guinea*. Nationwide drought affected over 700 000 people.

Sept 1997 Earthquakes. *Central Italy*. Two earthquakes, the most powerful measuring 5.7 on Richter scale. 11 people killed and more than 120 injured.

Sept 1997 Cyclone. *Bangladesh*. At least 47 killed and hundreds injured on islands off south-east coast.

Sept 1997 Earthquake. *Sulawesi, Indonesia*. 6.0 on Richter scale. At least 14 killed and 30 injured.

Oct 1997 Hurricane Pauline. *Mexico*. Acapulco devastated and widespread damage caused to state of Guerro. More than 111 people killed and 8 000 homeless.

Oct 1997 Earthquake. *Chile*. 6.8 on Richter scale. 8 killed, 98 injured, 15 000 left homeless.

Nov 1997 Earthquake. *Bangladesh*. 6.0 on Richter scale. Killed 11 people in port city of Chittagong. Thousands homeless.

Jan 1998 Flooding. *Peru*. 70 people killed and 22 000 homeless.

Jan 1998 Storms. *Canada*. Up to 100mm of freezing rain fell across eastern Ontario and Quebec. Ice load brought down about 1 000 power transmission towers and 30 000 wooden utility poles. Around 3 million people lost electricity and at least 25 people were killed. Over 700 000 insurance claims filed for property damage.

Apr 1998 Storms. *USA (Alabama, Georgia, Mississippi)*. 60 people killed.

May 1998 Forest fires. *Central America*. Vast tracts of land destroyed.

Natural Disasters *continued*

22 May 1998 Earthquakes. *Central Bolivia*. Series of earthquakes measuring up to 6.8 on Richter scale. At least 100 people killed.

30 May 1998 Earthquake. *Northern Afghanistan*. 3 000 killed.

27 Jun 1998 Earthquake. *Adana, Turkey*. More than 120 people killed.

30 Jun-2 Jul 1998 Storms and flooding. *USA (Wisconsin, Minnesota, Indiana, Ohio, West Virginia, Vermont)*. More than 20 people killed.

17 Jul 1998 Tidal wave. *Papua New Guinea*. 10 metres high. Generated by off-shore earthquake. Swept 2 km inland in Aitape district of north coast. At least 2 000 killed.

Jul-Aug 1998 Flooding. *China*. 21 million hectares of land damaged by severe floods following heavy monsoon rainfall. 13 million hectares suffered total crop loss. Extensive damage to road and rail networks. Almost 250 million people affected. 13.4 million relocated. Official death toll: 3 004. More than 5.5 million houses destroyed. A further 12 million homes damaged.

22 Sept 1998 Hurricane Georges. *Dominican Republic, Haiti*. 300 killed, mostly in floods and landslides.

Nov 1998 Hurricane Mitch. *Central America*. Wind speeds of up to 190 mph (300 km per hour). Widespread devastation of roads, homes and crops. In Honduras, 6 500 people killed, 11 000 reported missing and up to 2 million suffered loss of property. In Nicaragua, 1 000 people killed and 1 900 missing. Also deaths and extensive damage in El Salvador and Guatemala.

2-6 Jan 1999 Snow storm. *USA*. About 90 people killed as a result of severe storm on the eastern seaboard and in mid-western states.

14 Jan 1999 Landslide. *Tacabamba, Peru*. 40 killed. Several dozen village homes buried after volcanic activity caused landslide.

Jan 1999 Earthquake. *Colombia*. 6.0 on Richter scale. More than 900 people killed and 250 000 homeless.

11 Feb 1999 Earthquake. *Afghanistan (Wardak)*. 5.5 on Richter scale. 50 killed and more than 500 injured. Over 5 000 buildings destroyed.

23-24 Feb 1999 Avalanches. *Austria (Tyrol)*. Killed 38 people. Tens of thousands of people evacuated from the Alpine region.

29 Mar 1999 Earthquake. *India (Uttar Pradesh)*. 6.8 on Richter scale. At least 110 people killed and hundreds injured in foothills of Himalayas.

3 May 1999 Tornadoes. *USA (Oklahoma, Kansas)*. At least 47 killed and hundreds injured after dozens of tornadoes struck, some of which were 5km wide. Caused extensive property damage.

7 May 1999 Earthquake. *Shiraz, Iran*. 6.5 on Richter scale. At least 26 people killed and 100 injured. 20 villages damaged.

20 May 1999 Cyclone. *Pakistan (Sind)*. Winds of up to 275 km per hour caused widespread crop damage and submerged thousands of villages. At least 400 deaths.

15 Jun 1999 Earthquake. *Southern Mexico*. At least 19 people killed.

Jul 1999 Flooding. *Central and Southern China*. Widespread flooding along banks of Yangtze river following weeks of torrential rain. 725 people killed. 5.5 million evacuated. Caused US$8 billion worth of damage.

13 Jul 1999 Landslide. *Western Romania*. Caused by heavy rains and floods. 13 killed and 23 injured.

Natural Disasters *continued*

Jul-Aug 1999 Heatwave. *USA (Missouri, Iowa, Illinois, New York, Ohio, West Virginia)*. At least 20 people killed. Agricultural disaster areas declared in 15 states. Losses in West Virginia exceeded $80m.

Aug 1999 Typhoon. *North & South Korea, Philippines*. Typhoon Olga killed more than 165 people and made at least 100 000 homeless. Severe flooding left thousands of hectares of farm land submerged and infrastructure damaged.

Aug 1999 Earthquake. *Northwestern Turkey*. 7.4 on Richter scale. 14 095 people killed, 27 000 injured, 200 000 homeless and more than 72 000 buildings damaged.

Sept 1999 Flooding. *Central America*. 70 people killed and 100 000 homeless in Honduras, Guatemala and Nicaragua.

Sept 1999 Hurricane Floyd. *USA (Florida, Georgia, Carolina)*. A storm system the size of Texas brought heavy rains, severe flooding and high winds. Massive mandatory evacuation took place in preparation. 60 people killed.

Sept 1999 Earthquake. *Greece*. 5.9 on Richter scale. More than 120 people killed and 60 000 homeless.

Sept 1999 Typhoon. *Hong Kong*. Winds of up to 150km per hour. One person killed and 494 injured. Caused a cargo ship to sink.

Sept 1999 Earthquake. *Taiwan*. 7.6 on Richter scale. 2 256 people killed, 8 713 injured, 100 000 homeless and 404 000 homes left without water supplies. Temporary power cut throughout island. Most affected were Taichung, Taiwan's 3rd largest city, and mountain towns of Puli and Tungshi.

Sept 1999 Typhoon. *Honshu, Japan*. At least 26 people killed and 350 injured. 1 million homes left without power.

Sept 1999 Earthquake. *Oaxaca, Mexico*. 7.5 on Richter scale. At least 33 people killed.

Oct 1999 Flooding. *Mexico*. At least 341 people killed and 271 000 homeless.

Oct 1999 Cyclones. *Orissa, India*. Wind speeds of between 200 and 300 km per hour caused widespread destruction. More than 10 000 people killed, 1.5 million homeless and 323 000 hectares of land inundated by tidal wave that followed.

Oct-Nov 1999 Floods. *Vietnam*. At least 470 people died in floods following torrential rainstorms.

Nov 1999 Earthquake. *Northwestern Turkey*. Towns of Düzce, Kaynasli and Bolu devastated. Over 737 people died, 5 000 injured and tens of thousands left homeless.

Nov 1999 Flooding. *Southern France*. Torrential storms caused floods. Killed 31 people. Within 48 hours about 600 litres of water fell per square metre – the average rainfall for a whole year in southern France.

15-18 Dec 1999 Floods and mudslides. *Venezuela*. Up to 50 000 people killed after flash floods and mudslides struck 150km of coastline. Telecommunications and power supplies collapsed.

26-27 Dec 1999 Storms. *France*. Hurricane-force winds of over 150km per hour killed 88 people and severely damaged country's infrastructure.

15 Feb 2000 Tornadoes. *USA (Southwestern Georgia)*. Series of tornadoes killed 22 people and injured 100 in town of Camilla.

27 Feb 2000 Cyclone Steve. *Australia (Queensland, Northern Territory)*. Tropical cyclone Steve caused widespread damage. Two-thirds of the area's annual rainfall fell in just 36 hours.

Natural Disasters *continued*

Feb 2000 Flooding. *Mozambique, Botswana, Zimbabwe, South Africa.* Situation worsened by cyclone Eline hitting Mozambique on 21 February. Limpopo river rose 7 metres. Save and Sabi rivers also swollen. Thousands of people stranded in trees and on rooftops. Infrastructure severely affected; thousands of hectares of farmland washed away; 28 000 ha of crops destroyed; 800 000-1 million people homeless; 30 000 cattle drowned; official total of 640 deaths. In South Africa, 95 killed. Dams overflowed and 60 000 homeless in Botswana. 62 killed in Zimbabwe and 250 000 affected by floods.

Feb-Apr 2000 Cyclones. *Madagascar.* Cyclone Eline in February killed 7 people and left thousands homeless. On 27 February, Cyclone Gloria killed 130, left 10 000 homeless and 12 000 stranded. Cyclone Hudah hit in early April. Widespread cropland devastation.

Apr 2000 Drought and forest fires. *Ethiopia, Kenya.* Widespread crop devastation following 3 years of drought. Hundreds died daily through starvation.

5-10 Apr 2000 Flooding. *Hungary, Romania.* Flooding along several rivers. In Hungary 230 000 ha of arable land made unusable. In Romania 60 000 ha of agricultural land destroyed and 489 towns and villages cut off. At least 7 people killed.

May 2000 Flooding. *Indonesia.* Severe floods on border of East and West Timor, caused by monsoon rain and tidal surge. At least 148 people killed. About 20 000 homeless. Thousands of tons of harvested crops destroyed.

Jan 2001 Earthquake. *El Salvador.* Over 800 people killed, thousands homeless

Jan 2001 Earthquake. *India.* More than 20 000 people killed and hundreds of thousands homeless in a severe earthquake in the western state of Gujarat.

Jan 2001 Earthquake. *El Salvador.* 7.6 on the Richter scale. At least 844 deaths

Jan 2001 Earthquake. *India.* 7.9 on the Richter scale. Resulted in 13 805 deaths in western India, thousands more injured and devastating damage to property

Jan 2001 onwards Flooding. *Mozambique.* At least 115 fatalities with around 230 000 people displaced

Feb 2001 Landslides, flooding and storms. *Indonesia.* A minimum of 122 fatalities

Feb 2001 Earthquake. *El Salvador.* 6.6 on the Rochter scale. Resulted in at least 315 deaths and 3 400 people being injured

May 2001 Landslide. *China (Chongqing).* At least 74 people died when a landslide destroyed a multi-storey residential building

Jun 2001 Earthquake. *Peru.* An estimated 145 fatalities, including 64 people reported as missing (an unknown number died following a resultant tsunami)

Jul 2001 Typhoons. *The Philippines, China and Taiwan.* An estimated 270 fatalities and widespread displacement

Jul-Aug 2001 Flooding. *India (Orissa).* At least 100 fatalities as a result of heavy monsoon season rains

Jul 2001 onwards Heatwave. *USA.* At least 54 fatalities by the end of July

Jul 2001 Typhoon. *Taiwan.* Mudslides and floods killed more than 70 people and forced nearly 300 000 to abandon their homes

Aug 2001 Flooding. *Northeastern Iran.* At least 240 fatalities

Aug-Oct 2001 Flooding. *Vietnam (Mekong Delta).* At least 322 fatalities, the majority of them children

Natural Disasters *continued*

Oct 2001 Storms, Tidal Wave. *North Korea*. At least 110 fatalities with thousands of homes, roads and factories destroyed

Oct 2001 Cyclone. *Andhra Pradesh, India*. An estimated 170 fatalities

Oct 2001-Spring 2002 Cold weather. *Poland*. At least 129 fatalities

Nov 2001 Flooding. *Algeria*. At least 764 people killed and more than 400 injured

Winter 2001-2002 Cold weather. *Russia*. At least 232 fatalities

Winter 2001-2002 Wildfires. *Australia (New South Wales)*. Many homes destroyed.

Jan 2002 Earthquake. *Vanuatu*. 7.2 on Richter scale, many buildings were devastated

Jan 2002 Storms. *Senegal*. Much damage inland and many fishermen drowned off the coast

Jan 2002 Volcano. *Democratic Republic of Congo*. Mount Nyiragongo erupted, engulfing the town of Goma and killing more than 40 people

Feb 2002 Earthquake. *Western Turkey*. 6.0 on Richter scale, caused many deaths and much damage

Feb 2002 Storms and flooding. *Bolivia*. The capital was particularly badly hit

Mar 2002 Earthquake. *Central Asia (Hindu Kush)*. 7.2 on the Richter scale. Resulted in many deaths

Mar 2002 Earthquake. *Northern Afghanistan*. 6.0 on Richter scale, it caused over 600 deaths

Apr 2002 Landslides. *Papua New Guinea*. Caused several deaths

Apr 2002 Earthquake. *Northern Afghanistan*. 5.8 on Richter scale, causing several deaths

Apr 2002 Storms. *Bangladesh*. More than 50 people killed

Apr 2002 Flooding and landslides. *Rwanda, Kenya*. More than 100 people killed and crops destroyed

May 2002 Storms. *Bangladesh*. More than 350 people killed when the Salahuddin-2, a passenger ferry, sank

May 2002 Tropical cyclone. *Madagascar*. More than 40 people killed and widespread property damage

May 2002 Red tide. *China*. Large areas of sea affected by unnaturally large algae population growth

May 2002 Flooding and landslides. *Haiti, Jamaica*. Over 30 people killed

May 2002 Storm. *Lake Victoria, Africa*. At least 30 dead when a boat capsized

Jun 2002 Heatwave. *Nigeria*. At least 60 people died

Jun 2002 Storm. *Lake Victoria, Africa*. At least 70 dead when a ferry capsized.

Jun 2002 Flooding. *Southern Russia*. Over 100 people drowned in floods

Jun 2002 Earthquake. *Northern Iran*. Over 200 people killed in an earthquake registering 6.8 on the Richter scale

Jun 2002 Flooding. *India*. At least 150 people drowned in floods in Gujarat

Jul 2002 Snowstorms. *Peru*. At least 60 people died, many of them children

Jul 2002 Explosion. *Ukraine*. A coal-mine blast killed 20 miners

Jul 2002 Typhoon and mudslides. *India, Bangladesh, Nepal*. Over 800 people killed

Jul 2002 Mudslides. *Ecuador*. At least 60 people killed

Natural Disasters *continued*

Aug 2002 Typhoons, mudslides and flooding. *China (Hunan), South Korea, Iran.* Hundreds of people died

Aug 2002 Flooding. *Vietnam.* Many people killed when the Mekong river flooded

Sept 2002 Flooding. *Thailand.* Many people killed

Sept 2002 Storm. *Senegal.* Almost 2000 people drowned when a ferry capsized

Oct 2002 Cold weather. *Moscow, Russia.* Many people died who could not cope with the sudden drop in temperature

Oct 2002 Earthquake. *Italy.* A school collapsed, killing at least 23 7 and 8 year olds

Dec 2002 Cold weather. *Warsaw, Poland.* Hundreds of people were unable to cope with the cold weather

Jan 2003 Flooding and drought. *Malawi.* Thousands are displaced by floodwaters during a time of severe drought and famine

Feb 2003 Storms. *Democratic Republic of Congo.* At least 2 500 people killed

Feb 2003 Earthquake. *China (Xinjiang).* Over 260 people are killed and 10 000 homes destroyed

Mar 2003 Hail storms. *India.* More than 500 people killed by hail

Apr 2003 Earthquake. *Western Turkey.* Over 5.5 on the Richter scale. More than 100 people killed.

Apr 2003 Flooding. *Argentina.* More than 50 000 people are displaced when rivers rose by 50cm in 12 hours

May 2003 Earthquake. *Algeria.* More than 2 200 people killed near Algiers

May 2003 Tornado. *Oklahoma, USA.* Over $100 million worth of damage

Jun 2003 Heatwave. *Southern India.* Thousands die in temperatures of over 50C

Jul 2003 Floods. *Southern China.* 600 die with half a million homes destroyed.

Jul 2003 Forest fires. *France, Portugal, Spain, Greece.* Serious fires, some thought to be the result of arson, with many people evacuated and some deaths

Aug 2003 Heatwave. *Europe.* Many elderly people die during extremely hot weather; crops are devastated

Oct-Nov 2003 Heatwave. *USA (California).* Droughts and forest fires rage, thousands of homes destroyed

Nov 2003 Flooding. *Sumatra, Indonesia.* The village of Bukit Lawang is practically wiped out and an estimated 200 people killed

Dec 2003 Earthquake. *Iran.* At least 40 000 are killed and a large part of the historic city of Bam destroyed

Dec 2003 Storms. *Phillippines.* Mudslides and stormy seas killed around 270 people

Dec 2003 Natural gas explosion. *China.* 233 killed, thousands taken to hospital or evacuated

Jan 2004 Explosion. *Algeria.* A natural gas plant exploded killing 23 with 74 injured

Feb 2004 Drowning. *Morecambe Bay, UK.* 19 cockle-pickers drowned while working in a notoriously dangerous area of sea with no safety equipment

Feb 2004 Drought. *Southern Africa.* Hundreds of thousands of people in need of food aid

Feb 2004 Earthquake. *Morocco.* Remote areas were devastated with nearly 600 people killed. Many were trapped in villages with rescue missions unable to get to them easily

Manmade Disasters

Dec 1984 Gas Leak. *Bhopal, India*. Gas leak from pesticide plant. At least 2 000 killed and 220 000 treated for various ailments.

Apr 1986 Nuclear Explosion. *Chernobyl, Ukraine*. A hydrogen explosion caused radioactive debris to be showered 1 500 metres into the air. Operational errors blamed. All Eastern Bloc countries, much of Scandinavia and all of Western Europe except Spain and Portugal are known to have been affected in varying degrees. At least 30 people at Chernobyl died almost immediately from burns or acute radiation sickness. The number of people finally affected will never be known.

Nov 1986 *River Rhine*. Following a fire at a chemical plant over 30 tons of pesticides, fungicides and other chemicals were washed into the river by firemen dousing the flames. Mercury was the main chemical involved. For almost two days none of the governments along the Rhine knew the true nature of the chemicals flowing down Europe's largest waterway. 200 miles of Upper Rhine practically irrecoverable and it is estimated that it will take 10-30 years to restore it to life.

Sept 1987 Radioactive pollution. *Goiana, Brazil*. Radioactive caesium chloride powder from a cylinder stolen from a hospital radiotherapy unit and sold for scrap found on a rubbish dump. It was handled casually by children and others ignorant of its dangers. Only four people died but this does not take into account longer-term effects from radioactive pollution of area.

Mar 1989 Oil slick. *Alaska, USA*. The tanker "Exxon Valdez" ran aground off Alaska causing massive damage to the coastline, wildlife and habitat.

Aug 1989 Oil slick. *Liverpool, UK*. 156 tonnes of crude oil emptied into the Mersey estuary from a Shell oil pipeline causing a 10-mile slick, killing at least 300 birds and affecting 2 000 others.

Sept 1990 Explosion. *Kazakhstan*. An explosion and fire at a factory making nuclear fuels at Ulba in East Kazakhstan contaminated a large area with highly toxic compounds of beryllian metal. The health of up to 120 000 people potentially at risk.

Sept 1990 Gas Explosion. *Bangkok, Thailand*. 58 people died and 100 were injured when a truck carrying two tanks of liquefied petroleum gas crashed and exploded in the centre of the capital.

Early 1991 Oil Slick. *Persian Gulf*. During the Gulf War Iraqi forces allegedly released 5-10 000 000 barrels of oil into the Gulf creating a vast oil slick affecting 400 miles of coast and endangering both the marine environment and the livelihoods of local fishermen.

Early 1991 Oil well fires. *Kuwait*. 600 oilwells allegedly set on fire by Iraqi troops causing massive air pollution and contamination of agricultural land and water supplies especially in the fertile, well-populated Tigris and Euphrates valleys in Iraq. 'Black rain' damaged crops in Iran, Pakistan. Bulgaria and Afghanistan. The final well fire was capped in late 1991.

Apr 1991 Oil slick. *Genoa, Italy*. A Cypriot-registered tanker "Haven" exploded during a routine pumping operation in the Ligurian Sea off Genoa. The resulting oil slick caused pollution along the Mediterranean coast westwards towards Nice. The 40 km slick was broken up by gale-force winds which diminished damage potential.

Jun 1991 Pollution. *Chile*. The government ordered 40% of all cars off the streets in the capital. Santiago, one of the most polluted cities in the world. At least 1 465 children had been treated for breathing problems by 10 June.

Manmade Disasters *continued*

Jul 1991 Oil slick. *USA (Washington State).* After a collision with a Chinese ship, a Japanese fish-processing ship sank, disccharging 100 000 gallons of oil into the sea creating a slick threatening the Olympia National Park. Hundreds of birds were killed and rare species such as the bald eagle, peregrine falcon and sea otter endangered.

Aug 1991 Pesticide spill. *USA (California).* A tanker rail car spilled 19 500 gallons of metam sodium pesticide into the Sacramento River. It drifted 45 miles downstream, killing wild life. 200 people were admitted to hospital suffering from fume inhalation and skin irritation.

Dec 1991 Nuclear accidents. *Russia.* The then environment minister, Victor Danilov-Daniliyan, admitted that large parts of Russian territory had been made uninhabitable for decades to come by nuclear accidents and waste.

Jan 1992 Pollution. *Athens, Greece.* When smog in the capital exceeded emergency levels, the government banned all cars from the centre, industrial production was cut and central heating was turned off in public buildings except hospitals.

Jan 1992 Water pollution. *Turkey, Greece.* Hundreds of dead or dying dolphins were washed up on beaches, the victims of a virus linked with water pollution. The rare monk seal, of which only about 300 remain, is also at risk.

Dec 1992 Oil slick. *Spain.* A Greek-owned oil tanker ran aground and exploded off the northwestern Spanish port of La Coruna, spilling an estimated 70 000 tonnes of oil into the sea, with serious ecological consequences. Strong winds and heavy seas helped disperse much of the oil.

Jan 1993 Ozone layer. *World.* NASA research showed ozone levels lower than ever before. Levels were measured up to 14% below normal in the mid-latitudes of the northern hemisphere. In the second half of 1992, ozone levels were 2-3% lower than in any previous year. Global thinning of the ozone layer means a widespread threat to human health.

Jan 1993 Oil slick. *Malaysia.* A supertanker fully laden with almost 2 million barrels of crude oil collided with another tanker and started spilling oil into the sea off the northern tip of Sumatra.

Jan 1993 Oil slick. *Shetland Islands, UK.* The oil tanker "Braer", carrying 84 000 tonnes of light crude oil, was driven ashore. Less damage than originally feared as hurricane winds were effective in breaking down and dispersing the spill. Salmon farms, fisheries and wildlife adversely affected.

Apr 1993 Radioactive explosion. *Tomsk, Russia.* Explosion at the Tomsk-7 nuclear reprocessing plant released a cloud of radioactive gas over western Siberia. Reported to have contaminated 120 sq km of forest, although official reports claimed the amount of plutonium released was negligible.

Summer 1993 Toxic algae. *Europe.* Toxic green algae choked parts of the Mediterranean. Clumps of the weed, which grows following the pollution of the sea by chemicals that fertilize the water, stretched over 4.2 sq km. There were colonies as far apart as Majorca and Livorno, on the Italian coast. Holidaymakers in France, Spain and Italy were warned not to uproot it.

Feb 1994 Oil slick. *Russia (Komi Republic).* Oil spill polluted wide areas of tundra. Estimates of the leak from the 47km-long pipeline ranged from 14 000 to 200 000 barrels. It was initially contained by an earth dam but this was breached by heavy rains in August.

Manmade Disasters *continued*

Jun 1994 Oil slick. *South Africa.* Large oil slicks covered 16km of beaches near Cape Town. Many seabirds including an estimated 10 000 rare Jakass penguin chicks were killed. The crude oil is thought to have come from a Spanish supertanker that caught fire and sank 60 km off Cape Town in 1983.

Oct 1994 Oil slick. *Portugal.* The tanker Cercal hit rocks off Oporto and spilled up to 1 300 tonnes of crude oil, which washed ashore on Portugal's northern beaches.

Oct 1994 Oil slick. *UK.* A Russian fish factory ship, the "Pionersk", carrying 550 tonnes of diesel and fuel, ran aground on rocks south of Lerwick off the coast of Shetland. A 1.6km line of oil was reported stretching southwards from the ship.

Early 1995 Oil slick. *Russia.* A damaged pipeline leaked 3 500 tonnes of crude oil near the Siberian town of Tulun. The spill spread over the frozen Kurzanka River, which feeds into the Bratsk reservoir, an important source of fresh water and hydro-electricity for the whole region.

Summer 1995 Pollution. *Athens, Greece.* A morning-to-evening ban on cars was imposed on the centre of the city for three months to alleviate the severe pollution.

Jul 1995 Fuel spillage. *Australia.* Ore-carrying vessel ran aground off north coast of Tasmania, spilling over 300 tonnes of fuel. At least 8km of shoreline to east of Tamar river reported to have been polluted.

Jul 1995 Chemical spillage. *UK.* An estimated 20 tonnes of toxic acid spilled from a chemicals factory into a stream, feeding the Cuckmere River, near Hailsham, East Sussex. As the acid evaporated it left a 0.8km stretch of the stream completely lifeless. Hundreds of fish were killed.

Aug 1995 Chemical spillage. *Guyana.* Large area along Esseqibo river declared a disaster area after more than 4 000 000 cubic metres of cyanide-contaminated slurry seeped out from a gold mine at Omai into a tributary upstream.

Feb 1996 Oil slick. *UK.* The tanker "Sea Empress", carrying about 128 000 tonnes of light crude oil, ran aground near Milford Haven, SW Wales (an area of major wildlife significance). 72 000 tonnes of oil were spilt into the sea, most of it during the course of efforts to refloat the tanker and transfer its cargo to other vessels.

Apr 1996 Coral damage. *Egypt.* The cruise liner "Royal Viking Sun" hit and damaged the protected Red Sea coral reef off the Egyptian coast.

Nov 1996 Oil slick. *UK.* 4 000 leaking bottles of suntan oil contaminated Camarthen beach in the Bristol Channel after being lost from a container ship.

May 1997 Chemical spillage. *UK.* Thousands of fish killed by contamination of Medway estuary in Kent.

Jul 1997 Oil spillage. *Japan.* State of emergency declared after oil supertanker "Diamond Grace" ran aground in Tokyo Bay.

Aug-Sept 1997 Forest fire. *South-East Asia.* Thousands of forest fires generated a giant smog cloud covering countries from Malaysia and Indonesia to the Philippines, Brunei and Thailand. Despite warnings of a prolonged dry season, fires were lit as a cheap and convenient means of clearing land. Health of tens of millions of people jeopardised; long-term effects of smoke inhalation may be devastating.

Jan 1998 Industrial contamination. *Grand Canal, Eastern China.* A 40km stretch of canal was contaminated by industrial waste, mostly from paper mills.

Jan 1998 Oil slick. *UAE.* Barge ran aground, spilling thousands of tonnes of oil which affected over 80km of coastline.

Manmade Disasters *continued*

Apr 1998 Toxic waste. *Aznalcóllar, Spain*. Toxic waste from a mine flooded 40km of the River Guadimar in Doñana national park. Caused widespread loss of wildlife and natural habitats.

1999 Toxic weaponry. *Yugoslavia*. In March 2000, NATO admitted to widespread use of depleted uranium (DU) weapons during 1999 bombing campaign. DU shells were used routinely throughout Kosovo in about 100 missions. Each mission might have used between 10kg and 100kg of DU, which amounted to a 'toxicity risk'.

Jan 2000 Chemical spillage. *Northern Romania*. 100 000 tonnes of sludge contaminated by cyanide and heavy metals spilled over a dam at a gold mine in Baia Mare. Polluted the Somes river, which then carried pollution to the Tisza river in Hungary and the Danube. By 15 February more than 100 tonnes of dead fish had been recovered from the rivers. Environmentalists warned of serious long-term effects of heavy metals on the river system.

Sept 2000 Ozone layer. *Antarctica*. NASA reported the largest ozone hole ever seen over Antarctica, covering 11 million square miles (three times larger than the area of the USA) and stretching to the southern tip of South America. It is evidence that ozone-destroying chemicals continue to increase in the stratosphere, where the hole forms. Although production of these chemicals has been reduced by international agreement, they remain in the atmosphere and will continue to do so for years.

Jan 2001 Oil slick. *Galapagos Islands*. An ecological disaster was narrowly averted when a ship laden with oil ran aground on the Galapagos Islands.

Feb 2001 Train crash. *Selby, UK*. Ten people killed when their train collided with a goods train

Mar 2001 Train crash. *Belgium*. 8 people are killed in a head-on collision

Jul 2001 Plane crash. *Siberia*. 143 are killed in a Russian plane headed to Vladivostock

11 Sept 2001 Plane crash. *USA*. Terrorists hijacked 2 planes and crashed them into the World Trade Centre in New York, a 3rd into the Pentagon and a 4th outside Pittsburgh. Over 3 000 people were killed

Oct 2001 Plane crash. *Milan, Italy*. Two planes crashed on a runway in heavy fog killing 118

Nov 2001 Plane crash. *New York, USA*. A plane crashed just after take-off, killing all 260 people on board.

Jan 2002 Pollution. *Cornwall, UK* Oil tanker "Willy" grounded with the possibility of explosion

Jan 2002 Pollution. *Djibouti*. Shipment of pesticide leaking in port

Jan 2002 Pollution. *Australia (Queensland)*. Water contaminated with uranium leaking into aquifers

Jan 2002 Pollution. *Thailand*. Huge oil slick from grounded tanker

Feb 2002 Pollution. *Spain*. Tonnes of oil leaked into the Ebro river

Feb 2002 Train crash. *Cairo, Egypt*. At least 300 killed in fire on train

Spring 2002 Pollution. *USA*. Huge oil slick appeared off the coast of California, and traced to an old wreck

Apr 2002 Pollution. *USA*. Coal waste spilled into rivers in Kentucky

Apr 2002 Pollution. *Pacific Ocean*. An abandoned oil tanker leaked oil near mid-ocean atolls

Manmade Disasters *continued*

May 2002 Train crash. *Potter's Bar, UK* Seven people were killed and dozens more injured when a train derailed and smashed into a station

May 2002 Pollution. *Brazil.* Crude oil leaked into Ilha Grande harbour

Jun 2002 Train crash. *Dodoma, Tanzania.* At least 200 killed in a head-on train collision

Jul 2002 Pollution. *Kyrgyzstan and Uzbekistan.* Radioactive waste leaked into the Maylisu River

Jul 2002 Pollution. *Australia.* A tanker carrying diesel oil and fuel oil ran aground on the Great Barrier Reef

Aug 2002 Pollution. *Romania.* Crude oil flowed into the Prahova River, a tributary of the Danube

Aug 2002 Pollution. *Nigeria.* Oil pipeline ruptured in the Niger River delta

Sept 2002 Ferry sinking. *Senegal.* The state-run ferry, the Joola, sank off the coast of Gambia killing around 1 000

Sept 2002 Pollution. *Australia.* Oil run into the Maribyrnong River, near Melbourne

Oct 2002 Building collapse. *Syria.* Several people killed when a building collapsed in Aleppo

Nov 2002 Pollution. *Spain, France.* Oil tanker "Prestige" sank off Galicia, spilling more than 60 000 tonnes of oil and devastating local wildlife

Nov 2002 Explosion. *Bali, Indonesia.* A bomb in the holiday resort of Kuta killed at least 190, most of whom were tourists

Dec 2002 Pollution. *Falkland Islands.* Many penguins killed by an oil slick

Jan 2003 Pollution. *Saigon River, Vietnam.* Tanker damaged in a collision

Jan 2003 Plane crash. *Turkey.* 76 killed when the plane lost control coming in to land

Jan 2003 Train crash. *New South Wales, Australia.* A train derailed, possibly sabotaged, near Sydney killing 8.

Feb 2003 Fire. *Korea.* At least 125 people died in a deliberate fire set on the subway in Daegu

Feb 2003 Pollution. *Pacific Ocean.* Oil contaminated the sea round Midway Atoll after a pipeline valve broke

Feb 2003 Plane crash. *Iran.* All 276 people on board are killed

Feb 2003 Pollution. *Nigeria.* An old oil well exploded in the Niger Delta

Feb 2003 Space shuttle Columbia broke up on re-entry killing the 7 astronauts on board

Mar 2003 Pollution. *Australia.* A ruptured pipeline contaminated beaches near Brisbane

Mar 2003 Pollution. *UK* Seabirds covered with oil found on the Devon coast which had probably been dumped into the English Channel

Apr 2003 Ferry crash. *Bangladesh.* 2 separate ferries capsized in the same storm, killing more than 150 people with hundreds more unaccounted for

May 2003 Plane crash. *Democratic Republic of Congo.* The rear ramp of the plane came loose sucking out the 120 passengers and crew

Manmade Disasters *continued*

May 2003 Earthquake. *Turkey*. 6.4. on Richter scale. A school dormitory collapsed, killing more than 80 children.

May 2003 Train crash. *Hungary*. 33 were killed when a train hit a coach at a level crossing

Jun 2003 Chemical fire. *Nigeria*. A fuel line split and burst into flames while local people were trying to collect the spilling fuel. Over 120 died

Jun 2003 Train crash. *Spain*. At least 19 people died when a passenger train hit a freight train

Jul 2003 Plane crash. *Sudan*. 115 passengers were killed with only one survivor, a small child

Jul 2003 Pollution. *India*. Oil tanker MV Tasman Spirit ran aground discharging more than 30 000 tonnes of oil onto beaches near Karachi.

Oct 2003 Ferry crash. *New York, USA*. A passenger ferry crashed into Staten Island Pier killing 10 and injuring a further 34

Dec 2003 Plane crash. *Benin*. 135 people killed on Christmas Day en route to Lebanon

Jan 2004 Plane crash. *Uzbekistan*. A passenger plane crashed killing all 37 people on board

Jan 2004 Plane crash. *Red Sea*. All 141 passengers are killed on board an Egyptian charter flight.

Feb 2004 Train crash. *Nayshabur, Iran*. Carriages packed with volatile chemicals and fuel crashed leaving at least 295 dead, hundreds injured.

Feb 2004 Plane crash. *United Arab Emirates*. An Iranian plane crashed killing 40 people